A PRACTICAL GUIDE TO PUBLIC PROCUREMENT

A PRACTICAL GUIDE TO PUBLIC PROCUREMENT

ABBY SEMPLE

Consultant Editor
MARK COOK

Great Clarendon Street, Oxford, OX2 6DP,
United Kingdom

Oxford University Press is a department of the University of Oxford.
It furthers the University's objective of excellence in research, scholarship,
and education by publishing worldwide. Oxford is a registered trade mark of
Oxford University Press in the UK and in certain other countries

Published in the United States of America by Oxford University Press
198 Madison Avenue, New York, NY 10016, United States of America

British Library Cataloguing in Publication Data
Data available

Library of Congress Control Number: 2014959017

ISBN 978–0–19–871611–2

Printed and bound by
Lightning Source UK Ltd

Cover image: iStockphoto

PREFACE

Much of this book was written in the British Library. Not the reading room in the British Museum where Karl Marx wrote *Das Kapital*, but its modern red brick successor, opened to the public in 1998. While working there, I couldn't help noticing the fraught interaction between the public and private purposes which the space serves. The reading rooms are used by students, academics, writers, and researchers from every discipline, whose only common trait is a need of quiet and calm. The rest of the building is occupied by the library's collections, galleries, conservation centre, gift shop, cloakroom, and a café area split over two levels. In 2009, a concession was granted to a private company to operate the café, which serves posh food.

The café is always busy, but space is at a premium and writers and academics are notorious for their ability to nurse a single cup of coffee for an entire afternoon. Impecunious students are even worse—sometimes attempting to bring their own flasks in. A constant, low-level turf war takes place between the café management and those who seek to use the space without buying enough high-margin beverages and cakes. The scramble for space reaches a higher pitch during exam season. Stepping outside of the hushed reading rooms, one is confronted with a public institution which has been at least partially captured for private gain.

I am not suggesting that the coffee should be free or that the British Library should not have granted a concession to a private company. The cost of running the reading rooms, which are well staffed and efficient, and maintaining the building must be huge. These services are free to users and many good books would not be written without them. The question is whether in awarding the concession sufficient regard was given to the way in which public and private interests would be accommodated in the limited space available. This question replicates itself in libraries, museums, hospitals, schools, and many other public spaces across Europe and the world.

It is part of a broader question: how can the essential characteristics of public services be maintained when the private sector becomes involved? If we accept that there are some activities which the private sector is better suited to carry out (selling coffee may be one of them), then the need to engage in procurement becomes clear. The public sector's reach is by definition greater than its grasp, because there are many functions which we expect the State to vouchsafe without necessarily delivering itself. Expectations of public services in European countries are generally high, while expectations regarding the taxation which funds public expenditure are more variable.

Universal, free-at-point-of-access service models remain common in areas such as education, healthcare, and emergency services. However, direct payment by users for utilities, transport, civil justice, and other services is now widespread. Regardless of the delivery model, the areas in which the State is able to provide without any recourse to the market are very few. Large swathes of public service provision have been opened up to competition, together with the more traditional need for governments to procure supplies and works. The field of competition for these contracts has also extended beyond national borders and the European Union into the growing number of countries which are party to the World Trade Organization's Government Procurement Agreement. Public procurement is about managing this interaction with the market.

This book is an attempt to synthesize three distinct perspectives on procurement which often seem to be at cross-purposes: those of the lawyer, the practitioner, and the policy-maker. The recent reform of the EU public procurement directives provides an opportune moment for this work, as it has brought to the fore various conflicts between these three perspectives. Can cross-border competition for contracts be reconciled with the desire to support small businesses and local industries? Are environmental and social responsibility antithetical to value for money and efficiency in procedures? This book assumes that it is not possible to answer these questions from a purely legal, economic, or political standpoint. An understanding of how rules inform practice, both at the individual organization level and in aggregate, is essential.

Fortunately, this understanding is aided by a recent flourishing of interdisciplinary activity in the field of public procurement. The experience of practitioners, as reflected in quantitative and qualitative research, case studies, codes of practice, and professional qualifications, is increasingly referenced in procurement policy and law. Among theorists, the number pursuing a purely legal or economic understanding is perhaps diminishing—as the volume of recent publications on environmental, social, and innovation aspects of public procurement testifies. The advent of the 2014 directives effectively moves such 'secondary' aspects of procurement into the mainstream. At the same time, exchange with other jurisdictions continues to grow both in breadth and depth. It is an exciting time to be a procurement anorak.

The desire to write this book arose when an American colleague asked me for reading recommendations on EU public procurement. While several excellent texts sprung to mind, there seemed to be little that was accessible to those with an interest in the day-to-day practice of procurement, together with its legal and policy dimensions. With the finalization of the new directives imminent, I set myself the challenge of providing something which might go some way towards filling this gap. As the project took shape, I realized there was a certain vanity to my endeavour. How could a single volume capture all that is new in the 2014 directives, let alone what it means in practice or why it is important? The answer is, of course, that it cannot. In seeking to explain the rules, I have come across as many questions as answers, and am filled with renewed respect for the practitioners, academics, and legislators who dedicate themselves to understanding and applying procurement law.

The 2014 directives are far from perfect. Even the least cynical reader of these instruments will wonder at some of their idiosyncrasies and be pained by their linguistic infelicities—both of which are presently being transposed into 28 national legal systems. Their scope, complexity, and detail can be baffling, and yet they must be applied by thousands of individuals involved in public sector procurement across Europe. Each new generation of directives requires understanding of what has come before, as well as fresh interpretation. The steady stream of cases from the Court of Justice in Luxembourg, together with developments in the many related areas of law and policy with an impact on procurement, add to this palimpsest. Perhaps my American colleague had underestimated all this in her innocent request.

No one can predict where the most recent revision will lead to over the next decade, nor which countries will be at the table to negotiate future updates. We can, however, take a critical survey of the current landscape to identify the most advantageous routes to attain value for money and sustainability in procurement, as well as some potentially more treacherous ones. At the time of writing, the 2014 directives have not yet been transposed into national law in the Member States. While there are certain areas in which national legislators must make substantive choices, these are relatively few compared to the detailed common provisions which will prevail in all 28 Member States. If it is not then premature to analyse the substantive content of the new procurement rules at this stage, it is certainly too early to comment on their effect. Constant developments in practice and the case law of the Court of Justice mean that no book about public procurement can hope to remain current for very long. But as national governments and contracting authorities prepare to implement the new rules, consideration of both their overarching structure and their detail seems timely.

It has always been a conceit of the EU directives that they regulate the procedural aspects of procurement and leave the substantive choice of 'what to buy' up to the individual contracting authority. As I hope the following chapters will show, however, these two elements are everywhere entwined. Procedures, and especially the principles underpinning those procedures, shape the outcome of procurement. Over time, they also shape the way in which public contracts are conceived of, funded, and managed. This in turn invites the regulation of new forms of contracting, as can be seen in the coverage by the 2014 directives of concessions and various forms of public-public cooperation. Transparency and competition do not in themselves guarantee a fair use of space or reasonable prices for coffee in a public building. They do provide a structure for the mediation of public and private interests where the decision is taken to award a contract—the foundation on which so much of the public sector is now built.

ACKNOWLEDGEMENTS

In structuring this book, I had in mind both readers with advanced knowledge of procurement and those with a more casual or topical interest. I have been privileged to spend much of the past seven years discussing procurement with public sector workers, contractors, lawyers, consultants, activists, policy-makers, and academics, and have learned from each. If this book succeeds at all, I hope it is as a synthesis of these different perspectives. Within the pantheon of impressive procurement 'heads', I have encountered a few who deserve special acknowledgement here. Thanks go first to Mark Cook of Anthony Collins Solicitors, who as consultant editor shared his ample experience and insight into many of the topics covered. This project forms part of my graduate work at Birkbeck College, University of London, and I am particularly grateful to Professor Deborah Mabbett, my supervisor within the Politics Department, who challenged me to draw connections between procurement and a wider scholarship on public sector management. I am also grateful to Professor Dermot Cahill, Pedro Telles, and all at Bangor University's Institute for Competition and Procurement Studies, for providing encouragement and inviting me to their fabulous conferences.

I could not have written this book without the forbearance of my colleagues at London Fire Brigade, who kept me sane with their good humour and sense. At the European Commission, Robert Kaukewitsch and Bertrand Wert have shown energy and initiative in supporting projects which target the environmental and innovation aspects of procurement, and which have informed my work and that of many others. A number of people read and commented on drafts of this work or advised on particular points, among whom Roberto Caranta, Anna-Marie Curran, Omer Dekel, Daçian Dragos, Isabel Hyde, Lionel McCarthy, and Hans-Joachim Priess deserve special mention and gratitude. This book is dedicated to Jeanne Copeland and Lionel McCarthy of Achilles Ireland, who infected me with their passion for procurement and continue to challenge me with difficult questions.

I would also like to thank the anonymous peer reviewers who commented on both the proposal and final manuscript.

I remain solely responsible for each and every error contained herein.

Abby Semple, LL.B. (Dub)
September 2014

CONTENTS

TABLE OF CASES

References are to paragraph number apart from the Introduction, when Roman Numerals are used.

UNITED KINGDOM AND IRELAND

EUROPEAN UNION

TABLE OF LEGISLATION

References are to paragraph number apart from the Introduction, when Roman Numerals are used.

INTERNATIONAL

LIST OF ABBREVIATIONS

CETA	Comprehensive Economic and Trade Agreement
CJEU	Court of Justice of the European Union
CPN	competitive procedure with negotiation
CPV	common procurement vocabulary
CVD	Clean Vehicles Directive
DPS	dynamic purchasing system
ECI	European Citizens Initiative
EIA	Environmental Impact Assessment
EMAS	Eco-management and Audit Scheme
ESPD	European Single Procurement Document
EU	European Union
EU27	European Union of 27 Member States
GPA	Government Procurement Agreement
GPP	green public procurement
GPS	Global Positioning System
ICLEI	International Council for Local Environmental Initiatives
IMF	International Monetary Fund
ISO	International Organization for Standardization
ITT	invitation to tender
KPI	key performance indicator
LCC	life-cycle costing
MEAT	most economically advantageous tender
NPV	net present value
OECD	Organisation for Economic Cooperation and Development
OJEU	Official Journal of the European Union
PCR	Public Contracts Regulations
PFI	Private Finance Initiative
PIN	prior information notice
PPP	public-private partnership
PSC	public sector comparator
PWD	Posted Workers Directive
R&D	research and development
RoHS	Restriction of Hazardous Substances
RSC	Rules of the Superior Courts
SDR	Special Drawing Rights
SGEI	services of general economic interest
SLA	service level agreement
SMEs	small and medium-sized enterprises
SPP	sustainable public procurement
SROI	social return on investment

TCC	Technology and Construction Court
TED	Tenders Electronic Daily
TFEU	Treaty on the Functioning of the European Union
TTIP	Transatlantic Trade and Investment Partnership
TUPE	Transfer of Undertakings (Protection of Employment)
UCR	Utilities Contracts Regulations
UK	United Kingdom
VEAT	voluntary ex ante transparency notice
VfM	value for money
WEEE	Waste Electronic and Electrical Equipment
WTO	World Trade Organization

INTRODUCTION

Why Does Public Procurement Matter?

Public procurement is increasingly identified as a means of achieving policy objectives from carbon reduction to a more innovative, resilient, and inclusive economy. Many services traditionally provided by government are now carried out by external contractors, bringing focus to the way in which public contracts influence the wider market, as well as delivering societal needs. Public expenditure on goods, services, and works represents an average of 13 per cent of GDP in OECD countries, and amounts to some €2.5 trillion annually or 19 per cent of GDP in the European Union.[1] Competition to win larger contracts takes place under European Union and World Trade Organization rules, which aim to promote the free movement of goods and services across borders. At the same time, constraints on public spending mean that commissioning and procurement officers are under pressure to demonstrate greater value for money and, in some cases, to champion local or national firms. Policies which aim to leverage procurement must take account of these multiple strings pulling in different directions. This book seeks to critically examine the interaction between procurement law, policy, and practice within the structure provided by the 2014 procurement directives.

The recent reform of the EU legal framework has brought to light the manifold agendas to which public procurement is subject. As Member States implement the three 2014 directives,[2] this book analyses the new legislation in light of the experience of public authorities under the previous generation of directives adopted in 2004. What effect do the rules have on levels of competition, value for money, and social and environmental goals? How can legislators, policy-makers, procurers, and their advisers make use of the flexibilities in the new legislation to further their objectives? Answering these questions requires an understanding of how real

---

[1] *OECD Government at a Glance 2013* (total value of public expenditure on goods and services); *European Commission Public Procurement Indicators 2011* (total expenditure on works, goods, and services). An estimated €425 billion of this expenditure was advertised on Tenders Electronic Daily (TED) in 2011.

[2] Directive 2014/23/EU of the European Parliament and of the Council on the award of concession contracts (hereinafter, 'the Concessions Directive'); Directive 2014/24/EU of the European Parliament and of the Council on public procurement and repealing Directive 2004/18/EC (hereinafter, 'the Public Sector Directive'); and Directive 2014/25/EU on procurement by entities operating in the water, energy, transport and postal services sector and repealing Directive 2004/17/EC (hereinafter, 'the Utilities Directive').

public authorities and companies bidding for public contracts act, amid constraints on their time, capacity, and budgets. This perspective has often been missing from legislative and policy initiatives on procurement. Only in more recent years have statistical studies of procurement been supplemented with qualitative research carried out on a large international scale.[3] A number of references to this research are made in this text, to help place legal and policy concepts in the context of procurement practice in different Member States.

The central idea behind the chapters which follow is that the twin engines of legal compliance and policy leverage can serve to improve procurement practices and deliver better overall outcomes, including value for money. The primary mechanisms by which this is achieved are the greater transparency and competition brought to procedures by law, and the consideration of longer-term outcomes which social, environmental, and economic policies require. While many systems for organizing procurement subscribe to these objectives in theory, only where the governance framework for procurement encapsulates them can they be meaningfully tracked and enforced. This is not to say that better value and sustainability in public contracts follow automatically from policy and law; they are necessary but not sufficient conditions for progress towards these objectives. Three major themes emerge from this analysis, and run through the chapters that follow.

1. The breadth and depth of the procurement rules has shifted

The range of bodies (*ratione personae*) and contracts (*ratione materiae*) to which the EU rules apply has been addressed in a number of decisions of the Court of Justice of the European Union,[4] and may now be considered relatively clear. However, in several areas, the obligations arising under EU law have remained uncertain. The 2004 directives and their predecessors left a number of ambiguities and gaps regarding their scope which were ripe for judicial interpretation, as do their 2014 successors. The Court has delivered over 400 judgments on public procurement, with many more being issued by national courts and tribunals. One of the tasks

---

[3] Much of this research has focused on the strategic use of procurement, e.g. to achieve environmental and social goals. See in particular: Essig, M., Frijdal, J., Kahlenborn, W., and Moser, C. (2011) *Strategic Use of Public Procurement in Europe: Final Report to the European Commission* (Berlin: Adelphi); Centre for European Policy Studies and College of Europe (2012) *Monitoring the Uptake of Green Public Procurement in the EU27* (Brussels: European Commission); and O'Rourke, A., Leire, C., and Bowden, T. (2013) *Sustainable Public Procurement: A Global View*, Final report on behalf of the United Nations Environment Program. A series of studies on the economic impact of the 2004 directives carried out on behalf of the European Commission and published in 2011 are also cited in this text. They are available on the website of the Directorate General for Internal Market and Services.

[4] Hereinafter, 'the Court' or 'CJEU'.

of the revision process was to incorporate the Court's jurisprudence in a variety of areas, including public-public cooperation, modifications to contracts, award of service concessions, and use of social criteria.

Relatively few of the changes under the new directives can properly be called a codification of existing case law. Rather, they are an attempt to establish parameters for the Court's judgments which, taken together, expanded the scope of the procurement rules beyond what the 'reasonably well-informed and normally diligent' reader of the earlier directives might have understood them to cover.[5] Most prominently, the idea that contracts not covered by the directives might nevertheless be of certain cross-border interest, and thus subject to the Treaty principles and other positive obligations, has emerged from the Court's jurisprudence. The responsibilities which contracting authorities have where they enter into development agreements and public-private partnerships (PPPs), award contracts to an in-house company, or set up a shared service arrangement with other public bodies, have also been subject to the Court's interpretation. The new directives define the conditions under which award of contracts to an in-house (*Teckal*) company, or cooperation between public authorities to achieve common objectives (*Hamburg cooperation*), are exempt from the directives.

The 2014 directives set out detailed rules for when a modification to a contract after its award will necessitate a new competition, again drawing on the Court's case law, while not relying on it exclusively. The general principle that modifications will require a new competition is subject to numerous exceptions—the scope of which will no doubt be tested in the courts. The 2014 directives also create new exemptions for certain types of contract, such as the provision of legal services which are not considered to be of cross-border interest, and contracts awarded in the course of oil and gas exploration activity (previously covered by Directive 2004/17/EC).

In addition to contracts which are either fully covered or fully excluded, the 2014 directives encompass a lighter regulatory regime for social and related services, and for concessions. The new Concessions Directive seeks to regulate arrangements where, instead of a public body paying for services or works, a right is granted to a private operator who takes on the risk associated with the activity. Concessions are widely used for civil engineering and transport, energy and water projects, and to manage services such as waste collection. With over 25 cases coming before the

---

[5] The phrase was used by the Court in Case C-19/00 *SIAC v County Council of the County of Mayo* [2001] ECR I-07725 to describe the standard of transparency required for award criteria—with the 'reasonably well-informed and normally diligent' tenderer taking on a similar role to the 'man on the Clapham omnibus' in common law. The standard also appears in the 2014 directives to define the level of effort which can be expected from tenderers in producing data for life-cycle costing (see discussion in Chapter 7) and was recently considered by the UK Supreme Court in *Healthcare at Home Ltd (Appellant) v The Common Services Agency (Respondent) Scotland* [2014] UKSC 49 (see discussion in Chapters 4 and 8).

Court of Justice since 2000 on concessions, the need for regulation in this area was clear. The Concessions Directive replicates many—but not all—of the obligations found in the Public Sector and Utilities Directives relating to advertisement, time limits, specifications, selection and award criteria, notification of results, subcontracting, and modifications to contracts. Concessions valued at or above the threshold of €5,186,000 have also been brought within the scope of the Remedies Directives.

Almost as many cases came before the Court in relation to Annex IIB or 'non-priority' services—those which were considered to be of less cross-border interest and so were not subject to the full scope of obligations under the 2004 directives. Non-priority services no longer exist as a separate category under the 2014 directives. Many now fall under the separate, lighter regime for social and other specific services set out in Title III of the Directives. This may not in practice represent a significant shift in the duties of contracting authorities when awarding these services, as the basic requirements of advertising, acting transparently, and applying equal treatment are essentially those already articulated by the Court in respect of non-priority services.[6] However, Title III does create an additional obligation on national governments to ensure that contracting authorities can take into account:

> quality, continuity, accessibility, affordability, availability and comprehensiveness of the services, the specific needs of different categories of users, including disadvantaged and vulnerable groups, the involvement and empowerment of users and innovation.[7]

Member States may also stipulate that Title III contracts are not awarded on the basis of lowest cost or lowest price.

As the scope of coverage of the procurement rules has evolved, many public authorities have found that their strategies and decisions are affected in unexpected ways. The desire to avoid full application of the rules is often a motivating factor—but is this justified by cost or time savings? The need to obtain legal advice before treating a contract as exempt, and the cost implications of reduced competition, may outweigh any advantages gained. A consequence of the shifting landscape of regulated procurement is the need to update procedures and develop administrative capacity and expertise. Dedicated PPP units, for example, have emerged as one way of coordinating public sector strategies while complying with the rules. Centralized framework agreements and other forms of central purchasing may also continue to

---

[6] One difference is that contracts covered by Title III are not subject to the rules on formulation of technical specifications to which non-priority service contracts were subject, as discussed in Chapter 1. Higher thresholds also apply in respect of Title III services: €750,000 under the Public Sector Directive and €1 million under the Utilities Directive.

[7] Art 76(2) Public Sector Directive; and Art 93(2) Utilities Directive.

grow in popularity under the new directives, as these are seen as efficient ways of organizing procurement and benefiting from economies of scale.

International agreements affecting procurement

In parallel to the revision of the EU directives, the WTO Government Procurement Agreement (GPA) has been renegotiated. In 2011, revisions to the GPA were agreed which extend its coverage of sub-national authorities and those operating in the utilities sector, as well as updating the rules for award of contracts and use of e-procurement systems. Construction contracts have also been included for the first time. The revised agreement entered into force on 6 April 2014 following ratification of the Protocol of Amendment by Israel. In terms of direct impact on procurement practices, the changes are likely to be of greater significance outside of Europe, as compliance with the EU procurement directives generally implies compliance with the GPA. However, it is important for European contracting authorities to be aware of the list of countries which are party to the agreement,[8] in order to ensure that economic operators from those countries are given the same rights as EU operators. Ten countries, including China, are in the process of negotiating accession.[9]

Two other international developments are likely to shape public procurement in years to come. The first is the proposed free trade agreements between the European Union and Canada and the United States. The Comprehensive Economic and Trade Agreement (CETA) with Canada and the Transatlantic Trade and Investment Partnership (TTIP) with the United States both have the potential to expose public contracts to greater levels of transatlantic competition. As with the GPA, the impact of these agreements on procurement procedures is likely to be more noticeable outside of Europe, in particular if sub-national governments in Canada and the United States have to allow European businesses to compete for some contracts for the first time. However, the overall reduction in tariffs and trade barriers which these agreements envision will also mean more American and Canadian companies bidding for contracts awarded in Europe. CETA, for example, provides for the liberalization of trade in financial services, telecommunications, energy, and transport.

The second major development with the potential to affect both the economic and environmental aspects of public procurement is the negotiation of a legally binding global climate agreement under the United Nations Framework Convention on Climate Change. If successful, this would create new obligations on governments

---

[8] There are currently 14 accession parties in addition to the European Union: Canada, Japan, Korea, the United States, Hong Kong, Chinese Taipei, Armenia, the Netherlands with regard to Aruba, Norway, Iceland, Israel, Liechtenstein, Singapore, and Switzerland.

[9] In addition to China, the countries negotiating accession as of September 2014 are: Moldova, Montenegro, New Zealand, Ukraine, Albania, Georgia, Jordan, the Kyrgyz Republic, and Oman.

to reduce greenhouse gas emissions, linked to a comprehensive accounting system and financial or other sanctions for breaches. Needless to say, this would affect the way in which public contracts are carried out, as well as creating new markets for technologies linked to climate change mitigation and adaptation. At the time of writing, the content of the global agreement due to be adopted in 2015 and implemented by 2020 is not yet clear.[10] Europe has already committed to a second round of legally binding emission reductions under the Kyoto protocol. The extent to which the 2014 directives can assist governments in meeting climate change commitments is one of the questions addressed by this book.

2. Public procurement is being used to achieve a growing list of policy objectives

Governments have always seen public contracts as a means of achieving other policy aims, such as reduction of unemployment or support for particular industries, trades, or disadvantaged groups.[11] As the scope of procurement has expanded to encompass activities which were previously delivered directly by the public sector, the list of policy objectives associated with public contracts has also grown. The use of public contracts to promote economic, environmental, and social aims is often referred to as 'strategic' procurement—in that it serves one or more broader strategies in addition to obtaining the required goods, services, or works.[12] Not everyone has seen this as a positive development—either because they disagree with the specific policies being implemented, or because it is seen as a distraction from the core commercial functions of procurement. On this view, it is best not to fetter government-as-consumer with excess baggage.

Conversely, one may argue that the idea that governments can somehow step into the role of a private entity for the purpose of awarding contracts is chimerical: they are spending public money, and the manner in which they do so constitutes public policy as much as taxation or regulation does. In mediating between these two views of its role, there is perhaps a distinction to be made between public procurement as a *policy instrument*—subject to procedural guarantees of fairness,

---

[10] For consideration of the different top-down, bottom-up, and hybrid mechanisms to control emissions which the agreement may employ, see Edenhofer, O., Flachsland C., Stavins, R., and Stowe, R. (2013) *Identifying Options for a New International Climate Regime arising from the Durban Platform for Enhanced Action* (Harvard: John F. Kennedy School of Government).

[11] On policies linking procurement to social objectives in various jurisdictions over time, see McCrudden, C. (2007) *Buying Social Justice: Equality, Government Procurement and Legal Change* (Oxford: Oxford University Press).

[12] For discussion of various legal aspects of strategic procurement, see Arrowsmith, S. and Kunzlik, P. (eds) (2009) *Social and Environmental Policies in EC Procurement Law: New Directives and New Directions* (Cambridge: Cambridge University Press); and Caranta, R. and Trybus, M. (eds) (2010) *The Law of Green and Social Procurement in Europe* (Copenhagen: DJØF Publishing).

transparency, and competition—and procurement which is *political* in a sense which is not answerable to these principles. The 2014 directives aim to maintain this distinction, not least through the requirements that criteria be linked to the subject-matter of the contract, advertised in advance, and objectively verifiable. The coherence and fitness for purpose of these approaches is assessed throughout this book with reference to their practical effects.

Value for money and economic sustainability

The revision of the EU procurement directives came hard on the heels of Europe's worst economic crisis in several generations. With high rates of unemployment and stagnant growth, the case for using public contracts to aid recovery was made in many countries, while others focused on the need to reduce government deficits by cutting costs. Regardless of which route was chosen, renewed focus has been placed on the wider economic impact of public contracts. Some modes of contracting, such as public-private partnerships, have seen a retrenchment due to lower availability of private debt and equity financing. Other forms, such as public-public cooperation and central purchasing, appear to have grown in popularity as budgets and resources have been constrained.[13] At the same time, support for participation by small and medium-sized enterprises (SMEs) in public procurement has also strengthened at local, national, and European level. Several measures intended to encourage participation by SMEs have been included in the 2014 directives, such as division of contracts into lots, use of the European Single Procurement Document, and maximum turnover requirements. I examine how these may work in practice, while questioning the evidence that SMEs are seriously under-represented in EU-level tender procedures.

Value for money remains the foremost objective associated with public procurement in most jurisdictions. Finding the appropriate trade-off point between cost and quality, and long- and short-term value, remains a project for individual contracting authorities supported by national policy. Broader concepts of value for money look at the economic impact of procurement and ask whether it is sustainable. There are a number of ways of promoting economic sustainability in procurement, from ensuring that contractors are financially sound and tax compliant, to encouraging competition from a diverse range of enterprises, to assessing the effects which a public contract will have on local employment and wages. In the context of EU procurement, support for SMEs and local employment must be reconciled with the objectives of allowing cross-border competition and ensuring equal treatment of all operators. At present, levels of cross-border procurement remain very

---

[13] For a discussion of trends in centralized purchasing, see Albano, G. and Sparro, M. (2010) 'Flexible Strategies for Centralized Public Procurement' 1(2) *Review of Economics and Institutions* Article 4.

low indeed,[14] raising questions about the effectiveness of EU procurement law in achieving one of its central aims—that of free movement of goods and services.

The economic crisis has brought pressure to bear on free trade as a means of promoting greater economic welfare. In common with areas of competition law such as State aid, the reform of the procurement rules has sought to balance the removal of barriers to trade with the acknowledgement that government support for certain industries or types of activity also has a role to play in the economy. The creation of a lighter regime for social, health care, and educational services and the new ability to reserve certain contracts for competition by public service organizations fall under this heading. Depending on the standpoint of the commentator, these steps will either be construed as a welcome recognition of the social and local importance of public procurement or a regression to damaging protectionism. Regardless of which view is taken, the new rules provide for a markedly different approach to the award of such services from that which applies to a standard supply contract, for example.

A major feature of the revision is the enhanced ability for public authorities to negotiate aspects of their contracts. More flexible procedures may help to deliver value for money in certain cases—although this is entirely dependent on the ability of contracting authorities to negotiate effectively. Selection and award criteria can also be used to target financial and economic sustainability in tender procedures, such as by the exclusion of operators for non-payment of taxes or the rejection of abnormally low tenders, which is now mandatory where a tender is abnormally low due to non-compliance with applicable environmental, social, or labour obligations. However, considerable uncertainty still applies in this area due to the failure to agree a definition for abnormally low tenders at European level and the Court's jurisprudence regarding application of minimum wages and collective agreements in public contracts. Member States have the ability under the 2014 directives to extend obligations to subcontractors and to introduce provisions for their direct payment, either automatically or on request. The implementation of these provisions in a way which does not compromise or overly complicate liability for performance will pose challenges of its own.

Environmental and social sustainability

Sustainability is generally understood as encompassing three pillars: economic, social, and environmental. Impacts under each of these headings arise for most public contracts, with emissions of greenhouse gases, energy efficiency and development

---

[14] As of 2011, only 1.6 per cent of contracts advertised in the Official Journal were awarded to an undertaking established in another Member State. 11.4 per cent were indirectly awarded cross-border, eg via a subsidiary. Sylvest et al. (2011) *Final Report: Cross-Border Procurement above EU Thresholds* (Brussels: European Commission).

of renewable energy, fair working conditions, and tax compliance being among the most commonly targeted factors. The scope of government procurement is large—from routine supplies such as office IT equipment, to outsourced services such as training or waste collection, through to major infrastructure or military acquisitions. The range of social, environmental, and economic impacts associated with these contracts is similarly varied. Incorporating sustainability criteria directly into the award process has the advantage of maximizing their visibility and increasing the chances that competitors will take these seriously. At the same time, including sustainability criteria in the procurement process is largely meaningless if they are not backed up by effective verification techniques and contractual provisions which allow for monitoring and enforcement.

New rules on compliance with environmental, social, and labour law, use of third-party labels, life-cycle costing, and disclosure and monitoring of subcontractors have been included in the 2014 directives. These aim to address some of the key challenges associated with sustainable public procurement—the ability to effectively verify performance and to apply standards not only to main contractors, but also further down the supply chain. Procurement techniques which target environmental factors range from specification of more sustainable materials or production processes, to comparisons of carbon footprint or other metrics, through to energy performance contracting and other 'shared incentive' approaches to environmental management. The 2014 directives set out specific rules on life-cycle costing for the first time, including the possibility to monetize emissions and other environmental impacts. The rules on references to third-party (eco-)labels have been overhauled. I consider whether these rules will help or hinder the use of life-cycle costing and third-party labels, which are already relied on by many public bodies.

The 2014 directives also considerably enhance the scope for addressing social considerations in procurement. Approaches range from reserving contracts for enterprises employing a high percentage of disadvantaged workers, to awarding marks for fair trade products and enforcing contract clauses on minimum wages and working conditions. The extent to which social considerations can be taken into account in procurement is part of a wider debate on the social character of the internal market, which continues to play out in the Court's jurisprudence and is embodied in the different positions taken by the European Commission and Parliament in the reform process. Prominent incidences of substandard working conditions leading to injury and death—such as the collapse of the Rana Plaza factory in Bangladesh in 2013—have pushed many public sector bodies towards greater scrutiny of their supply chains. As with environmental considerations, the inclusion of social criteria can add complexity to tender processes, and in some cases carry additional costs, but many authorities consider socially responsible procurement essential both for ethical and reputational reasons. This book analyses approaches to socially responsible procurement which have emerged recently in

Europe, as well as those such as sheltered workshops and employment linkages which have a much longer pedigree.

3. Legal and professional skills are now essential for procurement

As is evident from the discussion of scope and policy objectives in this introduction, considerable complexity attaches to public procurement in Europe in the twenty-first century. In many public sector organizations, procurement is becoming increasingly professionalized, reflecting a change in its status from an administrative to a strategic function. The development of the Remedies Directives[15] has reinforced the extent to which in-house or external lawyers are involved in procurement procedures, with litigation or the threat of litigation a key concern. Nevertheless, most public sector workers with responsibility for commissioning and procurement are not lawyers. The sheer volume of legislation, case law, and guidance can make it difficult for practitioners to be confident that they have complied in many cases, much less that they have fully exploited the flexibilities and opportunities available to them.

The first EU directive relating to public procurement in 1970 weighed in at a mere three pages, the two 2004 directives each occupied over 100 pages, and the three 2014 directives cover more than 350 pages, supplemented by the separate directives governing remedies and defence procurement. While the total bulk of EU legislation still compares favourably to the nearly 2,000 pages of the US Federal Acquisition Regulation, for example, the addition of national implementing legislation in each of the 28 Member States tips the balance against us. This proliferation of legislation has been accompanied by, and to some extent reflects, the judicially driven development of rules governing the award of contracts which fall outside the full scope of application of the directives. However, it is worth pointing out that the complexity of the EU regime pales in comparison to the prospect of 28 separate systems for the award of public contracts.

The role of the Treaty principles and Court of Justice

The procurement rules have both a nucleus or core and a penumbra, and it is in this penumbra that the European Court of Justice has been most active. Often

---

[15] Directive 89/665/EEC on the coordination of the laws, regulations and administrative provisions relating to the application of review procedures to the award of public supply and public works contracts ('Public Sector Remedies Directive'); and Directive 92/13/EEC coordinating the laws, regulations and administrative provisions relating to the application of Community rules on the procurement procedures of entities operating in the water, energy, transport and telecommunications sectors ('Utilities Sector Remedies Directive') as amended by Directives 2007/66/EU and 2014/23/EU.

criticized for its terse or Delphic judgments, the Court has nonetheless contributed greatly to the development of public procurement as part of the broader body of Community law. At times, it has displayed a more progressive bent than the European Commission in its interpretation of the rules, perhaps most famously in the *Concordia* judgment which established the legitimacy of environmental award criteria and, more recently, the *Dutch Coffee* case which extended this approach to social criteria.[16] Throughout this book, the role of the Court's case law in contributing to a full understanding of the EU procurement rules is highlighted. As noted, the fact that many of these judgments have been encapsulated in the 2014 directives does not preclude further judicial developments, especially in areas which have been left open to interpretation, such as the rules on abnormally low tenders and modifications to contracts.

The principles which underlie the EU public procurement regime are the free movement of goods and services, mutual recognition, non-discrimination and equal treatment, transparency, and proportionality. While these principles are grounded in the Treaty on the Functioning of the European Union (TFEU), their specific application in the context of public procurement has been elaborated via the Court's case law. The principles of equal treatment and transparency in particular have been invoked to address gaps in the substantive rules provided by the directives. Proportionality has been developed as a test applicable to procurement measures, in particular where these are found to interfere with other principles or freedoms under the Treaty.

An understanding of the Treaty principles is therefore indispensable for practitioners, not least as they affect contracts both above and below the EU thresholds, and those which are not fully subject to the directives. Certain other principles contained within the Treaty also have the potential to influence public procurement—notably the requirements to integrate environmental and social protection into policy and legislation, and the principle of subsidiarity. The Charter of Fundamental Rights of the European Union, which came into effect with the Lisbon Treaty in 2009, is another source of obligations which may be found to be directly applicable in the award of public contracts. While the Charter has been referenced in a number of procurement judgments, the scope of its application to procurement measures has not been fully tested to date.

The growing need for procurement skills and expertise

As noted, the 2014 directives offer greater choice between procedures and make it easier for public authorities to engage in negotiation and dialogue with bidders. The new innovation partnership and competitive procedure with negotiation, and the revised competitive dialogue, all allow for a greater degree of interaction with

---

[16] Case C-513/99 *Concordia Bus Finland Oy Ab, formerly Stagecoach Finland Oy Ab v Helsingin kaupunki and HKL-Bussiliikenne* [2002] ECR I-07213; and Case C-368/10 *Commission v The Kingdom of the Netherlands*, not yet reported.

bidders as part of the contract award process. Choice of procedure is becoming more important as part of procurement strategy. The flexibilities offered in terms of choice of procedure may compensate in part for the growing scope of contracts which are subject to the directives. However, the new procedures also demand capacities which are not readily available within all public sector bodies, such as the ability to negotiate commercial terms or develop strategy related to intellectual property.

The innovation partnership procedure in particular will require application of legal and technical expertise. It aims at the development and subsequent purchase of innovative products, services, or works 'provided that they correspond to the agreed performance levels and maximum costs', through the award of one or more phased contracts. The intention is to help close the gap between research and development (R&D) services, which fall under an exemption to the directives, and the acquisition of the resulting solutions on a commercial scale. The State aid rules on R&D and innovation have recently been reformed, and specific funding opportunities for pre-commercial and commercial innovation procurement exist under the Horizon 2020 programme. Procurement of innovative goods and services is seen as a way of supporting broader economic development, while capturing the benefits of newly developed technology and processes to help meet public sector needs.

Rules on conflict of interest and the treatment of operators who have been involved in a pre-procurement procedure are set out in the 2014 directives for the first time,[17] but follow from the Court's interpretation of the principle of equal treatment. The merits of direct consultation with suppliers both before and during procurement have been recognized at many levels. However, pre-procurement activities can also pose challenges in terms of perceived advantages, integrity, and fairness. Similarly, the rules on confidentiality of tender submissions address what is sometimes seen as a lacuna in terms of the fair treatment of bidders. Many organizations have already developed standing orders and procedures which address these considerations; these will need to be reviewed to ensure their compliance with the 2014 directives and national implementing legislation. Choice of procedure, successful negotiation, and compliance with confidentiality and conflict of interest rules are all likely to add to the demand for more advanced procurement skills across the public sector.

Chapter Contents

Chapter 1 sets out the scope of application of the 2014 directives and the specific exemptions to them. The rules on valuation and thresholds, mixed contracts, and

---

[17] Art 24 Public Sector Directive; Art 42 Utilities Directive; and Art 35 Concessions Directive.

the specific exclusions which apply in respect of certain services and contracts in the defence and security sector are covered. It then turns to the new lighter regime in respect of social and related services (Title III services) and the separate rules for award of concessions under Directive 2014/23/EU. The rules on public-public cooperation (*Teckal* and *Hamburg* exemptions) are set out, together with those on public-private partnerships and land development agreements. Chapter 1 concludes with an analysis of the CJEU's jurisprudence on contracts which are of 'certain cross-border interest' and the extent to which this has expanded the scope of the procurement rules.

Chapter 2 examines the principles which underlie the EU public procurement regime and how these have been developed in the Court's case law. Free movement of goods and services, mutual recognition, equal treatment and non-discrimination, transparency, and proportionality are covered. The possibility of the equal treatment principle leading to a requirement for positive discrimination measures—for example, where an incumbent has an informational advantage over other competitors—is discussed. The wider implications of the transparency principle are also explored; for example, as the basis for open contracting, in which data about public contracts is made freely available on the internet. Chapter 2 also looks at the Court's case law for signs of how the obligations set out in the Charter of Fundamental Rights may take shape in the procurement context.

Chapter 3 presents each of the procedures, including the new innovation partnership procedure, competitive procedure with negotiation, and revised competitive dialogue. It identifies the changes which have been made to allow greater flexibility to contracting authorities in choice of procedure and in negotiating aspects of contracts. The timelines and stages for each of the procedures are set out, together with their resource implications and the situations in which they may be appropriate. The impact of the move to fully electronic tendering and use of the European Single Procurement Document are considered. Framework agreements are addressed in detail, with briefer sections on dynamic purchasing systems, design contests, electronic auctions, and electronic catalogues. Joint and central purchasing are also considered, together with the use of lots.

Chapter 4 focuses on the criteria which may be applied in tender procedures and how these affect procurement outcomes. Substantial revision has been undertaken regarding the mandatory and discretionary grounds for exclusion, selection of operators, technical specifications, and award criteria. Many of these changes are intended to contribute to more sustainable procurement or to the inclusion of SMEs, as well as streamlining procurement processes. However, in some cases they may actually make it more difficult to select suitable tenderers and award contracts. The rules on means of proof and verification are reviewed, with critical discussion of what they will mean in practice. The rules regarding treatment of abnormally low tenders are also discussed.

Chapter 5 looks at the form which public contracts take and how they are managed in practice. While standard-form contracts are still used by many public authorities, the evolution of the procurement rules and the inclusion of strategic elements demands a more sophisticated approach to contract drafting and management. The rules on modifications to contracts, incorporated in all three of the 2014 directives, provide a particular incentive for the inclusion of well-drafted contract review clauses which enable future changes to be made. I examine these rules in detail, asking how they relate to various situations which have previously been addressed by the Court in its case law, such as amendment of payment terms or a change of contractor or subcontractor. Practical application of the new subcontracting provisions, as well as some potential pitfalls, are discussed in Chapter 5.

Chapter 6 addresses a key concern of public procurement: how can value for money be achieved? Although this area is not directly regulated by the EU directives, it is affected by each stage of the procurement process from identifying and classifying needs through to contract management. Evidence regarding the impact of different procurement procedures on costs, including transaction costs, is analysed. Techniques are identified for evaluating longer-term costs such as life-cycle costing, use of a public sector comparator, and net present value calculations, with a consideration of how these function within the procurement rules. The effect of different public-sector budgeting practices such as performance-based and multi-year budgeting is also considered. Measuring the qualitative outcomes of procurement is difficult, and has often been ignored in policies which equate value for money with low costs. I argue that while the concept of value for money is subjective, there are a number of objective measures and principles in contract design, award, and management which consistently contribute to value. The chapter concludes with recommendations for how longer-term value can be incorporated into procurement processes.

Chapter 7 takes a critical look at environmental and social responsibility in procurement. Providing a greater ability to take these strategic elements into account was one of the key ambitions of the reform of the directives, with distinctly mixed results. There is a lack of mandatory measures addressing sustainability, but some enhancement of discretionary possibilities. The interaction between the possibilities in the directives, and the large volume of secondary EU legislation regulating everything from energy efficiency to equality is explored. The role of the broader legal and policy framework in supporting sustainable procurement—and at times in limiting it—is discussed with a particular critique of the 'link to the subject-matter' requirement developed in the Court's case law. Relevant approaches are identified for the prioritization of sustainable procurement activities, use of common criteria, and adaptation of e-procurement systems.

The scope for legal challenges under the Remedies Directives and via infringement actions by the European Commission is examined in Chapter 8, with consideration of how this influences procurement practice. CJEU case law highlights both the need for national rules to provide effective remedies and the discretion which exists over how this is done. The rules for challenging award of public contracts in the UK and Ireland are analysed, including case law on time limits, interim measures, disclosure, award of damages, and other remedies. Comparison is made between the UK and Irish courts' approach to the automatic suspension of contract award where a challenge is made under the remedies regime, and the conditions under which it may be lifted. The chapter concludes by highlighting the implications of this case law for procurement practice in terms of clarifications, evaluation procedures, and notification of outcomes. These areas have been fertile sources of legal challenge, and steps which can help to limit this risk are identified. Some observations are also made on the overall impact of the remedies regime on procurement and potential areas for reform.

1

THE SCOPE OF PROCUREMENT UNDER EU LAW

Public expenditure takes a wide variety of forms, not all of which are covered by the **1.01** EU procurement rules. This chapter identifies the range of activities and arrangements which fall within the 2014 procurement directives, and examines how the definition of contracts which are subject to some or all of the rules has evolved over time. The Treaty on the Functioning of the European Union (the Treaty) forms the basis in primary law for EU regulation of public procurement, in particular its provisions on free movement of goods and services, freedom of establishment, and the development of the internal market.[1] The application of these principles by the Court has formed the basis for the extension of the procurement rules into areas not explicitly covered by the text of previous directives, as discussed in the final section of this chapter. The origin and possible future developments in these principles as they relate to procurement are explored in Chapter 2.

In EU law, a 'public contract' is defined by who is doing the purchasing, what **1.02** they are buying, and from whom they buy it. The procurement directives cover central government, sub-central government, bodies governed by public law, and associations of one or more of these authorities or bodies. They also cover public undertakings and private or semi-private entities which have been granted special or exclusive rights in the water, energy, transport, and postal sectors, where they award contracts related to these activities. The directives apply to contracts with an estimated value above monetary thresholds which are linked to those under the WTO Government Procurement Agreement. Certain types of public expenditure fall outside of the EU and WTO rules, for example the purchase of land, social welfare payments, and employment contracts. Subsidies, grants, and contracts for research and development services are also excluded in most circumstances. Separate rules apply for defence procurement and, with the coming into force of the 2014 directives, to concessions and social, health care, and other specific services. The justification for these varying levels of regulation generally lies in the

---

[1] As set out in Arts 26, 28, 34, 49, and 56 of the Treaty.

lack of cross-border interest which is imputed to the contracts, or the impracticality of holding a tender competition, for example where a public authority wishes to purchase land or hire employees.

Definition of Public Contracts

1.03 Public contracts are defined in Article 2(5) of the Public Sector Directive as:

> contracts for pecuniary interest concluded in writing between one or more economic operators and one or more contracting authorities and having as their object the execution of works, the supply of products or the provision of services.

The concept of an economic operator, who forms one of the necessary parties to a public contract, includes any natural or legal person, grouping, or public entity which offers supplies, services, or works on the market. The inclusion of public entities in the definition is significant in light of the Court's case law on public-public cooperation. This has established that while in principle contracts for pecuniary interest between public bodies are covered by the procurement rules, certain defined exemptions to this rule exist where the relationship between the entities is one of control or genuine cooperation to fulfil a common objective. These exemptions are now encapsulated in the 2014 directives and are discussed at paragraphs 1.49 *et seq.*

1.04 The 'market' on which an economic operator must offer supplies, services, or works is not defined in the directives—if a public or private entity only offers goods or services to the contracting authority in question, it might be argued that it does not meet the definition of an economic operator and so the award of a contract to it would not be governed by the directives. However, the Court has placed emphasis on the 'pecuniary interest' aspect of the definition, suggesting that where this exists the nature and activities of an economic operator will not serve to remove a contract from the scope of the directives. In the *CoNISMa* case, which concerned the eligibility of a research consortium to tender for a public contract, the Court cautioned against a narrow interpretation of the concept of 'economic operator' and held that a continuous presence on the market was not required.[2] It also held that the concept of an economic operator could include entities which are not primarily profit-making and are not structured as a business.[3]

1.05 Contracting authorities means the State, regional or local authorities, bodies governed by public law, or associations formed by one or more of these authorities or bodies. A body governed by public law is one which: (i) has legal personality;

---

[2] Case C-305/08 *Consorzio Nazionale Interuniversitario per le Scienze del Mare (CoNISMa) v Regione Marche* [2009] ECR I-12129, paras 42–5.
[3] *CoNISMa*, paras 30–5.

(ii) has been established to meet 'needs in the general interest, not having an industrial or commercial character'; and (iii) is publicly financed or controlled.[4] The Court has held that the second condition is not met where a body carries out its activities in a competitive environment and is administered according to criteria of performance, efficiency, and cost-effectiveness.[5] However, the fact that a body carries out some of its activities in such conditions will not be sufficient to prevent it from being classified as a body governed by public law and thus subject to the directives in respect of all of its contracts, even if there is a separate accounting system in place for those activities which are subject to competition or carried out on a profit-making basis.[6] The proportion of activities which are carried out in a competitive or profit-making capacity is not relevant for the purposes of classification of a body governed by public law.[7]

The third condition requires that the body is publicly financed 'for the most part'— **1.06** that is, more than 50 per cent of its total income[8]—or that control is exercised by way of management supervision or a board more than half of whose members are public appointments. This condition may be met whether the public financing or control is direct or indirect—for example, where fees to a professional association or statutory fund are set by law, or approval from a public supervisory body is needed for certain decisions only.[9] It is possible for an organization to cease being a body governed by public law if the public finance or control condition is no longer met, for example where a university or research body ceases to receive public funding. The reference point for making this determination is the financial year when a procurement procedure begins.[10] A body may also come to fall within the scope of the definition even if it did not meet all three conditions at the time of its establishment.[11]

---

[4] Art 2(1)(4) Public Sector Directive; Art 3(4) Utilities Directive.

[5] Joined Cases C-223/99 and C-260/99 *Agorà Srl v Ente Autonomo Fiera Internazionale di Milano* [2001] ECR I-03605.

[6] Thus, in Case C-393/06 *Ing Aigner Wasser-Wärme-Umwelt, GmbH v Fernwärme Wien GmbH* [2008] ECR I-02339, a body set up to provide district heating from waste in Vienna and which enjoyed a 'virtual monopoly' in carrying out that activity was held to be a body governed by public law, even though it faced competition in respect of the activity to which the contract related.

[7] Case C-44/96 *Mannesmann Anlagenbau Austria and Others* [1998] ECR I-00073, para 25; Case C-373/00 *Adolf Truley* [2003] ECR I-1931, para 56; and Case C-18/01 *Korhonen* [2003] ECR I-5321, paras 57–8.

[8] Case C-380/98 *University of Cambridge* [2000] ECR I-8035, para 33.

[9] Case C-337/06 *Bayerischer Rundfunk and Others* [2007] ECR I-11173; Case C-300/07 *Hans & Christophorus Oymanns GbR, Orthopädie Schuhtechnik,v AOK Rheinland/Hamburg* [2009] ECR I-04779, para 57; and Case C-526/11 *IVD GmbH & Co KG v Ärztekammer Westfalen-Lippe*, judgment of 12 September 2013, not yet reported.

[10] Case C-380/98 *University of Cambridge*, para 44.

[11] In *Universale-Bau*, the Court held that a body which was not established to meet needs in the general interest, but which had subsequently taken responsibility for such needs, met the condition (Case C-470/99, at para 63). The wording 'established for the specific purpose of meeting needs in the general interest' remains in the 2014 directives.

1.07   Public contracts are divided into those having as their object: the design, execution, or realization by any means of works ('public works contracts'); the purchase, lease, rental, or hire-purchase of products ('public supply contracts'); and the provision of services ('public service contracts'). The concept of realization by any means of a work corresponding to requirements specified by a contracting authority has been subject to judicial interpretation in the context of development agreements, discussed at paragraphs 1.68 *et seq.* The classification of contracts which contain mixed elements of works, supplies, and services is examined at paragraphs 1.13 *et seq.* 'Pecuniary interest' has also been subject to the Court's interpretation, and may consist of payment which is limited to reimbursement of costs,[12] or which is in the form of a waived debt or charge due to the contracting authority.[13] It does not appear, however, to extend to payments made by third parties to the economic operator if the contracting authority does not incur any economic detriment.[14]

1.08   The first recital to the Public Sector Directive states that public contracts are subject to the Treaty principles of free movement of goods, freedom of establishment, freedom to provide services, equal treatment, non-discrimination, mutual recognition, proportionality, and transparency. It is an interesting formulation, inasmuch as it is limited to 'public contracts'. The equivalent recital in Directive 2004/18/EC referred to 'contracts concluded in the Member States on behalf of the State, regional or local authorities and other bodies governed by public law entities...'—which could include contracts without pecuniary interest or which did not relate to supplies, services, or works (for example, a contract *not* to do something or for the transfer of land). While the recitals are not binding in themselves, they express the intention of the legislator and may in this case signal an attempt to define the frontiers of applicability of the Treaty principles. It is not possible, however, for a directive (secondary legislation) to modify or limit the Treaty (primary law) or to curtail the Court's ability to interpret it. Interestingly, the Public Sector Directive also defines 'procurement' as acquisition by means of a public contract. The term 'procurement' was almost entirely missing from the 2004 directives (with the exception of the recitals), whereas it appears in several places in the 2014 directives—such as the sections on 'Principles of procurement'.[15]

---

[12] Case C-159/11 *Azienda Sanitaria Locale di Lecce, Università del Salento v Ordine degli Ingegneri della Provincia di Lecce and Others*, judgment of 19 December 2012, not yet reported, para 29.

[13] Case C-399/98 *Ordine degli Architetti delle Province di Milano e Lodi and Others v Comune di Milano and Others* ('*La Scala*') [2001] ECR I-05409, paras 83–6.

[14] Case C-306/08 *Commission v Kingdom of Spain* ('*Valencia Development Agreements*') [2011] ECR I-04541. The Court did not address this question directly, but AG Jaaskinen considered that the absence of a 'mutually binding relationship in the nature of an exchange of performance with a tangible economic value between the contracting authority and the economic operators executing the works or services in question' precluded a finding that a contract for pecuniary interest existed (AG's opinion at para 87).

[15] Art 18 Public Sector Directive; and Art 36 Utilities Directive. Art 1(2) of the Public Sector Directive states that: 'Procurement within the meaning of this Directive is the acquisition by means of a public contract of works, supplies or services by one or more contracting authorities from economic operators chosen by those contracting authorities, whether or not the works, supplies or

Thresholds and Valuation of Contracts

The 2014 procurement directives apply to public contracts which are valued above **1.09** defined monetary thresholds. These are set with reference to the special drawing rights (SDR) under the WTO Government Procurement Agreement, with the corresponding value in euro and other European currencies being fixed every two years. Central government bodies, which are specified in Annex I of the Public Sector Directive, are subject to lower thresholds for supply and service contracts than local government or bodies governed by public law (currently €134,000 as opposed to €207,000.) Utilities have a higher threshold for supply and service contracts (currently €414,000). All categories of contracting authority and entity are subject to the same higher threshold for public works contracts (currently €5.186 million.) This higher threshold also applies in respect of concessions, whereas Title III services are subject to intermediate thresholds of €750,000 for the public sector and €1 million for utilities.

The differentiation in thresholds reflects the historical development of both the EU **1.10** and WTO regimes, with authorities outside of central government being brought within the rules at a later stage and to a more limited extent, and lower value works contracts considered to be of little cross-border interest. Some Member State governments sought a general raising of the thresholds as part of the 2014 revision, but this was resisted. It has also been argued that, given the legal uncertainty regarding the application of the Treaty principles to below-threshold contracts, it would be preferable to have lower thresholds for application of the directives, below which no obligations would arise under EU law.[16] As it stands, the level at which the thresholds are set mean that roughly 20 per cent of all public expenditure on goods, services, and works is advertised in the Official Journal.[17]

The valuation of a contract for the purpose of determining whether the directives **1.11** apply is not always straightforward. In theory, any contract exceeding the relevant threshold which has not been advertised in the Official Journal may be subject to

---

services are intended for a public purpose.' However, in the author's view, the definition of public contracts is still the central point of reference for determining applicability of the directives. In particular, the use of the term 'acquisition' in the above definition of procurement should not be taken to overrule the Court's case law on 'realisation of a work by any means'. This view is supported by Recital 4 of the Public Sector Directive, which advises that 'acquisition' should be broadly interpreted.

[16] Telles, P. (2013) 'The Good, the Bad and the Ugly: The EU's Internal Market, Public Procurement Thresholds and Cross-Border Interest' 43 *Public Contract Law Journal* 1, 3–27.

[17] European Commission (2012) *Public Procurement Indicators 2011* gives an estimate of €425 billion for contracts published in the OJEU as opposed to general expenditure by government and utilities of €2,405 billion on goods, services, and works for the EU27 in 2011. However, the figures must be treated with caution due to the incomplete nature of information recorded in award notices and difficulties tracking overall spend. It is also the case that many authorities choose to advertise below-threshold contracts in the OJEU.

challenge either by a would-be bidder or by the Commission itself. Contracting authorities are thus obliged to exercise care when estimating the value of their expenditure or awarding contracts without a fixed price. A number of rules and principles govern the estimation of value for the purpose of applying the thresholds.[18] Chief among these is the prohibition on subdividing contracts in order to avoid application of the directives. The estimated value of a contract must take into account the total amount payable, net of VAT, including any form of options and any renewals. If there are various operational units within the contracting authority, the estimate must be calculated based on the aggregated value of their requirements, unless they are independently responsible for their own procurement or certain categories thereof.[19] Specific rules apply for calculating the value of service and supply contracts which are regular in nature or intended to be renewed within a given period, based on a reference period of 12 months. For service contracts without a fixed value, a reference period of 48 months applies, or the total estimated value over the full term if it is for less than 48 months.[20]

1.12 Rules on aggregating contract values between similar procurement categories are not established in the directives. So, for example, if a contracting authority wishes to award separate contracts for paper and envelopes, or for the design and construction of a building, this is only forbidden if such divisions are intended to avoid the application of the directives and are not objectively justified. The administrative inconvenience of such arrangements will often outweigh any perceived benefits in avoiding the need to conduct an OJEU-level tender. If similar contracts are awarded to the same operator, they may be subject to scrutiny by national authorities, other operators, or the Commission itself. In 2010, the Commission brought a challenge against Germany in respect of the award by a municipality of successive contracts to the same firm of architects for a renovation project realized in three separate phases.[21] The EU rules were not applied as the contracts were individually valued below the threshold, and the municipality argued that this was necessary for budgetary reasons. The Court found that the failure to tender was not justified as the services served a single economic and technical function.[22] Here, as in many other areas of its procurement jurisprudence, the Court has taken a purposive approach to the application of rules and principles; the designation or administrative structure of a contract is irrelevant.

---

[18] Art 5 Public Sector Directive; Art 16 Utilities Directives; and Art 8 Concessions Directive.
[19] Art 5(1)(a) Public Sector Directive; Art 16 Utilities Directive; and Art 8 Concessions Directive.
[20] Art 5(11) and (14) Public Sector Directive; and Art 16(11) and (14) Utilities Directive.
[21] Case C-574/10 *Commission v Germany*, judgment of 15 March 2012, not yet reported.
[22] This was the test set out in Case C-16/98 *Commission v France* [2000] ECR I-08315 to determine when works contracts should be aggregated.

Mixed Contracts

Some time and attention has also been dedicated by the Court to the proper charac- **1.13**
terization of mixed contracts, both those which involve a combination of services or
supplies and works, and those which contain some elements which are not covered
by the procurement directives. Many service or supply contracts involve an aspect of
works—for example, installation of medical equipment or parking metres. If such
contracts could be characterized as works, they would be subject to the higher threshold and many more would escape from the OJEU. The Court has held that it is the
main purpose of a contract which determines its classification.[23] The 2014 directives
incorporate the principles developed in case law regarding the classification of mixed
contracts in order to determine which rules apply. Under Article 3 of the Public Sector
Directive, for contracts which contain both fully covered services and services subject
to the new lighter regime set out in Title III, the element with the highest estimated
value determines the correct classification for the entire contract. The same rule applies
to supply contracts which involve a service element or vice versa, but as the rules and
thresholds for these contracts are the same, their classification is of little moment,
unless the service is one which would be subject to Title III.[24]

Another type of mixed contract is one which contains some elements which **1.14**
either fall outside of the EU procurement regime completely or are subject to the
Concessions Directive. For example, a contract for legal services may include representation or document certification services which are now excluded from the
scope of the Public Sector Directive. A contract to renovate an office building
might include a concession arrangement for car parking or catering. The relative
value of the different elements does not matter here. If the elements of the contract
are 'objectively separable', contracting authorities are free to decide whether to
award separate contracts for differently regulated elements, or to combine them.[25]

---

[23] See Case C-412/04 *Commission v Italy* [2008] ECR I-00619, paras 47–50. The Court held
that the main purpose must be determined by an objective examination of the entire transaction
to which the contract relates, and that the value of the various matters covered would be just one
criterion among others to be taken into account in that assessment.

[24] There was one exception to the identical treatment of supply and Part A service contracts
under Directive 2004/18/EC. Under Art 48(2)(f), an indication of the environmental management
measures which would be applied in carrying out a contract was an acceptable selection criterion—
but not for supply contracts. The origin or justification for this distinction was never entirely clear
and it has been removed in the 2014 directives, allowing environmental management measures to
be requested at selection stage for all contracts.

[25] The idea of the elements of a contract being inseparable or indivisible was developed by the
Court in its judgment in Joined Cases C-145/08 and C-149/08 *Club Hotel Loutraki AE and Others*
[2010] ECR I-04165, in which it held that the inclusion of requirements to provide certain works
and services in a contract for the privatization of a casino did not bring it within the scope of the
procurement directives, as the main object was the sale of shares in a public undertaking (paras
48–63 of judgment). Recital 11 of the Public Sector Directive emphasizes that the determination

If a combined contract is awarded, the 'red sock' principle applies—the inclusion of an element covered by the Public Sector Directive means that it applies to the entire contract. The only exception to this principle is where a mixed contract contains a concessions element, and the value of the element subject to the Public Sector Directive in itself is below the relevant threshold.[26]

1.15 If a mixed contract contains separate activities subject to the Public Sector and Utilities directives, then the treatment of the mixed contract depends on the activity for which the contract is principally intended.[27] If it is 'objectively impossible' to determine which activity this is, then the default position is to apply the strictest rules which would apply to any element.[28] If a contract contains elements which are subject to the Defence and Security Directive or exempt from the procurement rules under Article 346 of the Treaty, the question of whether these elements are objectively separable again comes into play. However, the default position is reversed—if the elements are not objectively separable, then the inclusion of an element which would be subject to the Defence and Security Directive or exempt under Article 346 means that the entire contract can be tendered subject to the lightest rules which would apply to any element.[29] If the elements are objectively separable, the contracting authority may still decide to award a mixed contract and to apply the lightest rules which would apply to any one element, provided this decision is justified by objective reasons and is not made for the purpose of avoiding application of stricter rules. Needless to say, the extent to which elements are objectively separable, or a decision to award a single contract is based on an objective justification, may be subject to review by national courts and the CJEU.

Contracts in the Water, Energy, Transport, and Postal Services Sectors

1.16 Contracts which are fully subject to the Utilities Directive are excluded from the scope of application of the Public Sector Directive. Each directive sets requirements both in terms of the characteristics of the organizations to which it applies (*ratione personae*) and the type and value of contracts covered (*ratione materiae*). Whereas the classification of the purchasing organization as a contracting authority is an essential prerequisite for the application of the Public Sector Directive, a

---

of whether elements of a contract are objectively separable must be carried out on a case-by-case basis, and that both economic and technical considerations may be relevant in this determination.

[26] Art 3(4) Public Sector Directive, final paragraph. The 'red sock' principle is a metaphor drawn from laundry—referring to the inclusion of a single element which requires special treatment of the entire load.

[27] Art 6(2) Utilities Directive.

[28] Art 6(3) Utilities Directive.

[29] Art 17 Public Sector Directive; Art 25 Utilities Directive; and Art 21 Concessions Directive.

broader range of entities may be subject to the Utilities Directive where they are carrying out one or more of the activities covered by it. The Court has held that the scope of application of the utilities rules is strictly circumscribed, so that contracting entities are not obliged to apply them in respect of any other activities.[30] The list of covered activities is set out in Articles 7 to 14 of the Utilities Directive, and closely resembles the list of covered activities under Directive 2004/17/EC, with a few changes.[31]

The term 'contracting entity' refers to a contracting authority, public undertaking,   **1.17** or any other body (public or private) if it has been granted special or exclusive rights by a competent authority of a Member State and is awarding contracts in pursuit of the covered activities. A public authority may be subject to the Utilities Directive for some contracts and to the Public Sector Directive for others. Private sector organizations which have been granted special or exclusive rights—for example, to extract oil, gas, or coal, or to operate transport networks—may be subject to the Utilities Directive. However, where the rights in question have themselves been granted based on a transparent and objective procedure, then the grantee will not be subject to the procurement rules unless it is a contracting authority or public undertaking.[32] There is specific EU legislation governing such rights in the oil and gas, electricity, transport, and postal services sectors.[33]

Contracts awarded in the utilities sector are subject to a less prescriptive set of rules than   **1.18** that which applies to public sector contracts. Notably, contracting entities enjoy higher thresholds, greater freedom in choice of procedure and timelines, and can establish framework agreements for a period of eight years rather than four. They also have greater flexibility to award contracts to an affiliated undertaking or joint venture,[34]

---

[30] Case C-393/06 *Ing Aigner Wasser-Wärme-Umwelt*.

[31] Exploration for oil and gas has been excluded on the basis that these activities are subject to adequate competition. Exemptions in the oil and gas sectors had already been granted to the United Kingdom, Denmark, Italy, and the Netherlands by decisions of the Commission. Extraction of these fuels is still covered. Certain activities in the postal services sector, namely, financial, logistics, philatelic, and added-value electronic services, have also been excluded from the scope of Directive 2014/25/EU based on their exposure to competition.

[32] Art 4(3) Utilities Directive.

[33] Directive 2009/73/EC of the European Parliament and of the Council of 13 July 2009 concerning common rules for the internal market in natural gas and repealing Directive 2003/55/EC; Directive 2009/72/EC of the European Parliament and of the Council of 13 July 2009 concerning common rules for the internal market in electricity and repealing Directive 2003/54/EC; Directive 97/67/EC of the European Parliament and of the Council of 15 December 1997 on common rules for the development of the internal market of Community postal services and the improvement of quality of service; Directive 94/22/EC of the European Parliament and of the Council of 20 May 1994 on the conditions for granting and using authorisations for the prospection, exploration and production of hydrocarbons; and Regulation (EC) No 1370/2007 of the European Parliament and of the Council of 23 October 2007 on public passenger transport services by rail and by road and repealing Council Regulations (EEC) Nos 1191/69 and 1107/70.

[34] Arts 29 and 30 of the Utilities Directive set out the conditions under which contracting entities may award contracts to affiliated undertakings and joint ventures without application of the directives.

in addition to the provisions for exempted public-public cooperation outlined below. There is provision under Articles 34 and 35 of the Utilities Directive for activities to be excluded from its scope if they are directly exposed to competition on markets to which access is not restricted. This principle has led to the gradual exclusion of more activities from the scope of successive utilities directives, notably telecommunications services and financial, logistical, or added-value electronic services provided by entities active in the postal sector.

1.19 The rules on award of concessions apply both to contracting authorities and entities; however, activities in the water sector are excluded from the Concessions Directive (for reasons discussed at para 1.47 *et seq*), as are concessions for air transport or public passenger transport services, which are governed by separate regulations.[35] Concessions awarded by contracting entities for the pursuit of their activities in a third country are also excluded, provided these do not involve the physical use of a network or geographical area within the Union.[36] Concessions for activities which are exposed directly to competition are excluded on the same basis as applies under the Utilities Directive.[37] In the case of mixed concessions covering some activities in the utilities sector and some in the public sector, these exclusions are not available.[38]

Specific Exclusions

1.20 The 2014 directives provide for a number of specific exclusions, some of which existed under previous generations of procurement directives and some of which are new. The rationale for each exclusion is normally given in the recitals. Employment contracts and contracts for the acquisition or rental of existing buildings, land, or other immovable property have always been excluded from the scope of the procurement directives. The impracticality of arranging tender competitions for such contracts is obvious, although in some cases the line may be blurred between employment and a consultancy arrangement, or between acquisition of existing buildings and a land development agreement (discussed below.) Where employment or acquisition of real property form part of a larger contract such as an outsourced service arrangement, the rules on mixed contracts will apply.

Services of general interest

1.21 Services of general interest are subject to special treatment under the Treaty and this is reflected in the public procurement and State aid rules applicable to them. They are divided into services of general economic interest (SGEIs) and

---

[35] Art 10(3) Concessions Directive.
[36] Art 10(10) Concessions Directive.
[37] Art 16 Concessions Directive.
[38] Art 22(3) Concessions Directive.

non-economic services of general interest, sometimes also known as social services of general interest. SGEIs are economic activities which deliver outcomes in the overall public good that would not be supplied (or would be supplied under different conditions in terms of objective quality, safety, affordability, equal treatment, or universal access) by the market without public intervention.[39] Activities which may, depending on their organization, be classed as SGEIs include transport, postal, water, energy, telecommunications, and other services subject to a public service obligation. The 2014 directives simply state that they do not affect the freedom of Member States to decide what are SGEIs and how they should be organized and financed, in accordance with the State aid rules.[40] Non-economic services of general interest are activities that are performed without any consideration, by the State or on behalf of the State, as part of its duties in the social field, for example.[41] They may include activities related to the army or police, air traffic control, compulsory social security services, education and childcare, or the operation of public hospitals. Non-economic services of general interest are explicitly excluded from the 2014 procurement directives (including the Concessions Directive)[42]—however, this may also be seen as simply a restatement of the definition of public contracts, which requires pecuniary interest to apply.

Public communications networks

The 2004 directives contained an exemption for the award of contracts for the **1.22** provision or exploitation of public telecommunications networks or services, that is, where a contracting authority itself acted as a telecommunications provider. Under the 2014 directives, the wording of this exemption has been changed to refer to 'public communications networks' and 'electronic communications services', while still applying only to contracts and concessions for the public provision or exploitation of such networks and services, as opposed to where a public body purchases services for its own use.[43] The exemption is justified with reference to

---

[39] Commission Staff Working Document, *Guide to the application of the European Union rules on State aid, public procurement and the internal market to services of general economic interest, and in particular to social services of general interest*, SWD (2013) 53 final/2, p 21. The vagueness of this 'definition'—which could extend to cover almost all public sector activity—probably reflects the discretion of Member States to decide what is an SGEI.

[40] Art 1(4) Public Sector Directive; Recital 9 Utilities Directive; and Art 4 Concessions Directive. Special rules regarding State aid apply to SGEIs: see *Communication from the Commission on the application of the European Union State aid rules to compensation granted for the provision of services of general economic interest* (2012/C 8/02); and Commission Decision 2012/21/EU *on the application of Article 106(2) of the Treaty on the Functioning of the European Union to State aid in the form of public service compensation granted to certain undertakings entrusted with the operation of services of general economic interest*.

[41] Case C-109/92 *Stephan Max Wirth v Landeshauptstadt Hannover* [1993] ECR I-06447.

[42] Recital 6 and Annex XIV Public Sector Directive; Art 1(6) and Annex XVII Utilities Directive; and Art 4(2) and Annex IV Concessions Directive.

[43] Art 8 Public Sector Directive; and Art 11 Concessions Directive. 'Public communications network' and 'electronic communications service' are defined in accordance with Directive 2002/21/EC on a common regulatory framework for electronic communications networks and services.

the exposure of this sector to competition, as well as the desire to facilitate rapid dissemination of broadband internet services in particular.

Contracts awarded under international rules

1.23 Contracts or concessions which contracting authorities or entities are obliged to award under international procurement rules are excluded from the 2014 directives.[44] In order to qualify for this exemption, the obligation must be set out in a legal instrument which has been notified to the Commission and the contract must be for works, supplies, or services 'intended for the joint implementation or exploitation of a project' by the parties to the agreement. There is a further exemption in the case of procurement financed wholly or for the most part by an international organization, where it has prescribed procurement rules. These exemptions could apply to contracts or concessions awarded on behalf of United Nations agencies, for example, or financed by the World Bank or European Investment Bank. A parallel exemption applies to contracts with defence or security aspects which are awarded under international procurement rules, which also includes agreements or arrangements for the stationing of troops.[45]

Specific exclusions for service contracts

1.24 A motley collection of services enjoy exclusion from the directives, with justifications ranging from the obvious to the obscure. The long-standing exclusion for award of contracts by audiovisual and radio media service providers for programme material, or for contracts awarded to these organizations for broadcasting time or programme provision, is replicated in the 2014 directives.[46] This has traditionally been justified on the grounds that such contracts involve distinct national cultural interests and thus should not be subject to cross-border competition. It has never been clear why the acquisition of printed or online media services, or the acquisition of audiovisual or radio material by authorities other than media providers, should not be subject to the same treatment or justification.

1.25 The pre-existing exclusion for arbitration and conciliation services is now accompanied by an exemption for certain legal services which are considered not to be of cross-border interest.[47] The latter include representation before a court or tribunal, advice given in immediate contemplation of such proceedings, notary or document certification services, and trusteeship or other court-appointed or official functions performed by lawyers. In practice, it may prove difficult for contracting authorities

---

[44] Art 9 Public Sector Directive; Art 20 Utilities Directive; and Art 10(4) Concessions Directive.
[45] Art 17 Public Sector Directive; Art 27 Utilities Directive; and Art 10(5) Concessions Directive.
[46] Art 10(b) Public Sector Directive; Art 21(i) Utilities Directive; and Art 10(8)(b) Concessions Directive.
[47] Art 10(d) Public Sector Directive; Art 21(c) Utilities Directive; and Art 10(8)(d) Concessions Directive.

to separate out these functions from more general legal services, which are subject to the lighter Title III regime. The rules on mixed contracts prescribe that the services with the greater estimated value should determine how the contract is classified;[48] however, accurate estimation of legal costs, particularly where these include elements linked to judicial proceedings, can be challenging. Authorities may opt to err on the side of caution and treat legal services contracts or frameworks as being covered by Title III, even where they include a considerable element of excluded services.

Financial services connected to the issue, sale, purchase, or transfer of securities or **1.26** other financial instruments—for example, for the issue of government bonds or public debt management—are excluded as under previous directives. This is now complemented by an exclusion for loans, regardless of their purpose, and for operations conducted with the European Financial Stability Facility and the European Stability Mechanism.[49] While the difficulty of arranging transparent competitions for these types of financial service transactions must be acknowledged, arguably this is an area in which further cross-border competition could provide real gains both to the public purse and to the market.

Civil defence, civil protection, and danger prevention services which are provided **1.27** by non-profit organizations—for example, a volunteer fire brigade or mountain rescue organization—are not covered by the directives.[50] This can be understood based on the strong involvement of voluntary organizations in such services in many Member States and the need for continuity in service provision. However, the exemption does not extend to public contracts for ambulance services, which have been the subject of a number of cases before the European Court of Justice. Patient transport ambulance services are covered by the Title III regime for social and other specific services. The award of contracts for public passenger transport by rail or metro is governed by a separate EU regulation adopted in 2007, and so is excluded from the 2014 directives.[51]

A final new exclusion relates to political campaign services when awarded by a **1.28** political party in the context of an election campaign.[52] In the recitals to the Public Sector Directive, we learn that political campaign and propaganda services, when delivered in the context of an election campaign, 'are so inextricably connected to the political views of the service provider' that the selection of that service provider cannot be made in accordance with the procurement rules.[53] In addition to the

---

[48] Art 3(2) Public Sector Directive.
[49] Art 10(e) and (f) Public Sector Directive; Art 21(d) and (e) Utilities Directive; and Art 10(8)(e) and (f) Concessions Directive.
[50] Art 10(h) Public Sector Directive; Art 21(h) Utilities Directive; and Art 10(8)(g) Concessions Directive.
[51] Art 10(i) Public Sector Directive; and Art 21(g) Utilities Directive.
[52] Art 10(j) Public Sector Directive; and Art 10(8)(h) Concessions Directive.
[53] Recital 29 Public Sector Directive.

importance of the service provider's political views, the exemption might be justified based on the impracticality of conducting a procurement procedure within the short timescales which may apply after an election is called. Political parties will often fall outside of the definition of a contracting authority in any event, but in some Member States they are bodies governed by public law and so would be subject to the directives for contracts valued above the relevant thresholds.

Research and development services

1.29 Contracts for research and development (R&D) services are excluded from the scope of the directives unless the benefits of these services are reserved exclusively to the contracting authority and it also pays for them in full.[54] The rationale here is to encourage spending on R&D which is either openly disseminated, attracts co-finance from other bodies, or both. The exemption, which also existed under the 2004 directives, has allowed for the development of 'pre-commercial procurement', a competitive process for the award of R&D service contracts which takes into account the State aid rules. The possibility of awarding contracts in this way was outlined in a 2007 Commission communication,[55] and several EU funding programmes have specifically encouraged its use, including Horizon 2020. However, pre-commercial procurement can by definition only relate to the R&D phases (up to a limited volume of first production)—meaning that if public authorities wish to acquire the outcomes of the R&D on a commercial scale, they must hold a separate competition. The innovation partnership procedure, discussed in Chapter 3, aims to close this gap by allowing for the award of phased contracts which cover both R&D activities and commercial acquisition, as well as intermediate stages such as prototyping or piloting. The 2014 directives also make specific provision for intellectual property rights, which were not mentioned in earlier directives, to be addressed in technical specifications.

Defence and security

1.30 Articles 15 to 17 of the Public Sector Directive and Articles 24 to 27 of the Utilities Directive deal with procurement which involves defence or security aspects. Contracts which are subject to the Defence and Security Directive[56] or specifically excluded from that directive are not covered by the Public Sector or Utilities Directives. Contracts may also be excluded where Member States invoke Article 346 of the Treaty due to the need to protect essential security interests, or where

---

[54] Art 14 Public Sector Directive; and Art 32 Utilities Directive.

[55] COM (2007) 799 *Pre-commercial Procurement: Driving innovation to ensure sustainable high quality public services in Europe*, SEC (2007) 1668.

[56] Directive 2009/81/EC of the European Parliament and of the Council on the coordination of procedures for the award of certain works contracts, supply contracts, and service contracts by contracting authorities or entities in the fields of defence and security, and amending Directives 2004/17/EC and 2004/18/EC.

contracts are secret or subject to special security measures, provided the protection of these interests and objectives cannot be attained by less intrusive means.[57]

The Defence and Security Directive aims to coordinate the award of contracts **1.31** for military equipment, services, and works, and contracts which are considered 'sensitive'—meaning they have a security purpose and involve classified information.[58] It applies to contracting authorities and entities as defined in the Public Sector and Utilities Directives, and adopts the higher threshold for supply and service contracts applicable in the utilities sector. The basic rules on advertising, procedures, specifications, and selection and award criteria are adapted to take account of confidentiality and security of supply issues in particular. Special provisions also apply in relation to subcontracting, where contracting authorities may require that up to 30 per cent of a contract is subcontracted and impose requirements for the selection of subcontractors.[59]

The Defence and Security Directive was intended in part to reduce reliance by **1.32** Member States on the exemption available under Article 346 TFEU from the normal rules on free movement of goods and services. Article 346 provides that Member States may refuse to disclose information where this would be contrary to their essential security interests, and may take other measures necessary to protect their security connected with the production of or trade in arms, munitions, and war material. Such measures cannot adversely affect the conditions of competition for products which are not intended for specifically military purposes. They also cannot extend beyond what is strictly necessary for the protection of the legitimate interests served by the exemption. The Court has interpreted and applied both of these conditions in order to limit the scope of applicability of Article 346 where contracts are for mixed civil and military purposes, or where the necessity of the measures to protect security interests is dubious.[60]

If mixed contracts contain some elements covered by the public sector or utilities **1.33** rules and some for which the Defence and Security Directive or for which Article 346 has been invoked, the least onerous rules applicable to any element will apply, provided that separate contracts cannot be awarded for objective reasons.[61] This contrasts with the 'red sock' principle discussed above, which applies to mixed contracts not containing defence or security aspects. Concessions relating to defence or security are covered by the Concessions Directive; however, a number of

---

[57] Art 15 Public Sector Directive; and Art 24 Utilities Directive.

[58] 'Contracts for the purpose of intelligence activities' which are not defined are excluded under Art 13 Directive 2009/81/EC.

[59] Art 21 Directive 2009/81/EC.

[60] See Case C-337/05 *Commission v Italy* ('*Agusta Helicopters*') [2008] ECR I-2173; Case C-284/05 *Commission v Finland* [2009] ECR I-11705; and Case C-615/10 *Insinööritoimisto InsTiimi Oy*, not yet reported.

[61] Art 16(2) and (3) Public Sector Directive; and Art 25(2) and (3), Art 26(2) and (3) Utilities Directive.

exemptions are available—for example, where applying the Directive would lead to the disclosure of information which would compromise essential security interests, or where the concession is awarded to another government authority.[62] Rules on the award of mixed concessions containing some defence or security aspects are also set out.[63]

1.34 While justifications for the exemption of defence and security contracts can always be found in the imperatives of national self-reliance and security of supply, the scope of the exemption and its effectiveness in achieving these objectives, as well as the higher costs and perhaps lower quality associated with limited competition in the defence field, deserve scrutiny. Increased costs are associated in particular with 'offsets'—requiring all or part of a defence contract to be fulfilled using domestic companies. Offsets have been found to increase contract prices due to shorter production runs, duplicated investments, higher domestic manufacturing costs, higher sales price from the contractor in order to compensate for lost work, and licence fees.[64]

1.35 Offsets are not permitted under EU law unless the exemption provided for in Article 346 TFEU is invoked. In July 2013, the Commission announced the 'rapid phasing out of offsets' as part of an effort to address distortions in the defence procurement sector.[65] Even if there is some need for protected national defence industries within the EU, questions of transparency, corruption, and value for money in the award of defence contracts are periodically cast into sharp relief—as with the grotesque levels of spending and graft linked to defence contracts in Greece which came to light during the latest financial crisis.[66] Efforts to reform defence procurement have been hindered by the strategic and economic importance attached to the defence industry in many European countries, although existing procurement policies may in fact jeopardize the long-term viability of these sectors.

The New Regime for Social and Other Specific Services

1.36 The distinction between priority and non-priority services (listed respectively in Annex II A and II B of Directive 2004/18/EC) has been abolished under the 2014 directives. In its place is a new lighter regime for service contracts which are deemed

---

[62] Art 10(6) and (7) Concessions Directive.

[63] Art 21 Concessions Directive.

[64] Heuninckx, B. (2014) 'Security of Supply and Offsets in Defence Procurement: What's New in the EU?' 22 *PPLR* 33–49.

[65] COM (2013) 542 *Towards a more competitive and efficient defence and security sector*.

[66] Daley, S. (2014) 'So Many Bribes, A Greek Official Can't Recall Them All', *The New York Times*, 7 February. While the alleged recipients of the bribes were Greek officials, several of the companies allegedly paying them were German—raising further questions about the 'national self-reliance' argument for defence exemptions.

to be of limited cross-border interest, set out in Title III of both the Public Sector and Utilities Directives. Services subject to the lighter regime are identified by their Common Procurement Vocabulary (CPV) code in Annex XIV of the Public Sector Directive and Annex XVII of the Utilities Directive. This includes most but not all of the categories formerly included in Annex II B such as health, social, educational, and cultural services; legal services to the extent they are not excluded; investigation and security services; hotel and restaurant services; and religious and other community services. It also includes certain other categories such as benefit and social security services, prison-related and rescue services (to the extent they are not excluded), services provided by certain international organizations, and postal services. Unlike the Annex II B list, it does not contain a residual category for 'other services'—an important change. Personnel placement services and transport services other than by rail or metro are also now subject to the full rules.

As noted, higher thresholds apply in respect of Title III services (€750,000 for **1.37** the public sector and €1 million for utilities). The scope of obligations above the thresholds is limited to publication of a contract notice or prior information notice, observance of the principles of transparency and equal treatment, and publication of a contract award notice. Procedures are not prescribed in the directives, but Member States may choose to do this provided they comply with the principles of transparency and equal treatment. The formulation of technical specifications for Title III services is not regulated under the 2014 directives, in contrast with the rules previously applicable to non-priority services. The intention to allow an approach to these contracts which is less economically driven, and more conducive to social value, is clear in the instructions to Member States to ensure that in their award:

> contracting authorities may take into account the need to ensure quality, continuity, accessibility, affordability, availability and comprehensiveness of the services, the specific needs of different categories of users, including disadvantaged and vulnerable groups, the involvement and empowerment of users and innovation.

Member States are also able to restrict the use of lowest cost or lowest price for the **1.38** award of Title III contracts, and to require contracting authorities to take quality and sustainability into account.[67] The provisions represent an interesting compromise between the autonomy of contracting authorities and that of national governments, with each being given certain discretion over the award of services which are often subject to high degrees of public scrutiny and political sensitivity. As these contracts remain subject to the Remedies Directive and to the Treaty principles, the scope for protectionism is also constrained.

More controversially, Article 77 of the Public Sector Directive allows contracts for **1.39** health, social, and cultural services to be reserved for competition by organizations

---

[67] Art 76(2) Public Sector Directive; and Art 91(2) Utilities Directive.

with a specific public service character. This provision was lobbied for by the UK Government in particular, where the formation of employee-led mutual enterprises is seen as a way of delivering public services, while reducing public sector employment. In order to qualify for the reservation, organizations must meet a number of conditions regarding their objectives, treatment of profits, and management or ownership structures. Contracts awarded pursuant to Article 77 have a maximum duration of three years, and organizations which have been awarded a contract for the same services by the same contracting authority within the previous three years are not eligible to avail of the reservation.

1.40 Unlike the reservation for sheltered employment programmes and workshops (discussed in Chapter 7), the conditions set out in Article 77 refer to the financial and management characteristics of an organization. This means that they cannot readily be met by any operator wishing to compete for public sector contracts let under this provision, but only those which have been established on particular terms. It thus runs contrary to the general treatment of social, environmental, and economic policy objectives in the directives—which is that they can be pursued inasmuch as they do not distort competition and the relevant requirements or criteria can be met, at least in theory, by any operator.

1.41 From a competition perspective, the use of reservations (also sometimes known as set asides) has the potential to foster monopolistic or oligopolistic market structures and can be seen as contrary to the principles of the Treaty. While an organization from another Member State which meets the requirements set out in Article 77 could technically still compete for a contract, it seems more likely that this provision will be used to award contracts to organizations which are more or less intimately related to the contracting authority in question. Unusually, Article 77 is subject to the Commission's review within a five-year period, perhaps suggesting a degree of uneasiness about its inclusion.

Concessions

1.42 A service concession is an arrangement in which a private operator is given the right to exploit a service and bears the associated risk. The payment for the service often flows directly to the operator from users, for example where residents pay a private contractor appointed by their local authority for collection of waste, or customers in a hospital cafeteria pay for their meals. In other cases, there may be no immediate payment to the economic operator, for example if a company is permitted to advertise on publicly owned property. The risk borne by the operator may relate either to the demand for the service or to supply-side factors such as cost or technical aspects of delivery. A works concession is an arrangement of the same nature, but with the object of executing and exploiting a work, for example the construction of a road or bridge on which tolls will be levied. Works concessions were covered by Directive 2004/18/EC, but subject only to a limited set of requirements regarding advertising and procedures.

The Concessions Directive seeks to establish a harmonized regime for the award of **1.43** such arrangements, and is applicable to both the public and utilities sectors. It sets a threshold of €5,186,000 for service and works concessions, below which national rules will apply.[68] The rationale for legislation in this area arose in part from the large volume of case law relating to concessions, and the recognition that this mode of contracting is often used in areas which are of considerable cross-border interest, such as major infrastructure projects. The Concessions Directive replicates many—but not all—of the obligations found in the Public Sector and Utilities Directives relating to advertisement, time limits, specifications, selection and award criteria, notification of results, subcontracting, and modifications to contracts. Concessions valued above the threshold are also now subject to the remedies regime, including the requirement to apply a standstill period prior to award and to notify candidates and tenderers of the outcome of their applications and tenders.

The duration of concessions must be limited and stated in the contract notice or **1.44** documents, unless duration forms one of the grounds on which operators are competing. If longer than five years, it must not exceed the period in which the concessionaire could be reasonably expected to recoup its investment and make a return on capital, assuming normal operating conditions.[69] The relatively open wording of the restrictions on duration of concessions suggests that should a challenge be brought on this ground by the Commission or a private party, the Court would likely apply a proportionality test to judge whether the concession period is justified in all the circumstances. This approach has been applied by the Court in its competition law jurisprudence, leaving a relatively wide margin of discretion available to public authorities to determine contract length.[70]

In terms of the assumption of risk by the operator which is a necessary feature of a **1.45** concession, Article 5 of the Concessions Directive states:

> The concessionaire shall be deemed to assume operating risk where, under normal operating conditions, it is not guaranteed to recoup the investments made or the costs incurred in operating the works or the services which are the subject-matter of the concession. The part of the risk transferred to the concessionaire shall involve

---

[68] Given the discussion in paras 1.74–1.82 of the application of the Treaty principles to excluded and low-value contracts, the possibility of cross-border interest arising in concessions below this threshold should not be dismissed.

[69] Art 18 and Recital 52 Concessions Directive.

[70] In the *London Underground* decision (N-264/02), for example, a 30-year duration for contracts awarded as part of a PPP for the upgrade and maintenance of the London Underground network was found to be proportionate based on the complexities of the project, the level of investment, and time needed to reach the agreed rates of return. It remains to be seen whether a similar approach will be taken in respect of concessions.

real exposure to the vagaries of the market, such that any potential estimated loss incurred by the concessionaire shall not be merely nominal or negligible.

The Commission issued a 'fact sheet' at the time of the adoption of the directives, stating that in its view such risks did not include those which are inherent in every contract, such as those linked to bad management, contractual default, or *force majeure*.[71]

1.46 The concept of concessions excludes arrangements where all operators fulfilling certain conditions are entitled to perform a given task without any selectivity, such as a voucher system for accessing medical or other services. It also excludes the granting of licences or a right of way over public immovable property where these are not accompanied by an obligation to carry out the specific activity. Contracts where the operator is remunerated solely on the basis of regulated tariffs calculated to cover operating and investment costs also fall outside of the scope of the Concessions Directive.

1.47 A number of other sector- and activity-specific exemptions apply to the Concessions Directive, including the total exclusion of concessions related to the supply of drinking water and associated engineering or sewage treatment works and services. The decision to exclude water was taken following a European Citizens Initiative (ECI) calling on the European Commission to recognize a human right to water and sanitation, promote their provision as essential public services and exclude them from liberalization or the application of internal market rules.[72] The ECI was organized by the European Federation of Public Services Unions and gathered some 1.8 million signatures—meaning that the Commission was obliged to take action to respond to it. This was achieved in part by way of a statement issued by Commissioner Barnier agreeing to exclude water from the scope of the Concessions Directive.[73]

1.48 It is questionable whether this served the purpose advanced by supporters of the initiative. Although it formed part of their demands, exclusion from the Concessions Directive does not in itself make it any less likely that supply of water will be privatized or subject to competition. Article 2 of the Directive enshrines the principle that national, regional, and local authorities are free to decide how best to manage services and works, including through use of their own resources. If anything, excluding water from the scope of the Directive means that concessions in this

---

[71] Fact sheet available at: <http://ec.europa.eu/internal_market/publicprocurement/modernising_rules>.

[72] See *Water and sanitation are a human right! Water is a public good, not a commodity!* Commission registration number: ECI(2012)000003, date of registration 10 May 2012, available at: <http://ec.europa.eu/citizens-initiative/public/initiatives/finalised>.

[73] Statement by Commissioner Barnier on the exclusion of water from the Concessions Directive, 21 June 2013, available at: <http://ec.europa.eu/internal_market/publicprocurement/news/index_en.htm>.

sector will continue to be subject to less transparency and greater legal uncertainty. While concerns about privatization of water services eroding public control over this vital asset are real, the background information supporting the initiative also suggested that it reflected a specific concern about water companies from other EU Member States being involved in the management of water.[74]

Public-Public Cooperation

As explained in paragraph 1.03, contracts between public authorities are not by their nature excluded from the directives. However, the Court has carved out an exemption for contracts considered to be 'in-house' or otherwise falling within the concept of legitimate 'public-public cooperation'. This includes both the award of contracts to controlled entities (*Teckal* companies) and shared service arrangements between public authorities, where certain conditions are met (following the *Hamburg* case). These conditions are designed to ensure that no private operator is given an advantage relative to its competitors by way of such arrangements. The new directives also incorporate relatively light rules for awarding contracts to public-private partnerships or through central purchasing bodies. The discussion which follows aims to elucidate the scope of these exemptions as they appear in the 2014 directives, with reference to their origins in case law.   **1.49**

Article 12 of the Public Sector Directive, Article 28 of the Utilities Directive, and Article 17 of the Concessions Directive contain the exemptions for different forms of public-public cooperation developed by the Court in its *Teckal* and *Hamburg* jurisprudence.[75] The award of a contract to an 'in-house' entity will not be covered by the procurement rules, where certain conditions are met: **1.50**

(a) the contracting authority exercises over the legal person concerned a control which is similar to that which it exercises over its own departments;

(b) more than 80 per cent of the activities of the controlled legal person are carried out in the performance of tasks entrusted to it by the controlling contracting authority or by other legal persons controlled by that contracting authority; and

(c) there is no direct private capital participation in the controlled legal person with the exception of non-controlling and non-blocking forms of private capital participation required by national legislative provisions, in conformity with

---

[74] See <http://www.right2water.eu>, which sets out the background and ambitions of the initiative. Two-thirds of the signatories were from Germany, perhaps reflecting a specific concern about large French water companies winning concessions in that country.

[75] Case C-107/98 *Teckal Srl v Comune di Viano* ('*Teckal*') [1999] ECR I-8121; and Case C-480/06 *Commission v Germany* ('*Hamburg*') [2009] ECR I-4747. The *Teckal* exemption was further developed by the Court in Cases C-26/03 ('*Stadt Halle*'), C-340/04 ('*Carbotermo*'), C-295/05 ('*Asemfo*'), C-324/07 ('*Coditel Brabant*'), and Joined Cases C-182/11 and C-183/11 ('*Econord*')—among others. The Hamburg principle was applied by the Court in Case C-159/11 ('*Azienda*'); Case C-386/11 ('*Piepenbrock*'); and Case C-15/13 *Datenlotsen Inofrmationssysteme GmbH v Technische Universität Hamburg-Harburg* ('*Datenlotsen*'), not yet reported.

the Treaties, which do not exert a decisive influence on the controlled legal person.[76]

1.51 The purpose of each of the three aspects of the test is to limit the 'in-house' exemption to prevent it from being used in cases where this would lead to a distortion of competition. If an entity is independent in its decisions, operates significantly on the market, or includes private participation, the ability to award contracts or concessions to it directly would create an unfair competitive advantage. It is worth noting that the restrictions on in-house award of contracts does not interfere with the ability of public authorities to provide goods, services, or works out of their own resources. It also does not mean that award of a contract to an entity not meeting the Article 12 conditions is impossible, only that the procurement rules would apply, unless another exemption is available.

1.52 The precise percentage of activities which a controlled entity must carry out for the controlling authority or authorities had not been decided in case law. In *Stadt Halle*, the Court left open the possibility that 80 per cent of such activities might be sufficient to meet the test, but did not resolve the issue conclusively. This 80 per cent threshold was ultimately adopted in the 2014 directives, and is to be calculated relative to the entity's average turnover over a period of three years prior to award of the contract. If the entity has not been established for that entire period, the 80 per cent may be calculated based on business projections or other 'credible' accounts of its expected activity. Chapter 8 considers the availability of remedies in cases where a company awarded an in-house contract is found not to meet the required conditions.

1.53 The level of control needed is 'a decisive influence over both the strategic objectives and significant decisions of the controlled legal person'. Case law following *Teckal* established that more than one public authority may exercise the requisite control over the entity and that it may carry out the essential part of its activities for those authorities collectively.[77] It also established that the exemption can apply where the controlled entity awards a contract to its controlling authority, or another legal person controlled by the authority awards the contract.[78] These 'collective', 'reverse', and 'indirect' *Teckal* modalities are also included in the scope of Articles 12 and 28 (and Article 17 of the Concessions Directive). In *Datenlotsen*, the Court found that the 'indirect' *Teckal* mode did not include the award by a controlled entity of a contract to another body controlled by the same 'parent'.[79] However, this situation

---

[76] Art 12 Public Sector Directive.
[77] Case C-340/04 *Carbotermo*.
[78] Case C-295/05 *Asemfo* and Case C-324/07 *Coditel Brabant*.
[79] Case C-15/13 *Datenlotsen*, paras 28–30. In that case, the requisite control did not in fact exist between the 'parent' and 'daughter' entity (the City and University), so the extension of the exemption to a 'sister' entity was moot.

is now specifically included in the scope of the exemption set out in Article 12(2) of the Public Sector Directive.

The second form of public-public cooperation exempted from the 2014 directives **1.54** relates to arrangements in which two or more authorities collaborate to achieve common objectives. This exemption was first articulated by the Court in the *Hamburg* case,[80] which concerned an agreement between the City of Hamburg Sanitation Department and four local authorities in the Lower Saxony region. Each of the four authorities had agreed to provide a certain volume of waste throughput to the incineration facility built by Hamburg. Payments were made to Hamburg to cover the cost of incineration, and it assumed responsibility for providing replacement capacity in certain circumstances and representing the authorities' interests against the private operator of the facility. A citizen concerned about the charges for waste management in the region made a complaint to the Commission, which brought the case upon learning that the arrangement between the authorities had not been subject to tender. The Advocate General in the case applied the *Teckal* logic and found that the arrangement did not qualify for the in-house exemption, as the control condition was not met.

The Court, however, considered that as the arrangement constituted a form of **1.55** genuine cooperation between the authorities, and was not intended to circumvent the procurement rules, it could stand. The *Hamburg* judgment was welcomed by many who felt that the *Teckal* exemption had become too narrow to accommodate forms of public-public cooperation which are in place in many Member States. Nevertheless, it was not clear to what extent the Court's judgment in *Hamburg* might be limited by the facts of that case. In particular, the Court emphasized that the arrangement aimed to fulfil specific obligations regarding waste treatment set out in European directives, that the facility would not have been built without the guarantee of throughput from the four authorities, and that a separate service contract was awarded by Hamburg for the operation of the facility. In subsequent cases in which this exemption has been invoked, the Court emphasized the requirement for each of the contracting authorities to be fulfilling the same public service function via the cooperation, rather than one authority procuring services from another.[81]

Public authorities wishing to set up or avail of the services of an in-house entity **1.56** or organize shared services have had cause to scrutinize the case law detailed in paragraphs 1.49 to 1.55, and may now take greater comfort in relying on their specific expression in the 2014 directives. Shared services have a particular role to play where there is a desire to realize efficiencies by availing of the capacity of other authorities. Collaborative or joint procurement—whether through a *Teckal*

---

[80] Case C-480/06 *Hamburg*.
[81] Cases C-159/11 *Azienda*, C-386/11 *Piepenbrock*, and C-15/13 *Datenlotsen*.

company or otherwise—is also considered to hold the potential for significant savings, both in terms of transaction costs and economies of scale reflected in contract prices.

1.57 A further exemption to be noted in the field of public-public cooperation is that which applies where a service contract is awarded to a contracting authority or association of authorities on the basis of an exclusive right which it enjoys. For example, if national legislation obliges public authorities to use a particular body for the provision of land appraisal, insurance, or pension services. Such rights must be set out in a law, regulation, or published administrative provision which is compliant with the Treaty.[82] The exemption is identical to that which appeared in Directives 2004/17/EC and 2004/18/EC.

Joint and Central Purchasing Arrangements

1.58 The potential is often touted for aggregated public sector demand to contribute to better-integrated markets and to generate economies of scale. Articles 37 and 38 of the Public Sector Directive address the possibilities for using central purchasing bodies and conducting occasional joint procurement with other public authorities. Article 39 aims to encourage joint procurement between authorities in different Member States, by removing national restrictions and setting principles for the allocation of liability and determining the applicable law. In practice, the barriers to joint procurement taking place across borders are often cultural and political as much as legal. Even at national level, the administrative challenges associated with joint or centralized procurement are formidable. However, it is possible that increased use of electronic tendering will facilitate more joint procurement taking place both within and across national borders, in particular where a shared language or similar public service structures apply.

1.59 While the procurement rules apply to contracts awarded jointly by two or more authorities, Article 37(4) contains an explicit exemption for the award of contracts for the provision of central purchasing and ancillary services to a central purchasing body. As such bodies are defined only by the fact that they carry out central purchasing and ancillary activities on a permanent basis, this would appear to be an easier approach to the *Hamburg*-type situation, if one contracting authority can simply be designated as a central purchasing body and then award contracts on behalf of other authorities. Notably, there is no requirement that central purchasing bodies provide services only to the public sector or that they do not carry out a range of other activities. Central purchasing bodies must themselves be contracting authorities; however, the directives will not apply to contracts awarded to

---

[82] Art 11 Public Sector Directive; and Art 22 Utilities Directive.

any entity providing central purchasing services, provided such contracts do not involve pecuniary interest.[83] This appears to sanction arrangements whereby a private operator could provide central purchasing services to contracting authorities and recoup its costs by way of charges to suppliers included on its frameworks, for example.

The 2014 directives recognize two distinct *modi operandi* for central purchasing **1.60** bodies.[84] They may either act as wholesale purchasers, buying goods, services, or works on behalf of other authorities or entities; or they may establish contracts, frameworks, or dynamic purchasing systems which are then used by authorities or entities to make purchases. Where the first method is used, the central purchasing body will be legally liable for compliance with the procurement rules, whereas in the second case it is only liable for those aspects of the procedure which it conducts itself. The directives also affirm the importance of central purchasing bodies by allowing Member States to render their use mandatory for certain contracts, and by requiring an earlier transition to fully electronic procurement on the part of central purchasing bodies.[85]

Given the expanding scope of applicability of the procurement rules, as well as **1.61** the expanding menu of procedures and new obligations and opportunities created under the 2014 directives, the role for dedicated and expert central purchasing bodies may grow. Central purchasing arrangements may be more or less formal or permanent, and a variety of different approaches can be observed across the Member States. Ireland, for example, has since 2013 entrusted a number of public sector purchase categories to a newly established Office for Government Procurement, with the explicit motive of making financial savings due to economies of scale.' Lithuania's Central Project Management Agency, set up in 2003, has gradually taken over responsibility for a wide range of public sector purchases. It is not only in smaller, centralized Member States that central purchasing bodies play a significant role: in Germany, France, the UK, and Italy, central purchasing bodies are also active and used by many national and sub-national contracting authorities.

Evidence regarding the short- and long-term impact of central purchasing on cost **1.62** and other procurement outcomes is relatively sparse. In theory, savings should accrue both in terms of transaction costs and by leveraging government spending power to achieve economies of scale. However, central purchasing may also have negative outcomes in terms of efficiency of transactions (where the size of contracts or frameworks makes them more difficult to award and manage in a cost-effective

---

[83] Recital 70 Public Sector Directive; and Recital 79 Utilities Directive.

[84] Recital 69, Arts 2(14) and 37 Public Sector Directive; and Recital 78, Arts 2(10) and 55 Utilities Directive. Central purchasing arrangements are not mentioned in the Concessions Directive; however, central purchasing bodies would be subject to the rules on award of concessions if they are contracting authorities or entities.

[85] Arts 37(1) and 90(2) Public Sector Directive; and Arts 55(1) and 106(2) Utilities Directive.

manner), fitness for purpose of the acquired solutions, and longer-term effects on competition and market structure.[86] The role which these and other factors have in influencing value for money in procurement are discussed in Chapter 6.

Public-Private Partnerships and Land Development Agreements

Public-private partnerships

1.63 Public-private partnerships (PPPs) take a wide variety of forms across the EU Member States. A large proportion of PPPs will now be covered by the Concessions Directive if they are valued above €5,186,000. According to the Commission, over 60 per cent of all PPPs in Europe can be qualified as concessions, with 6,169 concessions advertised in the Spanish national Official Journal between 2006 and 2010, 817 in Italy in 2008 alone, and approximately 10,000 operating in France.[87] Concessions appear to be less common at the higher value end of the PPP market, which is dominated by authority-pays projects. The UK leads the European market for award of such PPPs, followed by Italy and France.[88] The decline in availability of private and public finance led to a sharp drop in both the number and value of PPPs reaching financial close between 2007 and 2012, with 2013 levels still remaining well below their 2007 peak. However, the available data does not fully capture the range of partnerships entered into between the public and private sectors, being focused on the larger end of the market.

1.64 For PPPs which are not classified as concessions, the Public Sector or Utilities Directives will apply if the activities to be carried out under the PPP are covered. In a 2008 Communication, the Commission acknowledged the impracticality of carrying out a 'double tendering' procedure where a PPP takes an institutional form—for example, if a jointly owned company is set up. In this case, it is sufficient to have a competition at the outset to choose the private partner, and not necessary to tender for each subsequent contract awarded to the venture, provided the contracts fall within the advertised scope of the arrangement.[89] Alternatively,

---

[86] For an overview of situations in which centralized purchasing may lead to cost reductions—and those in which it does not—see Albano, G. and Sparro, M. (2010) 'Flexible Strategies for Centralized Public Procurement' 1(2) *Review of Economics and Institutions*.

[87] European Commission, MEMO/14/19 Directive of the European Parliament and of the Council on the award of Concession Contracts—Frequently Asked Questions, 15 January 2014.

[88] European PPP Expertise Centre (2014) *Market Update: Review of the European PPP Market in 2013*. The data relates to larger value PPPs (> €10 million) across 14 European countries reporting PPP activity. In 2013, 80 such projects reached financial close, valued at €16.3 billion, and over 90 per cent of these were authority-pays.

[89] COM (2007) 6661 *Commission interpretative communication on the application of Community law on public procurement and concessions to Institutionalised Public-Private Partnerships (IPPPs)*, 5 February 2008.

if no competition is held to establish the joint venture, any contracts awarded to it which fall within the scope of the directives must be subject to competition (which is likely to be less practical once the public authority has committed itself to the arrangement). In its judgment in the *Acoset* case, the Court endorsed this pragmatic approach to the establishment and operation of PPPs. It held that contracts could be directly awarded to an institutional PPP provided that the private partner was selected in an open and transparent procedure in which criteria specific to the service in question were applied.[90]

Curiously, the scope to award contracts via a joint venture or PPP may now be broader than the scope to award contracts to an in-house entity or via a shared service arrangement, if the latter arrangements do not meet the specific conditions set out in Article 12 of the Public Sector Directive. For example, if a public authority wished to award a contract to another public entity to which it was linked, but did not control, there is no clear basis for setting up an 'institutional public-public partnership' which would allow for the award of multiple contracts to such an entity. Arguably, this could be done on the same basis as set out in the Commission's 2008 Communication and approved by the Court in *Acoset*—however, the wording of Article 12 appears to preclude the direct award of a covered contract to another public body on terms other than those set out. The Court may yet have cause to revisit the scope of the *Teckal* and *Hamburg* exemptions if this asymmetry is considered pernicious. **1.65**

The Court again analysed the application of the procurement rules to joint ventures in a case concerning a Finnish municipal authority which established a company with a private operator for the purpose, *inter alia*, of providing occupational health and welfare services to its own staff. The Court found that the authority was not entitled to award a contract for those services to the joint venture company without a competition.[91] The city had intended to conduct a tender competition after a transitional period during which it entrusted the services directly to the company. However, it had not in the first place conducted a competition in order to choose the private partner involved, and the nature of the entity set up precluded application of the *Teckal* exemption. **1.66**

It should be noted that some joint ventures will be covered by the new provision in the 2014 directives allowing contracts for certain health, social, and cultural **1.67**

---

[90] Case C-196/08 *Acoset SpA v Conferenza Sindaci e Presidenza Prov Reg ATO Idrico Ragusa* [2009] ECR I-09913. It should be noted that the contract in question was treated as a services concession by the Court.

[91] Case C-215/09 *Mehilainen Oy v Oulun Kaupunki* [2010] ECR I-13749. The Court distinguished the earlier case of *Club Hotel Loutraki*, in which a Greek authority sold the majority of its shares in a casino to a private company which then assumed its management for a fee and undertook refurbishment work, on the grounds that in that case the public contract elements of the deal were objectively inseparable from the non-covered elements, whereas in *Mehilainen* there was evidence that the elements were separable.

services to be reserved for competition by public service organizations.[92] Such organizations are defined with reference to their objectives, treatment of profits, and employee-led or participatory ownership or management structures. An organization can only benefit from this reservation if it has not been awarded a contract for the services concerned by the same contracting authority within the past three years, and contracts awarded under this provision cannot exceed three years. The provision was lobbied for by the United Kingdom in particular, where the creation and award of contracts to public service mutuals is a preferred means of reducing public sector employment.

Land development agreements

1.68 Land development agreements may be considered either public contracts or concessions, or they may fall outside of the procurement rules altogether. Article 13 of the Public Sector Directive deals with civil engineering, building works, and associated service contracts subsidised by public funds. As in the 2004 directives, if the level of public subsidy is 50 per cent or less, the procurement rules do not apply to the award of contract by the private partner.[93] A grant of planning permission also does not, in itself, constitute a public contract. However, it may be combined with other elements, such as an undertaking on the part of the developer to execute works on the site in question or elsewhere, which do constitute a public contract or concession. The Court's case law indicates that where a work corresponding to the requirements of a public authority is realized, even if the public authority has not specified or paid for it directly, this may be sufficient to attract application of the directives.

1.69 In *La Scala*,[94] the Court ruled that the fact that a public authority did not specify a particular work or choose the contractor did not prevent a public contract from arising. In *Auroux*,[95] this approach was extended to a development agreement, raising the spectre that grants of planning permission might also attract application of the rules where these are linked to conditions regarding the nature of development. However, in the *Müller*[96] case, the Court ruled that the sale of land to a private undertaking which had, in the opinion of the town council, submitted the best plans for development of that land, did not constitute a public contract. In that case, the contract in question contained no provisions on the future use of the land and there was no direct economic benefit to the authority.[97] The Commission subsequently dropped a challenge to a development agreement where it could not

---

[92] Art 77 Public Sector Directive; and Art 94 Utilities Directive.
[93] Art 13 Public Sector Directive.
[94] Case C-399/98.
[95] Case C-220/05 *Jean Auroux and Others v Commune de Roanne* [2007] ECR I-00385.
[96] Case C-451/08 *Helmut Müller GmbH v Bundesanstalt für Immobilienaufgaben* [2010] ECR I-02673.
[97] Case C-451/08 *Helmut Müller*, Opinion of AG Mengozzi, at para 11.

be shown that any contract for the actual execution of works existed.[98] The requirement of a contract in writing existing for the works in question was also emphasized by Advocate General Mazak and the Court in the *Libert* case, which concerned a requirement to provide social housing under a Flemish planning decree.[99]

In *Commission v Netherlands*, the municipality of Eindhoven had entered into a **1.70** cooperation agreement with a private developer for the construction of a community centre and commercial and residential developments on a site belonging to the city. The council had decided in 2002 that the arrangement was not a contract for pecuniary interest and therefore not subject to the procurement rules.[100] However, the contract with the developer was not finally signed until 2007. The Commission argued that there had been a substantial amendment of the terms of the agreement during this time and after the coming into effect of Directive 2004/18/EC, under which the municipality would have had to hold a tender competition.

The Court dismissed the Commission's action on the basis that: (i) the applicable **1.71** law is 'the one in force when the contracting authority chooses the type of procedure to be followed and decides definitively whether it is necessary for a prior call for competition to be issued'; and (ii) the changes in the financial make-up of the contract, including the question of whether the municipality would purchase the works from the developer, did not constitute substantial modifications to the contract.[101] Arguably, the more precise rules on modifications to contracts set out in the 2014 directives would lead to a different finding—they are discussed in Chapter 5.

The approach taken by the Court in the case suggested that land development **1.72** agreements, which by their nature often take considerable time to conclude and require multiple decisions to be taken by public authorities, may be treated with some leniency in applying the procurement rules. In comparison with the approach taken to joint ventures in particular, the Court was willing to allow for a greater degree of flexibility in the scope of the agreement without finding the need for a new competition. It is also notable that the Court did not review Eindhoven's decision against the general Treaty principles of transparency and equal treatment, despite the Commission's invocation of Article 2 of Directive 2004/18/EC, which embodies these principles. No advertisement of the development opportunity had taken place.

---

[98] IP/08/867 *Public procurement: Commission closes infringement case against Germany concerning an urban development project in Flensburg*, 5 June 2008.

[99] Joined Cases C-197/11 and C-203/11 *Eric Libert and Others v Gouvernement flamande*, not yet reported.

[100] At which time the relevant procurement rules were those of Directive 93/37/EEC of 14 June 1993 concerning the coordination of procedures for the award of public works contracts (OJ 1993 L 199, p 54).

[101] Case C-576/10 *Commission v Kingdom of the Netherlands*, not yet reported, paras 45, 53, and 61.

1.73 However, two factors caution against a broad reliance on the Court's approach to development agreements in *Commission v Netherlands*. The first is that the relevant decision by the municipality pre-dated the 2004 directives. The second is that the Court's unquestioning use of the date on which the initial decision on procedure was taken to determine the applicable law is open to abuse. For example, contracting authorities may take decisions regarding the award of concessions in advance of the Concessions Directive coming into force. If such decisions are followed by long delays or substantial changes to the scope of the contract prior to award, they may well be challenged. Evidence of bad faith or intention to avoid the application of the directives could undermine attempts to rely on a decision which pre-dates the coming into effect of the new rules.

Cross-Border Interest and the Frontiers of EU Public Procurement Law

1.74 As is evident from the discussion so far in this chapter, the scope of applicability of the procurement rules has been subject to both judicial and legislative evolution. At times, the Court can be seen as attempting to tame the Commission's wilder single market fantasies, while still marshalling reluctant Member States to apply the principles behind the directives. This approach was particularly evident in a number of judgments in the 2006 to 2011 period relating to non-priority services.[102] However, it was the Court's case law—in particular on the question of whether contracts not covered by the directives were of 'certain cross-border interest' and thus subject to the Treaty principles—which created a particularly difficult situation for practitioners and others wishing to determine the precise scope of the rules prior to 2014.

1.75 Beginning with *Unitron* and *Telaustria*, the Court ruled that certain positive obligations applied in respect of service concessions and other excluded or partially excluded contracts, based on the application of the Treaty principles of non-discrimination and transparency.[103] This line of cases reflects the Court's general approach of offering a purposive interpretation of EU directives and the Treaty, in order to give effect to their broader meaning. The basic problem of the

---

[102] Case C-507/03 *Commission v Ireland ('An Post')* [2007] ECR I-09777; Case C-532/03 *Commission v Ireland ('Irish Ambulances')* [2007] ECR I-11353; and Case C-95/10 *Strong Segurança SA v Municipio de Sintra ('Strong Segurança')* [2011] ECR 1-01865. For discussion of the Court's variable applications of the cross-border interest test, see Arrowsmith, S. (2014) *The Law of Public and Utilities Procurement* Vol. 1 (London: Sweet & Maxwell) at 4-12-4-19.

[103] Case C-275/98 *Unitron Scandinavia A/S and 3-S A/S, Danske Svineproducenters Serviceselskab v Ministeriet for Fødevarer, Landbrug og Fiskeri* [1999] ECR I-08291; and Case C-324/98 *Telaustria Verlags GmbH and Telefonadress GmbH v Telekom Austria and Herold Business Data AG* [2000] ECR I-10745. The Court's approach in this case was foreshadowed to some extent in Case C-3/88 *Commission v Italy ('Re: Data Processing Contracts')* and was further developed in Case C-231/03 *Consorzio Aziende Metano (Coname) v Cingia de' Botti* [2005] ECR I-7287 and Case C-458/03 *Parking Brixen GmbH v Gemeinde Brixen and Stadtwerke Brixen AG* [2005] ECR I-8585.

cross-border interest jurisprudence was that the Court endorsed a test which involved submitting contracts to EU level advertisement and competition (either hypothetically or actually) in order to determine whether certain cross-border interest existed—thus begging the very question which most of these cases aimed to resolve. It was then left up to individual authorities and national courts to apply this impractical test. The Court found that cross-border interest could arise not only in contracts excluded from the full scope of the directives due to their nature (service concessions, non-priority service contracts), but also for those excluded due to their low value.[104]

The application of the Treaty principles to non-priority service contracts based **1.76** on certain cross-border interest created a legal puzzle, as the presumed lack of cross-border interest in non-priority services was the basis for their classification as such under the 2004 directives and their predecessors.[105] The scope of obligations arising from the Treaty principles was not limited to advertisement, but included rules relating to fair procedures and equal treatment. With its rulings in *Parking Brixen*, *SECAP*, and *Wall AG*, the Court left open the possibility that contracting authorities might be obliged to apply even to excluded contracts the rules relating to in-house arrangements, treatment of abnormally low tenders, and modifications to contracts. Based on these developments, some legal scholars identified a convergence between the rules applicable under the directives and those implied from Treaty principles.[106]

Unsurprisingly, Member States were not satisfied with this state of affairs and sought **1.77** retrenchment of the positive obligations applicable to such contracts. In 2006, Germany, supported by six other Member States and the European Parliament, brought an application for the annulment of the Commission's *Interpretative Communication on the Community law applicable to contracts not or not fully subject to the directives*,[107] which purported to set out the obligations arising from the Court's case law. The saga of the 2006 *Interpretative Communication* encapsulates the three-way tug-of-war between the Commission, Court, and Member States to establish the limits of the EU procurement rules. The Commission formulated it with a view to 'clarifying' the extent to which low-value contracts, service concessions, and other forms of contract not explicitly covered by the 2004 directives were subject to certain procedural rules—for example, a duty to advertise—based on its interpretation of the Court's case law.

---

[104] Joined Cases C-147/06 and C148/06 *SECAP SpA and Santorso Soc coop arl v Comune di Torino* [2008] ECR I-3565, para 31.

[105] A fact acknowledged by the Court in its judgment in Case C-507/03 *An Post*, para 25.

[106] See Brown, A. (2010) 'EU Primary Law Requirements in Practice: Advertising, Procedures and Remedies for Public Contracts outside the Procurement Directives' 18 *PPLR* 169–81, but see also Risvig, C. (2012) *Contracts Not Covered, Or Not Fully Covered, by the Public Sector Directive* (Copenhagen: DJØF), pp 188–94.

[107] [2006] OJ C 179/02 of 23 June 2006.

1.78 The *Interpretative Communication* emphasizes that certain contracts, despite falling outside the scope of the directives due to their value or subject-matter, are nonetheless subject to the general Treaty principles of transparency and equal treatment. In practice, this means that such contracts must be advertised and procedures followed to ensure the possibility of access for non-domestic operators and to avoid any form of direct or indirect discrimination. The scope of obligations outlined relate to publicity for contracts, procedures for selection, and award, setting appropriate time limits and the availability of legal remedies. The *Interpretative Communication* indicates that the degree of advertising and procedural guarantees required must be determined on a case-by-case basis—hardly a recipe for legal certainty and a difficult ground on which to formulate clear national rules.

1.79 While it provides guidelines on the type of advertising and procedures which might be deemed sufficient for excluded or partly excluded contracts where these are of certain cross-border interest, the *Interpretative Communication* does not address the question of how cross-border interest is to be identified. In *SECAP*, a judgment which came after the *Interpretative Communication* was issued, but prior to the determination of Germany's challenge to it, the Court stated that it would be permissible for local or national legislation to lay down objective criteria to determine if cross-border interest arose for a particular contract. These criteria would need to have regard not only to the value of the contract, but also to its technical characteristics and location—the Court indicated that even low-value contracts may be of cross-border interest where they are carried out in a conurbation which straddles national borders, for example.[108]

1.80 In its lengthy ruling dismissing Germany's challenge to the *Interpretative Communication*, the General Court reviewed the content against previous jurisprudence and found that it did not create any new legal obligations. Accordingly, the application for annulment was found to be inadmissible. Subsequently, there were some signs of a retrenchment in the Court's application of Treaty principles to non-priority service contracts. In *Irish Translation Services*, the Court held that failing to attribute weightings to award criteria in advance for a non-priority service contract did not constitute a breach of the equal treatment principle; however, altering the weighting *after* an initial review of tenders *did* constitute such a breach.[109] In *Strong Segurança*, the Court rejected the application of Article 47(2) of Directive 2004/18/EC (allowing reliance on the financial and technical capacity of other entities at selection stage) to a non-priority service contract, stating that such a broad approach to the principle of equal treatment risked rendering the distinction between priority and non-priority services entirely ineffective.[110]

---

[108] Joined Cases C-147/06 and C148/06 *SECAP*, para 31.
[109] Case C-226/09 *Commission v Ireland* ('*Irish Translation Services*') [2010] ECR I-11807.
[110] Case C-95/10 *Strong Segurança*, para 42.

The implications of this evolving case law for the treatment of contracts which   **1.81**
are below-threshold or otherwise excluded under the 2014 directives is difficult
to gauge. While some national rules already explicitly apply the Treaty principles
in respect of such contracts, this is uneven and often reflects pre-existing national
practices as much as the utterances of the Court and Commission.[111] A 2013 analysis of legislation and case law in three Member States found that while soft law such
as the *Interpretative Communication* had little discernible impact on national legislation or practices, the Court's interpretation of the Treaty principles in respect
of excluded or partially excluded contracts was increasingly being applied by
national courts.[112] In respect of certain principles such as proportionality, national
courts may even have gone further than the CJEU in their review of procurement
decisions—this is discussed further in Chapter 2.

There is no reason to believe that the adoption of the 2014 directives has brought   **1.82**
to an end the evolution in the case law of the Court arising from the fundamental
Treaty freedoms and principles. For example, does the exclusion of water services
from the scope of the Concessions Directive mean that the Court would hesitate
to apply the requirements of transparency and equal treatment as developed in its
previous case law to water concessions? Probably not. While the recitals to the 2014
directives express the intention to delimit the scope of their applicability, as noted
in paragraph 1.08, it is not possible to exclude the application of the Treaty principles, as these constitute the primary law of the Union. There is also the possibility
of further developments in the list of principles which are held to be applicable in
the context of public procurement—for example, where environmental protection,
social inclusion, or fundamental rights protected by the EU Charter are at stake.
The next chapter considers the role which the fundamental freedoms and principles have played in regulating public contracts to date, and the potential for such
future permutations.

---

[111] For analysis and comparison of the position in eight Member States, see Caranta, R. and Dragos,
D. (eds) (2012) *Outside the EU Procurement Directives—Inside the Treaty?* (Copenhagen: DJØF,).

[112] De Mars, S. (2013) 'The Limits of General Principles: A Procurement Case Study' 38(3)
European Law Review 316–34, looking at application of the Treaty principles in the United
Kingdom, Netherlands, and France. A full copy of the author's doctoral thesis on this topic is avail-
able from <http://ethos.bl.uk>.

2

PRINCIPLES

Appreciation of the general principles which underlie the procurement rules is not **2.01** an idle intellectual pastime. As outlined in Chapter 1, the scope of the rules has been subject to steady evolution, and this has most often been justified by reference to one or other of the principles set out in the Treaty which have specific application to procurement. The line of cases beginning with *Telaustria* established that these principles may apply even in respect of contracts fully outside of the directives. In its 2010 *Betfair* judgment, the Court applied requirements of transparency and equal treatment to the award of a licence,[1] and has indicated in other cases that the mere granting by a public authority of authorization for an activity, in the absence of any obligation to perform it, may also be subject to the same Treaty principles.[2]

The diversity of ways in which the public sector obtains goods, services, and works **2.02** means there will always be a need to consider whether arrangements which fall outside of the specific scope of the directives may attract cross-border interest and thus the application of the Treaty. Short of submitting every contract to EU-level advertisement and competition, it does not appear possible to exclude the potential for cross-border interest entirely. As long as the directives apply only to specific-ally designated public contracts, there will be the possibility that other contracts may be subject to the Treaty principles. The Court's more recent case law does, however, suggest that the scope of obligations implied for excluded or partially excluded contracts will be relatively low, while the burden of proof to establish certain cross-border interest in such contracts will be high.[3]

---

[1] Case C-203/08 *Sporting Exchange Ltd (t/a Betfair) v Minister van Justitie* [2010] ECR I-04695.

[2] Case C-221/12 *Belgacom NV v Interkommunale voor Teledistributie van het Gewest Antwerpen (Integan) and Others* ('*Belgacom*'), not yet reported, para 33.

[3] In two cases brought by the Commission against Ireland in relation to the award of non-priority services, the Court held that the Commission had not discharged the onus of proof upon it to establish a breach of the principles. Case C-507/03 *Commission v Ireland* ('*An Post*') [2007] ECR I-09777; Case C-532/03 *Commission v Ireland* ('*Irish Ambulances*') [2007] ECR I-11353; and in *Strong Segurança*, the Court also took a limited view of the obligations applicable to non-priority service contracts (Case C-95/10 *Strong Segurança SA v Municipio de Sintra* [2011] ECR 1-01865).

2.03 Beyond an understanding of how the procurement rules have evolved and may continue to evolve, the principles are also an essential aid to interpreting the obligations contained in the 2014 directives. For example, it is difficult to know how to formulate and apply award criteria which 'do not confer an unrestricted freedom of choice', are 'linked to the subject-matter of the contract', and 'ensure the possibility of effective competition' without some familiarity with the principles of free movement, transparency, and proportionality from which the Court has derived these concepts. Similarly, a contracting authority which wishes to limit the number of lots which a single operator may win based on 'objective and non-discriminatory criteria' will need to have an understanding of the principles of equal treatment and non-discrimination.

2.04 Free movement of goods and services, freedom of establishment, mutual recognition, equal treatment, proportionality, and transparency form part of the established scaffolding upon which the procurement rules are based. However, there are a number of other general principles and freedoms within EU law, not least those set out in the Charter of Fundamental Rights, which may also be found applicable in the procurement context. This chapter evaluates the relevance of such principles and identifies areas where future developments may occur. Consideration of the principles of environmental protection and social inclusion, which have also influenced the Court's procurement jurisprudence, is given in Chapter 7.

Free Movement

2.05 The recitals to the 2014 directives clearly invoke the free movement of goods and services, and freedom of establishment, as overarching principles which govern the award of public contracts. References to these principles can be found in the earliest procurement directives.[4] Together with free movement of workers and capital, they are the foundation for much of EU law and have been the subject of extensive academic commentary based on the Court's progressive interpretation of their meaning and effect. From its first incarnation as a customs union, the importance of removing barriers to trade for the European project has been clear. In the procurement context, eliminating national practices which directly or indirectly restrict access to government contracts for goods, services, and providers originating from other Member States was the primary motivation for development of coordinated procedures.[5] The other freedoms, of movement of workers and capital,

---

[4] Directive 70/32/EEC on the provision of goods to the State, local authorities and other official bodies refers to the free movement of goods; and Directive 71/305/EEC concerning the co-ordination of procedures for the award of public works contracts refers to the free movement of services and freedom of establishment.

[5] This is not to say that other motivations, such as reducing corruption, were not also influential. For a discussion of the history and objectives of the EU procurement directives, see Arrowsmith, S. (2005) *The Law of Public and Utilities Procurement* (London: Sweet & Maxwell), pp 120–51.

are also implicated in public procurement; however, they are not the basis on which the directives have been adopted. The specific interaction between the public procurement rules and free movement of workers as protected by the Posted Workers Directive is considered in Chapter 4 (paragraphs 4.36 *et seq.*).

Article 34 of the Treaty prohibits quantitative restrictions and measures having **2.06** equivalent effect.[6] Both direct and indirect restrictions on free movement are covered by this prohibition, and the Court has scrutinized the effect of various measures promulgated in the Member States, rather than their formal designation or stated purpose. This approach has also been taken to restrictions within procurement procedures. References to a particular product name or make, or to national standards in the absence of the words 'or equivalent', have been held to restrict the free movement of goods, whether contracts were above or below threshold and whether or not foreign products or suppliers were involved.[7] In certain cases, the Court has declined to apply free movement rules to low value or excluded contracts, but this does not seem to have cohered into a general *de minimis* exemption.[8]

As noted in the Introduction, the actual levels of direct cross-border public pro- **2.07** curement within the EU remain very low. There are, however, difficulties associated with measuring this accurately, and levels of indirect cross-border procurement, through subsidiaries or affiliates based in the country where the contract is awarded or through subcontracts, appear to be considerably higher.[9] Nonetheless, the norm remains for French public contracts to be awarded to French companies, Polish to Polish, British to British, and so on. Smaller Member States naturally award a greater percentage of their contracts to companies established abroad. In some cases, it may yet be too early to see the effects of truly coordinated public procurement rules on free movement of goods and services, if the 2004 directives are taken as a starting point. In others, it must be acknowledged that the removal of legal and procedural obstacles to free movement does not affect the political, economic,

---

See also McCrudden, C. (2007) *Buying Social Justice: Equality, Government Procurement and Legal Change* (Oxford: Oxford University Press), pp 95–113.

[6] According to the Court's jurisprudence, 'measures having equivalent effect' include any trading rules which are capable of hindering intra-Community trade directly or indirectly, actually or potentially (*Dassonville*). There are a number of recognized grounds on which such restrictions can be justified, including protection of the environment or consumers, public morality or security, or public health.

[7] Case 45/87 *Commission v Ireland* ('*Dundalk Water*') [1988] ECR 4929; Case C-359/93 *Commission v Netherlands* ('*Unix*') [1995] ECR I-157; and Case C-59/00 *Bent Mousten Vestergaard v Spottrup Boligselskab* [2001] ECR I-09505.

[8] In *Coname*, the Court held that the effects on fundamental freedoms were 'too uncertain and too indirect to warrant the conclusion that they may have been infringed'. For discussion of this approach, see Trepte, P. (2007) *Public Procurement in the EU* (Oxford: Oxford University Press), p 23; and (contrasting the applicability of free movement and the cross-border interest test) Risvig, C. (2012) *Contracts Not Covered or Not Fully Covered by the Public Sector Directive* (Copenhagen: DJØF Publishing), pp 149–58.

[9] Sylvest et al (2011) *Final Report: Cross-Border Procurement above EU Thresholds* (European Commission).

cultural, and language barriers which remain in place and limit cross-border public procurement.[10]

2.08 What, then, are the benefits of free movement of goods and services within the EU? The basic idea of free movement is that goods and services, as well as businesses and the people and capital they employ, should be able to move to the areas where they are most needed. This is expected to increase overall economic welfare both for the country of origin and the receiving State over time. One study of the overall impact of European integration found that this had been associated with an increase in GDP of only 5 per cent;[11] however, other studies have emphasized the difficulty of measuring this accurately.[12] The Commission's own evaluation of the impact of the public procurement rules in 2011 found that the savings associated with competition and transparency outweighed the administrative costs (for both suppliers and contracting authorities) by a factor of four to one—however, the magnitude of savings was also small, at just 4 to 5 per cent of the value of the contracts evaluated.[13]

2.09 The free movement principles are not absolute; restrictions can be justified where these are justified by imperative requirements in the general interest; suitable for securing the attainment of the objective which they pursue; and do not go beyond what is necessary in order to attain it. The conditions are cumulative and the last two amount to a proportionality test, discussed below. Cases concerning the free movement of goods and services often focus on whether these conditions have been satisfied. In the *Contse* case,[14] the Spanish National Health Institute had invited tenders for home respiratory treatment services, to be provided to patients within a particular area. An admission condition required tenderers to have at least one office open to the public in the provincial capital, and award criteria assigned marks based on the number of such offices which tenderers had open at the time of tendering, as well as the number of oxygen production facilities they owned within 1,000 kilometres of the province.

2.10 Two lower courts rejected the applicants' claim; however, the *Audiencia Nacional* in Madrid made a reference to the Court for a preliminary ruling on the compatibility of the admission and award criteria with EU law. As the contract related to non-priority services, and there was some contention that it might actually be a

---

[10] Language may be particularly important in this regard—as evidenced by the higher rates of cross-border procurement between Member States sharing a language.

[11] Boltho, A. and Eichengreen, B. (2008) *The Economic Impact of European Integration*, Discussion Paper 6820 (Centre for Economic Policy Research).

[12] See Pelkmans, J. (2011) 'European Union Single Market: Economic Impact' in S. Durlauf and L. Blume (eds), *The New Palgrave Dictionary of Economics*, online edn (Basingstoke: Palgrave Macmillan); and European Parliament Directorate-General for Internal Policies (2014) *Towards Indicators for Measuring the Performance of the Single Market*.

[13] European Commission (2011) *Evaluation Report: Impact and Effectiveness of EU Public Procurement Legislation*, SEC (2011) 853 final, p 156.

[14] Case C-234/03 *Contse SA, Vivisol Srl and Oxigen Salud SA v Instituto Nacional de Gestión Sanitaria (Ingesa), formerly Instituto Nacional de la Salud (Insalud)* ('*Contse*') [2005] ECR I-9315.

service concession, the Court made clear that its ruling was based on the Treaty principles as opposed to the directive then in force.[15] The Spanish Government argued that the admission condition and award criteria were necessary in order to safeguard the supply of essential medical equipment and services and in order to ensure the possibility of rapid restocking. The Court held that the measures restricted the freedom to provide services and, while it accepted that they were intended to protect the life and health of patients, found that they went beyond what was needed to attain this aim. Reliability of supply could have been attained by requiring the contractor to have an office open and emergency stocks of oxygen held locally at the point when the contract commenced.

The freedom of establishment and to provide services have also been important **2.11** as a basis for the development of procurement law within the EU. The idea that undertakings and individuals should be able to pursue economic activity in any EU Member State is essential for the internal market. If contracting authorities were able to insist on candidates or tenderers having a particular legal form under national law, or to have domestic offices or facilities, this would undermine free movement. The process of integrating service markets across Europe has lagged behind that for goods, and remains incomplete in a number of areas. Questions about the social character of public service delivery also remain central to the debate about the extent and manner of service market integration.[16] The Concessions Directive is one action aimed at further integrating service markets across the EU. Others have been advanced under the Services Directive, relating in particular to services of general interest and the designation of professions.[17] In these areas, the principle of mutual recognition is also of central importance.

Mutual Recognition

While harmonized standards exist for many of the goods and services moved **2.12** across the EU, in certain areas national or local standards continue to apply. Here, the principle of mutual recognition is important: products legally manufactured or marketed in one Member State should be accepted for sale in others. In the context of services, the principle of mutual recognition means that services which are legally offered in one Member State can also be provided in other Member States. Mutual recognition allows for a diversity of standards to exist, but requires equivalent standards from other Member States to be recognized. This means that an architect qualified in Italy should be able to offer services in Denmark, and

---

[15] Case C-234/03 *Contse*, para 23.
[16] Further discussion of this can be found in Chapter 8. For an excellent overview of this debate within different sectors and areas of EU law, see Cremona, M. (ed) (2011) *Market Integration and Public Services in the European Union* (Oxford: Oxford University Press).
[17] Directive 2006/123/EC of 12 December 2006 on services in the internal market.

construction products sold in Ireland should be sellable in Slovenia. Directives have been adopted in these areas which give effect to the principle of mutual recognition—for example, by requiring that Member States allow access to their markets for professionals who have attained a relevant qualification in another Member State.[18]

2.13 Mutual recognition seems like an elegant solution to the problem of diverse national rules and regulations on products and services. However, it has not always operated so smoothly in practice. The Court in *Cassis-de-Dijon*[19] left open the possibility of a 'lowest common denominator' approach to product standards in the absence of harmonization. This was tempered in subsequent case law by the acceptance of various justifications for higher national standards, either based on the nature and purpose of such rules or their effect. Rules could be justified by reference to mandatory requirements in the field of health, safety, or consumer protection, or if they did not in fact impede market access for goods from outside of the Member State applying the rule.[20] In the 1980s, the Commission adopted the 'New Approach' to harmonization in areas where national rules still applied. Directives are used to establish minimum health and safety requirements for product groups, and refer to the relevant European standards (EN) for that sector. Governments are obliged to presume that products which meet these standards comply with the minimum requirements, and to allow such products free access to their markets. Examples of areas where this approach applies are construction products, chemicals, and medical devices.

2.14 The effect of the harmonized legislation for medical devices on a procurement procedure was at issue in the *Medipac* case.[21] A Greek hospital had issued a tender for surgical sutures bearing the CE marking—which attests to their conformity with the requirements under the Medical Devices Directive.[22] Upon receipt of Medipac's tender, the hospital decided to reject its offer of sutures which bore the required marking, but which the hospital's surgeons considered unsuitable. The case turned on the interpretation of the Medical Devices Directive and in particular the safeguard provisions in the event that a product marked as compliant does not in fact conform to the relevant standards. In this event, the directive requires that the alleged non-compliance be notified to the competent national body, so that the product can be investigated and removed from the market if necessary.

---

[18] Directive 2005/36/EC of 7 December 2005 on the recognition of professional qualifications.

[19] Case 120/78 *Rewe-Zentral AG v Bundesmonopolverwaltung für Branntwein* ('*Cassis de Dijon*') [1979] ECR 649.

[20] See Joined Cases C-267/91 and C-268/91 *Criminal proceedings against Bernard Keck and Daniel Mithouard* [1993] ECR I-06097; Opinion of AG Jacobs in Case C-412/93 *Société d'Importation Edouard Leclerc-Siplec v TF1 Publicité SA and M6 Publicité SA* [1995] ECR I-179, and the discussion of these cases in Craig, P. and de Búrca, G. (2011) *EU Law: Text Cases and Materials*, 5th edn (Oxford: Oxford University Press), pp 649–90.

[21] Case C-6/05 *Medipac-Kazantzidis AE v Venizelio-Pananio* [2007] ECR I-4557.

[22] Council Directive 93/42/EEC of 14 June 1993 concerning medical devices.

The hospital in this case had informed the competent body of its concerns, which then carried out tests, finding that the sutures in question did in fact comply with the relevant standards. However, the hospital had already rejected the bid and awarded the contract to another company.

In the circumstances, both Advocate General Sharpston and the Court considered **2.15** that the rejection of the bid was unauthorized. The value of the contract in the case was below threshold, so the Court relied on the Treaty principles in reaching its conclusion that the correct process would have been to suspend the award of contract while any public health concerns about the sutures were addressed. If there was an urgent need to procure sutures in the interim, this could be done by way of a negotiated procedure as provided for in the directives. It is worth noting that the outcome of the case may well have differed if the technical specifications had contained additional requirements regarding quality, or if lowest price had not been the sole award criterion. In either case, the hospital would have been able to take account of the surgeons' concerns in its evaluation of tenders. The Court also noted the apparently widespread rejection of devices bearing the CE marking by Greek hospitals at the time, to the extent that the Commission had initiated infringement proceedings on this matter.[23]

The *Medipac* judgment, although unsurprising based on its facts, points to some of **2.16** the limitations of the principle of mutual recognition as embodied in harmonized directives. The safeguard procedure, which is designed to protect public health in particular, is somewhat slow and laborious. This is so even after the 2008 reforms to harmonization.[24] The burden of establishing non-compliance rests firmly with the Member State which wishes to limit access to its market of any suspect products. In the procurement context, this is reinforced by the obligation to accept equivalents where technical specifications are formulated with reference to standards. While the vast majority of products bearing the CE marking or other evidence of compliance with standards will in fact conform, contracting authorities are under a duty to ensure that they treat all bidders equally, while at the same time protecting public health or other essential interests.

This may require verification efforts beyond those envisioned in harmonized direc- **2.17** tives, particularly where the directives exclude considerations such as environmental protection or new health or safety threats. Such verification efforts would be impeded if the *Medipac* judgment is interpreted to mean that the existence of a safeguard procedure is always sufficient to protect essential interests. The ability of contracting authorities to make their own enquiries and address any concerns about health and safety or fitness for purpose may become of even greater

---

[23] Case C-6/05 *Medipac*, Opinion of AG Sharpston at para 38.
[24] Decision No 768/2008/EC on a common framework for the marketing of products; and Regulation (EC) No 765/2008 setting out the requirements for accreditation and market surveillance relating to the marketing of products.

importance as the scope of bilateral and plurilateral trade agreements offering access to public procurement grows. As noted, there is ample freedom under the EU procurement rules for authorities to set their own criteria and make decisions based on objective criteria—however, it is essential that they apply the principles of non-discrimination and equal treatment in doing so.

Non-Discrimination and Equal Treatment

2.18 The principle of non-discrimination underlies both the EU procurement regime and the WTO Government Procurement Agreement (GPA). Article IV of the GPA requires that the treatment afforded to products, services, and suppliers of any party to the agreement is no less favourable than that afforded to domestic suppliers or any other party. It also stipulates that locally established suppliers must not be discriminated against based on degree of foreign ownership, or the origin of the products or services they supply. In EU law, the principle of non-discrimination on the basis of nationality is explicitly linked to the free movement of goods and services within the internal market. An early application of this principle in the context of public contracts can be found in the *Beentjes* case, with the Court stating that an obligation to employ long-term unemployed persons on a public works contract could infringe the Treaty:

> if it became apparent that such a condition could be satisfied only by tenderers from the State concerned or indeed that tenderers from other Member States would have difficulty in complying with it.[25]

2.19 In the *Unitron* case,[26] the Court held that the principle of non-discrimination on the basis of nationality could not be interpreted restrictively, and was accompanied by an obligation of transparency in order to confirm compliance. References to the general principle of non-discrimination have become less common in the Court's judgments as the procurement directives have grown to encompass a larger number of specific rules which give effect to it. For example, the detailed rules on references to labels contained in both the 2004 and 2014 directives can be seen as an expression of the prohibition on discrimination to the extent that they insist on recognition of equivalent labels. The Court has repeatedly found that the principle of equal treatment in public procurement goes beyond the requirement not to discriminate based on nationality, and arises regardless of whether there are any foreign bidders involved[27] and whether or not the contract is covered by the directives.[28] Equal

---

[25] Case 31/87 *Gebroeders Beentjes BV v State of the Netherlands* [1988] ECR 04635, para 30.

[26] Case C-275/98 *Unitron Scandinavia A/S and 3-S A/S, Danske Svineproducenters Serviceselskab v Ministeriet for Fødevarer, Landbrug og Fiskeri* [1999] ECR I-08291.

[27] This point was established in the *Wallonian Buses* case: C-87/94 *Commission v Belgium* [1996] ECR I-2043.

[28] See, eg, Case C-458/08 *Parking Brixen GmbH v Gemeinde Brixen and Stadtwerke Brixen AG* [2005] ECR I-8585, para 48; and Case C-410/04 *Associazione Nazionale Autotrasporto Viaggiatori*

treatment, which implies positive as well as negative obligations, has superseded non-discrimination in much of the Court's recent jurisprudence. The *Storebaelt* case may be seen as the turning point in this regard, as the Court held that, despite not being explicitly mentioned in the directives, the principle of equal treatment lay at the very heart of them.[29]

There are several references to equal treatment and equality in the Treaties and, lat- **2.20** terly, the Charter of Fundamental Rights. The clearest textual reference relates to equality between men and women in the context of employment; however, it can and has been interpreted as a general principle of EU law.[30] What does equal treatment mean? A distinction is normally made between formal equality—rules, criteria, and processes applying in the same way to everyone—and substantive equality, in which the effect of the rules is also considered. This is also sometimes expressed as the difference between equality of opportunity and equality of outcome. In the procurement context, the Court has interpreted equal treatment as requiring that:

> comparable situations must not be treated differently and different situations must not be treated in the same way, unless such treatment is objectively justified.[31]

The potential consequences of this definition for the idea of substantive equality in procurement are explored here. It should be noted at the outset that 'equality of outcome' may appear paradoxical in the procurement context: there can normally be only one winner in a tender competition. It is, however, possible that procurement policies aim to achieve substantive equality between different groups in the aggregate, so that the total benefit of public contracts is more evenly distributed among different groups within society. The legality and desirability of this approach is considered below.

Equal treatment in practice—neutralizing advantages

Arguably, the second limb of the Court's definition ('different situations must not **2.21** be treated in the same way') implies an element of substantive equality. One example of how this has been enforced by the Court relates to the treatment of incumbents in a tender procedure. Incumbents typically have access to information about

---

(ANAV) v Comune di Bari and AMTAB Servizio SpA [2006] ECR I-3303, para 20. Both cases concerned service concessions, at the time exempt from the directives.

[29] Case C-243/89 *Commission v Denmark* [1993] ECR I-3353, para 33.

[30] See Tridimas, T. (2006) *The General Principles of EU Law*, 2nd edn (Oxford: Oxford University Press), pp 59–135; Craig and de Búrca, *EU Law*, pp 854–91. Arrowsmith and Kunzlik consider that the textual foundation is too thin for a generally applicable principle of equal treatment to exist in procurement. It should be noted however that the authors were writing prior to the elevation of the legal status of the Charter of Fundamental Rights, which took place with entry into force of the Treaty of Lisbon. Arrowsmith, S. and Kunzlik, P. (eds) (2009) *Social and Environmental Policies in EC Procurement Law: New Directives and New Directions* (Cambridge: Cambridge University Press), pp 86–7.

[31] Joined Cases C-21/03 and C-34/03 *Fabricom SA v État belge* [2005] ECR I-01559, para 27.

contractual requirements which goes beyond that of their competitors. Depending on the nature of the pre-existing relationship, they may also have information about the contracting authority's plans, strategies, and financial position which is sensitive or confidential. This places other tenderers at a competitive disadvantage, one which the contracting authority must aim to remedy. The question is what steps an authority must take, and how issues of commercial sensitivity or intellectual property should be dealt with in aiming to create a level playing field between incumbents and other operators.

2.22 In a case brought against the European Commission in respect of its award of a large IT services contract, an unsuccessful bidder argued that the principle of equal treatment had been breached on two grounds.[32] The contract was technically complex, involving the development and hosting of the Commission's existing online platform for the coordination of its R&D funding ('CORDIS'). The tender documents provided for a three-month running-in period during which any new contractor would work with the incumbent for the handover of services. This period was to be unpaid on the part of the newly appointed contractor, while payment to the incumbent would continue under the previous contract. The applicant argued that this provision gave the incumbent an unfair financial advantage. It also argued that the Commission's failure to provide adequate specifications, including the source code for the existing platform, meant that it was placed at a technical disadvantage vis-à-vis the incumbent.

2.23 The case was heard by the then Court of First Instance, which considered the scope of duties arising under the principle of equal treatment. The Commission's procurement is governed by the Financial Regulation, which contains similar provisions on non-discrimination to those found in the Treaty and procurement directives. The Court found that this meant that the 'potential advantages of the existing contractor... must be neutralised, but only to the extent that it is technically easy to effect such neutralisation, where it is economically acceptable and where it does not infringe the rights of the existing contractor...'[33] A balance had to be struck between the interests involved, and in the case at hand the decision to have an unpaid running-in period was an appropriate way to manage these various interests. However, in relation to the information made available to non-incumbent bidders, the Commission had not gone far enough to neutralize the incumbent's advantage by providing full technical information to all bidders in good time. The award of contract was annulled.

2.24 The fact that the Commission was in possession of the relevant source code may have influenced the outcome of the case—as suggested by the Court's choice of wording on the extent to which advantages must be neutralized (technically easy,

---

[32] Case T-345/03 *Evropaïki Dynamiki v European Commission* [2008] ECR II-34.
[33] Case T-345/03 *Evropaïki Dynamiki*, para 76.

economically acceptable, and does not infringe existing rights). This test could apply to other situations in which a particular operator has an 'inherent de facto advantage'.[34] For example, a similar problem of information dissymmetry can arise in tenders for service contracts to which the Transfer of Undertakings Directive[35] applies, such as for cleaning or security. Unless robust conditions have been included in the existing contract regarding the handover of data on employees' terms and conditions of employment, it can be very difficult for non-incumbent competitors to price their bids taking these liabilities into account. This issue is considered further in Chapter 5.

Another situation in which authorities may need to proactively redress information **2.25** dissymmetry is where one or more bidders have been involved in pre-procurement activities. The 2014 directives contain specific rules regarding the actions to be taken where an operator may have gained an advantage from such involvement.[36] First, if a candidate or tenderer has advised the authority or otherwise been involved in the preparation of a tender, the authority must take 'appropriate measures to ensure that competition is not distorted by the participation of that candidate or tenderer'. Such measures include communicating relevant information to other candidates or tenderers and allowing adequate time for them to prepare their submissions.[37] Second, a contracting authority may exclude an operator from a competition where its participation would lead to a distortion in competition which 'cannot be remedied by other, less intrusive means'.[38] In this case, the operator must be given the opportunity to demonstrate that its participation is not capable of causing such distortion. These provisions may create an incentive for incumbent operators to cooperate in making information available in the run up to a tender, as failure to do so would create a risk of exclusion. They will not, however, remove the need for provident drafting of handover clauses in contracts, as discussed in Chapter 5.

Scope of obligations arising from equal treatment

If it is accepted that inequalities in the information available to candidates or ten- **2.26** derers may in some cases create positive obligations on contracting authorities to

---

[34] The terminology used by the Court at para 70 of its judgment.

[35] Directive 2001/23/EC, implemented in Ireland by the European Communities (Protection of Employees on Transfer of Undertakings) Regulations 2003 and in the UK by the Transfer of Undertakings (Protection of Employment) Regulations 2006 ('TUPE').

[36] Art 41 of the Public Sector Directive and Art 59 of the Utilities Directive, both headed 'Prior involvement of candidates or tenderers'. The *Fabricom* case concerned a situation of this nature.

[37] The time available to non-incumbent operators was at issue in Case T-345/03 *Evropaïki Dynamiki*. Despite the allowance of a relatively long tender period of three months, relevant technical details and clarifications were only issued by the Commission shortly before the deadline for tenders, impeding the applicant's ability to incorporate them in its bid.

[38] Art 57(4)(f) of the Public Sector Directive, which may be applied under Art 80 of the Utilities Directive. This ground for discretionary exclusion is omitted from Art 38 of the Concessions Directive.

level the playing field, the question naturally arises of whether this applies to other inequalities. A small company and a large one will be in different situations regarding their turnover, human, and technical resources. If the same selection criteria are applied to both, this would mean they are being treated in the same way despite their differences. However, in this case, the specific rules set out in the directives contradict any such general interpretation of the equality principle. The directives require that the same pre-defined and objective selection criteria be applied to all candidates, regardless of their size or corporate structure. There is no room for positive discrimination within the confines of the selection procedure itself. Extra points cannot be assigned to any candidate based on criteria other than those authorized by the directives.

2.27 There are, of course, numerous ways in which contracting authorities can encourage the participation and increase the chances of success for SMEs or other businesses which have been identified as being under-represented in contract awards. This applies both to general activities outside of the procurement process such as market consultation and engagement, and to the design of contracting opportunities such as division into lots or use of multi-supplier frameworks, as well as the choice of selection and award criteria. The 2014 directives also provide the possibility to reserve competition for certain contracts to businesses which employ a minimum percentage of disadvantaged or disabled workers or which are classed as public service organizations.[39] These are exceptions to the general rule that any undertaking must be able to compete regardless of its corporate form or other activities.

2.28 Could more active approaches to inclusion of SMEs or, as exists in other jurisdictions such as the United States and Canada, businesses owned by women and minorities, be accommodated within the EU procurement regime? In other areas where the Treaty equality principle applies, notably employment law, the Court has gradually moved from a formal interpretation to one which leaves room for positive discrimination in some cases.[40] The Charter, which attained legal force with the Treaty of Lisbon in 2009, also contains a statement of the principle of equality which may be taken as the basis for positive discrimination, at least where gender inequality exists. Article 23 states that 'equality between men and women must be ensured in all areas, including employment, work and pay'. It then goes on to provide that:

> The principle of equality shall not prevent the maintenance or adoption of measures providing for specific advantages in favour of the under-represented sex.

---

[39] Arts 20 and 77 of the Public Sector Directive; Arts 38 and 94 of the Utilities Directive; and Art 24 of the Concessions Directive.

[40] Tridimas, *The General Principles of EU Law*, pp 111–18. See also De Búrca, G. (2012) 'The Trajectories of European and American Anti-Discrimination Law' 60 *American Journal of Comparative Law* 1, analysing recent trends.

If, for example, a public authority were to determine that men were severely under- **2.29**
represented among contractors providing care services, or that women were severely
under-represented among construction contractors, could this be a grounds for
discriminating in favour of contractors who were able to remedy such imbalances?
The Charter also contains strong wording on the integration of people with disabilities, acknowledging their right to:

> benefit from measures designed to ensure their independence, social and occupa-
> tional integration and participation in the life of the community.

While the Charter formally has the same legal status as the Treaty, its scope of
application is limited to Union bodies and to Member States when they are implementing Union law. It does not create any new competences for the Union or Court
of Justice. If, however, a Member State or contracting authority adopted measures
in procurement designed to favour the under-represented gender or ensure the
integration of disabled people, the Court could have regard to the Charter's fundamental status in evaluating the legality of such measures.

To date, the Court has cited Charter principles including academic freedom,[41] **2.30**
the right to respect for private life,[42] the right to good administration,[43] and collective bargaining rights[44] in its procurement jurisprudence. Advocate General
Mengozzi's opinion in the *Datenlotsen* case illustrates how the Charter may
directly impact procurement decisions. Asked to consider the scope of the *Teckal*
exemption in relation to a university which was controlled in some of its decisions only by the City of Hamburg, the Advocate General opined that in order
for entities such as universities to be eligible for the exemption, it could not be
required that control be exercised over their teaching and research activities, as this
would conflict with the principle of academic freedom enshrined in the Charter.[45]
In *SECAP*, Advocate General Ruiz-Jarabo Colomer considered the scope of the
right to good administration and specifically the right to be heard in the context
of a decision about the existence of an abnormally low tender.[46] In both cases, the
Court appeared to accept the opinions on these points, without however, directly
citing the Charter in its judgments.

The 2014 directives contain specific provisions aimed at the integration of persons **2.31**
with disabilities, both in terms of accessibility requirements forming part of technical specifications and in the possibility to reserve certain contracts for sheltered

---

[41] Case C-15/13 *Datenlotsen Inofrmationssysteme GmbH v Technische Universität Hamburg-Harburg* ('*Datenlotsen*'), not yet reported.
[42] Case C-450/06 *Varec SA v État belge* [2008] ECR I-00581.
[43] Joined Cases C-147/06 and C-148/06 *SECAP SpA v Comune di Torino and Santorso Soc. coop. arl v Comune di Torino* ('*SECAP*') [2008] ECR I-03565.
[44] Case C-271/08 *Commission v Germany* [2010] ECR I-07091.
[45] Opinion of AG Mengozzi, Case C-15/13 *Datenlotsen*, para 73.
[46] Opinion of AG Ruiz-Jarabo Colomer, Joined Cases C-147/06 and C-148/06 *SECAP*, paras 49–54.

workshops or other enterprises employing disabled or disadvantaged workers. They do not contain provisions aimed at integrating women, minorities, or youth in the workforce, unless they are considered to be disadvantaged workers and thus eligible for the reservation of contracts via dedicated enterprises, workshops, or employment programmes—the term 'disadvantaged worker' is not defined in the directives.[47] In countries where public sector employment policies specifically target greater inclusion of these groups, the effect of fiscal consolidation and reduction in public sector employment can disproportionately affect their overall levels of participation in the economy. Public contracts then become one of the few instruments available to implement positive discrimination policies. Are such policies possible within the EU procurement rules, and if possible, desirable?

Positive Discrimination Policies in Procurement

2.32 There is a need here to distinguish between different procurement measures which fall under the broad heading of positive discrimination. The first are set-asides: where a contract or group of contracts is reserved for competition by a particular type of undertaking. The provisions for reserved contracts cited in Chapter 1 (paras 1.39 to 1.41) are examples of set-asides; however, these are exceptions to the general prohibition of such measures under the directives. The second approach is preferences, where marks are either added in the evaluation process for organizations which meet the targeted characteristics, or deducted from those which do not. Such approaches are only permissible under EU law if the characteristics being targeted are included in the definition of selection or award criteria (see Chapter 4). The same is true of contract performance clauses—for example, requiring employment of a certain percentage of disadvantaged workers—although the rules regarding such clauses are not as tightly defined as those which apply to selection and award criteria or technical specifications. Other measures, such as training programmes or capacity building, are not covered by the directives, but could be subject to challenge if they are found to violate the Treaty principles and cannot be justified as proportionate restrictions (see discussion of the proportionality principle below).

2.33 The use of government contracts to promote more inclusive employment practices where there is evidence of long-term structural imbalance and under-representation is attractive, although it remains controversial. No one wishes to be employed simply because of their race, gender, religion, age, or disability status. Much less

---

[47] The term 'disadvantaged worker' is not defined in the 2014 directives, but has traditionally been associated with disabled workers and the long-term unemployed. Recital 98 of the Public Sector Directive does provide that: 'Contract performance conditions might also be intended to favour the implementation of measures for the promotion of equality of women and men at work, the increased participation of women in the labour market and the reconciliation of work and private life…'

does anyone wish to be unemployed based on any of these factors. However, public sector employment policies in many parts of Europe acknowledge the need to take specific steps to integrate certain groups into the workforce, and where this is the case it may be considered anomalous that such policies cannot be pursued where contracts are awarded to a private operator. McCrudden has analysed the use of procurement linkages to promote equality in a number of jurisdictions, and draws a distinction between measures addressing status inequality which depend on protectionism or discrimination against foreign contractors, and those which do not.[48] Such a distinction may be considered particularly relevant within EU procurement law.

There are, of course, a number of arguments against adopting positive discrimination within public procurement. Leaving aside for a moment critiques based on the impact of such policies on costs or levels of competition,[49] three *a priori* objections to positive discrimination in procurement can be identified. I will call them the efficacy, fairness, and floodgates arguments, respectively. The efficacy argument is that positive discrimination policies in procurement are ineffective, or at best inefficient, at achieving the objectives they target.[50] In most cases, these objectives will be to redress discrimination against certain groups and/or to correct the imbalance in their representation among the ranks of government contractors. Wider objectives may include promoting growth in a particular sector of the economy or region. While the immediate objective of increasing representation may be well served by set-asides or preferences, the extent to which they are really capable of redressing long-term imbalances is debatable. **2.34**

One of the reasons for this is that the lifespan of such measures is usually uncertain, and businesses which come to rely on them or even adapt their ownership structure in order to be eligible for such schemes may find themselves disadvantaged once again after the policy ends. Unlike affirmative action in employment, for example, companies appointed pursuant to such policies will not be in a position to attain a critical mass and thus eventually change the management of the contracting organization. If the societal factors which cause such groups to be under-represented among government contractors continue to exist, the measures should not be seen as merely transitional. It may be possible for some 'trailblazing' to take place, in that once a contract has been entrusted to a smaller or woman- or **2.35**

---

[48] McCrudden, *Buying Social Justice*, p 112.

[49] The scope for making and refuting such arguments is severely limited in the European context, due to the lack of consistent long-term collection of data on the effect of procurement linkages. The legal uncertainty which attaches to these measures has served to exacerbate this lack of evidence since the 1990s.

[50] A more radical critique is that such policies assume that different groups subscribe to the same ideals of employment, whereas what may be needed is a rethink of the nature and conditions of employment. See Somek, A. (2011) *Engineering Equality: An Essay on European Anti-Discrimination Law* (Oxford: Oxford University Press).

minority-owned business, the possibility of doing so in other areas becomes clearer to the authority. But given the essentially iterative nature of procurement—contracts are awarded for a few years before being subject to competition again—the effect of positive discrimination on long-term diversity may be limited.[51]

2.36 If, on the other hand, a long-term commitment to positive discrimination policies is made, the second argument of fairness comes to the fore. Is it fair that certain businesses should have a long-term advantage over their competitors? Unlike individuals, businesses are capable of changing their stripes—a small business may grow into a large one; a large one may subdivide or its ownership or employee profile may change. Businesses don't deserve to win government contracts because of what they are, but because of what they can offer. The counter-argument to this is that large businesses owned and staffed by able-bodied white males already enjoy multiple advantages, which it is disingenuous to consider they have earned through merit alone. Carefully designed positive discrimination measures which address a specific deficit among government contractors may be considered fair by many public sector organizations, and by the taxpayers who fund them.

2.37 Finally, it may be argued that any form of positive discrimination in favour of SMEs or other types of under-represented business risks 'opening the floodgates' to many different interest groups arguing that they too deserve some form of advantage. So, for example, in the United States, preferences or set-asides are available to small businesses, those owned by veterans, women or minorities, and those employing prisoners or disadvantaged workers.[52] In Canada and Malaysia, preferences or set-asides are available to aboriginal-owned businesses[53] and in Korea to those employing disabled people or veterans, and well as SMEs.[54] However, there is always a need to treat floodgate or slippery slope arguments with caution. It is quite possible to justify positive discrimination in favour of some groups without admitting all such claims, provided the grounds for such treatment are clear. Each of the measures mentioned has a specific rationale, and claims from other groups without such justification are normally rejected.

---

[51] Some evidence of this effect can be seen in the implementation of affirmative action policies for federal contractors in the United States. A 2012 study comparing federal contractors with similar firms over a 30-year period found that while affirmative action policies were associated with gains in the workforce representation of women and minorities which persisted after contracts were complete, the effect of such policies declined over time, in part due to changes in political support. Kurtulus, F. (2012) 'The Effect of Affirmative Action on the Employment of Women and Minorities over Three Decades: 1973–2003' 51(2) *Industrial Relations: A Journal of Economy and Society* 213–46.

[52] These are in addition to the Federal 'Buy American' provisions. On US state and local preferences in procurement, see Cummings, G. Lloyd, R., Qiao, Y., and Thai, K. (2007) 'State and Local Procurement Preferences: A Survey' (Herndon, VA: National Institute of Governmental Purchasing).

[53] McCrudden, *Buying Social Justice*, pp 175–82 and 232–43.

[54] Under the Act on Contracts to which the State is a Party, Special Act on the Preferential Purchase of Products Manufactured by Persons with Severe Disabilities and SME Promotion Act.

Overall, while the fairness and floodgates arguments may hold limited water **2.38**
against positive discrimination measures in procurement, the efficacy argument
raises serious questions about whether such measures should be admissible within
the EU procurement rules. The work done to eliminate discrimination against
operators from other Member States must not be underestimated—and yet it is
vulnerable to relapse, especially during economic downturns. Positive discrimination policies should only be admitted where there is strong evidence that these
would achieve their legitimate objectives and not go beyond what is needed to
achieve them. This second requirement arises from another fundamental Treaty
principle with applications in procurement, that of proportionality.

Proportionality

Proportionality is perhaps the most far-reaching of general principles in EU law. **2.39**
It appears throughout the Court's case law under many headings, and often
acts as a standard of review in challenges to decisions or actions of government.
Proportionality requires that measures: (i) are appropriate to achieve the objectives
they pursue; and (ii) do not go beyond what is needed to attain those objectives. The
question of whether the objectives themselves are legitimate is in theory a separate
question, although in practice it is often conflated with the question of 'appropri-
ateness' in the Court's jurisprudence. A third limb to the test, in which the Court
asks if the measure places an excessive burden on rights *despite* being appropriate
and necessary, has also been identified by some commentators;[55] however, this is
not clearly seen in its procurement case law.[56] Proportionality first appeared as a
limit on the actions of the European institutions themselves, but has developed as
a general standard of review which applies equally to measures taken by Member
States. Its earlier origins as a legal principle lie in Prussian administrative law and
post-war German constitutional law.[57]

The determination of whether a given measure is appropriate, and if appropri- **2.40**
ate, necessary (ie could the same objective be attained by less onerous means?)
leaves considerable room for judicial manoeuvre. The first limb implies that the
means chosen must be linked to the ends, although does not normally extend to an
empirical analysis of whether the ends have been achieved in practice. The second
limb can invite a much broader analysis—to establish whether there are any other

---

[55] See de Búrca, G. (1993) 'The Principle of Proportionality and Its Application in EC Law' 13
Yearbook of European Law 105–50.
[56] See Cases C-376/08 *Serrantoni and Consorzio stabile edili v Comune di Milano* [2009] ECR
I-12169 and C-358/12 *Consorzio Stabile Libor Lavori Pubblici v Comune di Milano*, not yet reported,
for the Court's approach to proportionality in procurement cases.
[57] For a discussion of these origins, as well as the global spread of the principle and its effect on
judicial power, see Stone Sweet, A. and Mathews, J. (2008) 'Proportionality Balancing and Global
Constitutionalism' 47 *Columbia Journal of Transnational Law* 72.

means which might achieve the targeted ends without infringing the competing interests in question—normally in procurement cases the free movement rules or equal treatment. Thus, in the *Medipac* case,[58] the Court held that the rejection of the applicant's bid was disproportionate because the legitimate aim of protecting the health of patients could have been attained by suspending the procedure. The Court has also actively applied the principle in cases regarding the exclusion and selection of candidates in a procurement procedure.

Exclusion from procedures

2.41 Proportionality may be breached where an undertaking is excluded from a procedure either automatically or based on a contracting authority's decision. Automatic exclusion has arisen under a number of national laws, most of which pre-dated the 2004 directives. In *Fabricom*, the Court found that a Belgian law which provided for automatic exclusion of bidders who had been involved in pre-tender work was disproportionate as the contracting authority could instead carry out a case-by-case assessment to determine if any unfair advantage arose.[59] The *Michaniki* case concerned a provision of the Greek Constitution prohibiting the award of public contracts to individuals or companies with links to media ownership.[60] The Court found that this went beyond what was needed to attain the legitimate objective of protecting the award of public contracts from the influence of the media. The objective could be met by a law which allowed the risk associated with individual links between contractors and media organizations to be taken into account.

2.42 A similar factual situation arose in *Assitur*, in which an Italian authority had invited tenders for courier services. Two of the three bidders were linked in terms of ownership, and Assitur argued that this meant they must be excluded under an Italian law intended to prevent collusion. A preliminary reference was made to the Court regarding the compatibility of the Italian law with the procurement rules, given that it appeared to establish grounds for exclusion other than those set out in the directives. The Court again held that such a law was disproportionate, as it afforded no opportunity for the bidders to establish that their relationship did not give rise to a risk of collusion. In *Serrantoni*, the Court applied the same approach in respect of a below-threshold contract.[61]

2.43 The four cases cited in paragraphs 2.41 and 2.42 all involved proportionality review of national laws—however, the test has also been applied directly to procurement decisions taken by contracting authorities. In *Hochtief Construction*, the applicant's

---

[58] Case C-6/05.

[59] Joined cases C-21/03 and C-34/03 *Fabricom SA v État belge* [2005] ECR I-01559.

[60] Case C-213/07 *Michaniki AE v Ethniko Simvoulio Radiotileorasis and Ipourgos Epikratias* [2008] ECR I-9999.

[61] Case C-376/08 *Serrantoni Srl and Consorzio stabile edili Scrl v Comune di Milano* [2009] ECR I-12169.

expression of interest was rejected on the grounds that it did not meet the financial standing criteria set out in the tender documents. The authority had applied a rule that bidders could not have sustained a loss in more than one of the previous three financial years, as evidenced by their balance sheet. Hochtief was subject to a profit transfer agreement with its German parent company, meaning its profit/loss balance was typically zero or negative. The main part of the judgment related to the ability of the bidder to rely on the financial capacity of its parent company; however, the Court also stated that the contracting authority was entitled to apply specific financial standing criteria provided that their

> level is adapted to the size of the contract concerned in that it constitutes objectively a positive indication of the existence of a sufficient economic and financial basis for the performance of that contract, without, however, going beyond what is reasonably necessary for that purpose.[62]

This confirmed the applicability of the proportionality test to selection criteria **2.44** chosen by contracting authorities, even where these fall within the strict limits set by the directives. In *Tideland Signal*, the Court of First Instance applied a proportionality test to the decision of the Commission to reject a tender rather than seeking clarification of a minor clerical error. Faced with a choice between clarifying an ambiguity regarding the validity period of the tender and rejecting it, the Court found that the second option was disproportionate and constituted a manifest error of assessment.[63] Interestingly, however, in other cases where the Court might have invoked the test, it has relied instead on the requirement that criteria be linked to the subject-matter of the contract—which may in fact serve as a truncated version of the proportionality test in the procurement context. The 'link to the subject-matter' concept, prominent in the 2014 directives, is explored further in Chapters 4 and 7.

In *EVN and Wienstrom*, the contracting authority had allocated 45 per cent of the **2.45** available marks at award stage for bidders' capacity to produce renewable electricity in amounts which exceeded the volume required under the contract.[64] The award criteria were challenged on a number of grounds, and the Court looked to the then recent *Concordia* judgment to assess their validity.[65] It upheld the 45 per cent weighting for the renewable energy criterion, but found that the focus on

---

[62] Case C-218/11 *Edukovizig and Hochtief Construction AG*, not reported in ECR, para 40.
[63] Case T-211/02 *Tideland Signal Ltd v Commission of the European Communities* [2002] ECR II-03781, para 43.
[64] Case C-448/01 *EVN and Wienstrom* [2003] ECR I-14527.
[65] Case C-513/99 *Concordia Bus Finland v Helsingin kaupunki and HKL-Bussiliikenne* [2002] ECR I-07213. That case set out requirements for award criteria which were subsequently written into the 2004 directives, namely: (i) they must be linked to the subject-matter of the contract; (ii) they may not confer an unrestricted freedom of choice on the authority; (iii) they must be expressly mentioned in the contract documents or the tender notice; and (iv) they must comply with the fundamental principles of equal treatment, non-discrimination, and transparency. These rules are discussed in Chapters 4 and 7 (see latter for link to the subject-matter test).

volumes of electricity which exceeded the authority's requirements, together with its inability to verify the criterion as it was formulated, violated the principles of equal treatment and transparency. The contracting authority in *EVN* argued that the focus of the award criterion made sense due to the seasonal variation in production capacity for renewable electricity—assessing production volumes in excess of its total annual requirement was aimed at ensuring reliability of supply.

2.46 The Court seemed to accept this argument in principle, but held that the formulation of the award criterion—higher renewable electricity production leading to higher marks without any upper ceiling—was likely to give an undue advantage to larger operators.[66] A proportionality test is implicit in the Court's assessment. If the authority had instead awarded marks based on a defined margin above its requirements, provided this was accompanied by verification, this may well have withstood the Court's scrutiny. The Court also specifically disavowed the requirement that the criterion be effective in attaining its objective, in this case increasing the proportion of renewable electricity available on the market. I have argued that effectiveness should be taken into account when evaluating strategic procurement measures, and will take up this argument again in Chapter 7 in the specific context of environmental criteria.

2.47 The relative paucity of cases in which the Court has directly applied the proportionality test to criteria or other procurement measures adopted by contracting authorities, as opposed to those mandated by national laws, may stem in part from the nature of cases which it hears. This is a combination of preliminary references from national courts under Article 267 of the Treaty and infringement actions brought by the Commission against Member States. In the former cases, the Court is not normally asked to determine the validity of individual criteria directly, although it may give its opinion on these, as in *EVN*. In the latter cases, the Commission tends to challenge either the decision *not* to apply the procurement rules or national legislation which conflicts with them, as opposed to individual criteria. One expects that the Court would be reluctant to directly substitute its assessment of the proportionality of criteria or decisions for that of the contracting authority, unless evidence of a breach of one of the other Treaty principles or substantive provisions of the directives exists. One reason for this relates to the subsidiarity principle, discussed below. National courts, on the other hand, have not faced such qualms. The direct application of a proportionality test to procurement decisions can be clearly seen in case law from the United Kingdom and Ireland.

2.48 English courts have invoked proportionality most often in relation to the question of clarification of tenders. In *JB Leadbitter & Co Ltd v Devon County Council*,[67] the claimant had omitted to submit an essential part of its tender through the

---

[66] Case C-448/01 *EVN*, paras 69–71.
[67] [2009] EWHC 930 (Ch).

electronic submission system by the deadline. It argued that the Council's decision to reject its tender was disproportionate, despite being in accordance with the stated conditions. This claim was unsuccessful; however, Mr Justice Roberts specifically endorsed the application of a proportionality test to procurement decisions, based on the *Tideland Signal* judgment, and rejected the idea that such review was only suitable for legislative measures.[68] In several subsequent cases concerning legal services tenders, the High Court has reiterated the proportionality test—however, it has appeared to equate this with a test for manifest error and has not, on the facts, found any of the challenged decisions to be disproportionate.[69] In *J Varney & Sons*, Mr Justice Flaux held that the principle of proportionality did not imply a margin of appreciation for contracting authorities regarding compliance with the procurement rules, but that where the rules left room for discretion to be exercised, this was subject to review to confirm the absence of any manifest error.[70]

In *Baxter Healthcare Ltd v Health Service Executive*,[71] the Irish High Court also **2.49** applied the *Tideland* proportionality test, finding that the contracting authority had not committed a manifest error by refusing to seek clarification of the claimant's response to a question regarding its proposed level of staffing for a contract. Mr Justice Peart drew a distinction between an 'ambiguity' such as that which arose in *Tideland*, and a failure on the part of the tenderer to respond adequately to a scored question.[72] Clarification was not required in the latter case. In line with the approach in *J Varney & Sons*, Peart J also confirmed that the margin of appreciation available to the contracting authority only applied where there was no breach of the procurement rules.[73] In a case pre-dating the 2004 directives, the Irish High Court found that a requirement for bidders to have carried out at least one roadworks contract with a minimum value of £10 million during a four-year period was not a disproportionate selection criterion, in the context of a contract valued at £25 million.[74] Kelly J appeared to take account of the fact that the contracting authority had acted on expert advice in setting this criterion.[75]

The 2014 directives explicitly state that selection criteria must be proportionate to **2.50** the subject-matter of the contract, as did their 2004 predecessors.[76] Proportionality

---

[68] Paras 50–5 of judgment.

• [69] *Azam Co v Legal Services Commission* [2010] EWCA Civ 1194; *Harrow Solicitors and Advocates, R (on the application of) v The Legal Services Commission* [2011] EWHC 1087; and *All About Rights Law Practice, R (on the application of) v The Lord Chancellor* [2013] EWHC 3461 (Admin).

[70] *J Varney & Sons Waste Management Ltd v Hertfordshire County Council* [2010] EWHC 1404 (QB), 103–8.

[71] [2013] IEHC 413.

[72] *Baxter* [2013] IEHC 413, paras 151–3.

[73] *Baxter*, para 155.

[74] *Whelan Group (Ennis) Ltd v Clare County Council* [2001] IEHC 33.

[75] Para 29. Although, in the event, the Council did not act on the expert advice received, setting a lower threshold for the value of previous contracts than that advised.

[76] Art 58(1) of the Public Sector Directive and Art 44(2) of Directive 2004/18/EC.

also appears as one of the general principles applicable to procurement set out in Article 18 of the Public Sector Directive, and in a number of other places throughout all three directives. It features prominently in the rules applicable to communication in tender procedures. As part of the move to fully electronic tendering, it is understood that technical and security measures will be put in place which may require some adaptive effort for both procurers and suppliers. Who should bear the cost of such measures? Can candidates or bidders be expected to invest in new systems for the purpose of a single contract? Although specific rules are set out in relation to the accessibility of systems, use of electronic signatures, and so on, a general proportionality requirement is also included, with reference to the level of security prescribed for communications.[77] Systems which involve unduly onerous security measures or costs may be subject to challenge under this provision.

Transparency

2.51 Most procurement practitioners around the world appreciate the importance of transparency in tender procedures. Conceptually, it makes sense to distinguish between transparency for the participants in a tender, and transparency for the public at large. Both may be important in ensuring compliance with the other objectives of procurement—value for money, absence of corruption, sustainability, fairness, etc. Transparency for participants in tender procedures also serves the purpose of facilitating access to legal remedies where applicable, which has been identified as one of its most important roles by the European Court of Justice.[78] The concept tends to serve as a proxy in its procurement judgments for principles commonly encountered in national administrative law systems—such as the duty to give reasons. Transparency for the benefit of the public at large has not, as yet, formed part of the Court's review of procurement measures, although it does arise as a by-product of the rules set out in the directives regarding publication of notices, as well as national freedom of information laws. More profound developments in the public transparency aspect of procurement which have taken hold in other jurisdictions—and towards which voluntary inroads can be seen in some EU countries—are considered below.

2.52 In the Court's jurisprudence, then, transparency has developed as a secondary or supporting principle in order to give effect to non-discrimination, equal treatment, and proportionality. However, it has also taken on a life of its own, aided not least

---

[77] Art 22(6)(b) of the Public Sector Directive and Art 40 of the Utilities Directive. The recitals to both directives also invoke proportionality as a general principle applicable to electronic communication.

[78] See, eg, Case C-285/99 *Impresa Lombardini SpA v ANAS* [2001] ECR I-9233, para 38; Case C-19/00 *SIAC Construction Ltd v Mayo County Council* [2001] ECR I-7725, para 41; Case C-470/99 *Universale-Bau AG* [2002] ECR I-11617, para 91; and Case T-345/03 *Evropaïki Dynamiki*, para 142.

by the presence of transparency as a fundamental concept in national administrative law systems. In the procurement context, transparency implies that: (i) contracts will be given a sufficient degree of advertising/publicity; (ii) procurement documents will be published and adequate time allowed to take account of any additional information issued; (iii) selection and award criteria will be published in advance, with weightings; (iv) criteria and specifications will be clearly formulated; (v) notification of cancellation of a procedure will be provided to candidates or tenderers, with reasons; (vi) candidates and tenderers will be notified of the outcome of their expressions of interest and tenders; and (vii) modifications to a contract after its award will not be substantial, or will have been provided for in advance. Each of these elements of transparency is considered briefly here.

Sufficient degree of advertising/publicity

The most elementary transparency obligation is that of advertising contracts in advance **2.53** of their award. For contracts covered by the Directives, the form and content of notices is prescribed—either a contract notice or prior information notice (PIN) may be used as a call for competition. These contain details regarding the scope, nature, estimated value, and common procurement vocabulary (CPV) codes applicable to the contract or framework, as well as the procedure to be used, deadlines, and high-level description (at least) of the selection and award criteria. Notices are published in the supplement to the Official Journal, and are available online via the Tenders Electronic Daily (TED) platform. A summary version of notices is published in all official EU languages, and search and notification features are available for contractors wishing to identify relevant opportunities. In practice, contracting authorities typically submit notices via national or sector-specific e-procurement systems, which act as recognized senders of notices. The 2014 directives aim to ensure the primacy of OJEU notices over those published at national level by: (i) requiring that publication does not occur at national level until a notice has been published in the OJEU, or until 48 hours have passed from the time of receipt of the notice; and (ii) stipulating that national notices may not contain any information beyond that included in the OJEU notice.[79]

For contracts not covered by the directives, there is a requirement to engage in a **2.54** 'degree of advertising sufficient to enable the services market to be opened up to competition and the impartiality of procurement procedures to be reviewed'.[80] This requirement originated in the Court's case law on concessions, but in *Germany v Commission* (challenging the *Interpretative Communication*), the Court confirmed that the transparency obligation applied equally to other contracts which, despite not being covered by the directives, were of relevance to the internal market.[81]

---

[79] Art 52 Public Sector Directive; Art 72 Utilities Directive; and Art 33 Concessions Directive.
[80] Case C-324/98 *Telaustria Verlags GmbH and Telefonadress GmbH v Telekom Austria and Herold Business Data AG* [2000] ECR I-10745, para 62.
[81] Case T-258/06 *Germany v Commission* [2010] ECR II-02027, para 83.

The *Interpretative Communication* states that it is for the contracting authority to determine this relevance, taking into account factors such as the value and nature of the contract, the market sector, and location of performance. If the contract is deemed to be relevant to the internal market, it should be advertised on websites, or in newspapers or journals, which are accessible to operators from other Member States. Advertisement in the OJEU may also take place on a voluntary basis.[82] Directly inviting selected operators to tender, or merely responding to requests for information about the contract, is insufficient.[83]

Publication of procurement documents

2.55 In addition to publishing a notice, contracting authorities are obliged to provide a description of their requirements. The 2014 directives are more prescriptive than their 2004 counterparts regarding the content of procurement documents and the timing of their publication. Under Article 53 of the Public Sector Directive, 'unrestricted and full direct access free of charge to the procurement documents' must be made available from the date of publication of the notice or, where a PIN is used, the invitation to confirm interest. This contrasts with the prevailing practice of many contracting authorities in multi-stage procedures, which is that tender documents are only finalized following selection of candidates. Derogations from the Article 53 requirement are possible on grounds of confidentiality or where documents cannot be published electronically for specific reasons; however, it seems clear that these are intended to be exceptional.[84] They are also accompanied by requirements to extend the period for receipt of tenders.

2.56 It is possible that the wording of the Article 53 requirements was formulated in contemplation of the open procedure and cannot be applied strictly to multi-stage procedures. For example, the competitive dialogue procedure clearly envisions that successive documents will be generated refining the authority's requirements, and not all of these could be published at the same time as the notice. The definition of 'procurement documents' is a broad one, and Article 53 could be read to refer to those specific parts of the procurement documents which form part of the initial stage of the competition.[85] What would be the consequences of the contrary

---

[82] Disturbingly, in *Irish Translation Services*, the Court referred to the fact that the contract had been published in the OJEU as evidence that it might be of relevance to the internal market, raising the possibility that voluntary publication will attract the responsibility to comply with the Treaty principles (Case C-226/09 *Commission v Ireland* [2010] ECR I-11807, para 33). However, in that case, bids from other Member States had also in fact been received.

[83] [2006] OJ C 179/02 of 23 June 2006 at para 2.1.1.

[84] Arts 21(2) and 22(1) Public Sector Directive; Arts 39(2) and 40(1) Utilities Directive; and Art 34(2) Concessions Directive.

[85] More precise definition of the contents of invitations to tender, to participate in dialogue, and to confirm interest are found in Annex IX of the Public Sector Directive, which allows that in the case of competitive dialogue and innovation partnership these need not contain the deadline or language for tender submission. However, the use of the broader term 'procurement documents' in

interpretation? Arguably, a lesser degree of transparency, due to the inevitable need to clarify and amend tender documents as the contours of a competition emerge. The directives make specific provision for extension of the tender deadline where additional information is issued; however, this may not fully compensate for time lost preparing tenders based on incomplete or inaccurate information.[86]

In relation to contracts not covered by the directives, the *Interpretative Communication* **2.57** states that a short description of the essential details of the contract to be awarded and the award method is sufficient. Time limits must be 'long enough to allow undertakings from other Member States to make a meaningful assessment and prepare their offers'.[87] The risks associated with excessively short tender periods, which can now be reduced to ten days or less with the agreement of bidders, are discussed in Chapter 3.

Criteria and weightings published in advance

The advance disclosure of selection and award criteria is a key pillar of transparency in procurement. The CJEU and national courts have had many occasions **2.58** to consider the precise degree of disclosure required, and in particular the question of whether weightings for criteria and sub-criteria must also be published in advance.[88] This is now regulated by Article 67(5) of the Public Sector Directive, which provides that the relative weighting of award criteria must be published in advance unless the contract is to be awarded on the basis of price alone. Weightings may be expressed as a range of values with an appropriate maximum spread. There is an exception to the requirement to publish weightings in advance if this cannot be done for objective reasons, in which case the obligation is to list criteria in decreasing order of importance. In *Irish Translation Services*, the Court held that the requirement to determine and publish weightings for award criteria in advance did not apply in respect of a non-priority service contract—finding that such an obligation did not flow directly from the principle of transparency. However, the

---

Art 53 seems to suggest that the invitation document together with technical specifications (where relevant) must be published at the outset.

[86] Art 47(3) of the Public Sector Directive requires the time limit for receipt of tenders to be extended where: (a) additional information is not provided at least six days prior to the deadline (four in an accelerated procedure); or (b) significant changes are made to the procurement documents. The period of extension must be proportionate to the importance of the additional information or change.

[87] European Commission, *Interpretative Communication on the Community law applicable to contracts not or not fully subject to the directives*, [2006] OJ C 179/02, paras 2.1.3 and 2.2.1.

[88] Case C-470/99 *Universale-Bau and Others* [2002] ECR I-11617; Case C-331/04 *ATI EAC and Viaggi di Maio v ACTV Venezia SpA* [2005] ECR I-10109; *Harmon CFEM Facades (UK) Ltd v The Corporate Officer of the House of Commons* [1999] EWHC Technology 199; *J Varney & Sons Waste Management Ltd v Hertfordshire CC* [2011] EWCA Civ 708; and *McLaughlin and Harvey Ltd v Department of Finance and Personnel* [2011] NICA 60.

Court found that *altering* the weightings of the award criteria after an initial review of tenders constituted a violation of equal treatment and transparency.[89]

2.59 The Court has also held that any sub-criteria which will be applied in the evaluation must also be disclosed, although the contracting authority is able to specify aspects of sub-criteria at a later stage.[90] The position regarding disclosure of weightings for sub-criteria remains less clear. In *ATI*, the Court held that weightings for sub-criteria need not be disclosed in advance if these did not alter the main criteria, did not contain elements which could have influenced the preparation of bids, and did not give rise to discrimination against any tenderer.[91] A similar ambiguity applies to the disclosure of weightings for selection criteria. Under Article 65 of the Public Sector Directive, selection criteria must be published in the notice or invitation to confirm interest, together with the minimum number of candidates which will be selected and, where appropriate, the maximum. It does not state that weightings for selection criteria must be disclosed. However, in *Universale-Bau*, the Court held that where weightings for selection criteria had been determined in advance, these must be published in order to ensure adequate transparency.[92] This position sits somewhat uncomfortably, as failure to determine weightings for selection criteria in advance could both obviate the need for publication and potentially give rise to weightings which were discriminatory. There may also be legitimate reasons for not publishing weightings for selection criteria or sub-criteria in advance.[93]

Clarity in technical specifications and award criteria

2.60 Beyond the obligation to make criteria, sub-criteria, and, in most cases, weightings known in advance, there is the question of how technical specifications and criteria are formulated. Multiple rules apply in respect of technical specifications, and the permissible scope of both selection and award criteria is also regulated in some

---

[89] Case C-226/09 *Commission v Ireland*, paras 43 and 66. The change in weighting amounted to only 5 per cent of the available marks and no evidence was presented that this would have led to a different evaluation outcome.

[90] Case C-532/06 *Lianakis and Others* [2008] ECR I-251; and Case T-70/05 *Evropaiki Dynamiki v EMSA* [2010] ECR II-313, para 32. The English courts have also considered the degree of disclosure required for sub-criteria, notably in *Letting International v London Borough of Newham* [2007] EWCA Civ 1522 and *Mears Ltd v Leeds City Council* [2011] EWHC 1022 (TCC).

[91] Case C-331/04 *ATI*, paras 26–32.

[92] Case C-470/99 *Universale-Bau and Others* [2002] ECR I-11617.

[93] For example, where it is not known if all candidates may be equally qualified under several criteria, in which case it would not be possible to limit the number invited to tender without weighting other criteria adequately. It is not clear whether the Commission or Court would in fact consider this a legitimate and objective reason for not ascribing advance weightings to selection criteria (or, for that matter, award criteria.) The judgment in *Irish Translation Services* suggests that *altering* weightings for award criteria after initial review of tenders will always be suspect, whereas *allocating* them at this stage may not be.

detail. These rules are discussed in Chapter 4. However, it is worth noting here the role which the transparency principle has played in the Court's interpretation and application of these rules. In *Nord Pas de Calais*, the Court found that the French region's reliance on the classification system for French contractors to designate the lots and qualifications for a works contract was 'so specific and abstruse that, as a rule, only French candidates are able immediately to discern their relevance'.[94] This fell short of the transparency requirements for technical specifications. In *SIAC*, the Court developed the idea of 'reasonably well-informed and normally diligent tenderers'—all of whom must be able to interpret award criteria in the same way.[95]

The requirement for clarity in specifications and criteria has been linked not only **2.61** to tenderers' ability to interpret them, but also that of the contracting authority to verify compliance and to apply them in the same manner throughout a procedure.[96] Criteria or specifications which are vague or which are applied in an inconsistent manner are thus vulnerable to challenge on transparency grounds. In the *Dutch Coffee* case,[97] the Court found that requirements to demonstrate 'sustainability of purchases' and 'socially responsible business' did not comply with the transparency obligation, as it was not clear to tenderers precisely what information they should provide. The relatively strict application of the transparency obligation in these cases contrasts with the Court's repeated assertion that contracting authorities have significant freedom to define the *subject-matter* of criteria. The consequences of this position in terms of choice and definition of criteria are explored in Chapter 4.

Notification of cancellation

Where a contracting authority or entity decides not to award a contract for which **2.62** it has issued a call for competition, it must notify candidates and tenderers of its decision. It is also obliged to provide the grounds on which the decision has been made. This must be done as soon as possible after the decision is made.[98] In *Embassy Limousines*, the Court confirmed that contracting authorities enjoy a broad discretion regarding the decision to award a contract, and may normally cancel the procedure at any time provided that the required notification and statement of grounds is provided.[99] In multi-stage procedures, it is not clear whether

---

[94] Case C-225/98 *Commission v France* [2000] ECR I-7445, paras 81–3.
[95] Case C-19/00 *SIAC Construction Ltd v Mayo County Council* [2001] ECR I-07725, para 42.
[96] Case T-345/03 *Evropaïki Dynamiki*, para 145; Case C-448/01 *EVN and Wienstrom* [2003] ECR I-14527, paras 50–3; and Case C-299/08 *Commission v France* [2009] ECR I-11587, paras 41–3.
[97] Case C-368/10 *Commission v The Kingdom of the Netherlands*, not yet reported.
[98] Art 55(1) Public Sector Directive; Art 75(1) Utilities Directive; and Art 40(1) Concessions Directive.
[99] Case T-203/96 *Embassy Limousines and Services v European Parliament* [1998] ECR II-04239, para 52.

it is necessary to inform only those operators who remain in the competition of the cancellation, or also those who have already been eliminated and who have received notification of this.[100] The decision to cancel a procedure must also be recorded in the individual tender report, and a form exists to register this on TED, although its use appears to be voluntary.

Notification of outcomes

2.63 Unsuccessful candidates and tenderers must be informed that they have not been successful as soon as possible after the decision has been taken. Upon request, they must also be given the reasons for their rejection and, if they have submitted an admissible tender, the name of the successful bidder and the characteristics and relative advantages of its bid, or of the progress of any ongoing negotiations or dialogue.[101] The duty to give reasons for rejection is not unlimited—information can be withheld if disclosure would be contrary to the public interest, prejudice the legitimate commercial interests of another operator, or impede fair competition.[102] The questions of precisely which information must be provided to unsuccessful candidates and tenderers, and whether this must be provided immediately upon notification of rejection or only upon request, are of great practical significance when it comes to the pursuit of remedies. These matters are examined in Chapter 8, together with the relevant time limits and provisions for automatic suspension of contracts under the remedies regime.

Modifications to contracts

2.64 A final dimension of the transparency requirement worth noting here is the rules on modifications to contracts after their award. Originally developed in the Court's case law,[103] these are now set out in detail in the 2014 directives. The starting point is that changes to contracts after their award will require a new tender competition to be held—however, the exceptions to this are numerous. These are discussed in more detail in Chapter 5, but the main headings under which modifications to

---

[100] The obligation applies to candidates and tenderers—the definition of a 'candidate' under the directives includes any operator who has sought an invitation or been invited to take part in a multi-stage procedure, a classification which does not appear to end by virtue of an expression of interest being rejected.

[101] Art 55(2) Public Sector Directive; Art 75(2) Utilities Directive; and Art 40(1) Concessions Directive. An 'admissible' tender is one submitted by an operator who has passed the exclusion and selection criteria, which conforms to the technical specifications and which is not irregular, unacceptable, or unsuitable. These terms are defined in Art 35(5) of the Public Sector Directive (curiously, as it relates to electronic auctions—but it seems likely that the same definitions would apply generally under the directives).

[102] Art 55(3) Public Sector Directive; Art 75(3) Utilities Directive; and Art 40(2) Concessions Directive. See also Case T-70/05 *Evropaïki Dynamiki v EMSA* and Case T-195/08 *Antwerpse Bouwerkken NV v European Commission* [2009] ECR II-04439 considering the scope of the duty to give reasons in the context of contracts awarded by EU bodies.

[103] Case C-496/99 P *Commission v Italy (Succhi di Frutta)* [2004] ECR I-3801; Case C-454/06 *presstext Nachrichten GmbH* [2008] ECR I-04401; and Case C-91/08 *Wall AG* [2010] ECR I-02815.

a contract can be justified are where: (i) they have been clearly provided for in a contract review clause; (ii) they are brought about by economic or technical necessity or unforeseeable circumstances; (iii) they arise due to corporate succession or the authority itself stepping in to perform the contract; or (iv) their value or nature renders them non-substantial. The potential for modifications to contracts to undermine the transparency of public procurement is enormous. It would be inconsistent if the extensive rules implementing transparency in the award of contracts were to have no counterpart in the post-award stage—however, this was largely the case prior to the Court's intervention in the cases cited in note 103. The rules on modifications now go some way to preventing abuse of this process to evade competition for public contracts.

As noted in paragraphs 2.51 and 2.52, the rules on transparency in procurement **2.65** are intended primarily to safeguard the application of the other principles and the rights of economic operators. However, the broader societal value of transparency in government contracts is also acknowledged in most jurisdictions, whether as a bulwark against corruption and cronyism or to promote public engagement, accountability, and legitimacy. In the digital era, the potential for access to information about public contracts to encourage innovation is also touted—although the quality of data often lags behind the ideals promoted. There are good reasons for this as well as bad ones. Public procurement is both a commercial and an administrative activity, and disclosure of details such as contract prices may in some cases impede competition and value for money (see discussion of the 'anchoring effect' in Chapter 6). It can also result in undue attention being focused on those details of contracts which are most likely to be picked out by the media or civil society—to the possible neglect of more mundane details which are equally essential to effective public contracts. For example, a contract awarded to a company with a record of tax avoidance may legitimately attract public anger, while one awarded to a company which is about to go bankrupt may not.

Nevertheless, the arguments against disclosure of details of public contracts have **2.66** been largely superseded in an era when sharing information has become the norm. In Europe, this has been driven in part by freedom of information laws which have a much broader scope of applicability than public procurement, but which are subject to numerous limitations. Meanwhile, the idea of openness in public contracts has gathered momentum in various international fora, such as the World Bank-supported Open Contracting initiative, and the Sunlight Foundation, both of which promote greater transparency in public contracts across developed and developing countries.[104] International organizations such as the OECD and Transparency International have also been active in tracking and reporting on

---

[104] See <http://www.open-contracting.org> and <http://sunlightfoundation.com> for information on these initiatives.

openness in contracting. The transformative effect of such initiatives on public procurement should not be underestimated, with the potential to foster public demand for comprehensive online data. In Europe, steps in this direction can be perceived particularly in Estonia and the United Kingdom, both of which have stated policies of publishing all public contracts online. At EU level, the OpenTED initiative has been instrumental in providing access to data on OJEU notices which can be more easily analysed by journalists, civil society groups, or private companies.[105]

Subsidiarity

2.67 The limits of the European Union's competence to legislate have been subject to considerable tension, with fear of 'competence creep' and federalist tendencies periodically coming to the fore. The principle of subsidiarity, introduced under the Maastricht Treaty and refined by the Lisbon Treaty, is intended to place some limits on the exercise of EU powers. It requires that in areas which do not fall within its exclusive competence (of which public procurement is one), the Union shall only act to the extent that the objectives of the action cannot be sufficiently achieved at national, regional, or local level and can be better achieved at Union level.[106] In practice, subsidiarity is normally addressed at the impact assessment stage for new EU legislation. Subsidiarity does not provide a general ground upon which either Member States or contracting authorities can rely in order to make decisions in the field of procurement, if such decisions would be contrary to EU law. It does, however, provide a potential ground for challenging actions of the European Union where their benefits have not been sufficiently well established or go beyond its realm of competence.

2.68 Interestingly, subsidiarity was not one of the grounds relied on by Germany and other Member States when they brought a challenge against the Commission's 2006 *Interpretative Communication*. Direct references to subsidiarity in the Court's procurement jurisprudence appear to be confined to several opinions of Advocates General. The *Michaniki* case, discussed in paragraph 2.41, concerned the compatibility of an automatic exclusion provision contained in the Greek Constitution with the list of exclusion grounds set out in the directives—which the Court has repeatedly held to be exhaustive. In *Michaniki*, however, both the Advocate General and the Court found that it was in theory possible to apply additional grounds of exclusion based on specific national concerns. The difference in the Advocate General's and Court's approach to the problem in *Michaniki* is instructive. Advocate General Maduro's opinion included the statement:

---

[105] See <http://ted.openspending.org>.
[106] Art 5(3)–(4) of the Treaty on European Union.

it is appropriate to grant each Member State, subject to review by the Court, a certain discretion concerning the definition of the grounds of exclusion suitable to ensure transparency and equal treatment in procedures for the award of public contracts. The Member State concerned is the best placed to assess which are, in the national context, the conflicts of interest most likely to arise and to threaten the principles of transparency and equal treatment which must be observed when public contracts are entered into.[107]

The Court, however, focused on the possibility that an additional ground of exclusion might be needed to give effect to the principles of equal treatment and transparency—perhaps afraid of the potential wider implications of citing subsidiarity or national discretion on matters explicitly regulated by the directives.[108] Exclusion on the basis of conflicts of interest is now explicitly permitted under the 2014 directives where the conflict cannot be remedied by other, less intrusive means.[109]

Subsidiarity was also invoked by Advocate General Sharpston in her opinion in **2.69** *Commission v Finland*, concerning the application of the principles of transparency and non-discrimination to a below-threshold contract for catering equipment. She considered that setting detailed publicity requirements at Community level for low value contracts was incompatible with the principle of subsidiarity.[110] The Court, however, did not rule on this point, finding the case inadmissible on a technicality. It would seem, then, that there is little evidence as yet of the principle of subsidiarity operating in the same way as equal treatment and transparency have, to allow challenges to procurement measures (or, as in *Michaniki* and *Commission v Finland*, to defend challenges to national measures) which are not subject to coordination under the directives. This is in line with other fields of EU law, in which subsidiarity primarily functions as a grounds for review of the procedures used to adopt legislation.[111]

The somewhat anaemic presence of subsidiarity in the Court's case law may yet **2.70** be transformed by shifting political majorities at national level—especially where these reflect eurosceptic sentiment. The Treaty of Lisbon introduced a more robust mechanism for national or regional parliaments to challenge proposed EU laws on subsidiarity grounds. If at least a third of eligible parliaments submit a reasoned opinion regarding a proposal, the Commission or other originating EU body is obliged to reconsider the subsidiarity case for action.[112] However, an eight-week time limit applies for submission of reasoned opinions, and this *ex ante* control

---

[107] Opinion of AG Poiares Maduro, Case 213/07 *Michaniki*, para 28.

[108] Case 213/07 *Michaniki*, paras 43–9 of judgment.

[109] Art 57(4)(e) Public Sector Directive; Art 80(1) Utilities Directive; and Art 38(7)(d) Concessions Directive.

[110] Case C-195/04 *Commission v Finland*, opinion of AG Sharpston, para 88.

[111] See Craig, P. (2012) 'Subsidiarity: A Political and Legal Analysis' 50 *Journal of Common Market Studies* No S1, 72–87.

[112] As provided for under Treaty Protocol No 2 on the application of the principles of subsidiarity and proportionality—this is known as the 'yellow card' procedure.

mechanism has only resulted in two legislative proposals being withdrawn by the Commission in the five years from 2009 to 2014. Of potentially greater significance in the realm of procurement law is the possibility for a Member State to bring an action in the CJEU on behalf of a parliament alleging a breach in the subsidiarity principle. If, for example, significantly lower thresholds were to be proposed for application of the procurement directives, such an action might be envisioned.

3

PROCEDURES

The use of defined procedures is a hallmark of procurement regulated under **3.01** the EU directives. Coordination of procedures under the directives represents an attempt to bring divergent national and organizational practices into greater sync—although particularities remain. The 2014 revision introduced two new procedures and a number of changes to the four existing ones. The stated intention was twofold: to simplify procedures and to provide greater flexibility for contracting authorities and economic operators responding to tenders. The compatibility of these two agendas is open to question. The availability of greater choice, both between procedures and in terms of the timelines and techniques which are applied within them, increases complexity in public procurement. Intelligent use of the various possibilities available under the directives may achieve better results in terms of value for money or the broader strategic objectives of procurement. The existence of rules for a procedure is only a starting point for being able to attain such results, but familiarity with a range of procedures is likely to be advantageous for most contracting organizations.

This chapter explores the procedures as set out in the 2014 directives, with par- **3.02** ticular attention to the new competitive procedure with negotiation, innovation partnership, and revised competitive dialogue. The open and restricted procedures remain largely unchanged from their incarnations in the 2004 directives, with the exception of revised timelines and the rules on selection and award criteria, which are considered in Chapter 4. For the first time, Member States are obliged to transcribe all of the procedures (with the exception of the negotiated procedure without prior publication) into national law. The Concessions Directive does not prescribe detailed procedures, but does include a number of procedural guarantees related to specifications, selection and award criteria, and providing information to candidates and tenderers. New provisions have also been introduced regarding the operation of framework agreements and dynamic purchasing systems, including rules on indicating how future contracts will be awarded under frameworks. These are discussed below, together with the use of lots, electronic auctions, and electronic catalogues, tools which can be used within procedures and which are appropriate for certain categories of procurement.

Choice of Procedure

3.03 Under the 2014 directives, contracting authorities and entities may choose from the procedures and techniques for procurement detailed in Table 3.1.

Table 3.1 Availability of procedures and techniques under 2014 directives

Procedure/Technique	Limitations on use (public sector)	Limitations on use (utilities)
Open	None	
Restricted	None	
Competitive procedure with negotiation	Must justify	None
Competitive dialogue	Must justify	None
Innovation partnership	None[i]	
Negotiated procedure without prior publication	Exceptional	
Design contest	None	
Framework agreements	Maximum four years	Maximum eight years
Dynamic purchasing system	Standardised purchases only[ii]	
Electronic auction	Cannot be used for design of works or other service/works contracts involving intellectual performances	
Electronic catalogues	None	

[i] No explicit constraints are placed on innovation partnership, but it is expressed as being applicable where the needs of the contracting authority/entity cannot be met by solutions already on the market (Article 31 of Public Sector Directive; Article 49 of Utilities Directive).

[ii] Under Article 34 of the Public Sector Directive and Article 52 of Utilities Directive, DPS may be used for 'commonly used purchases the characteristics of which, as generally available on the market, meet the needs of the contracting authorities [entities]'.

3.04 The grounds on which the public sector may justify use of the competitive procedure with negotiation and competitive dialogue are set out in Article 26:

(i) the needs of the contracting authority cannot be met without adaptation of readily available solutions; or

(ii) they include design or innovative solutions; or

(iii) the contract cannot be awarded without prior negotiations because of specific circumstances related to its nature, complexity or legal and financial make-up or because of the risks attaching to them; or

(iv) technical specifications cannot be established with sufficient precision by the contracting authority with reference to a standard, European Technical Assessment, common technical specification or technical reference; or

(v) only irregular or unacceptable tenders are received in response to an open or restricted procedure.

For the first time, examples are provided in the directives of what may constitute **3.05** an irregular or unacceptable tender. Tenders which do not comply with the procurement documents, which are received late, where there is evidence of collusion or corruption, or which have been found by the contracting authority to be abnormally low are to be considered irregular. Tenders submitted by tenderers who do not have the required qualifications, or whose price exceeds the contracting authority's budget as determined and documented prior to starting the procurement procedure, are to be considered as unacceptable. In cases where only irregular or unacceptable tenders are received, the contracting authority is entitled to enter into negotiations/dialogue without publishing a further notice, provided that:

- it does so only with tenderers who have met the exclusion and selection criteria for the original procedure, and who have submitted tenders 'in accordance with the formal requirements of the tender procedure'; and
- it invites all such tenderers to participate.[1]

The reference to the 'formal requirements of the tender procedure' is ambiguous— **3.06** it implies that tenders which were submitted late or which did not comply with the procurement documents in some respect should not be included in the subsequent negotiations or dialogue. In cases where only such tenders are received, it is not clear whether a new competition is required. This would tend to defeat the purpose of allowing reversion to negotiation or dialogue in cases where only irregular tenders are received. It is possible that compliance with the 'formal requirements of the tender procedure' should be read more narrowly, so that some tenders which are irregular would nonetheless be deemed to meet these requirements, but it is difficult to see how late or incomplete tenders could meet this description.

By contrast, the grounds for justifying the use of competitive dialogue or competi- **3.07** tive procedure with negotiation from the outset appear relatively easy to invoke. For procurement which involves anything other than routine or standardised purchases, there will normally be an element of adaptation or design. There are also many procurements for which the use of standards in technical specifications is not appropriate. Choice of procedure then largely becomes a question of strategy for the contracting authority, taking account of the different time and resource commitments required by each procedure, and the structure for competition which it provides. These considerations are examined below.

Time Limits

The minimum time limits for all procedures have been reduced under the 2014 **3.08** directives. In late 2008, the Commission published a memo to the effect that,

---

[1] Art 26(4)(b) Public Sector Directive.

in light of the financial crisis, use of accelerated procedures was acceptable without particular justification for all major public projects during 2009 and 2010.[2] During the revision process, governments and the private sector lobbied for shorter standard timelines for procedures. The Public Sector Directive now provides that sub-central contracting authorities may use a PIN as a call for competition and, where Member States so permit, may set time limits for tenders by agreement with all bidders in both the restricted procedure and competitive procedure with negotiation.[3] In the absence of such agreement, a minimum of ten days must be allowed for tender submission. Days are to be counted starting on the first day after the relevant notice or invitation is issued.[4]

3.09 Contracting authorities are obliged to take account of the complexity of a contract and the time required to prepare tenders when setting time limits in a procedure. They are also obliged to extend the time limits in a proportionate manner if additional information is not made available at least six days prior to the deadline for tenders (four in an accelerated procedure) or if any significant change is made to the documents.[5] The minimum time limits for procedures under the 2014 directives, net of the various adjustments which are available, are shown in Table 3.2. These reflect the time periods and reductions available under Article XI of the revised WTO Government Procurement Agreement.

3.10 The term 'days' in the procurement directives always refers to calendar days, so the fact that the prescribed period may include non-working days is not taken into account, unless the period ends on a non-working day (in which case, it is extended to the end of the following working day). If an invitation to tender is published on the Friday prior to a public holiday, it is quite conceivable that only five working days would be available for the preparation of tenders, which seems unfeasibly short for most requirements and likely to be detrimental to SME participation in particular. It remains to be seen whether such situations might lead to a more robust enforcement of the proportionality requirement for time limits by the Commission or national courts. In any event, it is unlikely to reduce the total time taken to complete many procedures, as shorter time limits for tenders often imply a longer period for evaluation and clarification due to lower quality submissions.

---

[2] European Commission, *Public procurement: Commission recognises need for accelerated procurement procedure*, IP/08/2040 19/12/2008.

[3] Arts 48(2), 28(4), and 29(1) (last indent) Public Sector Directive.

[4] Recital 106 Public Sector Directive and Recital 112 Utilities Directive stipulate that time limits are to be interpreted in accordance with Regulation No 1182/71 of the Council, Art 3 of which sets out three relevant rules: (i) 'days' includes public holidays, Saturdays, and Sundays; (ii) a period expressed in days begins on the day after the relevant event occurs; and (iii) if the end of a period expressed in days occurs on a Saturday, Sunday, or public holiday, the period is extended to the end of the following working day.

[5] Art 47 Public Sector Directive. Recital 81 to the Directive also states that any changes must not be such that additional candidates would have qualified for selection or been attracted to the competition.

Table 3.2 Time limits under the 2014 directives—public and utilities sectors

Procedure	Min. days for expressions of interest	Min. days for tenders	Min. days for tenders w/electronic submission	Min. days for tenders w/PIN[(i)]	Min. days for tenders if urgency invoked
Open	N/A	35	30	15	15
Restricted	30/15[(ii)]	30[(iii)]	25[(iii)]	10[(iii)]	10[(iii)]
Competitive procedure w/ negotiation (PS only)	30/15[(ii)]	30[(iii)]	25[(iii)]	10[(iii)]	10[(iii)]
Negotiated procedure w/prior publication (utilities only)	30/15[(ii)]	10[(iii)]	10[(iii)]	10[(iii)]	10[(iii)]
Competitive dialogue	30	None	None	None	None
Innovation partnership	30	None	None	None	None
Dynamic purchasing system	30	10	10	10	10
Concessions	30	22	17	17	17

[(i)] Provided the PIN is published at least 35 days and no more than 12 months in advance of the contract notice, and contains all relevant information such as estimated start date for the procedure, CPV codes, and short description of the contract.

[(ii)] The reduction to 15 days is available for the public sector in 'urgent situations duly substantiated by the contracting authority'—and not for the competitive dialogue or innovation partnership. For utilities, the conditions under which the reduction can be made are less clear, with 30 days being the 'general rule', but 15 days cited as the absolute minimum for expressions of interest.

[(iii)] Time limits for receipt of tenders may be set by agreement with all tenderers by utilities and, if provided for in national implementing legislation, by sub-central contracting authorities.

Pre-procurement

The pre-procurement stage is not strictly regulated by the directives; however, care **3.11** must be exercised to avoid prejudicing a future procurement in any way. The potential benefits of pre-procurement are broadly recognized: it can allow for more targeted, efficient, and effective procedures by engaging the market at an early stage. Procedures, specifications, and criteria can be chosen in better knowledge of market capacity, and suppliers gain the opportunity to prepare in advance of formal competition. This is likely to grow in importance given the very tight timescales with which most procedures can now be conducted and the requirement to publish full procurement documents at the outset of multi-stage procedures.[6] The benefits of pre-procurement are, of course, dependent on intelligent management on the part of the public authority, as well as the willingness of potential contractors to engage. Despite being less closely regulated, pre-procurement is not without its own risks.

---

[6] See discussion of this requirement under Art 53 Public Sector Directive at paras 2.55–2.56.

3.12 One such risk is that of an unfair advantage arising for operators involved in the pre-procurement stages, which then carries through to the subsequent competition. This scenario is now addressed specifically in Article 41 of the Public Sector Directive, following a number of cases in which the question of exclusion of bidders who may have gained such an advantage arose.[7] Article 41 provides that where the prior involvement of a candidate or tenderer in pre-procurement activities will distort competition, they may be excluded from the competition, but only where there is no other means of ensuring equal treatment, and then only with a right of objection to the proposed exclusion. Alternative measures which may secure equal treatment in such situations include the sharing of information exchanged at pre-procurement stage with all candidates or tenderers and allowing adequate time for them to prepare their submissions in light of this.

3.13 Given the potential need to share such information, it is important to clearly state the scope of confidentiality which will be afforded to submissions made by undertakings in the course of market consultation or other pre-procurement activities, and the conditions under which such information may be disclosed. In general, the information shared will be that emanating from the contracting authority itself, but these lines can sometimes become blurred, especially where an incumbent contractor is involved, as discussed in Chapter 2. The 2014 directives contain specific provisions on confidentiality in procedures, creating a presumption that information designated as confidential by economic operators or by the contracting authority itself should not be disclosed. However, this is expressed as being subject to national laws on access to information and to any specific disclosure requirements which arise under the directives, including the obligation to notify candidates and tenderers of the outcomes of evaluation and to publish a contract award notice.[8]

3.14 Although pre-procurement can be extremely useful in the case of first-time procurements or those which involve elements of innovation or other complexities, it is not a panacea. In some cases, operators may fail to take it seriously without the definite prospect of a contract being awarded, and in others poor coordination or follow-through on the part of the contracting authority will limit the value of the exercise. Due to its exclusion from the directives, it is difficult to gather data about the frequency with which pre-procurement is used or its outcomes. Chapter 6

---

[7] See Joined Cases C-21/03 and C-34/03 *Fabricom SA v État belge* [2005] ECR I-01559, Case T-345/03 *Evropaïki Dynamiki v European Commission* [2008] ECR II-34, and the discussion of these cases in Chapter 2.

[8] Art 21 Public Sector Directive; Art 39 Utilities Directive; and Art 28 Concessions Directive. In all three directives, confidentiality is expressed as being subject to the specific requirements of disclosure set out in the directives, as well as national legislation regarding access to information. Article 28 of the Concessions Directive also states that confidentiality 'shall not prevent public disclosure of non-confidential parts of concluded contracts, including any subsequent changes'.

looks in more detail at approaches to pre-procurement and their potential impact on value for money.

Open Procedure

The open procedure accounts for over two-thirds of contracts advertised in the **3.15** OJEU, and for many organizations is the sole procedure they use regularly. The average time taken under the 2004 directives to conduct an open procedure was 53 working days from advertisement through to award decision.[9] The key distinguishing feature of the open procedure is the possibility for any interested operator to submit a tender without the need to demonstrate its suitability or capacity in advance. Absence of grounds for exclusion and possession of the relevant financial, professional, and technical capacity ('eligibility') are still evaluated, but not for the purpose of selecting candidates to tender. The precise order and manner in which eligibility is assessed in open procedures varies; however, the 2014 directives make clear that this assessment may take place after the substantive evaluation of tenders against the contract award criteria.[10] The practicality of this approach will depend on the number of tenders received and the nature of the evaluation criteria. Where a large number of tenders are submitted and their evaluation is likely to be time-consuming, it is sensible to determine eligibility in advance of undertaking tender evaluation.

The transaction costs associated with the open procedure are potentially higher **3.16** than for other procedures due to the greater number of tenders which are prepared and evaluated. However, in practice, this is probably compensated for by the shorter time periods involved in most open procedures. The Commission's 2011 evaluation also revealed that the average number of tenders received in open procedures was just 5.7, only marginally more than the number typically received in restricted procedures. This finding must be seen in the context of the much lower average contract values for open procedures, mentioned above. Overall, the open procedure has much to recommend it for the procurement of low value or uncomplicated goods and services. One of the perceived disadvantages of the procedure, that it requires the publication of a full specification at the outset, now appears to apply equally to multi-stage procedures, due to the requirement to make procurement documents available electronically at the time of publishing a notice. The implications of this are discussed below.

---

[9] Strand, I., Ramada, P., and Canton, E. (2011) *Public Procurement in Europe: Cost and Effectiveness* (PwC, London Economics, and Ecorys), p 103. The study analysed some 540,000 procurements advertised in the Official Journal over five years (2006–10) from 30 countries.

[10] Art 56(2) Public Sector Directive; and Art 76(7) Utilities Directive. Member States may opt to restrict this option in their implementation of the directives.

Restricted Procedure

3.17 The restricted procedure has traditionally been favoured in the UK and Ireland, although more recent years have seen a shift towards open procedures. By providing for a discrete selection stage, it allows greater control over the size and nature of a competition. Qualitative selection criteria are used to evaluate and shortlist candidates to be invited to tender, with a minimum of five being required in most circumstances. Use of the restricted or other multi-stage procedures allows for the application of selection criteria which are weighted and scored, whereas in the open procedure eligibility can be assessed on a pass or fail basis only.[11] The minimum number of candidates who will be invited to tender must be stated in the contract notice, although this is subject to a sufficient number of suitably qualified candidates being available. It is also possible to state a maximum number, although if two or more candidates achieve the same score under the qualitative selection criteria, they must each be invited unless an objective and non-discriminatory rule for selection in event of a tie has been provided in advance. Multi-stage procedures are naturally longer, with an average of 160 days taken to conduct a restricted procedure under the 2004 directives. The average number of bids received in restricted procedures was 5.5, according to a 2011 evaluation.[12]

3.18 A major change affecting all multi-stage procedures is the requirement to have full procurement documents available electronically at the time a notice is published. As noted in Chapter 2, this is presumably intended to increase the transparency of tender procedures and perhaps also to reduce the wasted transaction costs associated with operators submitting expressions of interest for contracts which are not, on closer inspection, relevant or attractive to them. However, the absence of any explicit acknowledgement of this shift in the recitals to the directives suggests that its significance in the context of the restricted and other multi-stage procedures may not have been fully appreciated. One possible effect of this change would be that it ushers in a new era of leaner, more efficient procurement. Contracting authorities will engage more actively in pre-procurement in order to develop their requirements fully prior to publishing a notice, and businesses will start preparing their tenders at an earlier stage, improving their quality. Subcontractors will also have better access to information about contractual requirements, allowing them to develop their capacity and approach potential partners.

3.19 In contrast to this Panglossian scenario, it is possible that the procurement documents published by contracting authorities at the outset will be little better than rough first drafts. Companies will continue to wait until they receive an invitation to tender before starting to prepare their bids, and delays will arise in the process of

---

[11] Art 65 Public Sector Directive, which allows for the reduction of the number of otherwise qualified candidates, does not apply where the open procedure is used.

[12] Strand et al, *Public Procurement in Europe*, p 94.

clarification and major revisions to documents. The shorter time periods available for tendering will decrease possibilities for SMEs to negotiate effective partnerships or submit a bid themselves. The reality is naturally likely to rest somewhere between these two extremes, but neither scenario is precluded by the rules set out in the 2014 directives. One relative certainty is that the frequency with which the restricted procedure is used will fall, due to the increased flexibility of the open procedure and greater availability of other multi-stage procedures, in addition to the more onerous publication requirements now associated with the restricted procedure.

Competitive Procedure with Negotiation

The competitive procedure with negotiation (CPN) replaces the old negotiated **3.20** procedure with prior publication for the public sector (the latter remains in place for the utilities sector). The major feature distinguishing the CPN from the negotiated procedure is the greater ease with which its use may be justified by the public sector. Overall, the 2014 directives display a much diminished suspicion towards the idea of public authorities negotiating their contracts. That said, the CPN provides a structure within which there is a limited scope for negotiation, and only at certain designated points within the procedure. A diagram of the procedure as outlined in the 2014 directives is shown in Figure 3.1.

Unlike the competitive dialogue—and this is the key point of distinction between **3.21** the two procedures—it requires the contracting authority to develop a specification of its requirements in advance of inviting submissions from bidders, and to

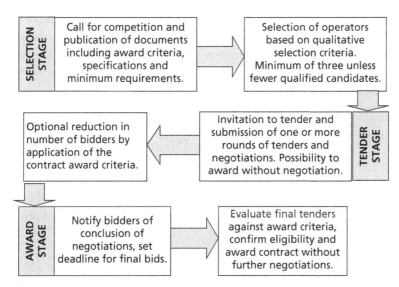

Figure 3.1 Competitive procedure with negotiation

structure the negotiation around these requirements.[13] Recital 45 of the Public Sector Directive refers to 'physical, functional and legal' characteristics or conditions as examples of minimum requirements. In contrast, in competitive dialogue, the descriptive document may simply identify needs without prescribing the nature or characteristics of solutions to be offered. Progressive identification of these solutions takes place within the competitive dialogue, whereas in the CPN an authority must have a clear concept of what it is buying from the outset. It is thus probably less suited to truly innovative or complex requirements, but may be effective for those which have certain commercial or technical features which are difficult to secure without some intercourse with bidders.

3.22 For example, the CPN may be well suited to service contracts involving the transfer of employees in accordance with the Transfers of Undertakings Directive, or where materials or commodities which are subject to price fluctuations form a significant part of the contract cost. Insurance services where these involve specific assessment of liabilities may also prove amenable to CPN—although the imperative to make information available to all bidders who have not yet been eliminated from the procedure must be borne in mind in such cases. Use of the CPN in each of these scenarios could likely be justified with reference to 'circumstances related to the nature, the complexity or the legal and financial make-up [of the contract] or because of the risks attaching to them' as provided for in Article 27(4)(a)(iii) of the Public Sector Directive.

3.23 The other point of distinction between CPN and competitive dialogue is that CPN does not allow for the same level of engagement with the preferred bidder to clarify, specify, and optimize the final tender submitted. The extent to which this has been liberalized under the new formulation of the competitive dialogue is discussed below. Both procedures emphasize the need to ensure equal treatment of bidders, and in particular not to make information available in a discriminatory manner between them. This is, however, subject to the confidentiality provisions set out in the 2014 directives, which allow limited grounds for refusing to disclose information designated as confidential by either economic operators or the contracting authority itself.[14]

Competitive Dialogue

3.24 The competitive dialogue procedure was introduced for the public sector in the 2004 directives. Although it was not formally included in the old Utilities Directive, contracting entities could apply it as a form of the negotiated procedure,

---

[13] Art 29(1) Public Sector Directive.
[14] Art 21 Public Sector Directive; Art 39 Utilities Directive; and Art 28 Concessions Directive.

which they were and are entitled to use without justification. It is now included explicitly in the Utilities Directive. For the public sector, competitive dialogue was envisioned as a kind of 'halfway house' between outright negotiation and the constraints of the open and restricted procedures. Its use could be justified for 'particularly complex contracts' where Member States took the option of implementing the procedure in national law. Twenty-four Member States implemented the procedure; however, of these, just two (the UK and France) were responsible for the large majority of competitive dialogues advertised in the OJEU in the period from 2006 to 2011. Although it accounted for less than 1 per cent of procedures advertised in the OJEU over this period, the value of contracts awarded via competitive dialogue was much higher: 8.6 per cent of the total, with an average contract value of over €40 million, compared to €2.2 million for the open procedure and €8.2 million for the restricted procedure.[15]

3.25 This reflects the intention for the procedure to be used for large and complex contracts, particularly those which involve an element of private finance or public-private partnership. Much has been written about competitive dialogue and in particular the somewhat enigmatic provision in Article 29 of Directive 2004/18/EC that tenders could be 'clarified, specified and fine-tuned' following submission, to the extent that this did not 'involve changes to the basic features of the tender or the call for tender'.[16] The imperative to stop short of wholesale negotiation of bids was clear—however, in practice, it has often proved difficult to tie down all aspects of contracts prior to the preferred bidder stage, in particular where third-party finance or other sensitive and contingent factors are involved. In the 2014 directives, the ability to 'fine-tune' tenders has been replaced by the ability to 'optimize'—perhaps implying greater flexibility.[17] The ability to engage in successive rounds of dialogue with participants prior to the preferred bidder stage, and to do so in a structured way, is a key appeal of the procedure. It allows, at least in principle, for competitive tension to be maintained while the technical and commercial features of bids are fleshed out.

3.26 The lengthy duration of many competitive dialogues, and its occasional misuse, led to something of an official backlash in the UK. In 2010, the Treasury completed a review of the competitive dialogue in which it recommended, *inter alia*, that it should not be seen as the 'default' procedure for all complex procurements.

---

[15] Strand et al, *Public Procurement in Europe*, p 18.

[16] See Arrowsmith, S. and Treumer, S. (eds) (2012) *Competitive Dialogue in EU Procurement* (Cambridge: Cambridge University Press); and Kennedy-Loest, C. (2006) 'What Can Be Done at the Preferred Bidder Stage in Competitive Dialogue?' 15 *PPLR* 316; and *Public Procurement Law Reviews* and *European Procurement & Public Private Partnership Law Reviews passim*.

[17] Although 'optimize' does raise the question of whether bids may be downgraded as well as upgraded. Some commentators on the 2014 directives have interpreted 'optimize' as implying more flexibility than 'fine-tune'. See Kotsonis, T. (2014) 'The 2014 Utilities Directive of the EU: Codification, Flexibilisation and Other Misdemeanours' PPLR 3, at 176.

This was based on its findings that many public sector bodies lacked the skills to conduct the procedure efficiently and that its resource demands were often dispro-portionate to the length and value of contracts awarded.[18] Under a further review carried out by the Efficiency and Reform Group within the Cabinet Office, this appeared to harden into a 'presumption' against the use of the procedure, in line with the focus on reducing procurement timescales to 120 working days for all but the most complex projects.[19] The Cabinet Office position contrasted with the Treasury findings that, on the whole, competitive dialogue was considered to be an effective procedure by both the public and private sector organizations familiar with it. The Cabinet Office approach emphasized the role of pre-procurement mar-ket engagement, including something called 'boot camps' to ready suppliers and procurers prior to OJEU publication.

3.27 The change in UK policy does not appear to have led to a significant reduction in the proportion of above-threshold contracts awarded using competitive dia-logue, which remained steady at around 3 per cent of procedures advertised in the period from 2009 to 2014.[20] The primary concerns expressed by the Treasury, namely, those relating to skills and the time and resource commitment required for competitive dialogue, would likely be exacerbated by a decline in the number of competitive dialogues being carried out. Its relatively high rates of use in the UK may be explained in part by the low rate of use of the negotiated procedure compared to other EU countries, and by the greater prevalence of large-scale out-sourcing and private finance initiative contracts. In France, a procedure similar to the competitive dialogue existed under the *Code des marchés publics* prior to the 2004 directives, elements of which appear to have inspired the wording found in Article 29 of Directive 2004/18/EC.[21] That France has the highest absolute num-ber of competitive dialogues is thus unsurprising, although it still accounts for less than 1 per cent of OJEU level contracts advertised in that country. Other Member States such as Poland and the Netherlands have also embraced the procedure with relative gusto.[22]

3.28 It is difficult to predict the impact which the introduction of two other, more flexible, procedures under the 2014 directives will have on the use of competi-tive dialogue. All three of these procedures are available more or less freely, with the grounds for justifying their choice being capacious enough to accommodate

---

[18] HM Treasury (2010) *HM Treasury Review of Competitive Dialogue*, pp 10–11.

[19] Cabinet Office (2012) *Government Sourcing: A New Approach Using LEAN*, p 5.

[20] The author's analysis of calls for competition published on TED between 2009 and 2014 shows competitive dialogue accounting for between 2.5 and 3.3 per cent of procedures advertised in the UK during this period.

[21] De Mars, S. and Olivier, F. (2012) 'Competitive Dialogue in France' in Arrowsmith and Treumer, *Competitive Dialogue in EU Procurement*.

[22] See Nagelkerke, M. and Muntz-Beekhuis, J. (2012) 'Competitive dialogue in the Netherlands' and Gorczynska, A. (2012) 'Competitive Dialogue in Poland' in Arrowsmith and Treumer, *Competitive Dialogue in EU Procurement*.

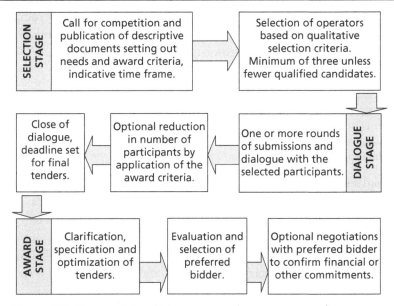

Figure 3.2 **Competitive dialogue procedure**

all but the most routine of procurements.[23] Familiarity with the competitive dialogue (despite the changes noted below) may work in its favour, although it also appears to have bred some contempt in the UK context. While it is no longer the only non-exceptional procedure allowing a greater degree of interaction with bidders, it continues to offer a particular balance between negotiation and structured competition. Most importantly, it allows contracting authorities to refine—and in some cases define—their requirements based on focused engagement with potential contractors, which I have argued above is not always possible in the context of pre-procurement. (See Figure 3.2.)

Challenges to the decision to use the competitive dialogue under the 2004 directives appear to be exceedingly rare. However, given the high value and complexity of contracts awarded, challenges to aspects of its application, in particular the sharing of information and reduction in the number of participants, naturally arose both at national and EU level.[24] The revisions to the procedure which appear in the   **3.29**

---

[23] Recital 43 of the Public Sector Directive indicates that competitive dialogue and competitive procedure are not to be used '[i]n respect of off-the-shelf services or supplies that can be provided by many different operators on the market'.

[24] Eg Case C-299/08 *Commission v France* [2009] ECR I-11587 (concerning the *marchés de définition*), *Montpellier Estates Ltd v Leeds City Council* [2013] EWHC 166 (QB), and *Baxter Healthcare Ltd v Health Service Executive* [2013] IEHC 413. In Italy, use of the competitive dialogue was suspended due to concerns about its potential to invite litigation (see Racca, M. and Casalini, D. (2012) 'Competitive Dialogue in Italy' in Arrowsmith and Treumer, *Competitive Dialogue in EU Procurement*, pp 458–90).

2014 directives aim to resolve some of the ambiguities associated with competitive dialogue and the complaint that in some cases it has been used to unfairly share participants' ideas with their competitors. Article 30 of the Public Sector Directive stipulates that:

> contracting authorities shall not reveal to the other participants solutions proposed or other confidential information communicated by a candidate or tenderer participating in the dialogue without its agreement. Such agreement shall not take the form of a general waiver but shall be given with reference to the intended communication of specific information.

3.30 The second sentence represents a strengthening of the confidentiality requirements over the 2004 directives. Unlike the general confidentiality provisions included in the 2014 directives, it is not expressed as being subject to freedom of information or other legal obligations of disclosure which may arise for public authorities. Although derogations from disclosure are generally possible for reasons of commercial sensitivity, it is conceivable that the confidentiality provision set out in Article 30 will conflict with such laws.

3.31 Perhaps in response to complaints about the length of some dialogues, there is now a requirement to provide an 'indicative timeline' in the notice or tender documents—although it is not entirely clear whether this relates to the dialogue or the contract itself. The other notable change in the procedure is that negotiations with the preferred bidder are now permitted to:

> confirm financial commitments or other terms contained in the tender by finalising the terms of the contract provided this does not have the effect of materially modifying essential aspects of the tender or of the public procurement, including the needs and requirements set out in the contract notice or in the descriptive document and does not risk distorting competition or causing discrimination.

This somewhat breathless provision acknowledges that not all aspects of solutions may be fully agreed at dialogue stage, and so brings the procedure closer to the reality of its practice in many cases. As previously, contracts awarded under competitive dialogue must take qualitative aspects into account as part of the award criteria and so cannot be awarded on the basis of lowest price or cost only. A minimum of three participants are to be invited to dialogue (assuming a sufficient number of qualified candidates exist) and the number invited to submit final bids must allow for 'genuine competition in so far as there are enough tenders, solutions or qualified candidates'.[25] Reduction in numbers can only take place by applying the award criteria, which must be stated at the outset.

---

[25] Art 66 Public Sector Directive.

Innovation Partnership

Public procurement of innovative goods and services is seen as having benefits **3.32** both for the public sector organizations engaging in it and the broader economy. For the purchasing organizations, it offers the ability to take advantage of new technologies or systems which may improve efficiency and enable better delivery of public services. It can also lead to economic growth in the sectors supplying the innovation, as seen clearly in the case of the aerospace and defence sectors, as well as health sciences. It is often pointed out that the internet, touch screens, GPS, voice recognition, and other technologies which have become widespread originated as part of government-funded projects.[26] There is a difference between governments supporting basic research activity and providing a market for the eventual outcome of this activity—and it is in the latter arena that the public procurement rules are most relevant. As noted in Chapter 1 (paragraph 1.29), an exemption exists for the purchase of research and development services, but this does not extend to acquisition on a commercial scale of the resulting goods or services. It is this gap which the innovation partnership procedure is intended to address.

An innovation partnership aims at the development and subsequent purchase **3.33** of innovative products, services, or works 'provided that they correspond to the agreed performance levels and maximum costs'. It is an application of the competitive procedure with negotiation to set up a partnership with one or several operators, with additional rules regarding the structure and phasing of contracts. Partnerships are to be structured in successive phases, including intermediate targets and payment in instalments.[27] Unlike pre-commercial procurement, which is available under the exemption from the directives for research and development services only, the innovation partnership allows for procurement from the early R&D stages up to and including acquisition on a commercial scale. This should, in theory, help public authorities to apply the benefits of R&D activities they finance or co-finance in their own operations.

The structure of the procedure is illustrated in Figure 3.3, although this represents **3.34** only one possible application of the rules set out in Article 31 of the Public Sector Directive.

---

[26] See Mazzucato, M. (2013) *The Entrepreneurial State: Debunking Public vs. Private Sector Myths* (London: Anthem Press), discussing the instrumental role of public contracts in fostering innovation in the United States. For the European context, see Edler, J. and Georghiou, L. (2007) 'Public Procurement and Innovation—Resurrecting the Demand Side' 36(7) *Research Policy* 949–63; Uyarra, E. and Flanagan, K. (2010) 'Understanding the Innovation Impacts of Public Procurement' 18(1) *European Planning Studies* 123–45; and Semple, A. (2014) *Guidance for Public Authorities on Public Procurement of Innovation*, Procurement of Innovation Platform, available at <http://www.innovation-procurement.org/about-ppi/guidance/>.

[27] Art 31 Public Sector Directive; and Art 49 Utilities Directive.

Competitive procedure with negotiation to set up partnership with one or more operators.

Partner A Phase I: R&D activities	**Partner B** Phase I: R&D activities	**Partner C** Phase I: R&D activities
↓	↓	↓
Intermediate target and payment for R&D phase	Intermediate target and payment for R&D phase	Intermediate target and payment for R&D phase
	↓	↓
	Phase II: Prototyping Intermediate target & payment for prototype	Phase II: Prototyping Intermediate target & payment for prototype
		↓
		Phase III: Test series or pilot Intermediate target & payment for pilot
		Purchase of resulting supplies, services or works

Figure 3.3 Innovation partnership procedure

3.35 The selection criteria applied must address the candidates' capacity for research and development activities and developing and implementing innovative solutions. The procurement documents are to define intellectual property arrangements and the sequence of activities required to develop an innovative solution. While these provisions may seem overly prescriptive given the unpredictable nature of the outcomes of R&D, it is worth noting that the procedure was adjusted from that in the Commission's original proposal to make it more flexible (and possibly less likely to have State aid implications) by removing the requirement to ensure an 'adequate profit' for the private partner(s).[28] However, it may still prove difficult to define requirements and select appropriate partners at the outset for what will often be long-term projects, with the possibility of commercial acquisition only arising at the end.

3.36 Facilitating public procurement of innovation has proven to be a complex process, and funding under Horizon 2020 and other EU programmes is being targeted to encourage public sector innovation procurement in various sectors, including health, construction, and IT services and equipment.[29] Many of the matters affecting rates of innovation procurement fall outside the scope of the procurement

---

[28] European Commission, *Proposal for a directive of the European Parliament and the Council on public procurement* (COM (2011) 896 final), p 60.

[29] For an overview of these funding opportunities, see <http://ec.europa.eu/programmes/horizon2020>.

directives, relating, for example, to the State aid rules and intellectual property law. Risk-aversion is also often cited as a factor limiting public sector willingness to act as a launch customer for innovative products and services. Innovation partnerships are designed to take some of the risk out of innovation procurement by providing for phased engagement with suppliers and the ability to terminate one or more of the contracts at the end of each phase. It seems likely, however, that other procedures will continue to be used to target innovation in many cases, including pre-commercial procurement and the competitive dialogue.

Negotiated Procedure without Prior Publication

The negotiated procedure without prior publication of a notice is available in excep- **3.37** tional cases only. The example given in the recitals to the Public Sector Directive is that of a natural catastrophe requiring immediate action. However, the grounds set out in Article 32 of the Public Sector Directive are somewhat broader, encompassing nine distinct situations:

    (i) Failure of an open or restricted procedure due to no, or no suitable, expressions of interest or tenders being received.

   (ii) Absence of competition due to artistic, technical, or intellectual property factors.

  (iii) Extreme urgency which is unforeseen by, and unattributable to, the contracting authority.

  (iv) Procurement of research or test products on a small scale.

   (v) Additional supplies which replace or extend original supplies where change of contractor is not feasible either due to technical incompatibility or the disproportionate technical difficulty this would cause in operation or maintenance. The maximum duration of such contracts is three years.

  (vi) The repetition of previous services or works which are entrusted to the same operator and which form part of the same basic project. The possibility of awarding additional contracts in this way must be included in the original notice along with their estimated value and can only be availed of within three years of the original contract award.

 (vii) For supplies quoted and purchased on a commodity market.

(viii) For supplies or services purchased on particularly advantageous terms, for example, due to liquidation of a contractor's assets.

  (ix) For award of a contract following on from a design contest. If there is more than one winner of the contest, all must be included in the negotiations.[30]

---

[30] Art 32(2)–(5) Public Sector Directive (summarized); and Art 50(a)–(j) of the Utilities Directive includes all of the above grounds for use of the negotiated procedure without prior publication and in addition: (i) the award of contracts which are purely for research, experiment, study, and development; and (ii) bargain purchases.

3.38 With regard to the first ground, this is formulated in a similar manner to the provision on irregular or unacceptable tenders discussed in paragraph 3.05, but with two notable differences. A tender is defined as being unsuitable where it is 'irrelevant to the contract, being manifestly incapable, without substantial changes, of meeting the contracting authority's needs and requirements as specified in the procurement documents' and an expression of interest is unsuitable if it fails to meet the prescribed exclusion or selection criteria. However, unlike the rules regarding justification of reversion to the CPN or competitive dialogue, there are no rules about which tenders are included in the subsequent negotiations.

3.39 It is not necessary to determine whether tenders or expressions of interest rejected as unsuitable meet the 'formal requirements of the tender procedure' prior to including them in negotiations—suggesting late or incomplete tenders could also be included. There is also no requirement that all of the tenders be included in the negotiations. This seems inconsistent, but could perhaps be justified by the stricter grounds for identifying an unsuitable tender. In the exceptional cases where only unsuitable tenders are received, contracting authorities may decide which of those tenders merit inclusion in subsequent negotiations. It is open to Member States to develop more detailed rules regarding implementation of this provision, which may also assist in determining how to proceed when no tenders are received.

3.40 Grounds (v) and (vi) are similar to those which existed under Articles 31(2)(b) and 31(4) of Directive 2004/18/EC for additional or repeated supplies, services, and works. However, the ability to award additional services or works which have become necessary due to unforeseen circumstances, up to a maximum of 50 per cent of the original contract value, is gone. In contrast, the sixth ground cited above requires foresight of the possible need to award further contracts to the same contractor and explicit mention of this in the original notice. It is difficult to see why reversion to a negotiated procedure would be needed in such cases, as an option to extend could simply be included in the notice. These grounds must also be read in conjunction with the rules on permissible modifications to contracts after their award, which are examined in Chapter 5.

Design Contests

3.41 A design contest involves the selection of a plan or design by a jury following a competition. They are most often used for architectural purposes; however, the 2014 directives also mention the possibility of applying them to engineering, data processing, or to obtain plans for 'financial engineering'. The latter is referred to in the recitals in the context of developing plans for the implementation of EU-funded SME support programmes.[31] Design contests may be used as a preliminary stage prior to award of a

---

[31] Recital 120 Public Sector Directive, making specific reference to the JEREMIE programme.

public service contract and/or for the award of prizes or payments to the competitors. For the purpose of advertisement, their value must be calculated taking account of all such prizes or payments *and* any subsequent public service contract envisioned. A specific form of notice is provided for the advertisement of design contests, which includes details of the procedures to be followed, selection and evaluation criteria, and whether the jury's decision will be binding on the contracting authority.

Article 80 of the Public Sector Directive provides that procedures may be adapted **3.42** for the purpose of conducting a design contest; however, certain basic safeguards are provided. Where a selection stage is included, the criteria for selection must be clear and non-discriminatory and the number selected must make for genuine competition. The jury members must be independent of the contestants and the jury act autonomously in its decisions and opinions. If membership of a particular profession is required to compete, at least a third of the members of the jury must belong to that profession. Anonymity of contestants is to be maintained during the evaluation, with the jury recording its ranking along with any comments or clarifications to be taken up with contestants following sign-off by the jury. Any such dialogue with the designated winner(s) must be minuted. The combined effect of these provisions is to indicate that there is limited scope for refining plans in consultation with contestants. Design contests are thus suitable for projects where the value and quality of plans can be readily assessed based on an initial submission. For other contracts involving design, competitive dialogue or CPN may be more appropriate.

Framework Agreements and Dynamic Purchasing Systems

Framework agreements are a means of organizing the award of multiple contracts, **3.43** either to a single operator or among a number of operators who have been admitted to the framework. They may also be established and used by a single contracting authority or by several, with central purchasing organizations often establishing frameworks on behalf of others. Frameworks are important instruments both for the aggregation of procurement (pooling demand) and for the award of repeat or phased contracts, for example, where award will depend on successful completion of a first phase or pilot. They are not the only such instruments—joint purchasing, dynamic purchasing systems, and contracts with options or stages may also fulfil some of the same functions—however, frameworks are in broad use across Europe and their efficiency for delivering these functions is acknowledged in the 2014 directives. In 2011, frameworks accounted for one-quarter of the value of procurement advertised in the OJEU.[32]

---

[32] Thomassen, G., Orderud, P., Strand, I., Vincze, M., de Bas, P., van der Wagt, M., and Yagafarova, A. (2014) *SMEs' Access to Public Procurement Markets and Aggregation of Demand in the EU* (PwC, ICF-GHK, and Ecorys), p 7.

3.44 Criticism has occasionally been levied at frameworks due to their potential to limit competition or, in some cases, to exclude smaller operators. Despite this, the requirement that a minimum of three economic operators be admitted to a multi-operator framework has quietly been dropped in the 2014 directives.[33] For the public sector, frameworks remain limited to a maximum duration of four years, unless a longer duration can be justified in exceptional circumstances. A maximum framework duration of eight years has been introduced in the utilities sector for the first time under the 2014 directives, perhaps in response to concerns about the potentially anti-competitive use of frameworks in that sector. Several other new provisions aim to clarify aspects of the use of frameworks in both sectors. Article 33 of the Public Sector Directive provides that frameworks may be used to award contracts where:

(i) the contracting authority has been clearly identified in the notice;
(ii) the economic operator or operator(s) are only those admitted to the framework following the initial competition; and
(iii) the contracts do not entail substantial modifications to the terms set out in the framework agreement.

3.45 Contracts awarded within a framework may outlive the framework itself,[34] although precisely how much longer they may last is uncertain. The general requirement is for contracts awarded under frameworks to fall within their scope as defined in the original notice and competition, together with the prohibition on using frameworks in a manner which would 'prevent, restrict or distort' competition. The directives do not prescribe a maximum duration for contracts, with the exception of the Concessions Directive, which limits the duration of concessions to five years or the 'time that a concessionaire could reasonably be expected to take to recoup the investments made in operating the works or services together with a return on invested capital'.[35] Very lengthy contracts may, however, be subject to challenge on competition grounds.[36] Factors which may legitimate longer contracts include the time needed for their performance, where maintenance of equipment with an

---

[33] Article 32(4) of Directive 2004/18/EC stipulated that a multi-operator framework must be concluded with at least three operators, provided that this number satisfied the selection and award criteria.

[34] This is confirmed in Recital 62 Public Sector Directive.

[35] Art 18(2) Concessions Directive.

[36] In the *London Underground* decision (N-264/02), the Commission found that a 30-year duration for contracts awarded as part of a PPP for the upgrade and maintenance of the London Underground network was proportionate based on the complexities of the project, the level of investment, and time needed to reach the agreed rates of return. The Commission also noted that the continuous review of payments by an independent arbiter, procedures for the award of subcontracts, and safeguards against use of assets to distort competition in ancillary markets helped to establish the proportionality of the arrangements (paras 104–10).

expected useful life of more than four years is included, or where extensive training of staff to perform the contract is needed.[37]

In a single-operator framework, the contracting authority may request the oper- **3.46**
ator to supplement its tender in writing to reflect the requirements of a particular contract. In a multi-operator framework, contracts may either be awarded without reopening competition if all of the terms are set out in the framework agreement itself, or by reopening competition among the operators admitted to the frame-work (known as a mini-competition). The 2014 directives clarify that both options may be used within a given framework, provided that the objective criteria for choosing between the two methods are set out in the procurement documents, together with an identification of the terms[38] which will be subject to reopened competition. Recital 61 states that such objective criteria may:

> relate to the quantity, value or characteristics of the works, supplies or services con-cerned, including the need for a higher degree of service or an increased security level, or to developments in price levels compared to a predetermined price index.

These provisions are presumably intended to provide greater transparency in the way in which frameworks are used, following in part from the Court's judgments regarding the use of *marchés de définition* in France.[39]

Rules regarding the conduct of mini-competitions are set out in Article 33(5) and **3.47**
are largely unchanged from the 2004 directives. Article 33(5)(d) specifies that the award criteria for contracts awarded in a mini-competition must be those set out in the procurement documents for the framework agreement. This raises the question of to what degree contracting authorities may vary the award criteria, sub-criteria, and weightings applied in mini-competitions. Guidance published by the Commission in 2005 indicated that it was possible to apply different award cri-teria for the establishment of the framework agreement itself and the award of indi-vidual contracts thereunder.[40] The reasons for doing this are clear, as the specific requirements under individual contracts will vary. Article 33(5)(d) means that at least the top-level award criteria must be indicated in the procurement documents for the framework itself—however, it does not necessarily mean that all of these

---

[37] Recital 62 Public Sector Directive; and Recital 72 Utilities Directive.

[38] Confusingly, the English text of Art 33(4)(a) and (b) uses 'terms' in two distinct senses. The first is 'terms and conditions of the framework agreement' and the second is 'terms governing the provision of the works, supplies and services concerned'. This distinction in itself is not problematic; however, Art 33(4)(b) then goes on to state that only where all of the terms governing provision are set out in the framework agreement can the authority choose between awarding based on these terms and reopening competition. If all of the terms governing provision have been agreed, then it is difficult to see what scope there is for reopening competition. The French and German texts, respectively, use *conditions* and *Bedingungen* in the same dual sense.

[39] Case C-340/02 *Commission v France* ('*Le Mans*') [2004] ECR I-9845; and Case C-299/08 *Commission v France* [2009] ECR I-11587.

[40] European Commission [2005] Explanatory Note—Framework Agreements—Classic Directive, pp 9–10.

criteria are applied in the initial competition. It may also be possible to apply distinct sub-criteria and weightings in the context of a mini-competition—for example, if 'Technical Merit' has been specified as an award criterion in the original procurement documents for a framework under which various engineering works will be purchased, then it would make sense to specify sub-criteria and weightings which are appropriate to the works in question.

3.48 While further guidance on these points may be imminent, it is clear that the prohibition on substantial modifications will play a role in determining the extent to which the criteria and other terms for contracts awarded under frameworks can deviate from those applied in the initial competition. The definition of substantial modifications is explored in Chapter 5. Article 50(2) provides that it is not necessary to publish a contract award notice in respect of each contract awarded under a framework. Member States may allow contracting authorities to publish such award notices on a quarterly basis, in which case they are to be grouped and sent within 30 days of the end of the quarter. This provision seems to be aimed at reducing the administrative burden associated with frameworks used to award a high volume of contracts.

3.49 A key feature of framework agreements is that their membership is fixed for their duration and new operators or contracting authorities may not be admitted. The situation where a framework contractor is replaced by a process of legal succession is governed by the rules on modifications set out in Article 72—which allow substitution where this has either been specifically provided for in an unambiguous contract review clause or where it results from restructuring, insolvency, or other unforeseen events, provided it does not entail other substantial modifications and the replacement contractor meets the original selection criteria.[41] If greater flexibility to admit new operators to a purchasing arrangement is desired, the establishment of a dynamic purchasing system as provided for in Article 34 may be more appropriate. Dynamic purchasing systems (DPS) existed under the 2004 directives, but were not broadly used due to the cumbersome nature of the advertisement process. While some attempt has been made to streamline the arrangements for operating a DPS in the 2014 directives, they still require the publication of multiple OJEU notices to establish the system and for each contract awarded.

3.50 DPS are intended for standardised purchases,[42] and all candidates who meet the selection criteria must be admitted to the system. A restricted procedure is used to establish the system, but requests to participate may be submitted at any time, with the contracting authority being obliged to process these within a maximum of 15 working days. All candidates who have been admitted to a DPS must be

---

[41] See Chapter 5 for discussion of this and other grounds for justifying modifications to contracts.
[42] Article 34 of the Public Sector Directive and Art 52 of the Utilities Directive refer to 'commonly used purchases the characteristics of which, as generally available on the market, meet the needs of the contracting authorities [entities]'.

invited to tender for each contract, or where the option to divide it into categories has been taken, all candidates within that category. A minimum of ten days must be allowed for tenders, which are to be fully electronic. Although this represents a leaner process than that described in the 2004 directives, the ongoing management of a DPS still requires a level of administration which goes beyond that of a framework. They may be suitable for high frequency, repeated contracts where the contracting authority wishes to avail itself of new suppliers entering the market. Although it is not explicitly stated in Article 34, it appears from the provisions regarding joint and centralized purchasing that a DPS may be used by multiple contracting authorities.

Lots

As part of the effort to foster greater SME involvement in public procurement, the **3.51** mandatory division of contracts into lots was proposed during the revision process. Lots are used with varying frequency across the Member States, on average in just under 30 per cent of OJEU procedures during the period from 2009 to 2012.[43] To require all contracts to be subdivided in this manner would thus have required a major shift in practices—one which was ultimately rejected during the revision negotiations. The compromise position is set out in Article 46 of the Public Sector Directive, which allows Member States to mandate division into lots for certain contracts, and requires contracting authorities to include a statement of their reasons for not dividing into lots for all other contracts. Authorities may limit the number of lots to be awarded to any one operator or combine lots, by stating the objective criteria by which they will do so in advance. Under the Utilities Directive, the obligation to explain does not apply, but the same ability to limit lots awarded to one operator or to combine lots exists.[44]

Such initiatives appear to be premised on the idea that SMEs are significantly **3.52** under-represented in the award of public contracts—however, the available data offers very limited support to this proposition. SMEs account for some 56 per cent of contracts awarded via the OJEU, and an estimated 45 per cent of aggregate contract value.[45] This compares to a 58 per cent SME share of total value added in the European economy; however, as SMEs win a greater proportion of below-threshold contracts, and OJEU level tenders account for only around a fifth of procurement spend, it seems that any under-representation in terms of overall volume or value of contracts is very small. In certain sectors, and some Member States, SMEs are over-represented in the award of public contracts compared to their share in the

---

[43] Thomassen et al, *SMEs' Access to Public Procurement Markets*, p 53.
[44] Art 65 Utilities Directive.
[45] Thomassen et al, *SMEs' Access to Public Procurement Markets*, pp 5–6.

relevant sector of the economy. Although other good reasons may exist to support greater SME involvement in public procurement, the idea that the existing rules systematically discriminate against them does not seem to withstand scrutiny, at least at the overall European level.

3.53 The evidence does suggest that division of contracts into lots improves SME success rates, even when contract value is controlled for.[46] It also suggests that framework agreements are not usually detrimental to SME chances of success.[47] Where a framework is awarded in multiple lots, the effect is that multiple framework agreements exist, with operators only able to win contracts which fall within the lot(s) to which they have been admitted. The rules on selection criteria make clear that these are to be set with reference to the value and nature of individual lots. However, where there is a possibility that an operator may win multiple lots which are to be performed at the same time, the minimum turnover required may be set with reference to the value of these multiple lots.[48] The effectiveness of the turnover limits introduced in the 2014 directives is considered in Chapter 4.

3.54 The development and application of objective criteria for limiting the number of lots to be awarded to any one operator may not be straightforward. If it is merely desired to limit the number of lots awarded to any one operator without regard to the optimal combination of lots, this can readily be achieved by indicating the maximum in the notice. However, the more likely situation is that the authority wishes to limit the number of lots awarded to one operator based on cost or quality considerations which cannot be fully known until tenders are evaluated. The starting point is that evaluation of tenders is done on a per-lot basis, with the individual winner for each lot being awarded the contract. If the authority wishes to deviate from this, it must indicate the criteria which it will apply to do so. Possible approaches would be to refer to the financial and technical capacity which the tenderer has demonstrated during the selection stage (ie lots will be awarded up to a maximum ratio of the assessed capacity), or to the minimum number of operators to be appointed to a contract or framework. If award to the highest scoring tenderer against the award criteria for a lot would not meet these previously stated rules, award to the runner-up for that lot would be possible under Article 46.

3.55 It is also possible under Article 46(3) and Recital 79 of the Public Sector Directive to award based on the outcome of evaluation of combinations of lots, rather than individual ones. Recital 79 states that where awarding a combination of lots to a single operator would fulfil the award criteria better than awarding the lots in isolation, contracting authorities may opt for this approach provided they have carried out a comparative assessment showing this to be the case. It is thus similar to the

---

[46] Thomassen et al, *SMEs' Access to Public Procurement Markets*, p 53.
[47] Thomassen et al, *SMEs' Access to Public Procurement Markets*, p 8.
[48] Art 58 Public Sector Directive.

evaluation approach which applies where variants are authorized. This provision may counteract the use of lots to encourage SMEs, as it is more likely to favour larger operators who can offer volume discounts if multiple lots are awarded to them. It may, however, be instrumental in attaining greater value for money where suppliers are able to offer economies of scale in this way.

Overall, while the provisions in Article 46(2) and (3) (which are replicated in **3.56** Article 65(2) and (3) of the Utilities Directive) offer greater flexibility to make decisions about award of lots which take into account broader strategic objectives, they also have the potential to add considerably to the complexity of such decisions and open up ground on which legal challenges may be advanced. The net effect in some cases may be to discourage use of lots, contrary to the intention of these provisions.

Electronic Auctions and Electronic Catalogues

Electronic auctions and catalogues, like lots, are techniques which may be applied **3.57** in any procurement procedure rather than procedures in themselves. The 2014 directives aim to facilitate use of these techniques as part of the general push towards e-procurement. Reverse auctions may help to target more competitive pricing and have been used successfully for both standardised commodities and more complex requirements—although their use for service or works contracts involving intellectual performance (such as the design of works) is prohibited under Article 35 of the Public Sector Directive. The auction process takes place after tenders are evaluated for compliance with technical specifications and, where relevant, performance against the qualitative award criteria. Tenderers are informed of the outcome of this evaluation at the time of being invited to participate in the auction, allowing this to influence their pricing strategy. They must also be informed of the formula which will be used in the auction to determine rankings, which are to reflect all of the award criteria. Auctions must preserve the anonymity of tenderers, raising the possibility that an in-house bid or stalking horse might be included in the auction.[49]

The rules on electronic auctions set out in the 2014 directives reflect those in the **3.58** GPA, but provide additional detail intended to facilitate the uniform conduct of auctions in procurement. In particular, they emphasize that only 'admissible' tenders may be included in an auction—meaning those which are unsuitable, irregular, or unacceptable cannot be. The proliferation of these terms in the directives, along with the fifth concept of a tender which 'does not meet the formal requirements of the tender procedure' discussed in paragraph 3.06, is regrettable.

---

[49] Art 35(7) Public Sector Directive; and Art 53(7) Utilities Directive.

However, in the case of auctions, the objective is clear: any tender which might be rejected for any reason should not be included in the auction, as this would invalidate the results and prevent award of the contract on the basis of the outcome of the auction. A factor which may still undermine the finality of an auction result is the submission of an abnormally low tender requiring the contracting authority to investigate in accordance with the provisions set out in Article 69, discussed in Chapter 4.

3.59 Electronic catalogues may be used as a means of collecting prices or other product information from suppliers—for example, in the context of a framework agreement or dynamic purchasing system.[50] Notification of the intention to collect this information from catalogues must be sent to the participating suppliers, who are also given an opportunity to contest or confirm the information which will form part of their tenders. Electronic catalogues may be used in the same manner by the public and utilities sectors. Member States are also able to make their use mandatory for certain types of procurement. As with dynamic purchasing systems, they are likely to be of greatest use for standardised or repeated purchases where the market offering corresponds closely to the authority's needs.

3.60 The effectiveness of electronic auctions and catalogues in procurement is largely dependent on the electronic platforms which support their use. The accessibility of such systems is protected by Article 22, which requires that they be 'non-discriminatory, generally available and interoperable with the ICT products in general use', and that any security requirements be proportionate. However, these rules alone do not guarantee that systems will be user-friendly and efficient in the way they are designed. Fortunately, the market for providing e-procurement systems is a healthy one, with about 300 such systems in use across Europe. A study carried out on behalf of the Commission in 2013 identified a set of good practices in the design of e-procurement systems, although it did not address auctions or electronic catalogues in detail.[51]

---

[50] Art 36 Public Sector Directive; and Art 54 Utilities Directive.

[51] Bausa Paris, O., Kourtidis, S., Liljemo, K., Loozen, N., Rodrigues Frade, J., and Snaprud, M. (2013) *e-Procurement Golden Book of Good Practice: Final Report* (European Commission), available at <http://ec.europa.eu/internal_market/publicprocurement/e-procurement/golden-book/>.

4

SPECIFICATIONS, SELECTION, AND AWARD CRITERIA

Beyond choice of procedure, the manner in which contracting authorities define **4.01** their requirements and preferences is at the heart of procurement under the directives. This area is the focus of much procurement strategy, and a considerable proportion of legal challenges. Rules on technical specifications formed part of the earliest procurement directives, and have evolved noticeably between 2004 and 2014. Criteria for exclusion and selection of candidates in tender procedures, and for the award of contracts, have also been redefined in various ways, with an emphasis on the means of verification which may be required to demonstrate compliance or performance against such criteria. This chapter analyses the changes to technical specifications and criteria set out in Chapter III of the Public Sector Directive. These changes also apply (with a few noted exceptions) under Chapter III of the Utilities Directive, whereas the Concessions Directive prescribes only more limited procedural guarantees in respect of specifications and criteria.[1]

Two broad trends can be discerned in the changes made to specifications and cri- **4.02** teria in the 2014 directives. The first is that certain flexibilities have been introduced in the permissible scope of criteria and order of evaluation. Under this heading, we find confirmation that technical specifications and award criteria may relate to any stage of the life cycle and to characteristics which do not form part of the 'material substance' of the goods, services, and works being purchased. This resolves any lingering ambiguity regarding the possibility to specify or award marks for renewable electricity or organic products, for example. The order of evaluation has also been liberalized so that exclusion criteria may be applied at any stage within a procedure, and eligibility criteria applied after evaluation of tenders in the open procedure.[2] Award criteria may now address the experience of individuals proposed to deliver

---

[1] Chapter II (Arts 36–41) of the Concessions Directive covers technical and functional requirements, procedural guarantees, selection and qualitative assessment of candidates, time limits, provision of information, and award criteria.

[2] Arts 57(5) and 56(2) Public Sector Directive; and Arts 80(1) and 76(7) Utilities Directive.

a contract, resolving a difficulty which had affected service contracts in particular and was the basis for the much-criticized *Lianakis* decision.[3]

4.03 In contrast, there has been a tightening of the rules on verification of compliance with criteria. Some of these changes are designed to make the lives of suppliers tendering for public contracts easier, such as the European Single Procurement Document and the limits on turnover requirements and look-back periods for certain exclusion criteria. Others are designed to strengthen the credibility of environmental and social criteria, by extending the use of third-party labels and environmental management systems and setting procedural standards for life-cycle costing. The rules on abnormally low tenders also signify a tighter approach, requiring investigation and, in certain cases, rejection of bids where an abnormally low price has not been adequately explained. There is still much in these provisions which is left open to interpretation, and in some cases their drafting is such as to counteract the expressed intention. These ambiguities and shortcomings are explored below, together with ideas as to how criteria may be used most effectively by contracting authorities to achieve their strategic objectives.

Exclusion Criteria

Mandatory grounds

4.04 Like their predecessors, the 2014 directives contain both mandatory and discretionary grounds for the exclusion of economic operators from a tender procedure. The mandatory grounds of exclusion relate to certain serious offences which are deemed to preclude award of public contracts to an economic operator—at least for a period of time. These are:

(i) participation in a criminal organization;
(ii) corruption;
(iii) fraud;
(iv) terrorist offences;
(v) money laundering or terrorist financing;
(vi) child labour and other forms of trafficking in human beings; and
(vii) breach of obligations to pay taxes or social security contributions.

---

[3] Case C-532/06 *Lianakis v Dimos Alexandroupolis* [2008] ECR I-251. See PPLR 2009–10 for assorted critiques of the judgment. See also Arrowsmith, S. (2014) *The Law of Public and Utilities Procurement*, Vol 1 (London: Sweet & Maxwell), 7-183–7-194 for arguments in favour of some degree of overlap being permissible between selection and award criteria. Organization, experience, and qualifications of staff can now be taken into account at award stage 'where the quality of the staff assigned can have a significant impact on the level of performance on the contract' (Art 67(2)(b) Public Sector Directive; and Art 82(2)(b) Utilities Directive).

These offences are further defined in Article 57 of the Public Sector Directive **4.05** with reference to relevant EU and international legal instruments. The mandatory grounds of exclusion also apply to procurement by contracting authorities under the Utilities Directive.[4] Exclusion can only take place where the economic operator or a person who is a member of its administrative, management, or supervisory body, or has powers of representation, decision, or control over it, has been convicted by a final judgment of one of the offences. The mandatory exclusion grounds must be applied at any stage during a procurement procedure if the operator is in one of the situations set out. If an operator who should have been excluded under one of the mandatory grounds is awarded a public contract, contracting authorities must be able to terminate the contract.[5]

In the case of non-payment of tax or social security, a judicial or administrative **4.06** decision having final or binding effect is sufficient to warrant exclusion, and this may emanate either from the country where the operator is established or the country where the contract is awarded. This represents a considerable strengthening of the enforcement of tax obligations in the context of procurement procedures, as under the 2004 directives it existed as a discretionary exclusion ground only. However, it is limited in several respects: it does not apply to tax defaults in third countries (which may be significant in the case of multinational companies) and ceases to apply if the operator has paid or entered into a binding arrangement to pay the sums owed.[6] However, unlike all the other grounds of exclusion, both mandatory and discretionary, there is no general 'self-cleaning' or 'sunset clause' in respect of non-payment of tax or social security—meaning that where an operator remains in default, it will be more difficult for it to bid for contracts than an operator which has engaged in terrorist financing six years ago, for example. Member States are able to provide for derogation from this ground of exclusion where it would be disproportionate—for example, if only minor amounts of tax or social security payments are owing.[7] All grounds of exclusion may be derogated from for 'overriding reasons related to the public interest such as public health or protection of the environment'.[8]

---

[4] Art 80(1) Utilities Directive, 2nd paragraph.

[5] Art 73(b) Public Sector Directive; Art 90(b) Utilities Directive.

[6] Art 57(2) Public Sector Directive. This is derived from the Court's judgment in Joined Cases C-226/04 and C-228/04 *La Cascina Soc coop arl and Zilch Srl v Ministero della Difesa and Others* [2006] ECR I-01347.

[7] Notably, however, the Court has held that exclusion based on very small amounts of social security payments being unpaid at the time of a tender was *not* disproportionate (Case C-358/12 *Consorzio Stabile Libor Lavori Pubblici v Comune di Milano*, not yet reported). In that case, national legislation provided for exclusion where more than €100 or 5 per cent of the sums owed in respect of social security payments was outstanding.

[8] Art 57(3) Public Sector Directive.

Discretionary grounds

4.07 The circumstances justifying discretionary exclusion are more extensive, encompassing ten headings:

(i) breach of tax or social security obligations where this is established by any appropriate means (ie not requiring a judicial or administrative decision with final and binding effect);

(ii) violation of environmental, social or labour obligations as set out in Article 18(2);

(iii) bankruptcy, insolvency, administration, or analogous situations;

(iv) grave professional misconduct which renders integrity questionable;

(v) collusion or other agreements aimed at distorting competition;

(vi) conflict of interest which cannot be remedied by less intrusive means;

(vii) distortion of competition from prior involvement in the preparatory stages of a tender procedure, which cannot be remedied by less intrusive means;

(viii) significant or persistent deficiencies in the performance of a substantive requirement under a prior public contract, a prior contract with a contracting entity, or a prior concession contract which led to early termination of that prior contract, damages, or other comparable sanctions (the 'prior performance' ground);

(ix) serious misrepresentation or failure to submit evidence in response to exclusion or selection criteria;

(x) attempts to exercise undue influence, obtain confidential information, or negligently provide misleading information that may have a material influence on decisions concerning exclusion, selection, or award.

4.08 Member States may elect to make any of the above exclusion grounds mandatory. They are required to specify the maximum period during which exclusion will apply if this is not set out in a judgment against the operator, up to a maximum of five years from the date of conviction for the mandatory grounds and three years from the relevant event for the discretionary grounds. There is no maximum period specified for exclusion due to non-payment of tax or social security contributions. The maximum look-back periods are in addition to the 'self-cleaning' provision set out in Article 57(6), under which any operator may provide evidence that it has taken measures which demonstrate its reliability despite the existence of exclusion grounds. Contracting authorities are obliged to take such information into account in making decisions about exclusion.[9] Member States or contracting authorities may also authorize the inclusion of a candidate which is bankrupt, insolvent, or in a similar situation where it can demonstrate that it will be able to perform the contract.[10]

---

[9] Unless the operator has been excluded from participating in public procurement or concession procedures by a final judgment which is effective in the jurisdiction where the contract is being awarded.

[10] Art 57(4) Public Sector Directive, last indent.

With regard to the fourth ground of 'grave professional misconduct', the scope of **4.09**
activities which this may cover was examined by the Court in the *Forposta* case.[11] The
wording has been amended from the version which appeared in the 2004 directives,
to include the clarification that grave professional misconduct must be such as to render the integrity of the candidate questionable. This follows from the Court's finding
in *Forposta* that professional misconduct requires 'wrongful conduct which has an
impact on the professional credibility of the operator'.[12] The contracting authority in
Forposta had relied on a provision of Polish law allowing exclusion of a candidate if the
contracting authority had previously terminated a contract owing to circumstances
for which the candidate was responsible, and at least 5 per cent of the value of the
contract remained unperformed. While the Court held that deficiencies in performance of a prior contract could in theory constitute grave professional misconduct,
this required a specific and individual assessment of the operator's conduct.[13]

No explicit grounds for exclusion based on defective performance existed under the **4.10**
2004 directives; this has now been incorporated in a very limited form in the 2014
directives. In order to exclude an operator based on direct knowledge of defects in its
prior performance, there are four conditions: (i) the deficiencies must have been significant and persistent; (ii) they must relate to a substantive requirement of the prior
contract; (iii) they must have arisen in a public or utilities sector contract or concession;
and (iv) they must have led to early termination, damages, or other comparable sanctions. These cumulative conditions severely restrict the possibility to exclude an operator based on poor past performance. It is unclear what the justification for the third
condition may be, as serious deficiencies in performance of a private sector contract
may be just as pertinent as those occurring under a public contract. The need to have
detailed records in respect of any deficiencies is obvious, and an operator may seek
to establish its reliability under the self-cleaning provisions, despite the four conditions being established. Unless a judgment has been issued against the operator which
specifically bars it from public contracts for a longer period, the maximum exclusion
period under this provision is three years.[14]

The overall effect of the changes to the exclusion grounds is that while greater scope **4.11**
to exclude operators in dubious situations exists, this is accompanied by limitation
periods and the ability for operators to dispute the legitimacy of their exclusion based
on corrective actions taken. Article 57 of the Public Sector Directive[15] thus seeks to
balance the ability of contracting authorities to avoid unscrupulous or unstable contractors and the danger that certain undertakings will be blacklisted unfairly. For the

---

[11] Case C-465/11 *Forposta SA, ABC Direct Contact sp zoo v Poczta Polska SA*, not yet reported.
[12] Case C-465/11 *Forposta*, para 27.
[13] Case C-465/11 *Forposta*, para 31.
[14] Art 57(7) Public Sector Directive.
[15] Under Art 80 of the Utilities Directive, contracting entities may apply any of the exclusion
grounds listed in the Public Sector Directive, and may be obliged by Member States to apply certain
of them. Contracting authorities which award contracts under the Utilities Directive must apply
the mandatory exclusion grounds. Article 38(4)–(10) of the Concessions Directive replicate both

most part, this appears to have been achieved in the wording of Article 57, with the exception of the tax and social security provisions, which could be unfair to operators in certain circumstances,[16] and the 'prior performance' ground, which seems unduly tilted in favour of economic operators. While contracting authorities may take into account information other than that directly provided to them by candidates, it is still quite difficult to exclude an operator based on evidence of poor or negligent past performance. Given these limitations, elimination of candidates with poor records is more readily achieved through criteria for qualitative selection.

Criteria for Qualitative Selection

4.12 Criteria for qualitative selection ('selection criteria') allow for reduction in the number of candidates who will be invited to tender, or in the open procedure for eligibility for tender evaluation or award of contract to be determined. As a general rule, they are directed towards the past or present situation of an economic operator, whereas technical specifications and award criteria relate to what will be performed in the future. This distinction, belaboured by the Court in *Lianakis*, has been partially eroded by the provision in the 2014 directives, allowing experience to be evaluated at award stage in some cases.[17] Reforms to selection criteria under the 2014 directives are primarily aimed at addressing the concern that these are sometimes used unfairly to eliminate operators, and that they add a layer of bureaucracy in multi-stage procedures. Nevertheless, selection (or eligibility) criteria are an essential part of competitive procurement, as they allow for basic considerations about the suitability of an operator to be separated from consideration of its economic and technical offer.

4.13 The general headings under which selection criteria are organized—suitability to pursue the professional activity, economic and financial standing, and technical and professional ability—have not changed. The list of permissible selection

---

the mandatory and discretionary exclusion grounds found in the Public Sector Directive. Article 38(7)(i) of the Concessions Directive contains a further discretionary ground of exclusion in respect of defence and security sector concessions, where the operator has been found on the basis of any evidence not to possess the reliability to exclude risks to State security.

[16] Eg where an amnesty or change of law means that although payments are technically outstanding, there is no fault on the part of the operator. It is a matter of national law whether in such situations the judgment or decision against the operator will still be considered to be 'final and binding' and the operator is still considered to be in breach of its obligations within the terms set out in Art 57(2).

[17] Article 67(2)(b) of the Public Sector Directive provides that the organization, qualification, and experience of staff can be evaluated at award stage 'where the quality of the staff assigned can have a significant impact on the level of performance of the contract'—surely the case in most contracts. However, where this option is taken, such matters cannot also be assessed at selection stage (Annex XII, Part II, point (f)).

criteria for public contracts continues to be an exhaustive one, in contrast to the list of award criteria, which is illustrative only.[18] Both types of criteria must be related to the subject-matter of the specific contract being awarded, but in the case of selection criteria there is an additional requirement that these be proportionate to it. Selection criteria may address:

Suitability to pursue professional activity

(i) enrolment on a professional or trade register;
(ii) for service contracts, authorization or membership of a professional organization if this is required in order to perform the service in the operator's country of origin;

Economic and financial standing

(iii) financial and economic criteria such as a minimum annual turnover, turnover in the area of the contract, and ratio of assets to liabilities;
(iv) appropriate levels of professional risk indemnity insurance;

Technical and professional ability

(v) criteria evaluating human and technical resources, including references regarding performance of previous contracts;
(vi) absence of any conflict of interest;
(vii) criteria evaluating skills, efficiency, experience, and reliability;[19]
(viii) evidence of quality assurance and environmental management systems in place.

The forms of evidence which may be requested in respect of these criteria are set **4.14** out in Annex XII of the Public Sector Directive. This includes the familiar forms of evidence from the 2004 directives such as statements of manpower or samples of products, together with a new possibility to require evidence of supply chain management and tracking systems. This reflects the general move under the directives to make it possible to extend verification of compliance beyond primary or first-tier contractors. There is also greater flexibility regarding the look-back period for previous contracts, with the possibility to take account of contracts carried out more than five years ago (for works contracts) or three years ago (for services and supplies) if this is necessary to ensure adequate competition.[20]

---

[18] Article 58(1) of the Public Sector Directive states that contracting authorities 'may only impose' the selection criteria listed in that article, whereas Art 67 provides that award criteria 'may comprise, for instance…' Greater flexibility is provided regarding choice of selection criteria under the Utilities Directive, with Art 78 merely stipulating that these must be objective and available to interested economic operators.
[19] With the exception of supply contracts which do not involve any element of siting or installation.
[20] Annex XII, Pt II(a) Public Sector Directive.

4.15   In relation to turnover, Article 58(3) stipulates that contracting authorities may not require a level greater than two times the contract value unless special justification applies—a measure intended to remove one barrier to SME access. However, this limit is expressed by reference to the 'estimated contract value'—as opposed to its annual value. If this is interpreted literally, the minimum turnover required in respect of any multi-year contract could still pose a significant barrier to SMEs. It is also possible for contracting authorities to set a minimum value for turnover related to the area of the contract, and no upper limit appears to apply to this value. For framework agreements involving mini-competitions, the turnover value is to be set by reference to the maximum size of contracts which may be performed at the same time, or if this is not known, the overall value of the framework. If a contract is awarded in lots, the turnover value can relate to the maximum number of lots which a candidate may be expected to perform at the same time.[21]

4.16   The drafting of the provisions on turnover therefore offer multiple ways to evade an 'SME friendly' approach. In addition to the exception for duly justified cases, the use of the total (multi-year) value of the contract as a reference, setting a requirement for turnover in the area of the contract only, or calculation based on the total value of the framework or multiple lots which may be performed simultaneously (even if the chance of an operator winning all such lots is minimal) would all effectively push the minimum turnover required upwards. This means that the utility of the turnover limit in promoting SME access is entirely dependent on the desire of contracting authorities, or indeed Member States, to apply it in the manner intended.[22] A further safeguard may be available through the general proportionality requirement which applies to selection criteria.[23]

4.17   In multi-stage procedures, additional criteria may be applied to reduce the number of candidates to be invited to the next stage, provided such criteria are objective and non-discriminatory.[24] The minimum number to be invited must be stated in the contract notice, subject to the absolute minima prescribed for each procedure, and it is also possible to set a maximum number. Where this is done, there is a need to consider how situations in which two or more candidates achieve the same score under the stipulated criteria will be dealt with. For example, if the fifth, sixth, and seventh highest scoring candidates in a restricted procedure all obtain the same score, it would be necessary to invite all three to tender unless a method for resolving such situations has been specified in advance, which accords with the principles of equal treatment and transparency. For this reason, contracting authorities often opt to state

---

[21] Art 58(3) Public Sector Directive.

[22] The intention of this provision to facilitate SME access is set out in Recital 83 of the Public Sector Directive.

[23] Article 58(1) of the Public Sector Directive provides that all selection requirements must be 'related and proportionate to the subject-matter of the contract'.

[24] Art 65 Public Sector Directive.

the maximum number as a range, or to omit the maximum altogether, allowing the cut-off decision to be made based on the 'natural breaking point' in scores. The latter approach does create some risk of an impractically large tender list arising.

The 2014 directives are silent on the weighting and scoring of selection criteria, **4.18** although the Court's judgment in *Universale-Bau*, discussed in Chapter 2, indicates that this may take place. The recitals to Directive 2004/18/EC stated that such criteria 'do not necessarily imply weightings'—thereby acknowledging that they may be weighted in some cases. In an open procedure, selection or eligibility criteria may only be assessed on a pass or fail basis, as no reduction of the number of qualified bidders is permitted under Article 65. In other procedures, providing the weighting of selection criteria in advance is likely to limit the potential for challenges on transparency grounds, although some thought must be given to the treatment of ties and cut-off points for selection as indicated in paragraph 4.17.

The question of *to whom* selection criteria are applied can in practice lead to some **4.19** difficulty. Groups of economic operators (including temporary associations) cannot be required to take any particular legal form during the tender procedure, although rules for how selection criteria will be applied to groups may be specified either in national legislation or by the contracting authority for a particular procedure.[25] Any such rules which are different from the conditions imposed on individual participants must be proportionate and justified by objective reasons. The 2014 directives also provide, as previously, that operators may rely on the capacity of others for the purpose of demonstrating their compliance with selection criteria, regardless of the links which exist between them.[26] This is subject to the operator demonstrating that it will have access to the capacities claimed during the actual performance of the contract. For example, if a company refers to the equipment or professional qualifications of its partner or subcontractor in an expression of interest, it may be required to provide a guarantee that the relevant people or machines will be made available for the contract in question. This principle has been developed in the Court's case law over a number of years,[27] with a functional approach being taken to determine whether economic operators are entitled to rely on resources claimed.

In most cases, application of the principle is straightforward; however, it does raise **4.20** the question of how the entities relied upon should be treated. If a parent company's finances are cited as evidence of possessing the relevant financial standing,

---

[25] Art 19(3) Public Sector Directive; Art 37(2) Utilities Directive; and Art 26(2) Concessions Directive.

[26] Art 63 Public Sector Directive; Art 79 Utilities Directive; and Art 38(2) Concessions Directive.

[27] See Cases C-389/92 *Ballast Nedam Groep NV v Belgian State* [1994] ECR I-01289; C-176/98 *Holst Italia SpA v Comune di Cagliari* [1999] ECR I-0860; C-314/01 *Siemens AG Österreich and ARGE Telekom & Partner v Hauptverband der österreichischen Sozialversicherungsträger* [2004] ECR I-02549; C-399/05 *Commission v Hellenic Republic* [2007] ECR I-00101; C-95/10 *Strong Segurança*

must the parent company's tax compliance also be examined as part of the selection process? In general, exclusion and selection criteria are to be applied to the economic operator applying for the contract, which may in some cases be a grouping or consortium. However, Article 63 of the Public Sector Directive makes clear that where reliance is placed on another entity, regardless of the links between it and the candidate, there is an obligation to verify that the entity complies with the mandatory exclusion criteria and any relevant selection criteria. If not, the authority may require that the entity be replaced. The same principle applies if a grouping relies on one of its members for the fulfilment of a particular criterion. In relation to subcontractors, the 2014 directives offer the ability to extend application of exclusion and selection criteria 'downwards'—to cover other entities involved in the delivery of the contract, and to require the replacement of subcontractors who do not meet the stated criteria.[28]

4.21 Where an operator relies on the financial and economic standing of another, the contracting authority can insist on joint liability for performance of the contract. Authorities are also able to require the tenderer itself, or a particular member of a grouping, to perform certain 'critical tasks' which form part of a contract.[29] The concern of Article 63, then (and the corresponding provisions in the Utilities Directive), is to balance the freedom of operators to bid for contracts in various constellations, with the integrity of the selection process and security regarding contract execution. The provisions regarding application of criteria to entities other than the main candidate are more extensive than those which appeared in the 2004 directives. However, in practice, the ability to identify unsuitable or unqualified companies may be constrained by reliance on self-declarations, which the 2014 directives endorse as a form of evidence of compliance with criteria.

Means of Proof

4.22 The European Single Procurement Document (ESPD) is a form of self-declaration which may be used by economic operators to attest to their compliance with exclusion and selection criteria, including those applied to shortlist candidates. At the time of writing, the standard electronic form of the ESPD had not been published by the Commission, so its precise contents and the extent to which this will be adaptable by economic operators are not known. The intention is to provide a standard, electronic format which can be readily updated. Contracting authorities

---

SA v Municipio de Sintra [2011] ECR I-1867; and C-218/11 *Edukovizig and Hochtief Construction AG*, not yet reported.

[28] Art 71(6)(b) Public Sector Directive; Art 88(6)(b) Utilities Directive; and Art 42(4)(b) Concessions Directive. Further consideration is given to the provisions on subcontracting in Chapter 5.

[29] Art 63(2) Public Sector Directive; and Art 79(3) Utilities Directive.

are required to accept the ESPD as 'preliminary evidence in replacement of certificates issued by public authorities or third parties'. The suggestion that the ESPD replaces only 'certificates' contrasts with the idea that it will cover all forms of qualitative selection criteria. It is difficult to see how a standard form could adequately present the specific information regarding previous experience, qualifications, skills, and human and technical resources which may be relevant for a particular contract. In fact, over-reliance on such standard documents may be to the detriment of SMEs, inasmuch as it encourages a formalistic assessment of relevant capacities and experience.

As with the requirement to publish full procurement documents at the outset of **4.23** a multi-stage procedure, the introduction of the ESPD seems likely to introduce as many problems as it solves. If it is submitted in response to a pre-qualification questionnaire, for example, the contracting authority will have to determine which of the selection criteria can be satisfied by production of a certificate, and accept the ESPD as preliminary evidence of compliance with those criteria. In relation to other criteria requiring a more tailored or narrative response, the ESPD may not suffice. Such situations could lead to clarifications and delays to procedures, with the exception of those where only certificates are required. The ESPD contains a declaration that the supporting documents can be provided 'without delay' and an indication of any database from which they may be obtained.[30] The use of the central e-Certis database is mandated under the 2014 directives, albeit with the possibility for Member States to postpone application until 2018.[31]

Supporting documents may be requested at any point if this is necessary to ensure **4.24** the proper conduct of the procedure—unless they are available free of charge from a database or the contracting authority 'already possesses' the documents.[32] The concept of possession may be open to interpretation—for example, where documents were submitted some time ago or to another department or unit within the contracting authority. Article 59(5) seems to preclude a requirement to produce supporting documents even if those which the authority already possesses are out of date or deficient in some way. This contrasts with the general duty on authorities to verify compliance with exclusion and selection criteria.[33]

A further complication arises regarding reliance on the ESPD in multi-stage **4.25** procedures. Under Article 59, contracting authorities are required to accept the ESPD as preliminary evidence, with supporting documents being provided prior

---

[30] Art 59(1) Public Sector Directive. Article 61 creates a requirement to consult the EU online repository of such certificates, e-Certis (<http://ec.europa.eu/markt/ecertis>).

[31] Art 90(5) Public Sector Directive.

[32] Art 59(5) Public Sector Directive. Recital 85 states that this provision should not come into effect until fully electronic tendering is in place (facilitating access to documents previously submitted), and Member States are entitled under Art 90 to postpone application of this provision until 18 October 2018.

[33] Art 56(1)(b) Public Sector Directive; and Art 76(5) Utilities Directive.

to contract award. However, in any multi-stage procedure, this creates the possibility that a candidate will be invited to tender who does not, in fact, meet the stated exclusion or selection criteria. If this is only discovered at the preferred bidder stage, the natural solution would be to turn to the next highest-scoring bidder.[34] This may be open to challenge by candidates who have lost their opportunity to tender to an unqualified operator, who could demand that the tender stage be re-run instead. The frequency with which such situations may arise should not be underestimated, as candidates routinely fail to meet exclusion or selection criteria on inspection. The recitals to the Public Sector Directive seem to acknowledge this problem, suggesting that in multi-stage procedures supporting documents should in fact be requested prior to invitation to tender.[35] This solves the problem, but detracts from any administrative simplification which the ESPD may offer.

4.26 Beyond the ESPD, Article 60 sets out the various references and records which may be required as means of proof of compliance with exclusion and selection criteria. Article 62 governs the use of quality assurance standards and environmental management systems at selection stage. Contracting authorities may request[36] certificates from independent bodies to attest to candidates' compliance with such standards or systems, and must accept equivalent certificates. The ability to insist on third-party certification is strengthened in comparison to the 2004 directives, as operators may only rely on in-house systems if they can demonstrate that they had no access to such certificates, or no possibility of obtaining them within the relevant time periods, due to factors which are 'not attributable' to them. Environmental management systems can now be requested in respect of all contracts, whereas previously this was limited to services and works contracts.[37]

4.27 In contrast to the (preliminary) reliance on self-declarations invited by the ESPD, other provisions of the 2014 directives aim to enhance contracting authorities' ability to objectively verify compliance with criteria. Under this heading, we find the new provisions on labels and test reports, certification, and other means of proof.[38] The ability to request third-party labels has been extended to cover labels which concern social and other characteristics, in addition to eco-labels. As the volume and variety of such labels has grown, the ability to distinguish between those which are independent and objective and those which are industry fig leaves has become vital. It is not possible to insist on a particular label; however, references to

---

[34] Provided this possibility has been reserved in the tender documents: see discussion at paras 5.41 *et seq.*

[35] Recital 84 Public Sector Directive.

[36] The term 'require' is used in Art 62 and in Art 43 on labels; however, in both cases, this is accompanied by the ability of the operator to rely on equivalent certificates or labels and, in certain cases, in-house systems or technical dossiers—meaning a specific certificate or label cannot really be 'required'. See discussion at paras 7.32 *et seq.*

[37] Compare Annex XII, Part II, point (g) Public Sector Directive with Art 50 Directive 2004/18/EC.

[38] Arts 43 and 44 Public Sector Directive; and Arts 61 and 62 Utilities Directive.

specific labels are permitted in technical specifications, award criteria, and contract performance clauses if certain conditions are met, namely:

(i) the label requirements only concern criteria which are linked to the subject-matter of the contract and are appropriate to define characteristics of the works, supplies, or services that are the subject matter of the contract;

(ii) the label requirements are based on objectively verifiable and non-discriminatory criteria;

(iii) the label is established in an open and transparent procedure in which all relevant stakeholders, including government bodies, consumers, social partners, manufacturers, distributors, and non-governmental organizations, may participate;

(iv) the label is accessible to all interested parties; and

(v) the label requirements are set by a third party over which the economic operator applying for the label cannot exercise a decisive influence.

Equivalent labels must also be accepted, but the ability of tenderers to rely instead on a 'technical dossier' has been curtailed: this can only be done where the label is not available to the tenderer for reasons not attributable to it. Labels concerning matters which are not linked to the subject-matter of the contract—for example, general corporate practices or membership of a trade organization—cannot be requested directly, but the underlying criteria from such labels may be referenced.[39]

4.28 Test reports and certificates from conformity assessment bodies may also be requested to demonstrate compliance with technical specifications, award criteria, or contract clauses. Conformity assessment bodies play a key role in the practical implementation of mutual recognition both within the EU and with other countries such as Australia, Canada, Japan, New Zealand, the United States, and Switzerland. They are accredited under Regulation (EC) No 765/2008 to perform the calibration, testing, inspection, and certification of products which are subject to harmonized standards, including the use of the CE marking. As with labels, recourse by operators to test reports or certificates from equivalent bodies is possible, or to other appropriate means of proof if such reports or certificates

---

[39] The formulation of Art 43 can be read as only requiring that the criteria underlying a label be cited where the label also sets requirements which are not linked to the subject-matter of a contract. However, this contrasts markedly with the Court's statement in *Dutch Coffee* that the need to cite the detailed criteria underlying a label 'is indispensable in order to allow potential tenderers to refer to a single official document, coming from the contracting authority itself and thus without being subject to the uncertainties of searching for information and the possible temporal variations in the criteria applicable to a particular eco-label' (para 67 of judgment). Although the 2014 directives clearly envision a wider ability to rely on labels as a means of proof, in the author's view where the requirements of labels are used to formulate technical specifications, reference should be made to the underlying criteria, and not just the label itself. The position may be different where labels are referred to in award criteria and contract performance clauses, given the greater discretion which contracting authorities have over their formulation. See further discussion at paras 7.32 *et seq*.

are unavailable to it. The onus is on the operator to demonstrate equivalence or non-availability of certificates in such cases.

Technical Specifications

4.29 Technical specifications define the characteristics required of a good, service, or work. They are present in all procedures with the exception of competitive dialogue and design contests, where the characteristics of solutions are instead proposed by participants. In other procedures, if a tender does not meet the minimum requirements set out in the technical specifications, it must be rejected.[40] The careful formulation of specifications is therefore essential, and forms the core of most procurement documents. The rules on technical specifications often appear to relate more closely to supply contracts than services or works, but they are equally applicable to all three types of contract. Under the 2014 directives and their predecessors, technical specifications may either be formulated by reference to standards, technical assessments, or other technical reference systems; in terms of performance or functional requirements; or by some combination of these approaches.

4.30 The use of performance- or outcome-based specifications is seen as a means of encouraging innovation and wider competition for contracts. Instead of prescribing inputs or the precise manner in which supplies, services, or works are to be provided, such specifications focus on the outcome to be achieved, normally accompanied by minimum performance levels. The use of variants, whereby operators may propose alternative solutions to meet the contracting authority's minimum requirements, can also encourage innovation and competition. Submission of variants may be either mandatory or optional, and tenderers may be required to submit a non-variant bid alongside any variant.[41] The authorization of variants must be indicated in the contract notice, and the minimum requirements which they are to meet stated in the procurement documents. Variants are assessed against the same contract award criteria as non-variant solutions, allowing the authority to determine which solution best meets its needs. Variants may be used, for example, if an authority wishes to compare conventional diesel or petrol vehicles with alternative-fuelled, electric or hybrid options; or if it wishes to compare a managed print service with conventional printing.

4.31 Performance-based specifications and variants are particularly useful where the range of solutions available on the market is unknown or the authority wishes to

---

[40] Art 56(1)(a) Public Sector Directive; and Art 76(5) Utilities Directive. The obligation to reject tenders which do not meet the technical specifications was highlighted by the Court in Case C-243/89 *Commission v Kingdom of Denmark* ('*Storebaelt*') [1993] ECR I-03353, para 37 and Case C-561/12 *Nordecon AS and Ramboll Eesti AS v Rahandusministeerium* ('*Nordecon*'), not yet reported, paras 37–9.
[41] Art 45 Public Sector Directive; and Art 64 Utilities Directive.

compare different service models or technologies—to determine their effect on cost or quality. However, in some cases, they may simply postpone the point at which a decision needs to be made, while adding to the complexity of tender submission and evaluation. For example, if an authority specifies that it wishes to purchase cleaning services and does not specify any of the inputs (for example, person days or hours) or methods to be applied, it may receive a range of offers with very different levels of service provision. The same is true in a tender for vehicles—where unsuitable models may be proposed. The absence of detailed specifications or the inclusion of variants can prompt bidders to innovate, but it may also mean they do not fully appreciate the authority's needs and preferences. In order to evaluate and distinguish between tenders in terms of cost and quality, the contracting authority will rely on award criteria, the application of which can become difficult where bids have been submitted based on different cost or delivery models. The use of performance-based specifications or variants should therefore be accompanied by careful consideration of how the evaluation methodology will be applied and bids compared.

Approaches to devising technical specifications vary widely and are influenced **4.32** by the subject matter of the contract, institutional, and national practices. The overriding concern of the directives is to prevent technical specifications being used in a way which may discriminate against certain operators or unduly limit competition. These ambitions are shared by the rules on specifications set out in Article X of the GPA; however, there is one notable difference in their formulation. Whereas the directives afford pre-eminence to national standards transposing European standards, the GPA naturally prefers international standards.[42] This appears to create a conflict where a tender is subject to both regimes; however, in practice, it is likely to be resolved by the requirement to accept equivalents which applies under both instruments. The inclusion of environmental characteristics in technical specifications is also explicitly highlighted in the GPA. The opening up of European procurement markets under the GPA and bilateral trade agreements is likely to bring more focus to the ability of public authorities to include environmental and social requirements in technical specifications which go beyond legally prescribed minima.

The 2014 directives clarify that specifications may concern production processes or **4.33** other stages of the life cycle, as well as the transfer of intellectual property rights.[43]

---

[42] Art 42(3)(b) Public Sector Directive; Art 60(3)(b) Utilities Directive; and Art X(2)(b) GPA.

[43] The former provision is accompanied by the statement that production processes, etc. may form part of technical specifications 'even where such factors do not form part of their material substance, provided that they are linked to the subject-matter of the contract and proportionate to its value and its objectives' (Art 42(1) Public Sector Directive). To understand the meaning of this statement, one must be aware of the Commission's former stance regarding the need for production processes to materially alter the substance of what is being purchased, discussed at paragraph 4.42 below and in Chapter 7 in the context of environmental specifications.

A non-exhaustive list of characteristics which may be addressed in technical specifications is set out in Annex VII of the Public Sector Directive. Accessibility criteria for persons with disabilities must be included for all goods, services, or works which will be used by people. The effect of these provisions is to confirm that technical specifications may concern the totality of characteristics which define a particular good, service, or work. However, there is one area in which uncertainty remains regarding the permissible scope of specifications: social and labour conditions within the supply chain. Unlike environmental characteristics, no mention is made of social characteristics (other than accessibility for disabled users) in Article 42. Recital 99 of the Public Sector Directive provides that:

> In technical specifications contracting authorities can provide such social requirements which directly characterise the product or service in question, such as accessibility for persons with disabilities or design for all users.

4.34 Does this preclude technical specifications which require payment of a living wage, a fair trade premium, or observance of other social conditions not prescribed in legislation or collective agreements? The Commission has frequently asserted that such matters are best addressed in contract performance clauses—however, the Court in *Dutch Coffee* held that they can also be applied as award criteria. This may allow such considerations to be addressed effectively in many tenders; however, there is a good reason to examine whether they may also form part of technical specifications. Award criteria and contract performance clauses do not necessarily form the basis for rejection of tenders, whereas non-compliance with specifications does.[44] Inclusion of a living wage provision, for example, only in award criteria or contract clauses may leave open the possibility that a tenderer who does not adequately reflect this requirement in its pricing would be successful.

4.35 The Court held in *Dutch Coffee* that conditions which relate to the acquisition by a supplier of goods from the manufacturer did not meet the definition of technical specifications under Directive 2004/18/EC.[45] However, given that this definition has now been changed to explicitly include factors which do not form part of the material substance of the final product or service, and which may relate to methods of *provision* as well as production, an argument can be advanced that this includes social characteristics of the supply chain, such as fair trade criteria or payment of a living wage. In the case of services, the conditions under which labour occurs may be the only method

---

[44] Where a tender does not respond to a particular award criterion, it will simply fail to attain marks under that criterion. Unless a minimum score has been prescribed (an approach discussed below), it may still be the most economically advantageous tender. Contract performance clauses, according to Recital 104, 'constitute fixed objective requirements that have no impact on the assessment of tenders'. These two approaches may therefore be insufficient to address non-legislative social requirements in the context of a tender.

[45] Case C-368/10 *Commission v Kingdom of the Netherlands* ('*Dutch Coffee*'), not yet reported, para 74.

of provision.[46] Further support for this position is derived from the possibility under the 2014 directives to refer to both environmental and social labels in technical specifications.[47] Social labels generally address supply chain criteria such as decent wages and conditions of work. Advocate General Kokott made clear in her opinion in *Dutch Coffee* that such considerations were linked to the subject matter of the contract, provided they apply to the specific products or services being purchased rather than the general corporate practices of a tenderer.[48] If social labels meet the other requirements set out in Article 43 relating to transparency, they can now form part of technical specifications, subject to an obligation to accept equivalents.

Uncertainty regarding the ability to insist on labour standards or wages above legal **4.36** minima arose from the *Rüffert* case.[49] The case concerned a works contract which had been terminated by a German authority due to the failure of a subcontractor to comply with minimum rates of pay set out in a collective agreement. Public authorities were obligated under German law to comply with such agreements and to procure the compliance of their contractors and sub-contractors. The case turned on the compatibility of this obligation with the Posted Workers Directive (PWD) and Article 49 of the Treaty, on freedom of establishment.[50] The PWD requires that where workers are posted from one Member State to another, they must be guaranteed certain minimum terms and conditions of employment. The minimum terms are those set out in laws, regulations, or administrative provisions, as well as those contained in collective agreements which have been declared universally applicable, meaning they must be observed by all undertakings in the geographical area and in the profession or industry concerned. The Court held that as the law in question referred to collective agreements which were not universally applicable, and did not itself fix minimum wage rates, the authority was not entitled to impose the higher rate of pay on posted workers.[51]

The Court in *Rüffert* emphasized that imposing higher wage requirements on **4.37** posted workers had the potential to undermine the competitive advantage of undertakings based in lower-wage Member States and to impede the free movement of services. The Court did not consider case law arising under the procurement directives such as *Beentjes* and *Nord Pas de Calais*—which point to a wider discretion over terms and conditions of employment in the context of public contracts. Criticism of this judgment has emphasized this omission as well as the Court's

---

[46] Annex VII of the Public Sector, point 1(b) includes 'production processes and methods at any stage of the life cycle of the supply or service' in the definition of technical specifications.

[47] Art 43(1) Public Sector Directive; and Art 61(1) Utilities Directive.

[48] Case C-368/10 *Dutch Coffee*, Advocate General's opinion at paras 110–13.

[49] Case C-346/06 *Dirk Rüffert v Land Niedersachsen* ('*Rüffert*') [2008] ECR I-01989.

[50] Directive 96/71/EC of the European Parliament and of the Council of 16 December 1996 concerning the posting of workers in the framework of the provision of services.

[51] Case C-346/06 *Rüffert*, paras 24–35.

failure to consider the equal treatment implications where collective agreements are binding only on domestic contractors.[52] In *Bundesdruckerei*, the Court held that a contracting authority could not require compliance with minimum wage legislation on the part of subcontractors located in another Member State, while accepting that such a measure could in principle be justified based on the objective of protecting employees and avoiding social dumping.[53] The case concerned a contract awarded by the City of Dortmund for data entry services, in which the application of the minimum wage requirement was challenged by a bidder using a Polish subcontractor. The Court found that the minimum wage requirement was disproportionate inasmuch as it applied only to public sector contracts and bore no relation to the cost of living in other Member States, thus depriving them of a competitive advantage.

4.38 However, the wording of the operative part of the judgment is confined to cases in which 'a tenderer intends to carry out a public contract by having recourse exclusively to workers employed by a subcontractor established in a Member State other than that to which the contracting authority belongs'. This suggests that the situation would be different if a contractor intends to rely in part or wholly on workers in the Member State where minimum wage legislation or a collective agreement applies, provided it is universally applicable in accordance with the *Rüffert* judgment. *Bundesdruckerei* itself only deals with cases of extraterritorial application of minimum wages. A further case testing the limits of *Rüffert* was lodged with the Court in 2014.[54] Importantly, the 2014 directives now contain a specific ability for contracting authorities to reject tenders which do not comply with wage provisions or other labour conditions enshrined in collective agreements (or in national, European, or international law)—meaning that such conditions will have the same effect as technical specifications.[55] There is no explicit requirement that the collective agreements be universally applicable, although the recitals to the directives do state that this provision must be applied in conformity with EU law in general and

---

[52] See McCrudden, C. (2011) 'The *Rüffert* Case and Public Procurement' in M. Cremona (ed), *Market Integration and Public Services in the European Union* (Oxford: Oxford University Press), pp 117–48. McCrudden highlights the legal and political background to the case both within Germany and at EU level, as well as the trade union reaction to the ruling. He argues that the Court did not adequately consider the effect of the procurement directives and relevant case law, and that as both the PWD and procurement directives embody political compromises between the Treaty freedoms and social protections, the two must be placed on equal footing in resolving cases such as *Rüffert* (pp 130–3).

[53] Case C-549/13 *Bundesdruckerei GmbH v Stadt Dortmund*, not yet reported, paras 31–3.

[54] Case C-115/14 *RegioPost GmbH & Co KG v Stadt Landau* lodged on 11 March 2014. The questions referred to the Court relate to requirements for contractors and subcontractors to pay certain minimum rates of pay to people employed on public contracts and to make declarations to this effect during the tender procedure. No judgment had been issued at the time of writing.

[55] Arts 18(2) and 56(1) Public Sector Directive; and Arts 36(2) and 76(6) Utilities Directive. Where a tender is abnormally low due to non-compliance with an applicable collective agreement, there is an obligation to reject it under Art 69(3) Public Sector Directive and Art 84(3) Utilities Directive.

the PWD in particular, so the case law on this will remain relevant. [56] The wording of the rules on contract performance conditions has also changed, referring to the link to the subject-matter requirement rather than general compatibility with EU law, and explicitly including 'employment-related considerations'.[57] The effect of these changes is considered in Chapter 5.

In summary, there are good reasons to consider that the 2014 directives allow **4.39** greater scope for addressing payment of fair wages and other labour conditions in technical specifications as well as in award criteria and contract performance clauses. In order to comply with the rules on technical specifications (and the Treaty principles), care must be taken to avoid any formulation which is directly or indirectly discriminatory against undertakings established in other Member States. Arguably, however, where contracting authorities are effectively bound by collective agreements or administrative practices mandating the application of enhanced wages or employment conditions, including these in technical specifications affords a greater degree of transparency for all bidders than including them in contract performance clauses alone. If the application of such standards is truly voluntary, then it may be preferable to address them in award criteria, as this affords the opportunity to assess their impact on other qualitative aspects of tenders and costs.

Award Criteria

The 2014 directives have seen an overhaul of the way in which award criteria **4.40** are defined. The principles governing their formulation and application remain unchanged, however, and are largely the product of the Court's case law. Award criteria are often the linchpin of a procedure, and the way in which they are devised, weighted, and evaluated is of central importance to tenderers and contracting authorities alike. Under the 2014 directives, contracts must be awarded on the basis of 'most economically advantageous tender' (MEAT)—with the option of assessing the best price-quality ratio, or price or cost only. It is not permitted to exclude price or cost from the assessment, even if these are fixed for a given supply or service under national law or other provisions.[58] Member States in implementing the directives may choose to restrict the use of lowest-price or lowest-cost awards. During the revision process, removing the possibility to award based on lowest price from the new directives altogether was suggested by the European

---

[56] Recital 37 Public Sector Directive; and Recital 52 Utilities Directive.

[57] Art 70 Public Sector Directive; and Art 87 Utilities Directive.

[58] Article 67(2) indicates that, where this is the case, 'economic operators will compete on quality criteria only'—raising the question of why a cost element needs to be included in the criteria at all.

Parliament rapporteur and others; however, this was ultimately rejected.[59] The use of lowest price to award contracts for standardised supplies or highly specified works contracts is likely to continue in many Member States.[60]

4.41 The fact that 'most economically advantageous tender' now includes the award of contracts based on price or cost only may lead to some confusion, as under the previous directives it implied that factors other than cost were included.[61] Case law had established that under the old directives 'lowest price only' meant just that: no other criteria could be taken into account at the award stage.[62] This ruled out the use of more sophisticated cost assessment techniques such as life-cycle costing, unless MEAT was specified as the award basis. The term 'best price-quality ratio' is now used to designate award criteria which include qualitative as well as cost elements. Specific rules for life-cycle costing are set out for the first time, which include the possibility to take environmental externalities into account.[63] Other notable changes to the provisions on award criteria are the ability to take the experience of staff assigned to perform a contract into account, and—following from *Dutch Coffee*—processes for the provision or trading of goods, services, or works. Staff qualifications and experience can be evaluated where this can have 'a significant impact on the level of performance of the contract' (surely the case for most contracts) and provided it has not already been assessed at selection stage.[64]

4.42 The general requirements for award criteria derived from case law and incorporated in the directives are that they must: (i) be linked to the subject-matter of the contract; (ii) be clearly stated in the contract notice or tender documents; (iii) not be such as to confer an unrestricted freedom of choice on the authority; and (iv) comply with the Treaty principles. The concept of a 'link to the subject-matter' requirement for award criteria was first articulated by the Court in the *Concordia* case,[65] and was included in the 2004 directives in relation to award criteria only. It has now snowballed, appearing in relation to technical specifications, variants,

---

[59] European Parliament Committee on the Internal Market and Consumer Protection (Rapporteur: Marc Tarabella), *Report on the Proposal for a Directive of the European Parliament and of the Council on Public Procurement* (COM (2011) 0896-C7-0006/2012-2011/0438(COD)), p 150.

[60] Research carried out by the Commission in 2011 indicated that lowest price was being used in approximately one-third of procedures advertised in the Official Journal, whereas MEAT was used in the remaining two-thirds. European Commission, *Evaluation Report: Impact and Effectiveness of EU Public Procurement Legislation*, SEC (2011) 853 final, p 146. Lowest price only was used disproportionately for lower-value contracts.

[61] When lowest price or cost is used, some qualitative assessment of bids will still take place to determine whether they meet the specification. This is done on a pass or fail basis, rather than by assigning a score.

[62] Case C-19/00 *SIAC Construction Ltd v Mayo County Council* [2001] ECR I-07725.

[63] Art 68 Public Sector Directive; and Art 83 Utilities Directive.

[64] Art 67(2)(b) and Annex XII, Part II, point (f) Public Sector Directive; and Art 82(2)(b) Utilities Directive.

[65] Case C-513/99 *Concordia Bus Finland v Helsingin kaupunki and HKL-Bussiliikenne* [2002] ECR I-07213.

labels and contract performance clauses, as well as award criteria in the 2014 directives. What does it mean? Article 67(3) of the Public sector Directive provides that:

> Award criteria shall be considered to be linked to the subject-matter of the public contract where they relate to the works, supplies or services to be provided under that contract in any respect and at any stage of their life cycle, including factors involved in:
> (i) the specific process of production, provision or trading of those works, supplies or services; or
> (ii) a specific process for another stage of their life cycle, even where such factors do not form part of their material substance.

The reference to 'material substance' harkens back to the Commission's previous **4.43** stance on award criteria, under which some discernible impact on the end-product was required. This was rejected by the Court comprehensively in *Dutch Coffee*.[66] The 'link to the subject-matter' test effectively means that criteria must not concern the general practices of an economic operator, but only the specific goods, services, or works being purchased. For example, it would be possible to award marks based on the carbon emissions associated with a particular product being purchased, but not on the basis of a company's overall carbon footprint. The only case in which the Court has found the subject-matter link to be missing is *EVN and Wienstrom*, in which marks were awarded based on the ability of tenderers to supply renewable electricity in excess of the volume required by the contracting authority, and without any upper limit.[67] As the subject-matter link requirement now appears in several places throughout the directives, it may well be the subject of further consideration by the Court.

The second requirement to state award criteria (together with their weightings and **4.44** any sub-criteria) in the contract notice or tender documents follows from the transparency principle, the scope of which is discussed in Chapter 2. The requirement that award criteria do not confer 'an unrestricted freedom of choice' on contracting authorities is also linked to transparency and equal treatment. It was first mentioned by the Court in *Beentjes*, where it held that contacting authorities' discretion in awarding contracts must be exercised based on objective criteria.[68] The idea that such criteria must be capable of being interpreted in the same way by all 'reasonably well-informed and normally diligent tenderers' was introduced in *SIAC*, and in *EVN* the Court held that award criteria must be 'accompanied by requirements which permit the information provided by the tenderers to be effectively verified'.[69]

---

[66] Case C-368/10 *Dutch Coffee*, para 91. See also the opinion of AG Kokott in the case, who observed that: 'Of course the taste of sugar does not vary depending on whether it was traded fairly or unfairly. A product placed on the market on unfair conditions does however leave a bitter taste in the mouth of a socially responsible customer' (at para 110).

[67] Case C-448/01 *EVN and Wienstrom* [2003] ECR I-14527. See discussion at paras 2.45 *et seq*.

[68] Case 31/87 *Gebroeders Beentjes BV v State of the Netherlands* [1988] ECR 04635, para 26.

[69] Case C-448/01 *EVN and Wienstrom*, para 52.

The combined effect of these rules, together with the obligation to publish criteria in advance, is to reduce the risk of arbitrary or biased decisions. However, they should not be taken to mean that public authorities must perfectly anticipate every feature which will determine the relative value of bids.

4.45   Within these confines, contracting authorities enjoy considerable discretion over the formulation, weighting, and evaluation of performance against contract award criteria. The Supreme Court of the United Kingdom has held that the 'reasonably well informed and normally diligent tenderer' is an objective test, which does not turn on evidence of how actual or potential tenderers interpreted the criteria in question.[70] This is to be welcomed, in that it removes the risk that award criteria which are clearly and carefully formulated will be subject to challenge simply because tenderers have chosen to interpret them in different ways. Given that tenderers will naturally interpret criteria in the manner most likely to secure their own competitive advantage, expecting complete uniformity in interpretation is both unrealistic and likely to prolong court proceedings due to the volume of evidence needed to establish how each bidder interpreted the criteria in question. On the other hand, it is vital that courts look to the particular circumstances of a tender in order to interpret award criteria objectively—reviewing the entirety of procurement documents as well as any clarifications or communications with bidders.

4.46   With regard to costs, the 2014 directives emphasize that these may be assessed in a variety of ways—with the obligation to ensure equal treatment of tenderers being paramount. Chapter 6 looks at the way in which cost scores are calculated and how this may affect value for money. Rules regarding life-cycle costing (LCC) have been introduced in the 2014 directives; however, these allow considerable flexibility regarding the range of cost factors which can be included in LCC. Costs arising either for the contracting authority itself or for users may be included, which relate to the acquisition, use, maintenance, or end of life of the goods, services, or works being purchased.[71] LCC may also include costs assigned to environmental externalities, such as greenhouse gas emissions, although the inclusion of social externalities is not yet provided for.[72] In order to include environmental externalities, the authority must specify the method by which it will use to monetize these. The method must:

(i)   be based on objectively verifiable and non-discriminatory criteria;
(ii) be accessible to all interested parties; and

---

[70] *Healthcare at Home Ltd (Appellant) v The Common Services Agency (Respondent) Scotland* [2014] UKSC 49.

[71] Art 68(1) Public Sector Directive; and Art 83(1) Utilities Directive.

[72] Recital 96 of the Public Sector Directive calls for the examination at Union level of the feasibility of a common methodology for social life-cycle costing, building on the UN Guidelines for Social Life Cycle Assessment of Products.

(iii) require only data which can be provided with reasonable effort by normally diligent tenderers, including those outside of the EU.[73]

Where a common mandatory method exists at EU level for LCC in a specific sector, this must be applied. While this provision may assist in preventing fragmentation and help to harmonize sector-specific approaches to LCC, its success depends very much on the user-friendliness of methods developed at EU level. The list at present consists only of the Clean Vehicles Directive, and it may be some time before such measures are adopted in other sectors.

Qualitative award criteria afford even greater discretion to contracting authorities **4.47** to target those areas which are of greatest importance to them. Technical merit, aesthetic and functional considerations, and social, environmental, and innovative characteristics may all form part of the assessment of quality, weighted to reflect the authority's priorities. One point worth noting is that 'compliance with specification' should not be considered an award criterion, as failure to comply with technical specifications means a tender must be rejected, as explained in paragraph 4.29. Qualitative award criteria should relate to preferences rather than mandatory requirements, with the factors which will contribute to assessment under each criterion or sub-criterion explained in the procurement documents. The approach which will be taken to verify performance must also be clear, whether this is based on statements from tenderers or third-party evidence in the form of certificates, labels, or test reports. References and other indications of a tender's reliability or quality may also be assessed at award stage, provided their content and not just their number is taken into account.[74]

The relative weighting of cost and qualitative criteria can determine the out- **4.48** come of a competition. The impact of different weighting and scoring methodologies on evaluation outcomes is explored in Chapters 6 and 8. Assigning a high percentage of marks to cost criteria is sometimes adopted as a strategy to encourage greater price competition. This can leave the contracting authority vulnerable to the submission of a very low-cost tender which, while meeting its technical specifications, performs poorly on quality. To safeguard against such a situation, authorities may adopt a strategy of setting a minimum percentage which must be obtained under some or all of the qualitative criteria. Such an approach is not precluded by anything in the 2014 directives, provided it is published in advance and applied equally to all bidders. A further safeguard against unusually low-priced bids exists in the rules on treatment of abnormally low tenders.

---

[73] Art 68(2) Public Sector Directive; and Art 83(2) Utilities Directive.
[74] Case C-324/93 *The Queen v Secretary of State for Home Department, ex p Evans Medical Ltd and Macfarlan Smith Ltd* [1995] ECR I-00563, para 50; and Case C-315/01 *Gesellschaft für Abfallentsorgungs-Technik GmbH (GAT) v Österreichische Autobahnen und Schnellstraßen AG (ÖSAG)* [2003] ECR I-06351, paras 66–7.

Abnormally Low Tenders

4.49   The concept of abnormally low tenders has been recognized in the EU procurement directives since 1971.[75] Where a tenderer submits an unusually low-priced bid, this may be due to legitimate factors such as a competitive advantage it enjoys based on its greater efficiency, cheaper inputs, or even the ability to take a loss on the contract. It may also be due to illegitimate factors, such as underpayment of staff or subcontractors, or failure to abide by relevant legislation. Under previous directives, case law on abnormally low tenders tended to focus on the need to investigate the individual situation, as opposed to automatically eliminating a tender which appears to be abnormally low.[76] The High Court of England and Wales in *Varney* rejected the idea of a duty to investigate abnormally low tenders being owed to other bidders.[77] However, in *SAG Slovensko*, the CJEU found that a positive obligation applied to contracting authorities to investigate abnormally low tenders, even where they did not propose to reject them.[78]

4.50   This position has been written into the 2014 directives, so that contracting authorities are obliged to seek an explanation in respect of any tender which 'appears' to be abnormally low.[79] Unfortunately, this is not accompanied by any definition or example of what might constitute an abnormally low tender, leaving it to national measures, or in their absence to the contracting authority, to determine how such tenders will be identified. The Commission's original proposal contained a formula for identifying abnormally low tenders based on comparison with the average price or cost of all tenders received and the next lowest bid to that being examined—however, this was removed in later drafts of the directives.[80] The absence of an EU definition for abnormally low tenders raises a potential conundrum—it is only if the contracting authority itself identifies a

---

[75]   Art 29(5) Council Directive 71/305/EEC of 26 July 1971 concerning the co-ordination of procedures for the award of public works contracts.

[76]   Case C-103/88 *Fratelli Costanzo SpA v Comune di Milano*; Case C-295/89 *Impresa Donà Alfonso di Donà Alfonso & Figli v Consorzio per lo sviluppo industriale del comune di Monfalcone* [1991] ECR I-02967; Joined Cases C-285/99 and C-286/99 *Lombardini and Mantovani* [2001] ECR I-9233; and Joined Cases C-147/06 and C-148/06 *SECAP SpA v Comune di Torino and Santorso Soc coop arl v Comune di Torino* ('*SECAP*') [2008] ECR I-3565.

[77]   *J Varney & Sons Waste Management Ltd v Hertfordshire County Council* [2010] EWHC 1404 (QB).

[78]   Case C-599/10 *SAG Slovensko and Others v Úrad pre verejné obstarávanie*, not reported in the ECR, para 34.

[79]   Art 69 Public Sector Directive; and Art 84 Utilities Directive. Article XV(6) of the GPA allows authorities to seek explanations in respect of abnormally low tenders; however, it does not create an obligation to do so, nor any explicit right to reject an abnormally low tender.

[80]   European Commission COM (2011) 896 final *Proposal for a directive of the European Parliament and the Council on public procurement*, pp 93–4. The proposal stated that a tender should be considered abnormally low where it was more than 50 per cent below the average tender price or cost and more than 20 per cent below the next lowest tender, provided that at least five tenders had been submitted.

tender as abnormally low that an obligation to investigate arises. This may create a disincentive to apply the provision unless national legislation requires contracting authorities to do so in unambiguous terms. This position is far from ideal from the viewpoint of creating coordinated procedures throughout the EU, but it appears that divergences in national approaches to the identification of abnormally low tenders could not be overcome.

Once investigation of an abnormally low tender is undertaken, the authority must   **4.51** take into account explanations relating to a list of factors such as the economic and technical conditions applicable to the operator, its compliance with environmental, social, and labour laws and the rules applicable to subcontracting, and the possibility of it obtaining State aid.[81] The overall objective is to determine whether the tender is 'genuine'—which the CJEU has variously interpreted as meaning 'viable'[82] or 'reliable'.[83] The list of factors to be taken into account is in itself somewhat confusing, as it contains a mixture of those which may legitimate an abnormally low tender (such as exceptionally favourable conditions available to the operator) and those which may render it illegitimate (such as receipt of State aid which is not compatible with the Treaty). The determination of the effect of these factors is left to the contracting authority. Only where the tender is abnormally low due to non-compliance with environmental, social, or labour law is the contracting authority required to reject it.[84] This would include, for example, failure of the tenderer to take account of wage rates set out in applicable collective agreements, or to comply with the Transfer of Undertakings rules.

---

[81] Art 69(2) Public Sector Directive; and Art 84(2) Utilities Directive.
[82] Joined Cases C-147/06 and C-148/06 *SECAP*.
[83] Case T-4/01 *Renco SpA* [2003] ECR II-171; and Case T-148/04 *TQ3 Travel Solutions Belgium SA* [2005] ECR II-2627.
[84] Art 69(3) Public Sector Directive; and Art 84(3) Utilities Directive.

5

CONTRACTS AND MODIFICATIONS
TO CONTRACTS

EU procurement regulation emphasizes process over outcomes. The titles of the **5.01**
2014 directives, unlike their predecessors, do not refer to 'coordination of procedures'—however, the majority of their content still relates to activities which take
place prior to contract award. The small proportion which relates to matters arising after the award of a contract is, however, extremely important, given that it is
the performance of contracts which matters most to contracting authorities and
economic operators. While there are divergences in national law and practice on
the formation and execution of contracts, it is easy to see how the Treaty freedoms
and principles which underlie procurement regulation would be frustrated if the
directives ceased to apply at the moment a contract was signed.[1] The Court has
shown itself to be conscious of this problem in its jurisprudence on modifications
to contracts in particular.

Despite the emergence of more detailed EU rules relating to the contract perfor- **5.02**
mance stage, this remains an area in which considerations other than compliance
with the directives are likely to dominate. The design of contracts is influenced primarily by commercial and practical concerns, which determine whether options,
phased or conditional payments, incentives and penalties (where permissible),
social and environmental clauses, or other terms are used. The use of standardized
contract terms, and the leeway which individual contracting authorities have to
amend these, is also influential for many types of purchase. This chapter does not
attempt to give a comprehensive account of such matters, but rather, to examine
those aspects of public contract design and execution which do fall within the
scope of the 2014 directives. In addition to the basic distinction between contracts
and framework agreements, the 2014 directives set certain boundaries for contract
performance clauses, subcontracting provisions, and modifications to contracts

---

[1] For consideration of the policy arguments for and against allowing a broad discretion to
modify public contracts, see Dekel, O. (2009) 'Modification of a Government Contract Awarded
Following a Competitive Procedure' 38(2) PCLJ 401–26.

during their term. These represent a deeper incursion into post-award territory than earlier directives, but are still far from the comprehensive rules governing advertising and procedures.

5.03 This chapter begins with consideration of what makes a good contract, and how its content and structure may be shaped by procurement. Despite the heterogeneity of public contracts, certain common elements and even recommended provisions can be identified. The drafting of framework agreement terms poses additional complexities which are considered here. The 2014 directives require that certain contract clauses are published in advance as part of the procurement documents, raising the question of what role these may play in the award process. The rules on subcontracting and modifications to contracts are among the most elaborate provisions contained in the 2014 directives, and some space is devoted to analysing how they may operate in practice. While the provisions on modifications to contracts can in part be seen as a codification of earlier case law, they also go beyond the Court's judgments in an attempt to create comprehensive rules for when changes to a contract will be considered to amount to a new contract award. Naturally, the emergence of further case law on this subject will assist with their interpretation and practical application. Further aspects of contract and framework design and performance which are relevant in terms of value for money are examined in Chapter 6.

What Makes a Good Contract?

5.04 A good contract may be defined as one which expresses the parties' agreement, provides for the various eventualities which may arise, and creates the conditions under which problems can be resolved. Ideally, it is compendious. In the case of public procurement, it should also accurately reflect the outcome of the tender procedure—so that the benefits of competition are captured during the performance phase. While this may seem self-evident, there is often a disconnection between the basis on which bids are sought and evaluated, and the subsequent execution of the contract. This can be driven by different individuals, departments, or organizations being responsible for procurement and contract management, by the different incentives faced by the parties at each stage, or in some cases simply by the passage of time. Poor or incomplete drafting of specifications can also mean that those responsible for managing a contract are faced with a contractor who has not fully anticipated or priced for the authority's true requirements. While the rules on modifications allow some scope for change without triggering a new competition, this is limited and should, together with the obligation to publish tender documents at an early stage, prompt contracting authorities to better anticipate and express their needs.

As noted in Chapter 1, the definition of public contracts under the procurement **5.05** directives is a wide-reaching one. The essential elements, other than the requirement that the parties and subject-matter fall within the scope of the directives, are that a contract must be in writing and be for pecuniary interest. The completeness, fairness, or clarity of a contract, or the intentions of the parties entering into it, are generally not relevant for the application of the procurement rules—although they may result in the contract being invalid under national law. The Remedies Directives,[2] which provide the framework for challenges to contract awards, mean that contracts may be suspended, set aside, or rendered ineffective where a breach of the procurement rules occurs. Damages or other specific remedies may also be available to a party which successfully challenges award of a contract: this is considered further in Chapter 8.

One of the fictions upon which the procedural rules set out in the directives rest **5.06** is that a contract can be fully defined in advance of the selection of the economic operator who will perform it. Contracting authorities and entities are required to estimate the value of contracts in advance, and to specify the performance conditions within the notice or procurement documents. The accuracy of this information is often open to question, as even standardized contracts are typically subject to some degree of negotiation with the preferred bidder—for example, on start date or the precise manner of delivery. Perfect foresight of such matters, even if possible, is not necessarily desirable—as competition may lead to more favourable terms being obtained. The introduction of rules on modifications to contracts means that in many cases, contracting authorities will seek to define their contracts in a flexible manner which takes account of potential variations in the scope or quantity of goods or services required and avoids the need for a new competition by providing for these in contract review clauses.

The constraints placed on changes to contracts after their award will in some cases **5.07** also be to the contracting authority's advantage. Where contracts are continually subject to change or the possibility of renegotiation, this may result in reluctance from contractors to deliver according to the initial specifications—for example, where input prices or availability have changed. The 2014 directives make it clear that any change which increases the economic benefit received by a contractor in a manner not provided for in the original contract can create an obligation to re-tender—which may in turn reduce pressure from contractors for such variations or allowances to be granted unless they have been clearly anticipated in review

---

[2] Directive 89/665/EEC on the coordination of the laws, regulations and administrative provisions relating to the application of review procedures to the award of public supply and public works contracts ('Public Sector Remedies Directive') and Directive 92/13/EEC coordinating the laws, regulations and administrative provisions relating to the application of Community rules on the procurement procedures of entities operating in the water, energy, transport and telecommunications sectors ('Utilities Sector Remedies Directive') as amended by Directive 2007/66/EU and Directive 2014/23/EU.

clauses. Reluctance to trigger a new award procedure, the result of which will be uncertain, may exist on both sides. In the reverse situation where a reduction in pricing occurs, it is much less likely that a new tender will be required—again working to the contracting authority's advantage.

5.08 Given these considerations, three elements which are likely to be valuable within almost all public contracts can be identified. The first is carefully drafted contract review clauses which allow the public authority to avail of reductions in pricing or increases in quality, and also allow some scope for changes which may benefit the contractor where the cost of these is less than the cost of entering into a new procurement process for the authority. Estimation of these costs can be difficult, and may change during the period of the contract. As such, it is usually best for the contracting authority to reserve the right to approve such changes at its discretion, while defining the circumstances in which a request may be made. For example, in a works contract, there may be provision for price variations where the bill of quantities changes, particularly if the change is driven by the client. These may be capped at a certain level, either in absolute terms or as a portion of the overall contract value. The 2014 directives require a high degree of transparency and specificity in such clauses, as discussed below.

5.09 The second element which is likely to have a place in almost all public contracts is a provision to the effect that nothing in the contract will prevent the contracting authority from complying with its obligations under the public procurement rules. This may also be reflected specifically in termination clauses, ensuring that in a situation where modifications to a contract create an obligation for the authority to re-tender, it will not be prevented from doing so or be liable for damages to the appointed contractor. The 2014 directives require that termination in such circumstances must be possible under national law.[3] This type of clause is also essential where a contract which has already been awarded is subject to challenge under the Remedies Directives—for example, where the authority has been successful in having the automatic suspension of that contract lifted, but is then unsuccessful in a substantive challenge. The objective is to avoid a situation where the authority may be liable for damages or other payments to both the successful and unsuccessful tenderer.[4]

5.10 Finally, the obligations of the contractor at the end of a contract which has been subject to a procurement procedure should be such as to support the re-tendering of that requirement. For example, there may be a need to obtain specific information about the performance of the contract in order to place other potential bidders in a

---

[3] Art 73 Public Sector Directive; Art 90 Utilities Directive; and Art 44 Concessions Directive.
[4] The possibility of an authority having to 'pay twice' was treated as a factor militating against lifting the automatic suspension of contract award, due to the injury to the public purse which might arise, in *Covanta Energy Ltd v Merseyside Waste Disposal Authority* [2013] EWHC 2922 (TCC), para 60.

position of equality, as discussed in Chapter 2. Allowance for a running-in period may also be necessary to ensure efficient handover of contractual responsibilities to a new contractor. For service contracts, if handover involves the transfer of assets such as cleaning, catering, or security equipment or premises, this may bring it within the scope of the Transfer of Undertakings Directive.[5] While in strict terms this creates obligations only between the private undertakings involved, in practice most public authorities are anxious to ensure the smooth handover of services and the fair treatment of staff involved, for whom rights may arise under TUPE. It is therefore advisable to include specific handover obligations in public contracts which take account of the potential applicability of this legislation—for example, by requiring the contractor to provide information about employee numbers and conditions of employment at any point in time when this is requested by the contracting authority.

5.11 These three elements of course form only a small part of what will make an effective public contract. As with all contracts, the balance of power between the parties determines their ability to insist on individual terms, and to enforce them in practice. Other more mundane realities such as the amount of time and quality of legal advice available to either party may also be determinative. Given the greater opportunity under the 2014 directives to engage in negotiation, matters which have traditionally been subject to two-way exchanges between the contracting authority and preferred bidder may become part of the procurement procedure itself. Wholesale acceptance of contractual terms, which is often required as part of final tender submissions, can simplify the end stages of procurement and ensure that bidders review terms carefully prior to submitting their tenders. However, it can also result in a degree of risk-pricing or even a reduced number of tenders if the terms are unclear or perceived to be unduly weighted against the contractor. Negotiations may allow terms to be better tailored to the particular competitive dynamic which emerges during a procedure. Any amendments can then be issued to all bidders prior to inviting final tenders, reducing the need for prolonged exchanges at preferred bidder stage.[6]

Framework Agreements

5.12 Framework agreements provide a structure for the award of multiple contracts—either by a single authority or by a number who have each been identified in the contract notice. The directives stipulate that framework agreements must be established by application of one of the procedures, meaning that they

---

[5] Council Directive 2001/23/EC of 12 March 2001 on the approximation of the laws of the Member States relating to the safeguarding of employees' rights in the event of transfers of undertakings, businesses or parts of undertakings or businesses (commonly known as TUPE).

[6] An alternative approach may be to assess contractual aspects as part of the award criteria.

cannot be used simply as a means of selecting operators who will later be invited to tender for specific requirements.[7] There must be an element of competition in order to establish the framework itself, whether based on an initial contract, pricing in respect of potential future requirements, or some combination of these approaches. This requirement is reinforced by the use of the terms 'supplement its tender' (in respect of single-operator frameworks) and 'reopening competition' (in respect of multi-operator frameworks)—it is not possible to do these things if there has not been an initial competition involving tenders. Beyond this stage, there are potential variations both in the content of framework terms and in the way in which contracts are awarded under them.

5.13 The rules on frameworks are in large part unchanged from those in the 2004 directives, with the exception of the removal of the minimum of three operators in multi-operator frameworks. For both single and multi-operator frameworks, the directives clearly contemplate that not all terms must be fixed under the framework agreement. If they were, there would be no advantage to using a (single-operator) framework rather than a contract with options or phases. The level of specificity required for these terms, and the extent to which individual contracts awarded under a framework may have different terms, are not squarely set out in the directives. Article 33(2) of the Public Sector Directive does provide that:

> contracts based on a framework agreement may under no circumstances entail substantial modifications to the terms laid down in that framework agreement...

meaning that the terms of the framework itself must be known with reasonable certainty. No parallel provision exists in the Utilities Directive, although the rules on modifications apply to frameworks as well as contracts under both directives. It is possible to establish framework terms which provide a structure for the award of contracts without themselves involving any payment or obligation to provide goods, services, or works. In this case, the framework agreement is a self-contained structure which may survive the termination of an individual contract. Technically, it is not a public contract if it does not involve any pecuniary interest. However, framework agreements are themselves subject to challenge under the Remedies Directives.[8]

---

[7] Art 33(1) Public Sector Directive; and Art 51(1) Utilities Directive. The Concessions Directive does not contain specific rules for framework agreements, which should not be taken to mean they are prohibited given that it does not aim to comprehensively coordinate procedures, but only to establish certain procedural guarantees. Frameworks may be suitable for the award of certain types of concession—for example, where this is done centrally on behalf of a number of State bodies or to cover multiple assets such as railway franchises (provided these are not exposed to competition and thereby excluded under Art 16 of the Concessions Directive).

[8] Article 1(1) of Directive 2007/66/EC provides that: 'Contracts within the meaning of this Directive include public contracts, framework agreements, public works concessions and dynamic purchasing systems.' Services concessions are also subject to the remedies regime under Art 46(1) of the Concessions Directive.

Different approaches to establishment and operation of both single and **5.14** multi-supplier frameworks can be observed across the Member States, and with a few exceptions these variations in practice appear to be tolerated by the European Commission and CJEU. The Commission did challenge a French law allowing use of a single procedure for both the award of a contract to define the parameters of supplies, services, or works to be purchased (*marché de définition*) and the subsequent contract itself (*marché d'exécution*). The Court held that the initial *marchés de définition* did not adequately prescribe the subject-matter, selection, and award criteria to be applied in the subsequent *marchés d'exécution*, meaning that a separate award procedure was required. This suggests that a relatively high level of specificity is needed in the initial notice and tender documents where it is intended to award subsequent contracts based on framework agreements.

Nevertheless, framework agreements continue to offer a greater degree of flexibility **5.15** than contracts in terms of the scope and quantity of purchases and their timing. Where a single-operator framework is established, the operator may be invited to supplement its tender to reflect requirements which fall within the scope of the framework, but which have not been fully anticipated in the initial tender procedure. Such contracts must be 'within the limits of the terms of the framework agreement'—which leaves open the question of to what extent revisions in specifications, quantity, or pricing are allowed. In addition to the rules on framework agreements set out in Article 33 of the Public Sector Directive, this question must be resolved by reference to the definition of 'substantial modifications' discussed below. The rules on modifications provide that if the terms of a framework agreement contain clear, precise, and unequivocal pricing revision clauses, then this is permitted regardless of its monetary value.[9] This does, however, raise certain questions regarding value for money in a single-operator framework, given the lack of competition.

There are several ways in which contracting authorities may seek to address this in **5.16** their framework terms. The first is to reserve the right to go outside of the framework to purchase any individual requirement, regardless of its value or the ability of the framework operator to provide it.[10] Such external purchases would of course be subject to the procurement rules and involve a new tender procedure if they are above threshold. The second approach is to benchmark framework pricing against market prices for the particular goods or services being purchased, with the framework operator agreeing to match such prices or offer a set discount against them.

---

[9] Art 72(1)(a) Public Sector Directive; and Art 89(1)(a) Utilities Directive. Review clauses must be included in the initial procurement documents and must not alter the overall nature of the framework agreement.

[10] Recital 61 of the Public Sector Directive confirms that there is no obligation for contracting authorities to make any specific purchase under a framework agreement they have established. It is, of course, possible that the framework terms entered into by a contracting authority will create such an obligation.

The use of an indexation clause, to allow adjustments in line with inflation or deflation, can also help to protect both parties from the erosion of value during the framework period. The third approach is to seek and evaluate pricing in respect of all potential requirements as part of the initial tender procedure, and then fix the successful bidder's pricing as part of the framework terms. In this scenario, supplementary tenders may relate only to qualitative aspects or delivery terms, with pricing being drawn down from the agreed schedules. This approach has certain obvious advantages in terms of ensuring price competition on the full range of items which may be purchased under a single-operator framework. It is not without its own hazards, particularly if prices go down during the framework period. Contracting authorities may seek to include a clause whereby the contractor must automatically extend the benefit of any price reductions to supplies or services provided under the framework, while reserving the right to go elsewhere if they are not satisfied that best value is being offered.

5.17 Overall, then, there are numerous ways in which single-operator frameworks may be designed in order to limit any negative effects on value for money. The willingness of bidders to accept such terms will depend on the perceived volume and attractiveness of contracts awarded under a framework. The same is largely true in multi-operator frameworks; however, the possibility of running mini competitions among the members of the framework provides a further means to ensure best value is obtained, albeit within a limited field of competition. Not all multi-operator frameworks involve mini competitions.[11] In some cases, contracting authorities may apply a 'cascade' or 'preferred contractor' methodology, whereby the bidder who has scored highest in the initial competition has the first opportunity to deliver any requirements arising under a framework. Other members are effectively treated as reserves, invited to perform contracts only where the primary contractor cannot meet a particular requirement. Alternatively, competition may be reopened in accordance with specific rules. Contracting authorities may combine these different methods for award of contracts in a multi-operator framework. The Public Sector Directive states that if different modes of awarding contracts under a multi-operator framework are to be used, the objective criteria which an authority will use to choose between them must be specified in advance.[12]

---

[11] Article 33(4) of the Public Sector Directive distinguishes between multi-operator frameworks in which 'all of the terms governing provision of the supplies, services or works' are set out, and those where they are not. In the latter case, competition must be reopened in order to award contracts. However, the wording of this provision lacks clarity in some respects, see discussion at paras 3.46–3.48.

[12] Art 33(4)(b) Public Sector Directive. Article 51(2) of the Utilities Directive simply provides that award of contracts under framework agreements must be on the basis of objective criteria and rules set out in the framework procurement documents, without restricting the choice between different modes of award.

The question of whether it is permissible to rotate the award of contracts between **5.18** the members of a framework agreement sometimes comes up in practice. On the face of it, there is nothing to prevent this approach in the 2014 directives, provided the 'objective conditions' which will form the basis for rotation of contract awards are stated in the framework procurement documents. On the same basis, one might seek to justify the random selection of a framework member for the award of an individual contract, provided the method for random selection was stated in advance. Arguably, however, both of these approaches contravene the basic principle that contracts subject to the directives must be awarded on the basis of most economically advantageous tender. Although it is not explicitly stated that this applies to contracts awarded under frameworks, it seems likely to apply at least to those which are individually valued above the relevant threshold for application of the directives. A safer approach where the contracting authority wishes to distribute work between members of a framework without holding further competitions would be to establish the framework in multiple lots, with a single operator appointed under each lot.

Contract Performance Clauses

The ability to set 'special conditions for the performance of a contract' under the **5.19** directives is not new[13]—however, the requirement for such conditions to be linked to the subject-matter of the contract appears in the 2014 directives for the first time. Emerging from the Court's case law on award criteria, the application of the subject-matter link test to contract clauses is likely to rule out the use of terms setting general corporate responsibility requirements in public contracts.[14] A requirement for a contractor to participate in a carbon offsetting scheme or to invest in the local community outside of a specific contract might not withstand challenge on this basis. Similar requirements should, however, be permissible where they relate directly to the activities being carried out under the contract—for example, a requirement to offset carbon emissions caused by the goods or services being provided, or to provide certain community benefits linked to contract performance such as training and apprenticeships under a works contract. The directives require that such 'special conditions' be indicated in the call for competition or procurement documents, which effectively reduces the scope for challenges to such conditions at a later stage.[15]

---

[13] Similar provisions appeared in Art 26 of Directive 2004/18/EC and Art 38 of Directive 2004/17/EC.

[14] See further discussion of this point at paras 7.51 *et seq.*

[15] The precise scope depends on the time limits and other conditions prescribed for access to remedies at national level—of which more in Chapter 8.

5.20 The term 'special conditions' is not defined, although 'economic, innovation-related, environmental, social or employment-related considerations' are cited as examples. The extent to which *all* contract performance clauses must be publicised as part of the competitive process remains unclear—although in the case of clauses authorizing substantial modifications, this is now mandated under the rules discussed below. Most contracting authorities issue draft contract terms as part of tender documentation; however, these may be subject to substantial changes either during the procedure itself (especially where the negotiated or competitive dialogue procedures are used) or at the preferred bidder stage. In most cases, the final contract signed will incorporate the successful tender, so it is not possible to fully publicise all contract terms in advance. Following from the Court's application of the transparency and equal treatment principles to award criteria and modifications to contracts, the question of which contract clauses must be disclosed might well be determined based on their potential to attract additional competitors or alter the outcome of a competition.[16] These questions are by their nature hypothetical; however, it is worth considering their potential impact if it is proposed to introduce new contract terms at the preferred bidder stage.

5.21 It seems reasonable to surmise that while prior publication of all contract performance conditions is not required by the directives, those which may have a specific impact on the competition should be highlighted at an early stage. Indeed, this is good practice to avoid drawn-out contractual negotiations at the preferred bidder stage, and to ensure that pricing reflects the full scope of responsibilities which will form part of the contract. One approach which can be useful is to publish contract terms in draft form at an early stage, inviting candidates or bidders to review these and to submit any queries or objections prior to final tender submission. The authority may then re-issue contract terms to all bidders inclusive of any amendments or clarifications. All bidders are required to indicate their acceptance of these terms as part of their final bid, with a clear indication that no contract will be formed until they are executed. This requires a little more legwork at tender stage and may not be appropriate where contract terms are highly sensitive; however, it can help to place the contracting authority in a better position at the preferred bidder stage, and to avoid the risk of substantial modifications being sought.

5.22 How is a contracting authority to deal with a situation where a bidder advises that it will be unable to meet a contract condition published as part of the procurement documents? Article 56(1)(a) provides that contracting authorities are to verify compliance with, *inter alia*, the conditions set out in the procurement documents. If agreement to all contract terms is stipulated as a mandatory requirement within the procurement documents, this may create difficulty where a tenderer expresses

---

[16] This would reflect the Court's approach to prior disclosure of sub-criteria and weightings in *ATI* and to modifications of contracts in *pressetext* and *Succhi di Frutta*.

a relatively minor caveat or reservation regarding a contractual term. The need to reject a tender where it does not comply with conditions stated to be mandatory was confirmed by the Court in the *Manova* case[17]—indeed, it is easy to see how to do otherwise would violate the principles of transparency and equal treatment. Contracting authorities are therefore well advised not to require unconditional compliance with contract terms unless it is their firm intention to apply this to all bidders regardless of the circumstances or nature of caveats expressed. Where discretion over such matters is reserved in the procurement documents, it may be exercised provided this is done in a way which ensures equal treatment of bidders.

Subcontracting Provisions

The 2014 directives deal with three distinct aspects of subcontracting: **5.23**

(i) information about subcontractors to be provided by tenderers/the main contractor;

(ii) compliance of subcontractors with exclusion criteria and environmental, social, and labour law; and

(iii) the possibility to arrange for direct payment and liability of subcontractors.

Identical provisions appear in Article 71 of the Public Sector Directive and Article **5.24** 88 of the Utilities Directive. Article 42 of the Concessions Directive replicates these, but makes no explicit reference to direct payment of subcontractors, which is not to say that Member States (or indeed contracting authorities and entities themselves) could not provide for this. However, the absence of clear legislative provision for direct payment of subcontractors may create a risk that such payments would be deemed to constitute a separate public contract or concession. Although the new provisions expand considerably on the sparse mention of subcontractors in the 2004 directives, it is left almost entirely to the discretion of Member States to determine whether, and to what extent, to apply these rules.

The only mandatory aspect, which applies under all three directives, is the require- **5.25** ment for the names, contact details, and legal representatives of subcontractors to be provided to the authority in the case of works contracts or services carried out at a facility under its direct oversight. This information is to be provided by the main contractor following contract award and prior to performance commencing, inasmuch as it is known, and updated as necessary.[18] It applies in respect of all works

---

[17] Case C-336/12 *Ministeriet for Forskning, Innovation og Videregående Uddannelser v Manova A/S*, para 40. See also Case C-561/12 *Nordecon AS and Ramboll Eesti AS v Rahandusministeerium* ('*Nordecon*'), not yet reported; and Case C-42/13 *Cartiera dell'Adda and Cartiera di Cologno*, not yet reported.

[18] Art 71(5) Public Sector Directive; Art 88(5) Utilities Directive; and Art 42(3) Concessions Directive.

and services subcontractors regardless of the size of their contribution; however, it is expressed as not applying to suppliers unless contracting authorities or Member States specifically provide for this. Contracting authorities or Member States may also extend the requirement to cover sub subcontractors, or in respect of supply contracts or services carried out at external sites. Such extensions may assist, for example, in ensuring that minimum working standards are observed along the supply chain.

5.26 As under the 2004 directives, it is also possible to request information during the tender procedure itself about the proportion of a contract to be subcontracted and the identity of the proposed subcontractors. Interestingly, the Public Sector and Utilities Directives state that this can be requested only from tenderers, whereas the Concessions Directive allows this to be requested from applicants as well.[19] This raises the question of how to resolve situations where a subcontractor is found not to comply with exclusion criteria—for example, because they owe unpaid tax or social security contributions. The ability to request the European Single Procurement Document from subcontractors, and to apply both mandatory and discretionary exclusion grounds, is included in the 2014 directives. Where a subcontractor is found not to comply with one or more grounds, the main contractor can be required to replace them. It is not entirely clear when this verification process should take place, but given that details of subcontractors apparently cannot be requested at selection stage (other than for concessions), it seems the earliest it could occur is during tender evaluation.[20] If there is a change in any of the relevant information, or new subcontractors are introduced during contract performance, verification and, if necessary, replacement of any non-compliant subcontractors can take place.[21]

5.27 The effect of these provisions is to allow a greater degree of oversight of subcontractors and avoidance of those who are in breach of legal obligations or in dubious financial situations. This is to be welcomed, as opaque subcontracting arrangements may otherwise be used to circumvent basic requirements regarding the suitability of contractors. Where national laws allow for joint liability of contractors and subcontractors for performance of a contract, the obligation to comply with all applicable environmental, social, and labour laws, including collective agreements, is to be extended to cover subcontractors.[22] This contrasts with the more general

---

[19] Art 71(2) Public Sector Directive; Art 88(2) Utilities Directive; and Art 42(2) Concessions Directive.

[20] As previously, an indication of the proportion of the contract which an operator intends to (possibly) subcontract can be required at selection stage (Annex XII, Pt II, point (j) Public Sector Directive). It would also be possible to glean more information about subcontractors where the candidate is intending to rely on their financial, economic, technical, or professional capacity under Art 63.

[21] Art 71(6)(b) Public Sector Directive; Art 88(6)(a) Utilities Directive; and Art 42(4)(a) Concessions Directive.

[22] Art 71(6)(a) Public Sector Directive; Art 88(6)(a) Utilities Directive; and Art 42(4)(a) Concessions Directive. The literal meaning of this provision seems to be that if such laws on joint

statement at the outset of Article 71 that compliance with such obligations 'is ensured by appropriate action of the competent national authorities acting within the scope of their responsibility and remit'. The recitals offer the examples of labour inspection or environmental protection agencies as 'competent national authorities'—however, this must be read as additional to the direct ability of authorities to enforce joint liability and/or require replacement of a subcontractor in breach of such obligations.

As a counterbalance to this increased scrutiny and potential liability of subcontractors, the possibility for direct payment of subcontractors is referred to in the 2014 directives. Again, it is left up to Member States to determine if and how to implement this provision, which addresses a common SME complaint about prompt payment under public contracts. In practice, direct payment of subcontractors may be legally fraught if liability for overall performance of the contract still rests with the main contractor appointed pursuant to the tender competition.[23] The directives appear to recognize this by suggesting that the main contractor may be given a right to object to any direct payments to subcontractors, which is likely to detract from the expediency of such measures and their consequent value to SMEs. More effective protection of subcontractors might be achieved by way of a contract clause requiring the main contractor to pay its subcontractors within a certain maximum period, unless there are specific grounds for withholding such payment. **5.28**

Where national law provides for direct payment and (joint) liability of subcontractors, the question arises of whether a separate public contract exists between the subcontractor and the contracting authority. This may be important in several regards, not least the applicability of the Remedies Directives to such contracts. If a rival subcontractor has an interest in obtaining such a contract, it may seek to argue that it is subject to the directives, so that decisions regarding exclusion would be subject to review. The existence of a separate contract between the contracting authority and a subcontractor may also be relevant for the application of the rules on modifications to contracts, as discussed below. **5.29**

Overall, the subcontracting provisions help to address a lacuna which existed under the 2004 directives. However, as with other areas regulated explicitly for the first time, it is possible that in setting out detailed rules for dealing with subcontractors some of the flexibilities available previously have disappeared. For example, it is now necessary to specify any arrangements regarding the proposed direct payment of subcontractors in the procurement documents,[24] whereas previously this might have been agreed at preferred bidder stage or even subsequent to contract award. Likewise, the ability to apply the exclusion grounds to subcontractors is **5.30**

---

liability exist, compliance with the Art 18(2) obligations on the part of subcontractors is required even if no joint liability arrangement applies to the contract in question.

[23] Art 71(3) Public Sector Directive; and Art 88(3) Utilities Directive.
[24] Art 71(3) Public Sector Directive; and Art 88(3) Utilities Directive.

accompanied by a corresponding right of self-cleaning and is time limited from the date on which any particular transgression occurs. As with the rules on abnormally low tenders, the obligation to have a subcontractor replaced only arises where a contracting authority seeks to verify its compliance with the exclusion grounds, meaning that many authorities may choose not to make such enquiries unless they are compelled to do so by national legislation.

Modifications to Contracts

5.31 The question of how modifications to contracts after their award are to be dealt with was not addressed in the 2004 directives, leaving it to the Court to establish principles for this. It did so in three cases in particular, decided between 2004 and 2010. The first of these, *Succhi di Frutta*, concerned a contract awarded by the Commission for the supply of fruit juices and jams to Armenia and Azerbaijan.[25] Payment under the contract was to take the form of fruit withdrawn from the EU market under the Common Agricultural Policy. Bidders were to indicate the quantities of apples and oranges which they would accept as payment; however, when the contract was performed, the quantities of these fruits withdrawn from the market were insufficient to meet the Commission's liabilities under the contract. It was forced to substitute peaches. Succhi di Frutta, an unsuccessful bidder, argued that this deviated from the terms of the tender competition, which nowhere mentioned the possibility of peaches. It challenged the Commission's decision before the then Court of First Instance, which found in its favour.

5.32 On appeal, the Commission argued that the company lacked standing to challenge the substitution decision, as it was no longer concerned in the contractual relationship. The Court wholly rejected this line of argumentation, finding that a contracting authority was not at liberty to manage a contract with the successful bidder as it sees fit if this involves derogations from the terms set down in the invitation to tender which have not been provided for.[26] To do so would violate the principles of equal treatment and transparency. *Succhi di Frutta* had potentially far-reaching consequences for public contracts amended following award. It suggested that *any* changes which were not fully foreseen in tender documents could in theory result in the need for a new tender competition. Such changes to public contracts are made frequently, although often not in such a visible manner.

5.33 The direct application of this principle to a contract awarded under the procurement directives occurred in the *pressetext* case, concerning the purchase of press agency services by an Austrian authority.[27] The company providing the service transferred

---

[25] Case C-496/99 P *Commission of the European Communities v CAS Succhi di Frutta SpA* [2004] ECR I-03801.
[26] Case C-496/99 P *Succhi di Frutta*, paras 38–40.
[27] Case C-454/06 *pressetext Nachrichtenagentur* [2008] ECR I-4401.

the contract to its newly established wholly owned subsidiary, while maintaining joint liability for performance of the services. Further changes to the contract were made to reflect Austria's transition to the euro, updating of a price indexation clause, minor reductions in prices, and extension of a waiver of the right to terminate the contract. The applicant, a competitor in the press agency market, challenged these as de-facto contract awards which demanded a new tender procedure. The Court held that this would be required if the changes to the contract rendered it materially different in character from the original contract and therefore demonstrated the intention of the parties to renegotiate the essential terms of the contract. It gave three examples of where changes would be considered material: (i) if they would have allowed for the admission of, or award to, a different tenderer; (ii) if they extended the scope of the contract considerably to encompass services not initially covered; or (iii) if they changed the economic balance of the contract in favour of the contractor in a manner which was not provided for in the terms of the initial contract.[28] On the facts at hand, the Court held that no new contract had arisen.

Pressetext left several unanswered questions, such as whether the list enumerated **5.34** in paragraph 5.33 was an exhaustive one, and whether changes which were to the economic detriment of the operator could in any circumstances be considered material. The subsequent case of *Wall AG*, while confirming that the same principles applied in respect of modifications to a service concession, offered little further guidance on these points. The case concerned a change in a major subcontractor to be used in a service concession, whose name had been included in the successful tender. The Court found that a change in subcontractor might in exceptional cases constitute a material change, where the use of a particular subcontractor was a decisive factor in the award of the contract.[29] It did not consider whether the inclusion in the tender documents of a term allowing substitution of a subcontractor would make this permissible. The position regarding the scope for material changes to contracts both where they were publicised in advance and where they were unforeseen thus remained unclear.

Article 72 of the Public Sector Directive, which is replicated in its entirety in the **5.35** Utilities and Concessions Directives, now sets explicit rules regarding modifications to contracts. The starting position is that modifications to contracts awarded under the directives will require a new competition to be held, unless they can be brought within one of six exceptions to this principle.[30] The exceptions are:

(i) where the modification is provided for in a clear, precise, and unequivocal review clause which was included in the initial procurement documents;

---

[28] Case C-454/06 *pressetext*, paras 34–7.
[29] Case C-91/08 *Wall AG v La ville de Francfort-sur-le-Main and Frankfurter Entsorgungs- und Service (FES) GmbH* [2010] ECR I-02815, para 39.
[30] Art 72(5) Public Sector Directive; Art 89(5) Utilities Directive; and Art 43(5) Concessions Directive.

(ii) for additional works, services, or supplies where a change of contractor is not possible for economic or technical reasons and would result in significant inconvenience or substantial duplication of costs;

(iii) where the need for modification is brought about by circumstances which a diligent authority could not foresee and it does not alter the overall nature of the contract;

(iv) replacement of the original contractor by another under a review clause, universal or partial succession (for example, corporate restructuring or insolvency), or step-in by the authority;

(v) where the modifications, irrespective of their value, are not substantial;

(vi) for modifications valued below the threshold and 10 per cent of the initial contract value for supplies and services or 15 per cent of the initial value for works.

Further conditions, definitions, and examples are set out in relation to each ground. These are considered here, together with some analysis of how they may be applied in practice.

Contract review clauses

5.36 As discussed above, contracts and frameworks may contain clauses allowing for price revision, changes in quantity or delivery terms, or the exercise of options. In order to avail of such terms, if the proposed changes are substantial and cannot be justified under any of the other grounds, the 2014 directives set three conditions. The first is that the clauses must be included in the 'initial procurement documents'—so cannot be introduced at the preferred bidder stage. The inclusion of the term 'initial' raises the question of how this requirement is to be interpreted in multi-stage procedures. For example, in a competitive dialogue, the need for price revisions or other options may not become clear until after dialogue sessions are held—and in an innovation partnership, the need may not become clear until after research and development activities are carried out. A strict interpretation of Article 72(1)(a) would mean that including such clauses at these later stages, even if they are made known to all bidders or partners, is not sufficient. However, as with the Article 53 requirements regarding publication of procurement documents, it is possible that in multi-stage procedures this should be interpreted as referring to the *relevant* procurement documents—that is, those which set out the contract terms. The directives do not require full publication of contract terms in the context of a procedure, but it may be intended to provide a greater degree of transparency regarding terms which specifically authorize modifications.

5.37 The second requirement is that contract review clauses must be clear, precise, and unequivocal, and 'state the scope and nature of possible modifications or options as well as the conditions under which they may be used'. The intention here is to prevent contracting authorities from including clauses which would entitle them to modify contracts in ways which were not specifically envisioned and brought to the attention of bidders. In the case of a price revision clause, for example, it is probably necessary to state the specific situations in which it may be applied and to give some indication of the frequency of revisions and how their value will be calculated. Reserving the right for the contracting authority to authorize revisions at its discretion is unlikely to suffice. A high level of foresight is thus needed in order to draft contract review clauses, which may be difficult to achieve if publication of the relevant clauses is required at the very outset of a complex procedure. In return for this high degree of foresight, modifications pursuant to contract review clauses have the advantage of not being capped in terms of their monetary value. However, the third condition for their use is that they must not alter the overall nature of the contract. Very high value modifications may be vulnerable to challenge on this basis, particularly if they arise due to changes in what is being delivered under the contract.

Unforeseen modifications

In contrast, the second and third grounds on which modifications can be justi- **5.38**
fied relate to situations which have not been foreseen by the contracting authority. Article 72(1)(b)[31] echoes one of the grounds for use of the negotiated procedure without prior publication available under the 2004 directives.[32] It allows for additional works, supplies, or services which did not form part of the original contract to be provided by the original contractor where there are economic or technical reasons which prevent a change of contractor—for example, the need for interoperability with existing equipment. The contracting authority must also show that it would incur significant inconvenience or substantial duplication of costs by changing contractor—however, it is not necessary to show that the overall nature of the contract remains the same or that the requirement was *unforeseeable*. On first glance, Article 72(1)(b) appears to be one of the more generous grounds for justifying changes; however, one must be conscious of the Court's prior case law indicating that the existence of economic or technical reasons is to be interpreted strictly.[33]

Article 72(1)(c), on the other hand, requires that the change be necessitated by **5.39**
circumstances which a diligent authority *could not* have foreseen—one thinks of emergency situations or unexpected political events.[34] The requirement to show

---

[31] Art 89(1)(b) Utilities Directive; and Art 43(1)(b) Concessions Directive.

[32] Art 31(4)(a) Directive 2004/18/EC; and Art 40(3)(f) Directive 2004/17/EC.

[33] In Joined Cases C-20/01 and C-28/01 *Commission v Germany* [2003] ECR I-3609, para 58; Case C-126/03 *Commission v Germany* [2004] I-11197, para 23; Case C-26/03 *Stadt Halle* [2005] ECR I-0001, para 46; Case C-337/05 *Commission v Italy* [2008] ECR I-2173, paras 57–58; and Case C-601/10 *Commission v Hellenic Republic* [2011] ECR I-00163.

[34] It is also possible that this ground may be used to justify changes aimed at remedying deficiencies in the performance of contracts. A more restrictive clause dealing with such situations was removed from the draft Public Sector Directive. For a discussion of this, see Treumer, S. (2014) 'Contract Changes and the Duty to Retender under the New EU Public Procurement Directive' (3) PPLR 148.

that the need for a modification was unforeseeable represents a tighter test than that which applied under the 2004 directives for use of the negotiated procedure. Both Article 72(1)(b) and (c) allow for modifications up to 50 per cent of the value of the original contract, and importantly this cap applies to each modification individually rather than on a cumulative basis. It is therefore possible that high value changes may be justified under these grounds, although this is likely to be accompanied by stronger scrutiny of the reasons invoked. Unlike the other grounds justifying modifications, there is an obligation to publish a notice in the OJEU where Article 72(1)(b) or (c) (or their equivalents in the Utilities and Concessions Directives) are invoked—which makes such scrutiny by the Commission or eager competitors more likely.

5.40 An interesting question may arise as to whether events which are contemplated in contractual terms can be considered to be either unforeseen or unforeseeable. For example, it is common for contracts to include a lengthy, colourful list of occurrences which will constitute *force majeure* and allow performance to be suspended—with possible implications for both the duration and value of the contract. Such changes may be justifiable on the ground that they are covered by contract review clauses, although *force majeure* clauses are typically drafted in expansive terms to include all possible eventualities, so may fall short of the 'clear, precise, and unequivocal' standard required by Article 72(1)(a). Any attempt to justify such changes under Article 72(1)(b) or (c) would need to distinguish between what is provided for in a contract merely as a safeguard and what was foreseen or foreseeable.

Change of contractor

5.41 Situations where the appointed contractor is replaced by another are dealt with in Article 72(1)(d).[35] Such replacement may be provided for in a contract review clause, in which case the rules set out in paragraphs apply. It is also authorized where the replacement contractor is the universal or partial legal successor to the original contractor—for example, due to a takeover, merger, acquisition, or insolvency. In such cases, the replacement contractor must fulfil the criteria for qualitative selection applied during the procurement, and the succession must not entail other substantial changes to the contract or be intended to circumvent the application of the directives. It is also possible for the contracting authority itself to step into the role of the contractor by assuming its obligations to its subcontractors, if this has been provided for by national legislation implementing the directives' subcontracting rules. Article 72(4) provides that changes of contractor in other situations are to be considered substantial, and so would require a re-tender.

---

[35] Art 89(1)(d) Utilities Directive; and Art 43(1)(d) Concessions Directive.

The provisions on replacement of a contractor do not deal with the situation where, **5.42** following tender evaluation but prior to conclusion of a contract, events intervene which prevent award of the contract to the economic operator which has been identified as the preferred bidder (for example, if a takeover or merger occurs during this period, or if there is a sudden deterioration in the operator's finances which make it inadvisable to enter into a contract with it). Arguably, contracting authorities now have less room for manoeuvre in this period than they do after a contract is awarded—as the directives do not provide any explicit possibility to award a contract to an economic operator other than the one which has submitted the most economically advantageous tender.[36] Naturally, it is always possible to cancel a procedure at this stage, but this is far from expedient in most cases.

If the change in corporate structure is cosmetic only, or will in fact strengthen the **5.43** position of the contractor, the authority may wish to continue with the award. In other cases where the change in the identity or situation renders the contractor unsuitable, the logical solution would be designate the next highest scoring tenderer (runner-up) as the preferred bidder. The directives are silent as regards both possibilities, although they do contemplate at least one situation in which information discovered after evaluation is complete may prevent award of contract: where the designated preferred bidder is in violation of environmental, social, or labour law.[37] Given the allowance for replacement of appointed contractors where this is clearly provided for in a contract review clause, it seems that the inclusion of clauses in procurement documents, to the effect that where it is not possible to award a contract to the designated preferred bidder the contracting authority may award a contract to (i) its legal successor or (ii) the next highest-scoring bidder, is both acceptable and advisable.[38] In the first scenario, the inclusion of a requirement that the successor demonstrate compliance with the selection criteria is recommended.

Non-substantial and small value changes

The final two grounds on which modifications may be justified are more general. If the modification is not substantial, regardless of its value, then it can be permitted. Article 72(4) defines a substantial modification (in line with **5.44**

---

[36] Case T-48/12 *Euroscript—Polska Sp zoo v European Parliament*, not yet reported, casts some light on the constraints faced by contracting authorities when events during the standstill period or prior to contract award lead to a change in the identity of the preferred bidder. In that case, the evaluation panel revisited its marking and sought to appoint the runner-up as preferred bidder—however, the Court held that it was not entitled to do so without suspending the award of the contract and informing all concerned bidders of this.

[37] Art 56(1) Public Sector Directive; and Art 76(6) Utilities Directive.

[38] While a strong argument can be made for the ability to make changes in the pre-contractual stage which would be permitted under Art 72 in the post-contractual stage, contracting authorities should be aware of the need to inform other bidders of the new successful tenderer, and that time in respect of a challenge under the remedies rules may start to run again from this point. See discussion of these points and Case C-161/13 *Idrodinamica* in Chapter 8, paras 8.11 and 8.88–8.89.

pressetext) as one which renders a contract or framework agreement materially different from the one originally concluded. It then gives a non-exhaustive list of factors which would render a change substantial, namely, if: (i) it introduces conditions which would have attracted additional participants to a tender competition or resulted in a different selection or award outcome; (ii) it changes the economic balance of the contract in favour of the contractor, in a manner not provided for in the original contract or framework; (iii) it extends the scope of the contract or framework considerably; or (iv) a new contractor replaces the original one and this does not fall within the exception set out in Article 72(1)(d). In order to argue that a modification is not substantial, it would have to be shown that none of these situations applied—and other factors may also be taken into account.

5.45 The first two factors set a relatively low bar for what may be considered a substantial change; many changes have the hypothetical potential to attract additional participants or result in a different outcome, and even a small shift in the economic balance of the contract will be considered substantial—although it will normally be possible to justify on the *de minimis* grounds set out below. A potential loophole exists given the possibility for contracting authorities to pay subcontractors directly, and thus avoid shifting the economic balance in favour of the contractor itself where a need for additional payments arises. However, given that the list of changes which are to be considered substantial is non-exhaustive, reliance on this would be precarious. Changes which shift the economic balance in favour of a contractor or subcontractor, if sufficiently large, may also be vulnerable to challenge on State aid grounds.[39]

5.46 The final exception to the requirement to re-tender when a contract is modified is the *de minimis* provision, that is, where the value of the changes are sufficiently small to exclude this. In addition to being below threshold, they are capped at 10 per cent of the initial contract value for supplies and services and 15 per cent for works contracts.[40] Unlike the 50 per cent caps for modifications where a specific justification applies, the *de minimis* limits are calculated cumulatively based on all such changes. The question is likely to arise in practice of whether, where more than one modification to a contract takes place, the *de minimis* exception may be combined with another to justify changes in excess of the 10 or 15 per cent. For example, if a contract review clause is applied which allows an option to be exercised which increases the value of a supply contract by 20 per cent, could a separate modification worth another 10 per cent be justified? There is nothing in Article 72

---

[39] See Joined Cases E-10/11 and E-11/11 *Hurtigruten ASA, The Kingdom of Norway v EFTA Surveillance Authority*.

[40] Art 72(2) Public Sector Directive; Art 89(2) Utilities Directive; and Art 43(2) Concessions Directive.

to prevent this; however, the reference value for the *de minimis* limits remains the initial contract value, rather than that after any other permitted change has been made. Only if the contract includes an indexation clause can the reference value be updated to reflect this.[41] It is also provided that where multiple changes take place, it is their net value which matters—so an increase of more than 10 or 15 per cent may be justified where there has previously been a reduction against the initial contract value.

It is worth considering whether the modifications which took place in *Succhi di* **5.47** *Frutta*, *pressetext*, and *Wall* could have been accommodated within the current rules. The first question to be asked is whether the change is substantial: if it is not, then it can be accommodated within Article 72(1)(e) regardless of its value. A change of payment means which was not foreseen in contract review clauses might in theory attract additional competitors, and given that the award of the contract in *Succhi di Frutta* was based on the amount and type of payment which tenderers were willing to accept, it could also have altered the outcome. Even if evidence to counter these arguments was found, the aggrieved bidder would likely argue that it changed the economic balance in favour of the contractor. If a change is treated as substantial, it can be justified under Article 72(1)(c) if the need for it arose due to unforeseeable circumstances and it did not alter the over-all nature of the contract. However, this would be difficult to maintain on the facts of the case, given that availability of intervention stocks must frequently be subject to fluctuation and that in the circumstances a diligent authority could foresee the potential need to substitute different means of payment. Changes such as those in *Succhi di Frutta* would still require a re-tender.

Conversely, the changes in *pressetext* would be unlikely to trigger a new procedure **5.48** under the 2014 directives, as the definition of substantial changes is largely based on the Court's ruling in that case. A question might arise as to whether simply assign-ing a contract to a subsidiary in the absence of any specific corporate succession would justify the replacement of a contractor under Article 72(1)(d); however, it is likely that this would be covered by the existence of a contractual clause allowing assignment. This clause would then fall to be analysed against the requirements for clarity, precision, unequivocality, and prior publication set out in Article 72(1)(a). Finally, the situation in *Wall AG* would now be dealt with under the modification provisions in the Concessions Directive. Although these do not mention replace-ment of subcontractors, this could again be justified on the basis either that it did not constitute a substantial change, or that it had been specifically provided for in

---

[41] Art 72(3) Public Sector Directive; Art 89(3) Utilities Directive; and Art 43(3) Concessions Directive. The Concessions Directive also provides that where no indexation clause is included, the reference value shall be updated in line with average inflation in the Member State where the contract is awarded. In practice, the reference value may also be taken to include the cost of options if these are included in the value of the contract as indicated in the award notice. The term 'initial contract value' is undefined in the 2014 directives.

the contract terms. The former might be difficult to demonstrate on the facts of *Wall*, as the subcontractor's role was sufficiently prominent that it might well have altered the outcome of the competition.

5.49   As with the proliferation of terms such as 'irregular', 'unacceptable', and 'unsuitable' to describe tenders, it is somewhat unfortunate that various terms are used in Article 72 to describe changes which will require re-tendering. The concept of substantial changes is defined in some detail as set out above. However, nested within this concept we find a modification which 'extends the scope of the contract or framework considerably'—as just one example of a change which must be considered substantial. Elsewhere in the same article, references are made to changes which 'alter the overall nature of the contract or framework agreement'—with the implication that these go beyond substantial changes which may be justified in certain circumstances. While the recitals provide some guidance and examples in relation to these terms, the resolution of their meaning is likely to require further case law, whether at the suit of the Commission or economic operators challenging changes or extensions to existing contracts. Access to information about the scope and nature of contractual changes may, however, be an impediment to such challenges, despite the requirement to publish an OJEU notice in the case of substantial unforeseen changes.

Consequences of Modifications—Ability to Terminate Contracts

5.50   All three of the 2014 directives require that contracting authorities must be able to terminate contracts in certain circumstances, including where modifications have been made which cannot be justified on any of the above grounds. This represents the first time that the EU procurement directives have mandated, rather than simply authorized, specific contractual clauses. Notably, however, they do not create an obligation for contracting authorities to terminate a contract where modifications cannot be justified under the exceptions discussed above, but rather, simply aim to ensure that this is possible. If a modification is not authorized under the directives, it would appear that the appropriate legal remedy would be a declaration of ineffectiveness—as the contracting authority has failed to publish a contract notice in circumstances where this would be required under the directives—that is, a new contract has been directly awarded. It will also have breached the standstill period and deprived the claimant of access to pre-contractual remedies.[42] The case might

---

[42] These are two of the situations in which a contract must be considered ineffective under Art 2d of Directive 89/665/EEC (inserted by Directive 2007/66/EU). The English courts have to date been reluctant to apply ineffectiveness as a remedy for illicit modifications to contracts. Interestingly, in *Alstom*, Mann J rejected the idea that a *new* notice was required where substantial modifications

be different if the new contract itself were not subject to the directives—for example, because it is below threshold. In such cases, the *de minimis* exemption would sometimes, but not always, be available—for example, if a change worth €200,000 is made in a €1 million services contract, it is above the 10 per cent limit, but below the current non-central government threshold for supplies and services contracts. In such cases, a breach of the rules on modifications may not be sufficient to attract the remedy of ineffectiveness, but the new contract could still be set aside.

Where ineffectiveness is the appropriate remedy for unauthorized modifications **5.51** to contracts, this raises questions of how it will be applied in practice and how easy it will be for such claims to be made. The impact of a finding of ineffectiveness varies under national law, and may result in the retroactive cancellation of all obligations under the contract or in the cancellation of future obligations only.[43] In the latter situation, Member States must provide for either the payment of fines or the shortening of the duration of a contract as alternative penalties. Such remedies may well be better suited to illicit modifications to contracts than the payment of damages, the calculation of which is likely to prove difficult.[44] The time limits which apply in respect of challenges to illicit modifications may also need to be clarified—whether this is the longer six-month period for applications for ineffectiveness and whether publication of a voluntary *ex ante* transparency notice or contract award notice upon modification would shorten this. One further point worth noting in this regard is that modifications to contracts awarded

---

to a contract had been made, meaning that the remedy of ineffectiveness was not available to the claimant in that case. However, this rested on the defendant's use of a qualification system (*Alstom Transport v Eurostar International Ltd* [2011] EWHC 1828 (Ch), paras 33–43). In *J Varney & Sons v Hertfordshire County Council* [2010] EWHC 1404 (QB), Flaux J held that if the claim of an illegal modification had been made out, the only available remedy was a judicial review order to quash those changes. His reasoning was based on the impossibility of the authority terminating the contract in that case—an example of where the termination rule set out in Art 73(1) of the Public Sector Directive will be instrumental. It is submitted that both of these cases could be confined to their facts on the question of remedies for modifications, and that the position is in any event altered under the 2014 directives.

[43] Art 2(d)(2) Directive 89/665/EEC, inserted by Directive 2007/66/EU.

[44] This arises in part from the approach taken by courts in several Member States of calculating damages by reference to the chance which a bidder had to win a contract, were it not for the defect complained of. While this necessarily causes the court to engage with hypothetical questions, in the case of illicit modifications there will in fact have been no competition for the new contract, meaning that an extra layer of speculation must be entered into by the court (Would the contract have been advertised separately or as part of a larger contract? Would the claimant have been invited to tender? etc.). The question of the claimant's standing may also arise, although Art 1(3) of Directive 89/665/EEC requires that remedies be available to 'any person having or having had an interest in obtaining a particular contract and who has been or risks being harmed by an alleged infringement'—suggesting a low bar. For discussion of the availability of damages in procurement cases in different jurisdictions, see: Fairgrieve, D. and Lichère, F. (eds) (2011) *Public Procurement Law: Damages as an Effective Remedy* (Oxford: Hart Publishing).

prior to the 2014 directives coming into effect will be governed by the new rules, if the modification itself takes place after their implementation.[45] To the extent that the rules on modifications reflect the Court's existing case law, they may also be found directly effective prior to implementation of the 2014 directives in national law.

---

[45] The Court in Case C-576/10 *Commission v Netherlands*, not yet reported, confirmed that it is the law in force at the time the decision under challenge is taken which is relevant. In that case (discussed at paras 1.73–1.76), both the Court and the Advocate General considered that the modifications were not in fact substantial, meaning no new contract arose. As noted in Chapter 1, this approach seems open to abuse where decisions are taken in advance of new directives coming into effect.

6

VALUE FOR MONEY

Most public sector procurement identifies value for money (VfM) as a core objec- **6.01**
tive. Procurement decisions based on VfM may be distinguished from those based
on the lowest price, quality alone, or decisions made on some other basis such
as relationships with suppliers, political factors, or administrative expediency.
Procurement based on VfM is intended to deliver a better allocation of scarce
public resources among competing ends by weighing the cost and quality aspects
of different options and choosing the one which fully meets the purchaser's needs
at the lowest cost. This may be assessed both internally within a tender, by evaluating bids, and externally, by comparing the outcome of the competition with
other options such as in-house provision or availing of a shared service. There is no
universal formula for assessing VfM in procurement; the way in which both costs
and quality are measured and compared with other options varies widely. This
chapter examines the various approaches taken and offers a critique, in particular
of the tendency to focus on short-term costs to the exclusion of broader appraisals
of value.

The 2014 directives include specific rules on life-cycle costing, to ensure that this is **6.02**
done in a transparent manner which takes account of the ability of tenderers to provide information regarding the full life cycle of goods, services, or works. Where
common, mandatory methods for life-cycle costing in particular sectors are developed at EU level, authorities are obliged to apply these in their tenders—currently
only the case for road transport vehicles.[1] The provisions on award criteria and
life-cycle costing in the 2014 directives may help to bring the EU legal framework
into closer alignment with national definitions of VfM by emphasizing that these

---

[1] Under Directive 2009/33/EC of the European Parliament and of the Council of 23 April 2009
on the promotion of clean and energy-efficient road transport vehicles ('Clean Vehicles Directive'
or CVD) OJ L 120, 15 May 2009, pp 5–12. The directive requires contracting authorities and
entities to include energy/fuel consumption and environmental performance in their technical
specifications and/or award criteria when awarding contracts for road transport vehicles. Where
these impacts are monetized for inclusion in the purchasing decision, specific values are provided
for the costing of different types of emission. The application and impact of the CVD are discussed
in Chapter 7.

may address costs other than initial purchase price. UK Treasury guidance, for example, states that value for money 'means securing the best mix of quality and effectiveness for the least outlay over the period of use of the goods or services bought. It is not about minimising up front prices.'[2]

6.03 It may be argued that the methodology and precise criteria used to assess costs in procurement are of secondary importance to intelligent budgeting and commercial acumen. The exercise of these last two functions falls outside of the EU procurement regime.[3] Public sector budgeting is a science (or art) unto itself—with different traditions in evidence across Europe. It is sufficient for our purposes to make two broad observations here about the effect of public budgeting practices on procurement. The first is that efficiency, or allocation of scarce resources in an optimal way among competing ends, is an ongoing preoccupation of public sector budgeting. Efforts to root out spending which is identified as inefficient are perennial. The second is that it is more difficult to measure efficiency in the public sector context than for most private sector operations. This is because profitability, which often serves as a proxy for efficiency in private undertakings, does not apply—or if it does, it is tempered by the need to deliver public functions and objectives. There is no agreement across time, political wind changes, and financial systems as to how efficiency in public spending should be measured.[4]

Cost, Time, Quality, and Other Factors

6.04 Increasingly, public procurers are asked to balance a number of competing objectives: short- and long-term value, purchase price, innovation, social and environmental goals, economic and industrial policy—and to do all this in a manner which complies with the rules and attracts competition. In this environment, it may be difficult to 'act quickly and get the best deal'—a criticism often made when comparing public to private sector procurement. However, the assumption that private sector procurement is more driven by commercial considerations, and thus obtains better value for money, deserves some scrutiny. A 2011 study which analysed both public and private sector tender procedures found competition

---

[2] HM Treasury, *Managing Public Money*, July 2013, p 102.

[3] Public procurement regulation is based on the Treaty provisions relating to free movement of goods and services and the creation of an internal market, as opposed to the attainment of value for money by public authorities. However, the attainment of VfM has long formed the basis of national procurement policies, and the fact that the EU procurement directives have not sought to regulate this aspect of procurement directly should not be taken to mean that it is considered to be of lesser importance.

[4] Economists and international institutions such as the World Bank, IMF, and OECD have dedicated some effort to measuring and comparing efficiency in public spending practices. See under this heading Tanzi, V. (2004) *Measuring Efficiency in Public Expenditure* (World Bank website), acknowledging the difficulty in applying traditional input/output measures and surveying attempts to develop appropriate macro and micro indicators.

and price pressure may actually be weaker in many private sector procurement processes.[5] Corporate social responsibility also plays an increasingly prominent role in much private sector procurement, and in many sectors long-term relationships with suppliers are preferred to lowest-cost sourcing. The image of ruthlessly efficient private procurement, compared to softer, costlier public procurement is thus not a particularly instructive one.

Public tender procedures do on average require more person-days to conduct and **6.05** so incur greater transaction costs—in part a reflection of the larger number of firms participating. This indicates that there may be a trade-off between transaction costs and better value outcomes from the public buyer's perspective, to the extent that the latter are driven by levels of competition and associated price pressure. There is some evidence to support this view based on large-scale studies of the final purchase costs and number of bids achieved via different procurement procedures advertised in the Official Journal, discussed in paragraphs 6.22 and 6.23. Further research is needed to establish the overall effect which different procedures and levels of competition have on value for money, and particularly the extent to which transaction costs are effectively passed back to contracting authorities by suppliers.[6]

It is worth noting at the outset that, to the extent that public opinion has been **6.06** surveyed on the question, a majority of EU citizens appear to support use of factors other than price or cost in the award of public contracts. A 2011 Eurobarometer survey on perceptions of the internal market included a number of questions regarding public procurement, with a random sample of respondents over the age of 15 being polled across the EU. Fifty-six per cent of respondents considered that contracts for important projects should be awarded based on a mix of factors such as price, quality, environmental considerations, social aspects, and/or innovative aspects; with smaller numbers opting for award based on the cheapest offer, nationality of the bidding companies, or the quickest possible award to avoid delays to the project. Overall, only 13 per cent of respondents thought awarding to the cheapest

---

[5] Strand, I. Ramada, P., and Canton, E. (2011) *Public Procurement in Europe: Cost and Effectiveness* (PwC, London Economics, and Ecorys), pp 121–3. The study analyses some 540,000 procurements advertised in the Official Journal over five years (2006–10) from 30 countries. This data was supplemented by a survey of 7,300 authorities and firms and 150 in-depth interviews regarding different aspects of procurement procedures. Interviews were carried out with 20 large private sector construction and services firms regarding their own procurement, supplementing the survey responses from 1,882 firms.

[6] As discussed in Chapter 5, the 2014 directives incorporate the rules on modifications to contracts developed by the CJEU in cases such as *pressetext*, meaning that in theory there is less scope to make changes which increase the value of a contract after it has been awarded without triggering a new competition. If EU-level competitive tendering results in greater competition and price pressure on bidders, the outcomes should be 'locked down' in the contract which is awarded, with limited scope for suppliers to pass on transaction costs outside of what is included in their tendered price. However, in practice, there may still be ample room for post-award changes which affect contract value, particularly where these have been provided for by way of a contract review clause.

offer was the best approach, although there were significant regional disparities on this point (27 per cent of respondents in Portugal approved, compared to 4 per cent of respondents in the Netherlands, and 1 per cent in Sweden).[7] Policies based on appeals to the notional taxpayer seldom reflect such nuances in his or her understanding of value for money in public contracts.

How VfM is Addressed in Procurement

6.07 The most obvious consideration of VfM in procurement takes place in the scoring of bids against the award criteria. It is at this stage that price or cost is weighed against quality, according to the predetermined evaluation scheme. However, the decisions taken at many other stages can affect VfM as much as, if not more than, the final evaluation and selection of a preferred bidder. The design and execution of the procurement process typically encompasses a number of linked stages from needs assessment through to contract management. Brief consideration is given here to how each stage may influence the value obtained by contracting authorities and the evidence available from recent empirical studies of procurement in European countries.

Identifying and classifying a need

6.08 Should public hospitals keep stockpiles of vaccines? Are external legal services required for a project? Should early preventative maintenance be carried out on a road or bridge? These are examples of decisions which affect VfM at the initial stages of needs assessment. In some cases, they may do more to determine the cost/ quality outcome than decisions taken at any other point. Most public sector needs are not articulated by procurement departments in the first instance. They may either arise directly from the statutory functions of a public body, or be incidental to the discharge of those functions. Thus, the army must procure material, the fire brigade ladders and hoses, hospitals medical equipment—and all must procure computers and other supplies and services essential to modern administration. In some organizations, the commissioning function is separated from procurement, but there will inevitably be a high degree of interaction between them.

6.09 In addition to renewing contracts, the commissioning or procurement function may be responsible for identifying new needs or advising on the availability of replacement technology or services. Requirements in some procurement categories will be relatively fixed from year to year, others are linked to the number of staff or volume of services being delivered by the organization, and some are incidental to

---

[7] European Commission (2011) *Special Eurobarometer 363—Internal Market: Awareness, Perceptions and Impacts*, pp 113–19.

specific projects or operations. New procurement categories may replace previous ones—for example, multi-functional devices replacing separate purchases of printers, photocopiers, and scanners. Tensions often exist between the needs identified by internal users (for example, to acquire the latest technology) and the obligation of budget-holders and procurers to maximize value for money.

The role of needs assessment in VfM can be seen most clearly where failure to plan **6.10** ahead leads to emergency procurement. In December 2011, the Hammersmith flyover which carries one of London's major arterial roads was closed to traffic due to the need for emergency repairs. The flyover, built in the early 1960s, had suffered corrosion from a heating system which had malfunctioned many years previously. The total cost of the repair work, carried out in two instalments, was close to £60 million—not including the cost of disruption. If the maintenance had been carried out when the problem initially appeared, the real cost would have been much lower. Including anti-corrosion measures in the original construction contract would have been even cheaper. These are the type of considerations which contribute directly to value for money and which should be identified at the needs assessment stage—but are all too often only recognized in hindsight.

Market knowledge and pre-procurement

Once a requirement has been identified, intelligence about the market from which **6.11** it will be procured is needed. If it is a standard purchase in an established category, then the authority may feel confident to launch a tender or draw down from an existing contract or framework without carrying out any market research. However, markets are by their nature dynamic, and if a number of years have passed since the last purchase of the product or service, it is usually worthwhile to engage in some form of pre-procurement process. This can help to actively engage potential suppliers by notifying them of the upcoming tender, and seek answers to specific questions about their products or services. The publication of a Prior Information Notice in the OJEU announcing upcoming tenders is one way of engaging the market with a view to securing better competition. This may be complemented by supplier open days, market sounding questionnaires, or the publication of a prospectus. Other public sector organizations which have recently procured similar requirements may be contacted for advice or information. More passive approaches include web searches and consulting catalogues or online databases. The 2014 directives create explicit rules regarding preliminary market consultation for the first time, discussed in Chapter 3.

The pre-procurement phase can play a vital role in attaining value for money. The **6.12** more comprehensive and up-to-date an authority's knowledge of the market is, the less likely it is to make costly mistakes in choosing and executing a tender procedure. For example, if most suppliers of a given product or service are located abroad, it may be necessary to actively publicise the contract across borders or in other languages, to ensure a good response and adequate levels of competition. If suppliers will require lead time to build up their capacity to deliver the contract's requirements, tender deadlines and payment schedules should reflect this to ensure that the public sector client is not paying for something which cannot yet be delivered.[8] Alternatively, it may make sense to encourage the formation of consortia amongst bidders, to deliver the full range of requirements. All of these decisions can influence VfM, and all of them are more likely to be 'got right' when a contracting authority understands the market(s) from which it is procuring. Some public organizations employ a category management approach to develop closer understanding of their supply markets.

6.13 Engaging with suppliers at the pre-procurement stage may also help to increase levels of competition for a contract. An average of just over five tenders were received for procedures advertised in the Official Journal from 2006 to 2010; however, nearly 20 per cent of procedures received just one bid.[9] The short time frame associated with many calls for competition, and the difficulty which suppliers still encounter in obtaining detailed information about requirements, is likely to be to blame in some cases. Certain countries, such as Germany and Spain, have a higher average of eight tenders, and local government procurement tends to be more competitive than that of central government and utilities.[10] These variations between countries and types of authority suggest that levels of competition are not strictly due to the structure of supply markets, and that there is scope to influence the number of expressions of interest and bids received through market engagement at the pre-procurement stage.

6.14 Despite the much-touted virtues of pre-procurement, it is still the exception rather than the rule for most organizations. This may be due in part to the prevailing culture of procurement departments, which is oriented towards more structured interaction with suppliers. Engaging with suppliers during pre-procurement is less formal than selecting bidders or evaluating tenders, the activities which procurers are most familiar with. It can be difficult in practice to 'draw a line'—to go from discussing options and developing a rapport with suppliers to setting requirements and eliminating those who do not comply. Procurers may be wary, or may be specifically forbidden by organizational policies, to engage with suppliers outside of the formalized communication required for tendering.

6.15 The benefits of pre-procurement from a VfM perspective depend on the capacity of the organization to use the information gathered, while avoiding giving any company a real or perceived advantage. A supplier who believes it has already secured a contract at the pre-procurement phase is less likely to offer best value in its bid.

---

[8] Unless it is engaging in pre-commercial or innovation procurement, as discussed in Chapter 4.
[9] Strand et al, *Public Procurement in Europe*, p 6.
[10] Strand et al, *Public Procurement in Europe*, p 6.

A balance thus needs to be struck between engaging suppliers and maintaining competitive tension. It remains to be seen whether the move to full e-procurement under the 2014 directives will have the effect of increasing the levels of competition for contracts, and whether pre-procurement will also become fully electronic. Reliance on e-procurement systems to identify potential suppliers may limit more personal approaches to market engagement, such as speaking to suppliers directly or organizing an open day, unless the systems themselves encourage such activities.

Subject-matter, scope, and contract type

6.16 Should a framework agreement be set up to obtain legal services from multiple firms, or is it sufficient to have a contract with several lots? Does it make sense to procure spare parts at the same time as buying rolling stock or vehicles, or should these be provided under a service contract? These are the types of questions faced by procurers when determining the subject-matter and scope of a contract or framework. Consideration will normally be given to the exact nature of the authority's needs, any foreseeable future changes, past experience, and the way in which the market is structured. Equally important, but often overlooked, are the signals which decisions on subject-matter and scope give to the market. At the most basic level, choice of Common Procurement Vocabulary (CPV) codes determines how OJEU-level contract notices are classified and the title of the contract which potential bidders will see. Variations in e-procurement and notification systems mean that procurers do not always see a preview of the notice in the exact form in which it will appear to suppliers. This can lead to incomplete notices, poorer response rates, and, ultimately, poorer value outcomes.[11]

6.17 Prior to advertising, decisions must be made about the scope of a contract or framework in terms of estimated duration, total value, and any options or renewals. If a framework is chosen, the contract notice must indicate whether it will be with a single or multiple operators. While no maximum length for contracts is stipulated under the directives, disproportionately lengthy contracts may be challenged on competition grounds.[12] The maximum duration for a framework agreement is four

---

[11] Most e-procurement systems automatically notify registered suppliers regarding contracts advertised with the CPV codes they have selected. Companies may also subscribe to one or more notification systems which collect notices based on keywords, location, or the type of authority or contract. An increasing number of public authorities advertise all of their contracting opportunities on their own websites and regional or national portals—however, as discussed in Chapter 3, such advertising must not precede submission to Tenders Electronic Daily (TED), the electronic version of the supplement to the OJEU, or contain additional details.

[12] In its *London Underground* decision (N-264/02), the Commission found that a 30-year duration for contracts awarded as part of a PPP for the upgrade and maintenance of the underground network was proportionate based on the complexities of the project, the level of investment, and the time needed to reach the agreed rates of return. The Commission also noted that the continuous review of payments by an independent arbiter, procedures for the award of subcontracts, and safeguards against use of assets to distort competition in ancillary markets helped to establish the proportionality of the arrangements (paras 104–10 of the decision).

years for the public sector and eight years for utilities, although individual contracts awarded under a framework may have a longer duration. The effect of long contracts or frameworks on VfM depends on the nature of the requirements and market, as well as on the competitiveness of the tender outcome. Multi-operator frameworks can be effective in maintaining competitive tension to deliver best value when the precise quantity or nature of requirements is not known at the outset. However, there are transaction costs associated with conducting mini-competitions, and in some cases multi-operator frameworks may limit the volume discounts available from individual suppliers.[13]

6.18 Projects with high up-front capital costs or risks will normally benefit from longer contract periods, as the operator has time to recoup the initial investment made and pay off any external financing. Assuming that these costs will be passed on to the contracting authority in one form or another, the optimal contract period is one which allows sufficient time for payback while limiting the period of 'pure profit' for the operator. In contrast, some contracts may be highly profitable to operators at the outset with diminishing returns as time goes on—for example, where a licence fee is paid to a software vendor on installation. In these cases, public authorities may obtain better value by opting for longer-term contracts with fixed prices for additional services. There are a number of ways to build flexibility into contract periods, by including options for renewal, variants (to test the effect of different contracting periods on bid prices), or no-fault termination provisions. The scope of a contract in terms of the volume of goods or services to be delivered may also be made more or less flexible, with contracting authorities reserving the right to source requirements outside of the contract or framework.

Determining the procurement procedure

6.19 The various procedures available under the 2014 directives are discussed in Chapter 3. As these provide different ways of engaging with the market and structuring competition, one would expect choice of procedure to have some effect on VfM. However, isolating this effect is difficult, as choice of procedure will generally reflect the nature of the contract and the market from which it is being sourced. Thus, it is more common to use the open procedure for lower value contracts and standard supplies, whereas until recently competitive dialogue has been restricted to more complex requirements and the negotiated procedure was available only with special justification in the public sector.[14] The frequency with which each procedure is used also varies between Member States and types of contracting authority, so comparisons of the value obtained from different procedures needs to control for this.

---

[13] Further consideration of value within single and multi-operator frameworks is given at paras 3.43–3.49.
[14] Competitive dialogue is available in a wider range of circumstances under the 2014 directives: see paras 3.24–3.31.

Empirical research examining the impact of procurement procedures on cost and in particular on quality remains sparse, and the scope for direct comparison with non-EU jurisdictions is limited by differences in regulatory frameworks.

A 2011 econometric study carried out on behalf of the European Commission **6.20** attempted to analyse the relationship between the different procurement procedures and techniques available under the 2004 directives and their outcomes in terms of cost and number of bids received. This drew on contract award notices published in the TED database from 2006 to 2009. Cost outcomes were measured by comparing the values published in award notices against the initial estimate of contract value made by the contracting authority. As contract award notices are often either not published or exclude information about contract value, the results from the sample studied cannot be generalized to draw conclusions about all OJEU contracts, much less the total volume of public procurement.[15] However, the study's findings regarding different procedures and cost savings are still worth noting. Publishing an invitation to tender (ITT) alone was associated with a statistically significant saving of approximately 1 per cent in the value of the contract awarded against the initial estimate, with minimal variation in the percentage saving across different contract values. Using the open procedure was associated with an increase in this saving of some 3 per cent, whereas the additional saving from use of the restricted procedure was 1.1 per cent.[16] The procedures other than open or restricted were not individually evaluated.

A second study published in 2011 took a different approach to calculating the **6.21** costs and benefits of procurement procedures, assessing the number of person days required and monetizing this based on labour costs. This study found that the average OJEU competition required the equivalent of 123 person days of resources, or €28,000 in monetary terms. It also concluded that there was practically no relationship between contract value and procurement costs, except in the very high value range—meaning that transaction costs were comparatively high relative to contract value for smaller contracts. Transaction costs were found to be higher compared to contract value in Germany (4.8 per cent) and Sweden (3.8 per cent), and lower in Italy (1.0 per cent) and the UK (0.7 per cent)—findings which may be linked to the smaller average value of contracts in the first two countries and greater use of frameworks and central purchasing in the UK and Italy.[17] Transaction costs, of course, cannot be solely attributed to the EU procurement directives, as some would be incurred regardless of the regulatory regime or procedures followed.

---

[15] Europe Economics (2011) *Estimating the Benefits from the Procurement Directives: A Report for DG Internal Market*, pp 35–6. As the authors note, contract awards recorded in TED accounted for only some 18 per cent of the total value of public expenditure on goods and services during the relevant period, and their sample is the subset of TED notices for which all of the required information was available.

[16] Europe Economics, *Estimating the Benefits*, p 46.

[17] Strand et al, *Public Procurement in Europe*, p 90.

Table 6.1 Person-day costs for authorities and firms by type of procurement

Procedure/technique	Authority days	Firm days	Mean no. of bids	Median no. of days
EC funds	24	24	5.4	154
Restricted	28	19	5.5	130
Joint purchasing	20	18	5.9	126
EMAT (MEAT)	23	17	5.7	120
Framework (1st stage)	22	16	5.9	116
Negotiated	22	20	4.8	116
Average	22	16	5.4	108
Open	21	15	5.7	107
E-auctions	28	12	5.2	90
Lowest price	20	14	4.6	84
Accelerated restricted	21	13	4.8	83
Accelerated negotiated	22	15	4	82
Framework (all calls)	16	14	4	70
Negotiated without prior notice	18	20	1.8	53

Source: Strand, I., Ramada, P., and Canton, E. (2011) Public Procurement in Europe: Cost and Effectiveness (PwC, London Economics, and Ecorys), p 78.

6.22 The costs in terms of person days associated with each of the procedures available under the 2004 directives is shown in Table 6.1, and the average number of bids received using different procedures and techniques is shown in Table 6.2. While these figures do not allow a direct assessment of value attained via different procurement techniques and procedures, some inferences can be drawn based on the number of person days required (a proxy for transaction costs) and the number of bids received (a proxy for competitiveness). The firm days in Table 6.1 are per firm, so the median number of days in the right-hand column is the total calculated by multiplying this figure by the mean number of bids and adding the authority days. This should be distinguished from the average time elapsed from publication of a contract notice to award of a contract, discussed in paragraph 6.52.

6.23 Both framework agreements and joint purchasing can be seen to attract a relatively high number of bids, but joint purchasing requires a significantly higher investment in process. In order to determine the relative impact of these two approaches on overall VfM, additional factors would need to be known, such as the number and value of contracts awarded via these arrangements and the sectors involved. The relatively small difference in the number of bids received in open and restricted procedures appears surprising; however, this may be accounted for in part by the lower average value of contracts awarded via the open procedure in the sample studied. In contrast, the econometric study showed significantly higher bidder participation

Table 6.2 Number of bids received by procedure and technique

Procedure/technique	Mean no. of bids
Negotiated without prior notice	1.8
Accelerated	4.0
Competitive dialogue	3.9
Lowest price	4.6
EC funds	5.4
Negotiated	4.8
E-auctions	5.2
Non-framework	5.3
All procurement	5.4
Non-EC funds	5.4
Restricted	5.5
Open	5.7
EMAT (MEAT)	5.7
Framework	5.9
Joint purchasing	5.9

Source: Strand, I., Ramada, P., and Canton, E. (2011) Public Procurement in Europe: Cost and Effectiveness (PwC, London Economics, and Ecorys), p 94.

and savings against original estimates of cost where the open procedure was used.[18] Again, without controlling for the type of contract and type of authority, it is difficult to reach conclusions about the cost impact of the procedure itself.

What factors, then, should inform an authority's choice of procedure from a VfM **6.24** perspective? It is suggested that the level of interaction with operators needed to identify the best tender, together with the resources and expertise available to carry out the procedure, are core considerations. The competitive procedure with negotiation, which is available in a range of circumstances under the 2014 directives, provides the greatest flexibility to interact with operators in the post-tender stage, whereas the competitive dialogue offers greater flexibility at the pre-tender stage to refine requirements. Both have the potential to deliver good value, but the authority's ability to manage negotiations or dialogue and in particular to maintain competitive tension among a number of operators is key to their success. If the benefits of negotiation or dialogue are limited, the open or restricted procedures are likely to deliver better value by keeping transaction costs lower.

Preparing the specification

Technical specifications play three vital roles in procurement, each of which **6.25** has the potential to affect value for money. The first is that they influence the

---

[18] Europe Economics, *Estimating the Benefits*, p 52.

decision of suppliers to submit a bid. This is true whether the open procedure or a multi-stage procedure is used. In the latter case, shortlisted candidates may choose not to bid after reviewing the specification. While this information will not necessarily be known to other competitors, it still narrows the field of competition and may adversely affect the value obtained. A second function of technical specifications is that they determine which tenders will go forward for evaluation against the contract award criteria. Only bids which are valid and responsive to the technical specifications are eligible for such evaluation and contracting authorities are obliged to reject non-compliant bids, a point which was emphasized by the Court in the *Storebaelt* case.[19] Third, the substance of the technical specifications will determine what is offered by tenderers, and the price at which it is offered.

6.26 Specifications which are unclear or unnecessarily complex can compromise value for money by reducing the number of tenders or responsive tenders, by increasing prices, or by decreasing the quality of what is offered. They may also have a knock-on effect on costs at the contract management stage, if the goods, services, or works are not fit for purpose due to ambiguities or errors in the specification. This problem is encountered with particular frequency in IT contracts, where the nature of requirements is not fully or properly specified in the tender documents. This is one of the reasons why many organizations have moved from detailed, input-based specifications to outcome or performance-based specifications for IT contracts. By defining the required result, rather than the means of achieving it, procurers aim to avoid such pitfalls.

6.27 Regardless of whether a specification is defined with reference to inputs, outputs, or outcomes, the level of detail provided must be adequate to ensure that (i) bidders all have the same understanding of the requirements and (ii) this understanding matches that of the authority. In some cases, outcome-based specifications can simply disguise inadequate consideration of what is involved in a contract and how it will be delivered. This means that suppliers effectively take on the risk associated with defining these standards, and may do so in a way which does not meet the authority's needs or which detracts from overall value. The costs associated with ambiguities in specifications are usually passed back to the authority.

6.28 Some ambiguities in specifications may be unavoidable or intentional—for example, where they are used as a means of testing the market to see what can be delivered and what the cost implications are. The risk of this approach is that in most procedures bidders only get one chance to respond to the specification, with limited scope for subsequent negotiation of the content of bids. A better approach is to include priced variants or options in the scope of a tender, defining the minimum requirements which all tenders must meet and the way in which the variants or options will be assessed. Alternatively, the competitive dialogue does not require technical specifications to be developed in advance, but seeks proposals based on a description of the authority's requirements which can then be progressively

---

[19] Case C-243/89 *Commission v Denmark* [1993] ECR I-3353, paras 37–9.

refined. For complex contracts, this can save costs in the longer term, by ensuring that the purchased solution is fit for purpose and does not under- or over-perform against needs.

Selection criteria

As discussed in Chapter 4, the 2014 directives aim to reduce the burden of prov- **6.29** ing compliance with selection and exclusion criteria. This was mainly approached from the viewpoint of increasing SME participation and addressing complaints from suppliers regarding the bureaucratic and repetitive nature of selection procedures. If the European Single Procurement Document and other attempts to streamline selection are successful, and this translates into more competition for public contracts, then gains will accrue to public authorities. However, the purpose of exclusion and selection criteria is not only to limit the number of bidders for a contract, but also to ensure that those invited to bid[20] have the technical, financial, and professional capacity to carry it out. Failure to adequately assess this can compromise VfM in a variety of ways: for example, if a contractor becomes bankrupt and cannot deliver, or if losses arise from defective performance which could have been detected via more thorough investigation of previous contracts.

From a VfM perspective, then, it is vital to set the bar for selection at an appro- **6.30** priate level based on the specific requirements of the contract at hand. Selection approaches which are either under- or over-inclusive can undermine the value achieved at tender stage. For example, using an already-established framework agreement will exclude any new entrants to the market. The effect of this on VfM for a particular contract depends on how long ago the framework was set up and whether there are in fact more recent entrants who could offer better value. If, on the other hand, the authority uses a dynamic purchasing system or draws on a database of pre-qualified suppliers, both of which must be kept open to new applicants at any time, the pool will be larger, but likely to include some operators without relevant experience or capacity. Similarly, a standard form of pre-qualification questionnaire may not effectively eliminate candidates who are unable to deliver specific requirements. Inviting such candidates to tender incurs wasted transaction costs on both sides.

One criticism of the 2004 directives was that contracting authorities did not have **6.31** sufficient ability to take an operator's full record in delivering previous contracts into account. If an operator chose not to include a particular contract in its list of references, there was little scope to consider this unless it affected their overall reliability. The limited ability to exclude operators based on defective prior performance, discussed in Chapter 4, goes some way towards addressing this lacuna.

---

[20] Exclusion and selection criteria also apply in an open procedure, but are only assessed on a pass or fail basis to determine eligibility for tender evaluation or contract award.

A new provision dealing with situations where a candidate negligently provides misleading information regarding their previous experience or any other matter is also included in the 2014 directives.[21] The 2014 directives also create a clearer ability to evaluate the experience of specific staff assigned to the contract at award stage, thus putting to rest the much-criticised judgment of the Court in *Lianakis*, which appeared to rule out such considerations at award stage.[22]

6.32 It remains more difficult to exclude an operator based on specific knowledge of poor prior performance. The 2014 directives allow exclusion for defects in prior performance in individual cases where the operator has shown:

> significant or persistent deficiencies in the performance of a substantive requirement under a prior public contract, a prior contract with a contracting entity or a prior concession contract which led to early termination of that prior contract, damages or other comparable sanctions.[23]

As discussed in Chapter 4, the rationale for limiting the exclusion to deficiencies in performance of public contracts is not clear—termination of a prior contract delivered to the private sector seems equally relevant. The standard for exclusion is a high one, and is inevitably open to dispute. The period for exclusion is limited to a maximum of three years, and operators may also seek to establish their reliability despite the existence of this ground for exclusion (the self-cleaning proviso).[24] Avoiding an operator whom the contracting authority knows to have underperformed on prior contracts may be considered essential to delivering value. Time and resources spent documenting substandard performance, or availing of contractual remedies, inevitability detracts from other more productive activities in which both parties might engage. Nevertheless, there is a need to balance the ability to exclude poorly performing operators with fairness and the possibility that leopards change their spots, or their management.

Award criteria

6.33 Award criteria may relate to price or cost only, or the best cost-quality ratio. The role of award criteria and rules regarding their formulation and application are considered in Chapter 4. Any approach to comparing tenders must reflect the principles of equal treatment and transparency as developed in CJEU case law. Although contracting

---

[21] Art 57(4)(g) Public Sector Directive (also applicable under Art 80 Utilities Directive). The limitations of this provision are discussed at paras 4.10–4.11.

[22] Art 67(2)(b) Public Sector Directive. This is limited to where 'the quality of the staff assigned can have a significant impact on the level of performance of the contract'—a relatively low bar. Case C-532/06 *Lianakis v Dimos Alexandroupolis* ('*Lianakis*') [2008] ECR I-251. For a discussion of the Court's judgment, see Lee, P. (2010) 'Implications of the Lianakis Decision' 2 PPLR 47–56.

[23] Art 57(4)(g) Public Sector Directive.

[24] Art 57(6) Public Sector Directive.

authorities use a variety of formulae to award marks based on costs, the following is recommended:[25]

$$\text{Score Tender X} = (\text{Cost Tender L} / \text{Cost Tender X}) * \text{N}$$

Where:

Tender L = lowest valid and responsive tender;
Cost = total cost of all priced components of the tender; and
N = maximum points available for cost.

This yields a non-linear scoring outcome, with no possibility of a tender receiving a negative score.[26] The lowest valid and responsive tender receives full marks. A tender which is twice as expensive as the lowest one receives half as many marks. In contrast, a scoring approach which assigns zero marks to the highest bid and full marks to the lowest is less likely to yield a proportionate result—bids which are very close in value can receive vastly different scores. It is important that cost is assessed as a single figure, rather than different cost components being weighted or scored separately—as this could give a result in which the lowest tender overall did not receive the most marks. All separate cost components should be added together and this can then be compared with the sum for other tenders.   **6.34**

Applying the above formula to score costs means that where bids are clustered closely together, non-cost criteria become much more important in determining the final outcome. This is as would be expected, but in the opposite situation, where bid prices are highly dispersed, it may lead to undesirable outcomes, especially if the full range of marks available for qualitative criteria is not used. For example,   **6.35**

---

[25] This was the approach applied in Case C-513/99 *Concordia Bus Finland Oy Ab, formerly Stagecoach Finland Oy Ab v Helsingin kaupunki and HKL-Bussiliikenne* ('*Concordia*') [2002] ECR I-07213, para 22.

[26] A negative score would distort the published weighting of the award criteria, as it would detract from the marks awarded under other headings. In Case T-402/06 *Kingdom of Spain v Commission*, not yet reported, the Commission had made a financial correction of €6.8 million to aid granted under the Cohesion Fund to a Spanish authority, due in large part to procurement irregularities. The Commission successfully challenged the application by the authority of an 'average price' method of cost scoring, which the Court found violated the principle of transparency. The Court held that: 'Although the most economically advantageous tender is not always the tender with the lowest price, the fact remains that, where all tenders are perfectly equal as regards all the other relevant criteria, including technical criteria, a less expensive tender must be regarded, from an economic point of view, as being more advantageous than a more expensive tender' (para 77 of the judgment). The judgment is somewhat problematic in that the Court appeared to consider that the fact that tenderers did not know the average price to which their bid would be compared could, in itself, be a breach of transparency (paras 70–3). However, this is also true in relation to any cost-scoring model which relies on comparison with the lowest valid tender. The Commission, in correcting the amount of the grant, applied a linear cost-scoring model to determine which tender should have won. Under this model, the lowest valid tender received full marks, and the highest tender received the minimum marks under the cost criterion. The Court neither endorsed nor refuted this model, but found that Spain had not made out a sufficient case against it (para 123). The problem with a linear model such as that proposed by the Commission is that where the difference between the highest and lowest tender price is very small, this difference is exaggerated in the spread of cost scores, distorting the overall weighting of cost vs quality.

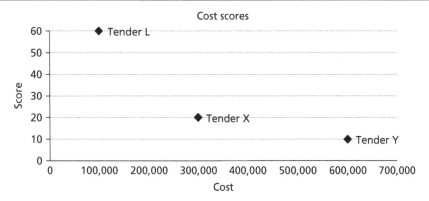

Figure 6.1 Cost scoring

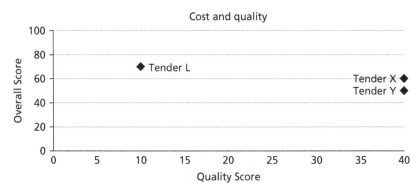

Figure 6.2 Cost and quality scoring

take the situation where cost is weighted at 60 per cent and three bids of €100,000, €300,000, and €600,000 are received (see Figures 6.1 and 6.2).

The three bids receive 60, 20, and 10 marks, respectively, out of the maximum of 60. Now, suppose that the 40 marks for quality are allocated as follows:

40—excellent response;
30—good response;
20—fair response;
10—poor response;
0—no response.

6.36   Even if the lowest-cost tender provides a poor response and the other two receive full marks, the former will still be the preferred bid—assuming it complies with the specification. One strategy to counter this type of outcome is to require a certain minimum mark in respect of qualitative criteria.[27] If a tender is abnormally

---

[27] This approach was approved by Treacy J in *Irish Waste Services Ltd v Northern Ireland Water Ltd and Others* [2013] NIQB 41, paras 21–30.

low, this may provide a separate ground for rejection; however, the 2014 directives leave the term 'abnormally low tender' undefined and there is a need to seek explanation from the bidder before contemplating rejection.

The example in paragraphs 6.35 and 6.36 illustrates the need for careful considera- **6.37** tion of both the weighting and application of award criteria and any sub-criteria, to ensure that they adequately reflect the relative importance of cost and quality considerations in a given tender. Contracting authorities may also employ more advanced approaches to calculating the overall cost of a tender. Life-cycle costing (LCC) broadens cost assessment to include operating and end-of-life costs, and may also include costs not directly incurred by the authority, such as environmental externalities. The role of LCC in furthering environmental policy through procurement is discussed in Chapter 7.

From a purely financial perspective, LCC can play an important role in identifying **6.38** the offer with the lowest real cost over its expected lifetime. It is not a new concept, and most tenders take some costs other than purchase price into account—for example, delivery fees, installation, and warranties. LCC goes beyond this and may be used in the planning stages to estimate budgets or evaluate different options for purchasing or leasing a particular asset, in addition to comparing the total costs of tenders received. Such applications may rely on the ability to make reasonably accurate predictions about future costs such as energy and water prices, interest rates, inflation, and wages. In some cases, the difficulty in gathering and verifying the data to support LCC calculations deters contracting authorities from taking this approach. It remains to be seen whether the provisions in the 2014 directives will lead to a broader uptake of LCC, which has the potential to enhance value for money in many public contracts.

Contract terms

Studies of value for money which do not look beyond the outcome recorded in a **6.39** contract award notice are missing a large part of the picture. In extreme cases, the contract may never have been carried out or may have been terminated early. In others, the final payment made to the contractor will be considerably higher or lower than the recorded price, due to a change in the contract period or deliverables. In theory, changes which represent a substantial modification to what was originally tendered and awarded require a new competition unless they fall within one of the exceptions discussed in Chapter 5. However, even if the changes do not meet this threshold, it is difficult to judge value for money without making some enquiry into the way in which the contract is delivered. Like specifications, contract terms can affect VfM in a number of different ways. First, as with specifications, they will influence the content and price of tenders. The procurement directives require publication of certain contract terms in advance as part of tender documentation.[28]

---

[28] Art 70 Public Sector Directive; and Art 87 Utilities Directive.

This is often done in draft format with scope for adjustments at the preferred bidder stage. In the negotiated and competitive dialogue procedures particularly, there may be considerable changes to contract terms in the post-tender phase. Contracting authorities must be vigilant to ensure that such changes do not tip the overall value equation in favour of the operator, especially where other competitors have already been eliminated.

6.40 For more routine purchases, standard terms and conditions may be used, which typically favour the purchaser on matters such as delivery, warranties, liability, and termination. Acceptance of such terms is often a condition of tender. The 'battle of the forms' is cut short in such cases: each valid tender is an offer to provide goods, services, or works on the specified terms which can be accepted by the authority without further recourse to the bidder. Any qualification to the terms contained in the tender documents may invalidate the tender. Aside from the question of fairness in this approach, it is worth asking whether it is conducive to VfM in procurement. The justification for such an approach lies in the need to ensure comparability of tenders (ie equal treatment) and transparency regarding the terms of the contract to be awarded. But it may also prompt bidders to inflate prices or agree to terms against which they cannot or will not actually deliver. An alternative approach is to allow variants regarding contractual terms, which can both encourage a more thorough review of the terms by bidders and identify any which are linked to bid inflation or risk pricing.

6.41 The second way in which contract terms affect VfM is by adding to the costs of executing a contract—for example, where legal, insurance, or financial services such as a performance bond must be obtained. As with selection criteria, it is important that any such requirements are appropriate and proportionate to the contract, rather than being standardized across a particular organization or procurement category. Usually, there will be some scope for adjusting these terms, but all too often they are included as standard, without consideration of their effect on costs. Similarly, terms governing intellectual property rights, termination, and liability may shift risks to operators without any real gains being achieved by the contracting authority, *a fortiori* where such terms are legally unenforceable. Conversely, well-drafted remedy clauses which are appropriate to the particular contract, such as step-in rights where a contractor defaults on performance, can save costs on both sides in the event they are called upon.

6.42 Another approach to building value into contract terms is to provide for financial incentives or penalties linked to performance levels. Financial incentives may be in the form of either a portion of the contract price held back pending satisfactory performance, or increments for performance beyond the required minimum, both of which are in common usage. Penalty clauses are somewhat more controversial. A study of the use of penalty clauses in the context of residential refuse collection contracts in the United States found that penalties for non-performance were strongly associated with an increase in unit costs.[29] Nevertheless, some authorities include them routinely in contracts, although their enforcement is less routine.

Other contract terms which effectively shift risk to the contractor are also likely to **6.43** carry some premium in terms of overall costs. This is one of the factors which has been seen to undermine value for money in Private Finance Initiative contracts in the UK and other forms of public private partnership: the transfer of excessive or inappropriate risk to the private sector. The financial repercussions of risk transfer grow larger where long-term contracts are awarded or the number of plausible competitors is low. It has become a truism to state that risk should be borne by the party best able to manage it, but that does not mean that this approach is always followed in practice. Blanket indemnities and provisions for liquidated damages are still to be found in many public contracts, despite the dubious cost-benefit profile of many such legal ingenuities.

How the contract is managed

The delivery stage of a contract falls outside of procurement as normally defined, **6.44** but ultimately determines the value obtained by the public authority. Poor delivery of a cleaning contract, for example, will quickly become more important than the initial price paid. On a larger scale, a public-private partnership to develop an area will almost certainly fail to deliver value if communication between the partners breaks down. No matter how good the initial deal is, the ability to verify outcomes and identify any problems at an early stage is dependent on effective management of the contract. If either side lacks the capacity or willingness to maintain the relationship, the value obtained during the tender phase becomes irrelevant.

While procurers may not be directly involved in managing contracts, they will be **6.45** affected by the outcomes. At the extreme end of poor delivery, termination of a contract will trigger a new procurement process. Even if a contract is allowed to run its course while delivering suboptimal value, the experience will influence the way in which it is eventually re-tendered. The most common way of monitoring contracts is through a service level agreement (SLA), which specifies the operational responsibilities of the parties and how performance will be measured. The quality of SLAs varies widely, as does the seriousness with which they are treated. Bidders may be asked to submit a draft SLA as part of a tender, which is then either incorporated into the contract or modified to reflect the authority's expectations. The inclusion of key performance indicators (KPIs) or financial incentives or penalties in a SLA can create a direct link to contractual value. Communication and the capacity to identify and act on service issues are equally important factors.

---

[29] Shetterley, D. R. (2000) 'The Influence of Contract Design on Contractor Performance: The Case of Residential Refuse Collection' 24 *Public Performance and Management Review* 1, 53–68.

Table 6.3 Key performance indicators

Contracting area	Sample environmental performance metrics
Vehicles/fleet	Fuel efficiency; maintenance events; actual emissions
Waste collection	Recycling rates; missed collections; route optimization
Cleaning	Use of cleaning products and water; packaging waste
Building design and construction	Energy performance; use of renewable energy sources

6.46 The metrics used to assess contractual performance will be more or less complex depending on the nature of the contract. KPIs which are expressed in simple terms (for example, 'user satisfaction') can prove more difficult to measure. Performance metrics are relatively well developed in the fields of health and education, but are in less common use for other areas of public service delivery. Contract managers and contractors may need to spend some time developing bespoke KPIs, especially where these are intended to address the secondary impacts of a contract as well as the basic 'what, where, who, how, and how much'. For example, the metrics shown in Table 6.3 might be used to measure environmental performance for different types of contract.

Even these relatively simple metrics have clear potential to influence both the cost and quality of what is being delivered. Provided both partners are willing to invest some time in applying them, such terms can enhance VfM considerably.

Public Sector Budgeting and VfM

6.47 The previous section highlighted the role played by the various stages of the procurement process in determining value for money. However, commissioning and procurement take place within a broader framework of public sector financial management, and it would be remiss not to consider the effect of budgeting practices in particular on procurement decisions. A move from input-based to output- or performance-based budgeting, for example, will influence how contracts are designed, awarded, and monitored. A full consideration of public sector financial management is beyond the scope of this chapter; however, the broad characteristics of public sector budgeting which can be seen to have an impact on VfM in procurement are identified here, and some consideration is given to their direction of influence.

Devolved versus centralized budgeting

6.48 Since the 1990s, there has been a trend among OECD countries to make public budgets more responsive to local priorities by transferring spending to subnational governments and adopting more flexible management practices.[30] At the

---

[30] Curristine, T., Lonti, Z., and Joumard, I. (2007) 'Improving Public Sector Efficiency: Challenges and Opportunities' 7(1) *OECD Journal on Budgeting* 5.

same time, there has been a continuing focus on competition between providers of public services and incentives to deliver cost-effective services. The ability to retain efficiency savings, although not always a feature of devolved budgeting, is much more common where contracting organizations are not linked to a central purse. An organization which is unable to benefit from its own procurement savings will usually be less motivated to achieve them. A literature review on devolved budget management among UK public sector organizations also found that the need for organizations to achieve their strategic aims within their budgets meant that tighter internal restrictions over spending were exercised when spending was decentralized.[31]

The appeal of decentralized budgeting in terms of the motivation it provides to organizations and managers to deliver savings may, however be tempered by the proliferation of controls within the organization itself—so that individual departments still do not realize any gains from procurement savings. As with centralized procurement, the benefits of devolved budgeting in terms of encouraging better value for money in procurement will vary between organizations and between procurement categories. And as with centralized procurement, there is a need to address organizational culture, as well as the mechanics of the process, if it is to yield lasting gains. **6.49**

Output- or performance-based budgets

Performance-based budgeting, which links funds allocated to measurable results, has been adopted for at least some government spending in the large majority of OECD countries.[32] Performance-based budgets are normally presented in terms of product or service groups, rather than revenues and expenditures.[33] In some cases, performance information is used to allocate budgets among competing departments or agencies, whereas in others it determines whether a particular programme or project retains funding. The metrics used to assess performance also vary widely, from purely quantitative indicators to those which include some element of quality assessment or user satisfaction. **6.50**

Outside of individual sectors such as health and education, comparison of the use and impact of different approaches to performance budgeting is impeded by a lack of robust data.[34] However, it seems clear that if performance-based budgets **6.51**

---

[31] Hamson, R. and Bird, L. (2008) 'Devolved Budgets in the Public Sector: A New Conceptual Framework for Consultancy Evaluation' 9(2) *Journal of Finance and Management in Public Services* 33.

[32] Hamson and Bird, 'Devolved Budgets', p 12.

[33] Bergmann, A. (2009) *Public Sector Financial Management* (Harlow: Prentice Hall).

[34] Curristine et al note that international comparison even of input-based budgeting presents difficulties, despite the ready availability of such figures in national accounts (Curristine et al, 'Improving Public Sector Efficiency', p 4).

are to support VfM in procurement, they must be based on a qualitative appraisal of outcomes rather than simply the numerical volume of outputs. Gathering this information can be challenging; however, it is facilitated where procurers use performance indicators and service level agreements as part of their own management of contracts. The impact of this information then depends on the extent to which budget holders have the resources and political wherewithal to assess and act on it.

Single versus multi-year budgets

6.52 The average time taken to conduct a procurement procedure is 108 days, and this does not include planning prior to the publication of a contract notice.[35] Smaller, simpler requirements or those procured using the open procedure typically require less time, whereas more complex procurement takes longer, especially where competitive dialogue is used.[36] For budgetary purposes, expenditure which is forecast for one period may easily slip into the next if any delays are encountered in the contract award process. It is also often difficult to forecast procurement costs accurately, given that this will reflect the particular competitive dynamic which emerges, as well as the market structure and specification. For these reasons, good practice regarding budgeting for procurement tends to involve some degree of temporal flexibility regarding when expenditure is incurred.[37] The ability to carry over unspent funds, or to borrow from future years, reduces the chance that procurement decisions will be based on short-term accounting considerations or that savings will be lost.

6.53 Lack of multi-year budgeting in many public sector bodies may also mean that the identification of procurement needs does not take adequate account of longer-term value considerations. For example, if an IT equipment budget cannot be carried over into the next financial year, then the fact that new tablets will be launched next year which could replace, rather than supplement, staff laptops is less likely to influence the timing and scope of purchases. The planning horizon for procurement is effectively reduced to match the budgetary horizon. While multi-year budgets are likely to encourage longer-term assessment of VfM in procurement, they in turn may create distortions if they do not adequately account for costs incurred outside of the multi-year budget time frame.

6.54 The very task of budgeting implies that expenditure will be constrained within a given period. A multi-year budget allows greater flexibility, but it too must end. Perhaps more important than the period covered by budgets is the approach taken to calculate budgets and the way in which procurement spend is estimated and

---

[35] Strand et al, *Public Procurement in Europe*, p 6.
[36] The average time taken to conduct a competitive dialogue comes in at 286 days (Strand et al, *Public Procurement in Europe*, p 103).
[37] Richard, A. (2003) 'Overview of Budget Systems and Public Procurement in OECD Countries' in *The Environmental Performance of Public Procurement: Issues of Policy Coherence* (Paris: OECD).

reconciled. One feature commonly associated with single-year budgets is that they are based on the previous year's expenditure, giving a strong incentive to spend to the maximum allocated level each year. This need not be the case, as single-year budgets may in theory be based on specific planning and savings carried over or placed in a dedicated fund. This may help to avoid some of the potential pitfalls of multi-year budgets, such as the uncertainty of macroeconomic forecasts.[38] Multi-year budgets offer a greater pay-off for the effort of detailed expenditure planning, but for many organizations planning beyond two to three years introduces more uncertainties than it resolves.

Separation of capital and current expenditure

Budgets often account separately for capital costs such as buildings or equipment **6.55** which have some value beyond the current accounting period. Depreciation may be recorded on the current (or revenue) account, although this is not nearly as prevalent in the public sector as in the private sector. Such budget conventions influence decisions about procurement, particularly where there is a division between appropriation, accounting, and liability for capital and current expenditure. When it comes to evaluating the life-cycle costs of an asset, the problem of split incentives may arise. For example, if a central Department of Education or Health is responsible for financing only the capital costs of schools or hospitals, whereas local school or hospital authorities are responsible for operational costs, there will be less incentive for the department to invest in energy-saving features which come with an initial capital cost premium.

Even where a single organization bears responsibility for both cost categories, their **6.56** differential treatment in its books may prejudice procurement decisions. Thus, one of the criticisms of the Private Finance Initiative in the UK was that public bodies were unduly influenced to adopt this mode of procurement as the capital costs could be recorded 'off balance sheet'.[39] As PFI and other forms of public-private partnership have matured, more countries are applying objective criteria to determine whether they feature on government balance sheets and to account for the contingent liabilities and costs associated with these projects.[40] Research suggests that the nature of service delivery, and in particular whether it has features such as low asset specificity (ie high levels of alternative uses for resources) and low

---

[38] Spackman, M. (2002) 'Multi-Year Perspective in Budgeting and Public Investment Planning', draft background paper for discussion at session III.1 of the OECD Global Forum on Sustainable Development, p 5.

[39] For a discussion of this in the context of hospital trusts, see Shaoul, J., Stafford, A., and Stapleton, P. (2008) 'The Cost of Using Private Finance to Build, Finance and Operate Hospitals' 28(2) *Public Money and Management* 101–8.

[40] Burger, P. and Hawkesworth, I. (2011) 'How to Attain Value for Money: Comparing PPP and Traditional Infrastructure Procurement' 1 *OECD Journal on Budgeting* 18. Accounting for contingent liabilities and costs was found to take place in 13 of 20 countries sampled in this study.

information costs, plays a strong role in determining how successful exposure to competition will be in increasing efficiency in service delivery.[41]

Discount rate policy

6.57 The rate at which future costs are discounted will affect any procurement for which a net present value (NPV) calculation is made. The higher the discount rate, the lower the present value of future cash flows. Capital appears less expensive where a low discount rate is used, which can encourage investment in larger and longer-term projects or the purchase rather than leasing of assets. Higher discount rates can favour more cautious investment and labour-intensive, rather than capital-intensive, investments.[42] They can also favour projects with high end-of-life costs—for example, decommissioning of a nuclear facility. A different discount rate is often applied for PPPs and other forms of procurement, with the rate more likely to be set at the individual project level for PPPs. This can affect both external and internal appraisals of value, that is, at the initial project approval stage and during the comparison of bids which may have varied payback periods and levels of capital investment. The discount rate applied can be particularly influential where a public sector comparator (PSC) is used to assess the relative costs of carrying out a project with or without private investment.

Allocation of procurement budgets

6.58 The budget available for an individual procurement will reflect all of the preceding choices, which are usually made by a separate department or body to that carrying out the procurement. Budgets may either be designated in advance for a particular procurement category or requirement, or may be allocated based on the outcome of a competitive procedure. The choice between these two approaches is often based on administrative considerations, and it is likely to have an impact on both the way in which procurement is conducted and the VfM achieved. There is also the question of whether the budget or reserve price for a procurement is made known to bidders. The effect of publishing a budget or ceiling for tenders has not been widely studied, but theoretical literature suggests that this may be a good strategy where it induces a more aggressive bidding strategy, even if it also reduces the number of competitors.[43] However, it may also lead to 'anchoring' or clustering of bids around the stated budget, detracting from economic efficiency. Contract notices published in the OJEU require an estimate of the total value or scope of the contract or framework, but these are not always an accurate guide to expected costs.

---

[41] Curristine et al, 'Improving Public Sector Efficiency', p 10.

[42] Richard, 'Overview of Budget Systems', p 118.

[43] Albano, G., Dimitri, N., Perrigne, I., and Piga, G. (2006) 'Fostering Participation' in Dimitri, N., Piga, G., and Spagnolo, G. (eds), *Handbook of Procurement* (Cambridge: Cambridge University Press), pp 267–92.

Contracting authorities may enter a range or value which exceeds the estimate or budget, in order to avoid having to re-tender if the value of the contract is higher than expected. Analysis of VfM based on comparison of the values published in contract notices and contract award notices must thus be treated with caution.

Public Sector Comparator

One further approach to assessing value for money in procurement decisions **6.59** deserves to be mentioned here: the use of a public sector comparator (PSC). The World Bank defines a public sector comparator as a tool 'used by a government to make decisions by testing whether a private investment proposal offers value for money in comparison with the most efficient form of public procurement' and which 'estimates the hypothetical risk-adjusted cost if a project were to be financed, owned and implemented by government'.[44] As such, it is often used to make a decision about whether to proceed with outsourcing a function or setting up a public-private partnership. The comparison may cover the in-house provision of the asset, publicly financed procurement as opposed to privately financed options, or both.

As with life-cycle costing, there is no single methodology used to calculate a PSC. **6.60** Both the way in which a PSC is calculated, and the use to which it is put, tend to reflect the preferences or prejudices of the contracting authority, as well as the realistic range of options which it has before it. Retaining an external firm to calculate a PSC may eliminate some, but not all, of these biases. In some cases, the calculated cost is published directly as part of the tender documentation in order to set a benchmark for the competition. However, using a PSC in this way requires a high degree of confidence that it is accurate. As is the case when bidders are told the budget or reference price for a procurement, there may be a clustering of bids close to the stated level. This is likely to compromise the value obtained, either by inflating bids if the PSC is too high, or by reducing quality if the PSC is too low.

Summary

Analysing value for money in public procurement throws up a number of concep- **6.61** tual as well as practical problems. How are costs measured and is this accurate? How is quality measured? Can costs be continuously reduced without jeopardizing quality and the competitiveness of markets? A further consideration, given the discussion in paragraphs 6.47 to 6.58 of public budgeting techniques, is what happens

---

[44] Kerali, H. (2011) 'Public Sector Comparator for Highway PP Projects' (World Bank). The use of a real, as opposed to hypothetical, public sector comparator was approved by Supperstone J in *Montpellier Estates Ltd v Leeds City Council* [2013] EWHC 166 (QB).

to money which is saved in procurement. It may or may not be reallocated in a way which is more efficient, or which brings greater benefits to the contracting authority, wider public sector, or citizens. Economists seek to model such scenarios based on (i) what the source of the savings is (profits, rents, income, subcontracts) and (ii) how it is reallocated (other contracts, future years, other functions within the organization, other public sector purposes, deficit reduction, private sector spending), but this raises as many questions as it answers. The purpose of introducing these questions here is simply to point out that despite the long-standing and wide-ranging emphasis on VfM as an objective of public procurement, there is little consensus on what it means or how it should be compared to other objectives such as transparency, fairness, competition, or wider economic, environmental, and social goals.

6.62 Nevertheless, the motivation to obtain value for money remains a cornerstone of public procurement. If we are to identify a framework conducive to optimizing VfM, it would contain the elements shown in Table 6.4.

Table 6.4 **Summary of practices contributing to VfM in procurement**

Phase	Practices
Budgeting and planning	Multi-year, performance-based budgeting; assess long-term needs in consultation with users; analyse life-cycle costs; calculate accurate reserve price or public sector comparator if in-house provision is an option.
Market consultation	Publicize need and seek detailed input from potential suppliers; consult other public or private sector clients; use information gathered to develop scope and specification for procurement; draw a line between consultation and procurement phases to avoid giving any (dis)advantage to individual competitors.
Choice of procedure	Consider level of interaction with market needed to identify best solution and time/resources available to conduct procedure; use frameworks or central purchasing to minimize transaction costs; competitive dialogue or negotiated procedures only if skills exist to manage these effectively.
Specification development	Develop unambiguous statement of requirements; allow variants to test effect on price; use competitive dialogue if specification requires input from potential suppliers.
Selection of tenderers	Apply selection criteria which are tailored to the specific need; check prior performance thoroughly; verify contents of European Single Procurement Document prior to tender stage.
Evaluation of tenders	Develop award criteria and weightings which reflect specific cost/quality considerations; model outcomes based on different score spreads; apply minimum score thresholds to quality criteria; use life-cycle costing where data is attainable.
Conditions of contract	Choose contract length based on levels of risk/investment; avoid standard terms which may inflate bid prices or fail to ensure adequate quality; allow bidders to comment on terms.
Contract management	Develop and apply appropriate KPIs as part of service level agreements; allocate sufficient time and resources to contract management; maintain good communication with contractor.

Many of these appear uncontroversial, yet they are routinely subsumed to other considerations such as administrative time and convenience, fear of legal challenges, price pressure, user demands, and political or organizational imperatives. In other cases, the structure or power of the supply market makes it difficult to obtain value despite the best efforts of procurers and policy makers.

7

ENVIRONMENTAL AND SOCIAL
RESPONSIBILITY

It is perhaps surprising that the inclusion of social and environmental aspects in **7.01** public procurement is still sometimes seen as a 'nice to have' rather than a core consideration. In other areas of public sector decision-making—such as planning and development or fiscal policy—impacts on longer-term human and environmental welfare are routinely taken into account. Evidence from across Europe suggests that such considerations are not yet fully integrated into procurement, although it is difficult to obtain a comprehensive view.[1] One reason for this may be that the commercial function of government is seen as being separate from its general responsibility to act in a manner which contributes to societal well-being. Another is that the 1990s in particular saw a retrenchment in the use of public procurement to attain policy objectives other than those linked to the internal market and competition.[2] The 2014 directives offer the opportunity for sustainable procurement to become more mainstream. However, as will be seen below, almost all of their environmental and social provisions remain optional for contracting authorities to implement and so progress is dependent on political will and incentives.

What is meant by sustainable procurement? Two concepts predominate. The first **7.02** is that of balancing current and future needs.[3] Resources should be managed in a

---

[1] A picture of the level of green public procurement (GPP) implementation across Europe is available from Centre for European Policy Studies and Council of Europe (2012) *The Uptake of Green Public Procurement in the EU27* (European Commission: DG Environment). The study found that 55 per cent of the contracting authorities surveyed had included at least one GPP criterion in the last contract awarded, and 26 per cent had included all of the EU core GPP criteria for that product or service group. In addition, some 54 per cent of local governments in the sample, and 41 per cent of central governments, reported that they 'always or often' include environmental criteria in their tenders. The latter was based on information about 230,000 public contracts in 26 Member States.

[2] For an account of this retrenchment in the EU, see McCrudden, C. (2007) *Buying Social Justice: Equality, Government Procurement and Legal Change* (Oxford: Oxford University Press), pp 331–63.

[3] The UN World Commission on Environment and Development (1987) *Our Common Future* (the 'Brundtland Report'), offered the following definition: 'Sustainable development is development which meets the needs of the present without compromising the ability of future generations to meet their own needs' (p 37).

way which ensures future generations are not deprived of their benefit. Impacts on the natural environment, whether in the form of greenhouse gas emissions, water and soil quality, or waste should be minimized. Costs should be assessed over the entire life cycle of an asset to avoid hidden expenses in the future. Activities which detract from common wealth, such as tax evasion, unfair commercial practices, or corruption, must be subject to censure. The second concept is that of balancing economic, social, and environmental objectives. Money spent on public contracts should contribute to objectives such as reducing unemployment, equality, and social inclusion. Uniforms for hospital workers should be cost-effective, comfortable, and ethically produced. Buildings should be designed in a way which is environmentally sound and affords access for disabled users. The basic tenets of sustainable procurement are often uncontroversial—however, there is obviously a wealth of complexity in its implementation. Like value for money, there is no consensus on how sustainability in procurement can best be measured, although as will be seen in the remainder of this chapter, a number of common tools and techniques have gained acceptance and are referenced within the 2014 directives.

7.03 This chapter identifies the legal and policy framework for incorporating environmental and social considerations in public procurement. This comprises both mandatory measures, such as those relating to energy-efficiency, vehicle emissions, and the treatment of abnormally low tenders, and voluntary initiatives, such as use of environmental management systems, life-cycle costing, and environmental or social labels. It then offers a critique of the effectiveness of the current legal framework, asking how it might be adapted in future to better secure sustainability objectives. The chapter concludes with some recommendations for practical steps which can be taken by contracting authorities and entities. A significant body of research, guidance, and other material focused on sustainable procurement has emerged in recent years and is referred to throughout this chapter.[4]

EU Legal and Policy Framework

Legislation

7.04 There can be little doubt that the concept of sustainability is embedded in the law of the European Union. Article 11 of the Treaty requires that:

---

[4] The author has had the opportunity to work with a number of national and international organizations on the development of sustainable procurement policy, criteria, and guidance, and would like to acknowledge the influence of these projects on this chapter, notably European Commission (2011) *Buying Green: A Handbook for Environmental Public Procurement* (2nd edn); SEAD Initiative (US Department of Energy) (2013) *Energy-Efficient Public Procurement: Best Practice in Program Delivery*; Irish Environmental Protection Agency (2014) *Green Procurement Guidance for the Public Sector*; and ICLEI—Local Governments for Sustainability (2014) *The Procura+ Manual: A Guide to Implementing Sustainable Public Procurement* (3rd edn).

Environmental protection requirements must be integrated into the definition and implementation of the Union's policies and activities, in particular with a view to promoting sustainable development.

Article 37 of the Charter of Fundamental Rights goes further, in providing that:

A high level of environmental protection and the improvement of the quality of the environment must be integrated into the policies of the Union and ensured in accordance with the principle of sustainable development.

Article 9 of the Treaty contains a similar imperative to integrate into EU policies 'requirements linked to the promotion of a high level of employment, the guarantee of adequate social protection, the fight against social exclusion, and a high level of education, training and protection of human health'. Article 10 states that in its policies the EU 'shall aim to combat discrimination based on sex, racial or ethnic origin, religion or belief, disability, age or sexual orientation'. While these articles might be considered only to create general obligations on the EU as opposed to the more specific rules regarding the internal market which apply directly to Member States, as noted in Chapter 2 the Court has interpreted them as creating positive obligations on Member States in certain cases.[5]

In furtherance of these objectives, a wide range of secondary legislation has been **7.05** adopted at EU level in the fields of environmental protection, sustainable development, energy, climate change, social inclusion, and equalities. While these instruments are too numerous to list in their entirety here, the ones which are of the most practical significance for public procurement are shown below. Naturally, others may be of relevance for specific types of procurement—for example, by contracting entities operating in the transport or water sectors. National implementing legislation exists for most of the measures detailed in Tables 7.1 and 7.2, with the exception of Regulations, which are directly effective.

As can be seen in Tables 7.1 and 7.2, secondary EU legislation addresses a wide **7.06** range of environmental and social matters (bearing in mind that the lists are not exhaustive), and its impacts on procurement are diverse. In some cases, it may merely be a question of reinforcing obligations which already rest on suppliers— for example, by including compliance with rules regarding disposal of waste or maximum working hours among the contract conditions. In others, however, secondary legislation creates a specific requirement within the procurement process—for example, that only equipment which meets minimum energy performance levels or which is accessible to disabled users can be procured. The Energy Efficiency Directive is particularly far-reaching in this regard, as it sets minimum requirements across a range of commonly procured goods and services,

---

[5] See discussion at paras 2.28 *et seq*. For consideration of the extent to which the environmental protection requirements set out in Art 11 TFEU and Art 37 CFR have been incorporated in other areas of EU law, see Kingston, S. (ed) (2013) *European Perspectives on Environmental Law and Governance* (London: Routledge).

Table 7.1 EU environmental legislation impacting public procurement

Policy area	Relevant instruments	Main impact on procurement
Waste	Waste Framework Directive (2008/98/EC)	Sets rules for the allocation of costs and responsibility for waste management.
	Packaging and Packaging Waste Directives (94/62/EC and 2004/12/EC)	Set requirements for the separation and recovery of packaging waste.
Energy	Energy Efficiency Directive (2012/27/EU)	Requires minimum energy efficiency standards to be included in procurement of supplies, services, and works (central government only).
	Renewable Energy Directive (2009/28/EU)	Requires guarantee of origin certificates to be recognized as evidence of renewable production; sets criteria for sustainable biofuels.
	Energy Performance of Buildings Directive (2010/31/EU)	Sets minimum energy-efficiency requirements for buildings owned or operated by public bodies.
	Energy Labelling Directive (2010/30/EU)	Establishes efficiency classes and labelling requirements for a range of common consumer appliances.
Water	Water Framework Directive (2000/60/EC)	Requires that the principle of recovery of costs of water services is applied.
IT, electronic, and electrical equipment	Energy Star Regulation (No 106/2008)	Sets minimum energy-efficiency standards for procurement of office IT equipment (central government only).
	Restriction of Hazardous Substances (RoHS) Directive (2002/95/EC)	Electrical and electronic equipment purchased cannot contain certain hazardous substances.
	Waste Electronic and Electrical Equipment (WEEE) Directive (2012/19/EU)	Sets requirements for producers to label equipment for recycling purposes and take it back at its end-of-life.
Wood and paper	Timber Regulation (No 995/2010)	Wood and paper products must be traceable to legally harvested sources.
Vehicles	Clean Vehicles Directive (2009/33/EC)	Lifetime energy consumption, emissions, and noise of road transport vehicles must be taken into account.
	European Emission Standards Regulation (No 715/2007)—Euro 5 and Euro 6	Sets maximum emission levels for vehicles placed on the market after a given date.
Certification	Ecolabel Regulation (No 66/2010)	Assists in identifying environmentally preferable products.
	EU Eco-management and Audit Scheme (EMAS) Regulation (No 1221/2009)	Provides a means for contractors to demonstrate compliance with environmental measures.
	EU Organic Regulations (Nos 834/2007 and 889/2008)	Set standards for organic certification and labelling.

Table 7.2 EU social legislation impacting public procurement

Policy area	Relevant instruments	Main impact on procurement
Employment	Transfer of Undertakings, Protection of Employees (TUPE) Directive (2001/23/EC)	Maintains the terms and conditions of employees on the transfer of an undertaking.
	Working Time Directive (2003/88/EC)	Sets minimum periods of daily rest, breaks, weekly rest, annual leave, and regulates aspects of night work and shift work.
	Posted Workers Directive (96/71/EC)	Certain minimum conditions of employment must be guaranteed to workers from other Member States.
Equality	Equal treatment of men and women (Art 157 TFEU and Directive 2006/54/EC)	Prohibits direct or indirect discrimination on grounds of sex in employment, training, and pay.
	Non-discrimination on grounds of racial or ethnic origin (Directive 2000/43/EC)	Prohibits direct or indirect discrimination on grounds of race or ethnicity in employment, training, and pay.
Disability	Equal treatment in employment and occupation (Framework Directive 2000/78/EC)	Employers must provide reasonable accommodation for disabled persons to have access to, participate in, or advance in employment.
	Council Decision on Rights of Persons with Disabilities (2010/48/EC)	Rights of disabled persons must be reflected in choice of means of communication, technical specifications, award criteria, and contract performance conditions.
Services of general interest[6]	Protocol No 26 to the Treaty (TFEU) on Services of General Interest	Recognizes the discretion of national, regional, and local authorities in providing, commissioning, and organizing services of general interest.
	Universal and Public Service Obligations (various directives)	Certain services in the postal, energy, transport, and telecommunications sectors may be remunerated under separate rules.
Health and safety	Health and Safety of Workers at Work Directive (89/391/EEC)	Sets basic rules on safety which must be observed in execution of contracts.
	Protection from Exposure to Asbestos Directive (2009/148/EC)	Requires working procedures which limit exposure to asbestos and the risks arising therefrom.

albeit that these are expressed primarily by reference to pre-existing standards such as those underlying the EU Energy Label, and that compliance with these standards is only required insofar as this is consistent with cost-effectiveness,

---

[6] Services of general economic interest (SGEIs) are economic activities which deliver outcomes in the overall public good that would not be supplied (or would be supplied under different conditions in terms of objective quality, safety, affordability, equal treatment, or universal access) by the market without public intervention. See discussion at para 1.21 and Commission Staff Working Document, *Guide to the Application of the European Union Rules on State Aid, Public Procurement and the Internal Market to Services of General Economic Interest, and in Particular to Social Services of General Interest* SWD (2013) 53 final/2.

economical feasibility, wider sustainability, technical suitability, and sufficient competition.[7]

7.07 It is somewhat unfortunate that the instruments listed in Tables 7.1 and 7.2—even those which explicitly create obligations in the context of public procurement procedures—are for the most part not referenced in the procurement directives. Article 18(2) of the Public Sector Directive[8] refers in a general way to social, labour, and environmental obligations which apply under Union law, as well as those which apply under national law, collective agreements, or specified international conventions.[9] On the one hand, this may help to avoid rapid obsolescence of any list of relevant laws and the risk that it would be incomplete. However, from a practical perspective, it can be difficult for contracting authorities and entities to identify social and environmental legislation which may apply when they are procuring certain goods or services for the first time or under a new contracting model or arrangement. As will be seen in paragraph 7.42, compliance with the laws referred to in Article 18(2) is invoked in a number of places within the 2014 directives, so it is important that contracting authorities have a clear idea of which social, labour, and environmental laws are applicable for a given procurement.

Policy environment

7.08 A majority of the 28 EU Member States have adopted policies on sustainable procurement, representing varying approaches and levels of ambition. Some include mandatory measures for procurement of greener products or services, while others set indicative targets only.[10] Where these policies refer to specific criteria to be applied in procurement, they are in many cases based on the common green public procurement (GPP) criteria developed by the European Commission, covering over 20 product and service groups. The Commission has actively supported GPP since the publication of its communication *Public procurement for a better environment* in 2008.[11] The common GPP criteria aim to address the key environmental impacts of each product or service based on its entire life cycle, taking into account the need to verify claims and ensure comparability of tenders and equal treatment. At national level, the criteria adopted often address social considerations in addition to the environmental impacts targeted by the EU criteria. Social considerations in this context include both characteristics of the final product or service, such as accessibility to all

---

[7] Art 6 and Annex III of Directive 2012/27/EU on energy efficiency ('Energy Efficiency Directive').
[8] Equivalent provisions exist in Art 36(2) of the Utilities Directive and Art 30(3) of the Concessions Directive.
[9] Set out in Annex X Public Sector Directive; Annex XIV Utilities Directive; and Annex X Concessions Directive.
[10] A summary of national policies, together with the EU GPP criteria and numerous other resources related to GPP, are available on the European Commission website at <http://ec.europa.eu/environment/gpp>.
[11] COM (2008) 400 of 16 July 2008.

users, and supply-chain characteristics such as exclusion of child labour or payment of a living or fair wage to those involved in the production process. Many local and regional authorities have adopted their own policies which go beyond the minimum requirements set out at national level.[12]

7.09 The most common means of implementing environmental objectives into regulated procurement procedures appears to be via technical specifications.[13] In the case of social considerations, contract performance clauses are the preferred route.[14] One likely reason for this is the legal uncertainty surrounding the inclusion of social considerations in the competitive stages of procurement, discussed in Chapter 4. Progress on socially responsible procurement is more fragmented and support from the European Commission has been less fulsome than that provided for GPP.[15] During the revision of the directives, the rapporteur on behalf of the European Parliament tabled a large number of amendments aimed at strengthening the social protection elements of the proposed legislation, but only a minority of these were accepted by the Council and Commission.[16] Nevertheless, the 2014 directives have a distinctly social flavour compared to their predecessors, including the emphasis placed on non-price considerations in contract award, enhanced ability to reserve contracts for sheltered workshops or social enterprises, the separate rules applicable to Title III services, and the explicit ability to take trading conditions into account in award criteria. The rules on abnormally low tenders and clearer ability to enforce compliance with social and labour law, including applicable collective agreements, also represent a shift. The scope of these provisions is examined in more detail below.

7.10 Despite the steps taken to facilitate sustainable procurement, a number of core challenges have emerged which have not been entirely resolved in the new directives. The first is that administrative frameworks for procurement have largely been designed without taking the broader environmental or social impacts of purchasing into account. Efficient procurement is understood to be that which delivers the required goods, services, or works and achieves the levels of competition, value for money,

---

[12] In this activity they have been supported by a number of regional and GPP and sustainable public procurement (SPP) European networks. In particular, the Procura+ Campaign has developed detailed guidance and supports its members, primarily local authorities, in the implementation of sustainable procurement (<http://www.procuraplus.org>). International organisations such as the United Nations and European Investment Bank have also adopted influential sustainable procurement programmes.

[13] Essig, M., Frijdal, J., Kahlenborn,W., and Moser, C. (2011) *Strategic Use of Public Procurement in Europe: Final Report to the European Commission*, p 8; and Centre for European Policy Studies and College of Europe (2012) *Monitoring the Uptake of Green Public Procurement in the EU27* (Brussels: European Commission), p 46.

[14] Essig et al, *Strategic Use of Public Procurement in Europe*, p 12.

[15] In 2010, the Commission published *Buying Social: A guide to taking account of social considerations in public procurement*, but much of this is concerned with what is *not* allowed under the EU rules. Updated guidance may be expected to reflect the significant expansion in social aspects under the 2014 directives.

[16] European Parliament Committee on the Internal Market and Consumer Protection (Rapporteur: Marc Tarabella) *Report on the proposal for a directive of the European Parliament and of the Council on public procurement* (COM (2011) 0896–C7-0006/2012–2011/0438(COD)).

and legal compliance expected within the organization or broader polity authorizing expenditure. As discussed in Chapter 6, this rather simplistic formulation belies the variability inherent in determining what represents value for money. The second challenge is that even where sustainability objectives are embedded into procedures (for example, to target energy or fuel efficiency), it is often difficult to meaningfully compare bids, verify performance, and enforce commitments over the duration of contracts. The 2014 directives attempt to address this problem in particular through the rules on third-party labels and life-cycle costing, but as will be seen in the remainder of this chapter, these provisions are not without their own difficulties.

Case law

7.11   As with other areas of procurement, the Court of Justice has played a prominent role in shaping the law relating to environmentally and socially responsible procurement. This is despite the relatively small number of cases in which it has had to consider such matters directly. Beginning with the *Beentjes* judgment in 1988, the Court has displayed a willingness to acknowledge the wider social function of public procurement.[17] That case concerned a tenderer for a Dutch works contract who had lost out to a more expensive bid which was considered by the authority to be more advantageous. One of the reasons for this was the preferred bidder's ability to meet a condition included in the tender documents regarding the employment of long-term unemployed persons in executing the works. The Court held that such a condition was acceptable provided it had no direct or indirect discriminatory effect on tenderers from other Member States, and was mentioned explicitly in the contract notice.[18] As the case was a reference for a preliminary ruling, the determination of the effect of the condition was left up to the national court.

7.12   In *Nord-Pas de Calais*, the Commission challenged the award in the French region of a number of school-building contracts which included an 'additional award criterion' relating to local employment.[19] The criterion was based on an inter-ministerial circular setting out French Government policy on reducing unemployment, under which this was to be taken into account where two tenders were of equal value. The Advocate General considered that such a criterion was precluded under the procurement rules and that *Beentjes* should be interpreted as relating solely to conditions for the performance of contracts which were not decisive in the award of contract.[20] However, the Court rejected this view, finding that a condition relating to unemployment could be applied as an award criterion provided it was consistent with the fundamental principles of Community law, in particular the principle of non-discrimination.[21]

---

[17] Case 31/87 *Gebroeders Beentjes BV v State of the Netherlands* [1988] ECR I-04635.

[18] Case 31/87 *Beentjes*, para 37.

[19] Case C-225/98 *Commission v French Republic* ('*Nord-Pas de Calais*') [2000] ECR I-07445.

[20] Case C-225/98 *Nord-Pas de Calais*, opinion of AG Alber, paras 43–9.

[21] Case C-225/98 *Nord-Pas de Calais*, paras 49–54 of judgment.

At the turn of the century, then, the Court had recognized a limited scope for social **7.13** considerations, particularly those related to employment, to be incorporated as award criteria and/or contract performance clauses in procurement procedures. It was clear that where such provisions were found to be discriminatory, they would not survive scrutiny.[22] Given that schemes to combat unemployment are generally national or regional in character, such measures, as well as related schemes such as sheltered workshops (discussed in paragraph 7.44), were vulnerable to challenge. However, developments in related areas of internal market law suggested that the Court was prepared to sanction discriminatory measures in certain cases where these were justified on environmental grounds.

In *PreussenElektra*, which concerned State aid in the renewable electricity sector, **7.14** Advocate General Jacobs considered the meaning of the Treaty commitment to sustainable development, finding that it imposed legal obligations and that there-fore special account must be taken of environmental concerns in interpreting the Treaty provisions on the free movement of goods.[23] He considered that environ-mental measures may in some cases be justified even where they are discriminatory in nature—due, for example, to the requirement to rectify harm at its source. The case concerned a German law which obliged energy supply companies to purchase renewable electricity generated in their area of supply, at specified minimum rates. The Court held that the measure was compatible with the Treaty given its aim, which was to combat climate change and the lack of integration of markets for renewable electricity at that time.[24] In doing so, it did not apply the normal propor-tionality test by asking first if the measure was appropriate to achieve its legitimate objective, and then whether it went beyond what was necessary to achieve it. The question was left open as to whether this indicated a special approach to the justi-fication of all environmental measures which discriminate based on nationality, or was confined to the case at hand.

In *Concordia*, the Court had the opportunity to consider the scope for taking **7.15** environmental factors into account in procurement decisions. The City of Helsinki had invited tenders for bus transport services, including nitrogen oxide emissions and noise levels among the criteria to identify the most economically advantageous tender. The Court held that such award criteria were legitimate provided that they were linked to the subject-matter of the contract, did not confer an unrestricted freedom of choice of the contracting authority, were explicitly mentioned in the contract notice or tender documents, and complied with the fundamental Treaty

---

[22] This followed in particular from the Court's judgment in Case 45/87 *Commission v Ireland* ('*Dundalk Water*') [1988] ECR 4929.

[23] Case C-379/98 *PreussenElektra AG v Schleswag AG, in the presence of Windpark Reußenköge III GmbH and Land Schleswig-Holstein* [2001] ECR I-02099, Opinion of AG Jacobs, paras 232–6.

[24] Case C-379/98 *PreussenElektra*, paras 73–81 of judgment. This differed from the approach of AG Jacobs, who considered that the measure would not be justified if allowing renewable electricity produced in other Member States would be equally effective in reducing greenhouse gas emissions.

principles, in particular non-discrimination.[25] The criterion relating to emissions could be justified notwithstanding that only a small number of operators were in a position to obtain full marks under it, due to restrictions on the availability of natural gas refuelling facilities.[26] At the time, there was no explicit mention of environmental factors as being among those which could be taken into account in award, so the case was welcomed by environmentalists and others inasmuch as it supported this ability. However, it is notable that, in comparison to the assessment of State aid measures in *PreussenElektra*, the Court placed more restrictions on environmental measures in the procurement context in *Concordia*.

7.16 In particular, the emphasis placed on the link to the subject-matter and the principle of non-discrimination suggested that it would not be possible to justify environmental award criteria if these had a discriminatory effect. Further light was cast on the link to the subject-matter requirement in *EVN Wienstrom*, concerning the purchase of renewable electricity by the Austrian Government. The Court found that an award criterion which looked at suppliers' overall capacity to deliver electricity from renewable sources, rather than the specific quantities required under the contract, lacked the necessary link.[27] It also cited the authority's inability to effectively verify performance under the criterion in determining that it was illegal.[28] However, it held that there was nothing to prevent a contracting authority from attaching a heavy weighting to an environmental criterion provided it was linked to the subject-matter of the contract and was capable of verification, regardless of whether the criterion actually served to achieve the objective pursued.[29]

7.17 The effect of the judgments in *Concordia* and *EVN* was that contracting authorities have been able to apply environmental award criteria provided they are confined to the specific goods, services, or works they are purchasing and do not concern general corporate policies or capacities. They must also meet the other requirements for award criteria in terms of transparency and precision (ie 'not conferring an unrestricted freedom of choice' on the authority). In *Dutch Coffee*, the Court applied the same approach in respect of award criteria addressing social characteristics of the supply chain.[30] It held that an authority was entitled to apply award criteria relating to organic agriculture and fair trade in a tender for the supply of tea and coffee, as these considerations were linked to the subject-matter.[31] It also held that there was no requirement for award criteria to relate to an intrinsic characteristic of a product or something which alters its material substance—thus putting

---

[25] Case C-513/99 *Concordia Bus Finland v Helsingin kaupunki and HKL-Bussiliikenne* [2002] ECR I-07213, para 64.
[26] Case C-513/99 *Concordia*, para 85.
[27] Case C-448/01 *EVN and Wienstrom* [2003] ECR I-14527. See discussion at paras 2.45 *et seq.*
[28] Case C-448/01 *EVN*, paras 67–71.
[29] Case C-448/01 *EVN*, para 51.
[30] Case C-368/10 *Commission v Kingdom of the Netherlands* ('*Dutch Coffee*'), not yet reported.
[31] *Dutch Coffee*, paras 89–92.

to rest an invidious distinction once championed by the Commission.[32] However, by only awarding marks to tenderers who possessed certain organic and fair trade labels, without citing the detailed criteria behind these labels, the authority had breached its obligations under the 2004 directives.[33]

Two judgments in 2014, in *Ålands Vindkraft* and *Essent Belgium*, again highlighted **7.18** the greater ability to justify restricting free movement on environmental grounds where this takes place outside of the procurement rules.[34] The cases relate to green certificate schemes operated in Sweden and Flanders, respectively, under which suppliers are obliged to surrender to regulators a number of certificates each year representing production of electricity from renewable sources. Both schemes only accept certificates demonstrating production in the territory of supply, so that suppliers cannot meet the quota by relying on renewable electricity produced in other Member States. The purpose of this restriction is to encourage development of renewable energy capacity within the area of supply, by creating a market for tradable green certificates which helps to finance such investment.[35] The Court held in both cases that, while the schemes constituted a restriction on the free movement of goods and were discriminatory in nature, they could be justified with reference to their specific environmental objectives. Unlike in *PreussenElektra*, the Court carried out an explicit proportionality assessment of the measures, although given that both cases were references for preliminary rulings, it was left to the national courts to determine the final outcome. The Court emphasized that any fines imposed on operators who failed to meet the quotas must be proportionate and not impose excessive penalties.[36]

It should be noted that the restrictions on free movement in *Vindkraft* and *Essent* **7.19** *Belgium* arose in the context of an activity specifically sanctioned by a directive, namely the operation of national support schemes for the development of renewable energy capacity.[37] Such schemes contribute directly to the realization of national

---

[32] For a discussion and refutation of the 'material substance' theory, see Kunzlik, P. (2009) 'The Procurement of "Green" Energy' in P. Kunzlik and S. Arrowsmith (eds), *Social and Environmental Policies in EC Procurement Law: New Directives and Directions* (Cambridge: Cambridge University Press), pp 392–401.

[33] Case C-368/10 *Dutch Coffee*, paras 93–7.

[34] Case C-573/12 *Ålands Vindkraft AB v Energimyndigheten*, judgment of the Court (Grand Chamber) of 1 July 2014, not yet reported; and Joined Cases C-204/12 to C-208/12 *Essent Belgium NV v Vlaamse Reguleringsinstantie voor de Elektriciteits- en Gasmarkt*, judgment of 11 September 2014, not yet reported.

[35] Although for the most part these schemes remain national in remit, on the basis that they are funded by national authorities, a cross-border green certificate scheme has also been developed between Sweden and Norway. Such joint support schemes are specifically envisioned under Art 11 Renewable Energy Directive.

[36] Case C-573/12 *Vindkraft*, para 116; and Joined Cases C-204/12 to C-208/12 *Essent Belgium*, para 114.

[37] Under Directive 2009/28/EC on the promotion of the use of energy from renewable sources ('Renewable Energy Directive').

renewable energy targets, which are mandatory in order to meet the overall EU target of 20 per cent renewable electricity by 2020. It is possible that actions which restrict free movement and which are discriminatory in nature but which do not have such clear backing from the EU legislature would be more difficult to justify on environmental grounds. For example, a scheme which supported nuclear power development on the grounds that it is less damaging to the climate than fossil fuels might not survive scrutiny on a similar basis. In both cases, the Court looked at the effect of the schemes in achieving the aim of increasing renewable energy production,[38] although it did not consider whether other measures which are less restrictive of free movement could be equally effective.[39]

7.20   The Court seemed to take favourable account of the fact that the schemes are themselves market-based mechanisms, which operate in a number of Member States and are not (yet) harmonized under EU law.[40] However, the Court also noted that 'it is essential that Member States be able to control the effect and costs of their national support schemes according to their potential, whilst maintaining investor confidence'[41]—which contradicts the idea that such schemes operate strictly on market principles. The reason for questioning the depth of the analysis here is that it may become relevant in challenges to environmental or social measures adopted in procurement decisions which are found to restrict free movement and to be discriminatory. As noted in Chapter 4, the 2014 directives maintain the 'link to the subject-matter' test for award criteria and extend it to cover technical specifications and contract performance clauses. This is one way of drawing the line between what are seen as legitimate efforts to address the environmental and social impact of public sector purchasing and illegitimate restrictions on free movement. It is not the only way of drawing this line, nor does it follow obviously from the wording of the Treaty or the Court's balancing of rights in other areas. Crucially, it may also undermine the effectiveness of environmental and social measures implemented through procurement. This argument is revisited in paragraphs 7.48 to 7.58.

---

[38] Case C-573/12 *Vindkraft*, para 112; and Joined Cases C-204/12 to C-208/12 *Essent Belgium*, para 110.

[39] A question may be raised about the effect of strictly national schemes on the longer-term development of the market for renewable electricity. Allowing green certificates to be redeemed on a cross-border basis could support the development of a European-wide grid with positive effects for the viability of renewable energy, which is by its nature subject to peaks and troughs in supply.

[40] Under Art 4 Directive 2001/77/EC on the promotion of electricity produced from renewable energy sources in the internal electricity market. It has been replaced by Directive 2009/28/EC, Recital 25 of which states that it 'aims at facilitating cross-border support of energy from renewable sources without affecting national support schemes'.

[41] Joined Cases C-204/12 to C-208/12 *Essent Belgium*, para 102, reiterating the observation made in Case C-573/12 *Vindkraft*, para 99. The wording precisely echoes the recitals of the Renewable Energy Directive.

Table 7.3 Environmental considerations at each procurement stage under the 2014 directives

Contract definition/ pre-procurement	Exclusion and selection criteria	Technical specifications/award	Contract performance
Assessment of total quantity or scope of contract	Discretionary exclusion: Compliance with EU, national, and international environmental law (57(4)(a))	Specifications may relate to production processes and methods or any other stage of life cycle (42)	Special environmental conditions linked to the subject-matter (70)
Preliminary market consultation to identify relevant environmental standards and labels (40)	Discretionary exclusion: Grave professional misconduct which renders integrity questionable (57(4)(c))	Third-party environmental certification (eco-labels) may be required (43)	Compliance with environmental law—main contractor (18.2)
Choice of procedure to target environmental considerations	Selection: Ability to apply specific environmental management measures (62(2))	Ability to apply life-cycle costing (58)	Compliance with environmental law—subcontractors (18.2/71)
	Selection: Technical capacity and prior experience (58/Annex XII)	Rejection of abnormally low tenders which do not comply with environmental law (69)	
		Refusal to award for non-compliance with environmental laws (18.2/56.1)	

Numbers in brackets are article references within the Public Sector Directive. Equivalent possibilities exist within the Utilities and Concessions Directives.

Environmental Considerations under the 2014 Directives

One of the challenges associated with green public procurement is identifying **7.21** and prioritizing the environmental impacts of purchasing. Some sectors such as construction or major infrastructure projects have their own frameworks in place for this, such as that provided by environmental impact assessment.[42] Others, such as chemical products, are closely regulated, meaning that fewer environmental decisions will need to be taken by the contracting authority itself. Environmental

---

[42] Under the recently overhauled Environmental Impact Assessment (EIA) Directive (Directive 2014/52/EU on the assessment of the effects of certain public and private projects on the environment).

decisions are complex because they almost always involve trade-offs between impacts which are neither visible nor, in most cases, fully measurable. For example, determining whether to replace a given item of equipment from an environmental perspective requires information about the relative efficiency of newer versus existing models, the embedded energy and emissions involved in production, the way in which current units will be disposed of, the expected lifespan of the new equipment, and any ancillary impacts of replacement such as transport, packaging, and installation. As with value for money, decisions made prior to initiating procurement may be just as important or more so than those made in the context of competition.

7.22 The 2014 directives do not provide an overarching system for environmental decision-making. However, they do provide a number of specific avenues for the incorporation of environmental considerations at each stage of a procedure. These are highlighted in Table 7.3. The emphasis on verification under the 2014 directives, while in theory useful from the perspective of underwriting environmental performance and avoiding greenwash, stops short of enabling contracting authorities to insist on third-party certification in most circumstances. Self-declarations must be considered—although not necessarily accepted—as evidence of compliance with criteria and specifications where a supplier is unable to obtain third-party evidence for specific reasons.[43] This creates a potential risk where more ambitious environmental criteria are applied, as those contractors who have invested in certification may question the reliance of their competitors on self-declarations or the decision of a contracting authority to accept them.

7.23 Despite the challenges associated with identifying and applying environmental criteria in tenders, there are also clear benefits in most cases. As noted in paragraphs 7.04 to 7.08, public authorities are subject to general sustainable development obligations and may also be subject to specific targets regarding energy and water use, as well as carbon emissions. Procurement is increasingly seen as an essential contributor to these targets and supply chains are unlikely to escape scrutiny as such commitments are tightened. The economic benefits of green procurement are also evident in a number of sectors, particularly where energy savings or increased durability lead to lower expenditure, or where costs associated with waste or pollution can be avoided.[44] In the transport sector, public

---

[43] See discussion at paras 4.22 *et seq* on means of proof. In particular, where a label, test report, or certificate is requested, contracting authorities must accept other appropriate means of proof if the economic operator concerned had no opportunity to obtain the label, test report, or certificate within the time limits for reasons which are not attributable to it (Arts 43(1) and 44(2) Public Sector Directive). The words 'appropriate' and 'not attributable' make decisions to accept or reject such evidence liable to dispute.

[44] Studies comparing costs between green and conventional procurement are relatively few in number and face methodological difficulties in isolating the effect of environmental criteria in a tender process. However, the evidence available suggests a small net saving is available for most

authorities may see multiple benefits from investment in more efficient vehicles or infrastructure, such as improved local air quality, and health and productivity gains from reduced traffic. Added to the ethical imperative towards environmental responsibility, these and other tangible gains are influential in bringing green procurement into the mainstream.

A further dimension relevant under the 2014 directives is the relationship between **7.24** environmental sustainability and innovation. Innovation procurement has been adopted as a policy goal at EU level in and of itself, primarily for economic reasons as it is seen as a way of leveraging public spending to assist in the development and commercialization of new products and services.[45] The need for specific new technologies to address climate change and other societal challenges such as resource efficiency and aging populations has also led to a significant commitment of funding to support the pre-commercial and commercial procurement of innovation which meets one or more of these challenges. In addition to the innovation partnership procedure, the use of preliminary market consultation, the exemption from the directives for research and development services, and functional and performance-based specifications are examples of approaches which may support innovation procurement. A growing literature exists in this area, together with dedicated support programmes both at the European and national levels. In many cases, these make an explicit link between innovation and environmental or social objectives.[46]

Environmental management systems

Environmental management systems are used in many public and private sec- **7.25** tor organizations to provide objective and continuous oversight of environmental impacts arising within their operations. The best-known systems in Europe are ISO 14001 and the Eco-management and Audit Scheme (EMAS). These systems require that documented procedures and instructions exist in relation to the organizations or sites accredited, and provide for regular inspections or audits. The precise scope of the system will reflect the sector in which the accredited body operates

---

commonly procured goods and services when life-cycle costs are taken into account. A 2009 study found an average 1.2 per cent reduction in life-cycle costs and 25 per cent reduction in CO_2 emissions based on the application of GPP criteria for nine product and service groups in seven EU countries (Pricewaterhousecoopers, Significant, and Ecofys (2009) *Collection of Statistical Information on Green Public Procurement in the EU* (European Commission)). In a large 2011 survey, purchasers implementing GPP reported increased purchase costs and constant or decreasing purchase costs in roughly equal numbers, but this did not take total life-cycle costs into account (Essig et al, *Strategic Use*, p 115).

[45] See European Commission (2011) *Horizon 2020—The Framework Programme for Research and Innovation* COM (2011) 808 final.

[46] For an overview, see Semple, A. (2014) *Guidance for Public Authorities on Public Procurement of Innovation* (Procurement of Innovation Platform) (available at <http://http://www.innovation-procurement.org/about-ppi/guidance/>).

and the activities it performs. Under the 2004 directives, it was possible to request certification at selection stage to attest to the environmental management measures which an operator would be able to apply within a contract. This was limited in two respects: first, it only applied to services and works contracts, and then only in 'appropriate cases'; and, second, contracting authorities were obliged to accept equivalent evidence of the operator's ability to apply the relevant measures, including in-house systems. In *Evropaïki Dynamiki v European Environment Agency*, the General Court held that the contracting authority was entitled to award different marks based on the quality of the evidence produced in respect of environmental management measures.[47]

7.26 Under the 2014 directives, the ability to request evidence of environmental management measures is extended to cover supplies contracts. The restriction of the ability to request third-party certification in respect of environmental management to 'appropriate cases' has been removed, indicating that such systems may no longer be considered as specialist in nature.[48] The ability of operators to rely on non-certified systems has been curtailed, although they may still do so where they can demonstrate that: (i) they had no access or no possibility of attaining certification within the relevant time limits for reasons not attributable to them; and (ii) the measures they propose are equivalent to those applicable under the requested environmental management system or standard.[49] Environmental management systems may also provide evidence of compliance with specifications or performance against award criteria where these require particular environmental measures to be applied.

Green specifications and award criteria

7.27 The wording of the 2014 provisions on technical specifications and award criteria reflects a move towards life-cycle thinking, part of the conceptual basis of sustainable procurement. We are told that technical specifications may refer to a specific production process or method, or to a specific process which is relevant to any other stage of the life cycle—even where such factors do not form part of the material substance of the goods, services, or works being purchased.[50] What this means is that specifications for organic food, renewable electricity, biodegradable packaging, recycled and recyclable construction materials, or a building with a minimum energy rating are all acceptable in principle. The general requirements which apply to technical specifications are that they afford equal access to economic operators, do not create unjustified obstacles to competition, are linked to the subject-matter

---

[47] Case T-331/06 *Evropaïki Dynamiki v European Environment Agency* [2010] ECR II-00136, para 76.
[48] Cf Art 48(2)(f) Directive 2004/18/EC and Annex XII, Pt II(g) Public Sector Directive.
[49] Art 62(2) Public Sector Directive; and Art 81(2) Utilities Directive.
[50] Art 42 Public Sector Directive; and Art 60 Utilities Directive.

of the contract, and are proportionate to its value and objectives.[51] Contracting authorities are given the (familiar) option of defining technical specifications by reference to performance or functional requirements, by reference to standards or other technical reference systems under a defined hierarchy, or by some combination of these approaches.[52] References to standards or (exceptionally) to any specific make, source, or process must be accompanied by the words 'or equivalent'.[53]

Contracting authorities and entities are under a general duty to verify compliance **7.28** with technical specifications prior to awarding a contract.[54] Where environmental specifications are applied, the question may arise of how compliance can be meaningfully verified during the tender process. This is particularly true where a functional or performance-based specification is applied, such as the example above of a minimum building energy rating to be achieved in the outcome of a works contract. Ultimately, it is for the contracting authority to satisfy itself that the requirements will be met, taking into account the methods, materials, and any third-party certification or evidence relied upon by bidders. As discussed in Chapter 4, performance-based specifications can be an effective way to encourage innovative and environmentally preferable solutions, but can also imply a more demanding tender evaluation and contract management process. Where the optimal levels of environmental performance are not readily prescribed in technical specifications, they may be targeted by allowing variants (for example, for a base tender to be accompanied by an environmentally enhanced offer) and/or by assessing environmental performance under award criteria.[55]

Environmental award criteria can take a variety of forms, within the legal confines **7.29** set out by the Court and encapsulated in the directives. The 2014 directives place emphasis on the ability to address environmental considerations in award criteria, again employing the idea of the entire life cycle of a good, service, or work. They establish that award criteria will be considered to be linked to the subject-matter where they relate to the works, supplies, or services to be provided under that contract in any respect and at any stage of their life cycle.[56] Reflecting the Court's judgment in *Dutch Coffee*, award criteria may concern the specific process of production, provision, or trading of the goods, service, or works being purchased, or a specific process for another stage of their life cycle even where such factors do not form part of their material substance.[57] As under the 2004 directives, there is explicit mention of the possibility to include environmental characteristics in

---

[51] Art 42(1) and (2) Public Sector Directive; and Art 60(1) and (2) Utilities Directive.
[52] Art 42(3) Public Sector Directive; and Art 60(3) Utilities Directive.
[53] Art 42(3)(b) and (4) Public Sector Directive; and Art 60(3)(b) Utilities Directive.
[54] Art 56(1)(a) Public Sector Directive; and Art 76(5) Utilities Directives.
[55] See discussion at paras 4.29–4.33.
[56] Art 67(3) Public Sector Directive; and Art 82(3) Utilities Directive.
[57] Art 67(3) Public Sector Directive; and Art 82(3) Utilities Directive.

award criteria, to which innovative characteristics and trading and its conditions are added.[58]

7.30 What distinguishes award criteria from technical specifications in addressing environmental factors? Two main distinctions can be drawn. The first is that technical specifications are minimum mandatory requirements which must be applied to all tenderers. They are therefore appropriate to address environmental characteristics which are essential for the contract, and where there is a degree of certainty about what the market can provide. Award criteria, on the other hand, offer a means of distinguishing tenders based on environmental performance, and may be used even where the minimum or maximum levels of such performance are not known in advance. For example, in a contract for waste collection, a large range of factors may have an effect on the environmental footprint of the service—including choice of vehicles and routes, methods for separating waste, frequency of collection, and the means of processing collected materials. While technical specifications may include minimum requirements in respect of any or all of these aspects, award criteria are better suited to analysing the overall impact of the methods proposed by tenderers, as well as any trade-offs between environmental factors. The rules on life-cycle costing also allow nominal costs to be assigned to environmental externalities, as discussed in paragraphs 7.37 to 7.40.

7.31 The second distinction is in terms of the discretion which contracting authorities have both in formulating and evaluating technical specifications and award criteria respectively. There are detailed rules regarding the manner in which technical specifications are expressed, and authorities are obliged to verify that tenders comply with their requirements, including where 'equivalent' standards, labels, or other means of proof are presented by bidders. Award criteria are not subject to quite the same degree of regulation. While they must be adequately precise and accompanied by verification provisions, it is only where doubt arises about whether a tenderer satisfies a criterion that the authority is obliged to verify the accuracy of the information and proof provided.[59] This does not change the obligations of equal treatment and transparency in respect of award criteria, which have been expanded on both in EU and national case law. It does mean, however, that award criteria may be more appropriate for addressing environmental considerations where the most effective means of delivering and verifying the desired outcome is not known in advance of publishing tender documents.

Labels

7.32 Many public authorities now seek third-party verification regarding environmental performance or attributes in the form of a product label or certificate. There has

---

[58] Art 67(2)(a) Public Sector Directive; and Art 82(2)(a) Utilities Directive.
[59] Art 67(4) Public Sector Directive; and Art 82(4) Utilities Directive.

been a proliferation of standards, labels, and certifications which address environmental sustainability. One of the objectives of the reform of the procurement directives was to enable contracting authorities to distinguish between bona fide independent schemes and those which are closely tied to, or controlled by, industry. To this end, new rules have been introduced regarding references to labels in technical specifications, award criteria, and contract performance clauses. The provisions attempt to balance the advantages offered by labels in terms of reducing the overheads associated with verifying environmental criteria, with the potential for their abuse. Labels or certification schemes may also be used to verify compliance with social criteria, such as minimum labour conditions and ethical production practices. The specific potential for requiring fair trade certification is discussed below.

Environmental or social labels may be used in two different ways as part of **7.33**
procurement:

(i) to define the technical specifications, award criteria, or contract performance clauses; and
(ii) to verify compliance with technical specifications, award criteria, and contract clauses.

The 2014 directives provide an enhanced ability to 'require a specific label as means of proof that the works, services or supplies correspond to the required characteristics'.[60] This wording is misleading because it is subject both to an obligation to accept labels meeting equivalent requirements, and to the possibility for operators to rely on other means of proof where they are not able to obtain a label within the time limits for reasons which are not attributable to them.[61] This mirrors the caveat in respect of environmental management systems. The meaning of 'time limits' in this context is not entirely clear—if it refers to the time between publication of tender documents and the deadline for tenders, then this will be insufficient in most cases for an economic operator to obtain a label. However, it does reflect a shift in the burden of proof compared to the 2004 directives, under which operators were entitled to rely on technical dossiers or other non-third-party evidence without special justification.[62] This shift is accompanied by a longer list of conditions regarding the type of labels which contracting authorities may so 'require'.

A distinction is drawn between labels whose requirements only concern criteria linked **7.34**
to the subject-matter of the contract and those which concern other criteria without this link. An example of the latter would perhaps be a label which, in addition to stipulating product-specific environmental or social characteristics, such as design features

---

[60] Art 43(1) Public Sector Directive; and Art 61(1) Utilities Directive.
[61] Art 43(1) Public Sector Directive; and Art 61(1) Utilities Directive, penultimate and final indents.
[62] Art 23(6) of Directive 2004/18/EC, final indent.

to reduce energy consumption or improve accessibility for disabled users, also requires its bearers to apply certain principles or practices in their overall business operations. In this case, the label itself cannot be required, but the appropriate criteria from the label may be referred to in technical specifications.[63] It is not clear whether the appropriate criteria may also form part of award criteria and contract performance clauses, but given the greater freedom which contracting authorities have in these areas, it seems this must be possible. It is also unclear whether the same rules regarding operators' ability to rely on other evidence apply in such cases, or whether they may do so without special justification.

7.35 For any of the above uses, labels must meet four requirements regarding their formulation:

(i) the label requirements are based on objectively verifiable and non-discriminatory criteria;

(ii) the label is established using an open and transparent procedure in which all relevant stakeholders, including government bodies, consumers, social partners, manufacturers, distributors, and non-governmental organizations, may participate;

(iii) the label is accessible to all interested parties; and

(iv) the label requirements are set by a third party over which the economic operator applying for the label cannot exercise a decisive influence.

7.36 While most Type I eco-labels[64] will meet these standards, contracting authorities do need to have a degree of insight into both the content and award process for any labels referred to. This can be seen as a positive development from the perspective of increasing the reliability of environmental labelling and ensuring its transparency. However, in the short term, it may also add to the overheads associated with implementing GPP. In particular, the ambiguity regarding the way in which labels which concern requirements not linked to the subject-matter can be used in award criteria and contract performance clauses may be seen as creating a risk of legal challenge where such labels are referred to.

Life-cycle costing

7.37 The idea of life-cycle costing (LCC), also sometimes referred to as whole-life costing or total cost of ownership, has a lengthy pedigree within public procurement.[65] For consumable assets or those which use energy, water, or other inputs, a large part of the costs may arise after the initial purchase price is paid. The 2014 directives

---

[63] Art 43(2) Public Sector Directive; and Art 61(2) Utilities Directive.

[64] According to the International Organization for Standardization (ISO) classification for environmental declarations and labels, ISO 14024.

[65] Eg the 1929 *Manual of the American Railway Engineering Association* refers to 'Total Cost of Ownership' of track.

define the parameters within which LCC can be applied in procurement and in particular make provision for the inclusion of environmental externalities in the calculation of costs. Such externalities are stated to include greenhouse gas or other pollutant emissions and 'other climate change mitigation costs', provided their monetary value can be determined and verified.[66] The latter element is of particular interest, in that it may point to inclusion of the cost of carbon offsets, sequestration, or other activities intended to limit the impact of climate change. It is clear that such costs need not be borne by the contracting authority itself in order to be included in LCC calculations.[67]

7.38 Rules regarding the methods used to calculate LCC have been introduced, reflecting the general principles of transparency and equal treatment, as well as the Court's case law on award criteria. Contracting authorities must indicate the methodology which will be used for LCC in the tender documents, and specify the data which is to be submitted by bidders. The method chosen must:

(i) be based on objectively verifiable and non-discriminatory criteria;
(ii) be accessible to all interested parties;
(iii) not require more than a reasonable effort by normally diligent tenderers in terms of data submission; and
(iv) follow any common, mandatory EU method for calculating LCC which applies in the sector.[68]

A number of established LCC tools and methodologies are available for procurement of goods, services, and works. It is also possible for contracting authorities to develop and apply their own methods, provided they comply with the above conditions.[69] Earlier drafts of the directives had also included the ability for operators to submit LCC calculations according to their own methods, but this was removed—presumably due to the difficulty it posed for applying the principle of equal treatment in cost comparisons.

7.39 As with labels, the introduction of more detailed rules regarding LCC in the 2014 directives is a double-edged sword. On the one hand, it confirms the validity of life-cycle costing and may provide specific encouragement to some organisations to apply it. On the other hand, it also creates specific rules and limits which were not present in the 2004 directives, and may thereby increase the legal complexity associated with applying LCC. That it was previously possible to assess life-cycle costs, including environmental externalities, cannot be in any doubt as this was

---

[66] Art 68(1)(b) Public Sector Directive; and Art 83(1)(b) Utilities Directive.

[67] This is evident from the wording of Art 68(1)(a) and (b). The former refers to 'costs borne by the contracting authority and other users', whereas the latter refers to 'costs imputed to environmental externalities' without specifying who bears these costs.

[68] This is currently limited to the methodology set out in the Clean Vehicles Directive (2009/33/EC).

[69] Recital 96 Public Sector Directive.

specifically envisioned under the Clean Vehicles Directive adopted in 2009. The idea that the methods for LCC must be based on objectively verifiable and non-discriminatory criteria and be accessible to all parties may also not be considered to be new, inasmuch as they follow from the general principles of equal treatment and transparency. However, the limitation of the data which may be requested to that which can be obtained with reasonable effort by normally diligent tenderers is new—and explicitly includes tenderers from GPA countries who may be able to argue that certain methods are too onerous on them.

7.40 A further notable feature of the new rules on life-cycle costing is that it is possible to include costs for environmental externalities generated during transport. This is clear from the definition of 'life cycle' given in the directives.[70] The potential for this to result in discrimination against suppliers or service providers located further away from the point of consumption is clear, although it will normally only form one part of a series of consecutive life-cycle stages taken into account in the monetization of emissions. It remains to be seen whether the Court might apply the same logic as obtained in *Vindkraft* and *Essent Belgium* to justify any such discriminatory effect, given that the inclusion of environmental externalities in procurement decisions is specifically sanctioned under the 2014 directives.

Social and Socio-Economic Considerations under the 2014 Directives

7.41 Social considerations in procurement encompass both supply-chain and end-user impacts. Supply-chain impacts are all of those which arise prior to the point of consumption: extraction of raw materials, working conditions of those involved in harvesting, manufacture, or processing, and the terms on which trade is carried out. End-user impacts include the features of a product, service, or work which determine its social utility, such as accessibility to all users or the added value associated with employment, training, or apprenticeships. The 2014 directives afford the opportunity to address both types of impact, together with others which may be considered to have mixed social and economic characteristics such as payment of taxes and access to contracts for SMEs, sheltered workshops, and social enterprises. As with environmental considerations, the extent to which such matters can be taken into account depends on a link to the subject-matter of the contract. As discussed in Chapter 4, the ability to include social considerations in technical specifications appears to be more limited than the ability to take account of environmental factors, with the exception of accessibility for disabled users.[71] (See Table 7.4 below.)

---

[70] Art 2(20) Public Sector Directive.
[71] See discussion at paras 4.34–4.38.

Table 7.4 Social considerations at each procurement stage under the 2014 directives

Contract definition/ pre-procurement	Exclusion and selection criteria	Technical specifications/ award criteria	Contract performance
Application of lighter regime for Title III services (74/Annex XIV)	Mandatory: Child labour, human trafficking, and tax and social security if final judgment (57.1)	Accessibility for persons with disabilities (42/67)	Special social or employment conditions linked to the subject-matter (70)
Reservation for sheltered workshops or employment programmes (20) / public service organizations (77)	Discretionary (may be made mandatory by MS): Compliance with social and labour law, tax, and social security (57.2)	Trading conditions or other social characteristics (67)	Compliance with social and labour laws (18.2)
Preliminary market consultation to identify social impacts of contract (40)	Technical capacity and prior experience with social aspects (58/Annex XII)	Rejection of abnormally low tenders (69)	Subcontracting—direct payment of subcontractors (70.3)
	Supply chain management measures (Annex XII)	Refusal to award for non-compliance with social or labour laws (18.2/56.1)	Subcontracting—names and details of subcontractors (70.5)

Numbers in brackets are article references within the Public Sector Directive. Equivalent possibilities exist under the Utilities and Concessions Directives.

Compliance with social and labour law

7.42 Article 18(2) of the Public Sector Directive[72] sets out a general principle that in the peformance of public contracts economic operators must comply with applicable environmental, social, and labour law obligations established by Union law, national law, collective agreements, and under a list of international conventions listed in an Annex.[73] While this is expressed as a general duty on Member States, Article 18(2) is also the basis for a number of more specific rules. In addition to the general duty, the 2014 directives create:

(i) a discretion for contracting authorities to reject tenders which do not comply with these laws;[74]

---

[72] Replicated in Art 36(2) Utilities Directive and Art 30(3) Concessions Directive.

[73] Annex X Public Sector Directive; Annex XIV Utilities Directive; and Annex X Concessions Directive. The Annex contains the eight core conventions of the International Labour Organization and four environmental conventions relating to protection of the ozone layer, hazardous waste, persistent organic pollutants, and hazardous chemicals and pesticides.

[74] Art 56(1) Public Sector Directive; and Art 76(6) Utilities Directive.

(ii) a discretion for contracting authorities, the exercise of which may be made mandatory under national legislation, to exclude operators from a procedure where violation of these laws can be demonstrated by any appropriate means;[75]

(iii) an obligation on contracting authorities to reject an abnormally low tender where the low price or cost is due to non-compliance with these laws and explanation has been sought from the tenderer in question;[76]

(iv) an obligation on competent national authorities to ensure compliance by subcontractors with these laws;[77]

(v) an obligation on Member States to ensure that, where national law provides for joint liability between main contractors and subcontractors, the relevant rules are applied in compliance with these laws;[78] and

(vi) a discretion for contracting authorities, the exercise of which may be made mandatory under national legislation, to verify the compliance of subcontractors with these laws and to require replacement of a subcontractor which does not comply.[79]

The applicable environmental, social, and labour laws (other than those at international level listed in the Annex) are not defined, but it is suggested that this could include any of the instruments listed above in Tables 7.1 and 7.2, provided they were relevant to the contract at hand. Article 18(2) thus appears to underwrite the ability of contracting authorities to insist on the application of equality legislation, for example, both by rejecting tenders which do not comply with it and by taking action against subcontractors who do not comply.

Reservation of contracts

7.43 The 2014 directives extend the ability for Member States to reserve competition for contracts to certain enterprises which are considered to meet social objectives. Article 20 creates the ability to reserve competition for sheltered workshops or employment programmes where at least 30 per cent of the employees are disabled or disadvantaged workers.[80] This represents an extension against the similar provisions in the 2004 directives, which were limited to workshops or programmes where 'most of the persons employed are handicapped persons who, by reason

---

[75] Art 57(4) Public Sector Directive, which may be applied under Art 80(1) Utilities Directive and Art 38(7) Concessions Directive.

[76] Art 69(3) Public Sector Directive; and Art 84(3) Utilities Directive.

[77] Art 71(1) Public Sector Directive; Art 88 Utilities Directive; and Art 42 Concessions Directive. The recitals to the Public Sector Directive indicate that 'competent national authorities' for the purpose of Art 71(1) may include labour inspection agencies or environmental protection agencies.

[78] Art 71(6)(a) Public Sector Directive; Art 88 Utilities Directive; and Art 42 Concessions Directive.

[79] Art 71(6)(b) Public Sector Directive; Art 88 Utilities Directive; and Art 42 Concessions Directive.

[80] Art 20 Public Sector Directive; Art 38 Utilities Directive; and Art 24 Concessions Directive.

of the nature or the seriousness of their disabilities, cannot carry on occupations under normal conditions'.[81] The term 'disadvantaged worker' is not defined, so it is possible that this provision could be used to reserve contracts for programmes which offer employment to long-term unemployed people or those who face labour market discrimination based on age, gender, ethnicity, or other factors. However, it is not a derogation from the requirement to advertise and apply the procedures set out in the directives. There is no ability to limit such reservation to national or regional programmes or workshops. This is significant in the light of the history of sheltered workshops and similar programmes across Europe.

Sheltered workshops exist in a number of Member States, including the UK, **7.44** Ireland, Germany, Netherlands, Belgium, France, Sweden, Poland, and Italy, employing disabled workers and in some cases prisoners or other persons with social disadvantages who would not otherwise be employed.[82] Prior to the 1990s, schemes aimed at awarding public contracts to such undertakings were usually restricted to national workshops, and in some cases the preference or reservation applied both above and below the EU threshold.[83] In the 1990s, pressure was brought to bear on these schemes, both by the Commission and, perhaps more influentially, by a lack of political will at national level to support their operation if there was some risk that they would be forced to extend to cover similar work-shops in other Member States. Concerns about the legality of awarding public contracts to such workshops is only one factor which can been seen to contribute to their decline, but in certain countries its effect was clear.[84] It will be interesting to observe the effect, if any, of the more generous reservation provisions on the volume of public contracts awarded in this way.

---

[81] Art 19 Directive 2004/18/EC. For discussion of this provision and possible interpretations of its wording, see Boyle, R. 'Disability Issues in Public Procurement' in Kunzlik and Arrowsmith (eds), *Social and Environmental Policies*, pp 333–43.

[82] The history of such workshops stretches back to sixteenth-century France, where they were operated primarily by religious institutions. By the eighteenth century, they had become an established part of the economy in Europe. In the decades following World War II, the number of such workshops grew across Europe and in other parts of the world, often with a particular focus on employing adults with intellectual disabilities. See Migliore, A. (2010) 'Sheltered Workshops' in J. H. Stone and M. Blouin (eds), *International Encyclopedia of Rehabilitation*, available online at: <http://cirrie.buffalo.edu/encyclopedia/en/article/136/>.

[83] See McCrudden, *Buying Social Justice*, pp 344–6 and 555–6 on the links between such schemes and the procurement rules.

[84] In certain jurisdictions, policy shifted towards supporting disabled adults to find employment on the open market, with mixed results. There is an ongoing debate about the benefits of sheltered workshops as against integration into more mainstream employment. In relation to this debate, it is worth noting two points about the possibility to reserve contracts under the procurement directives. The first is that the reservation may apply to any undertaking provided it employs at least 30 per cent disabled or disadvantaged workers—meaning that programmes which aim to integrate such workers with others can also benefit. The second is that the nature of the reservation envisions competition between such undertakings, which may be used, inter alia, to compare their success in integrating workers or attaining other objectives specific to their nature and purpose.

7.45 The 2014 directives also include a new ability to reserve contracts for social, health, cultural or other specific services for competition by enterprises with a public service mission linked to the activities in question.[85] There are specific requirements regarding the treatment of profits and the ownership structure of such enterprises, and contracts awarded in this way cannot exceed three years or be awarded to an enterprise which has benefited from the reservation in the past three years. This reservation was lobbied for by the UK, where social enterprises are seen as being an effective means of maintaining the character of public services where they are contracted out.[86] It is expressed as being subject to review and reporting by the Commission prior to April 2019. Where either of the two reservation options is used, this must be indicated in the call for competition published in the OJEU. A question may arise as to whether it is possible to combine the two reservations in a single procedure where an authority wishes to allow the opportunity for both social enterprises and sheltered workshops or programmes to compete, but not to allow other businesses operating on a fully commercial basis to do so.

Fair trade

7.46 The timing of the Court's decision in the *Dutch Coffee* case was opportune from the perspective of those wishing to ensure the ability of contracting authorities to choose fair trade products and services. As noted, while the Court held against the specific application of a fair trade label by the authority in that case, it made clear that terms of trade might be considered as award criteria in other circumstances. This position was then written into the 2014 directives, by the inclusion of 'trading conditions' among the characteristics which award criteria may address. The provisions on labels were also extended to cover social labels as mentioned in paragraph 7.32, although the extent to which fair trade labels can be required in technical specifications remains questionable. This is due to the lack of any explicit reference to trading conditions in the provisions on technical specifications, as well as the Court's view in *Dutch Coffee* that such considerations did not constitute technical specifications.[87] However, as I have argued in Chapter 4, the inclusion of methods of provision among the characteristics which can be addressed in technical specifications may leave room for the Court to revisit this interpretation.

7.47 Many public authorities prefer to purchase fair trade products such as tea, coffee, sugar, produce, and cotton. Fair trade certification typically addresses a range of factors relating to the organization and representation of labour, payment of a producer premium and/or minimum price, traceability of products, and auditing

---

[85] Art 77 Public Sector Directive; and Art 94 Utilities Directive.

[86] See House of Commons Public Administration Select Committee (2013) *Government Procurement (Sixth Report of Session 2013–14)*, available at: <http://www.publications.parliament.uk/pa/>.

[87] Case C-368/10 *Dutch Coffee*, para 74.

and inspection. Certification is available for both products and producer organizations.[88] Different standards will be applicable to an organization based on its activities, size, and position within the supply chain. For the purposes of public procurement and given the link to the subject-matter requirement, it is fair trade product certification which is relevant, but in practice many of the activities such as setting up worker representation and cooperative structures are obviously only achievable and auditable at the organizational level. It then becomes necessary to ask if product certification can truly be separated from producer certification, and whether this is a sensible way to approach the larger structural and social problems which fair trade aims to address. A strict interpretation of the link to the subject-matter requirement impedes the use of fair trade or other certifications where these aim to address the overall practices of producers, as opposed to those adopted for a particular contract.

Critique—Is the 'Link to the Subject-matter' Requirement Sustainable?

On one view, the 'link to the subject-matter' requirement does not restrict sustainability criteria inasmuch as contracting authorities are free to define the subject-matter of their contracts.[89] While this is true, it is clear from the judgments in *Concordia*, *EVN*, and *Dutch Coffee* that it does exclude certain considerations, namely those which relate to the overall business practices of an undertaking rather than what is being purchased in the contract at hand. This distinction is emphasized in the recitals to the 2014 directives.[90] It reflects a general reluctance under the procurement directives to sanction restrictions on *tenderers* as opposed to *tenders*, as is evident in the exhaustive list of exclusion and selection criteria which may be applied to economic operators.[91]   **7.48**

However, there are a number of exceptions to this approach, notably the provisions   **7.49** on reservation of contracts, and the ability under the 2014 directives to take qualifications, experience, and organization of staff into account at award stage. Such provisions recognize that the assessment of a contractor's suitability or capacity and its tender are not hermetically sealed processes. Similarly, the directives allow assessment at selection stage of the environmental and supply chain management measures which an operator 'will be able to apply' in carrying out a contract—as

---

[88] For an overview of the standards operated by Fairtrade International, the largest fair trade body, see <http://www.fairtrade.net/standards.html>.

[89] This argument is set out in McCrudden, *Buying Social Justice*, pp 522–31.

[90] Recital 97 of the Public Sector Directive, in setting out the link to the subject-matter requirement, states: 'Contracting authorities should hence not be allowed to require tenderers to have a certain corporate social or environmental responsibility policy in place.'

[91] See discussion at paras 4.04–4.21.

opposed to just a general statement of the policies or certifications which it holds.[92] These provisions reflect the reality of many procurement procedures: candidates do not spring out fully armed for a contract like Athena from Zeus's forehead. There is often an iterative process whereby capacity or resources are put in place only at contract award stage. This is particularly true in the case of SMEs.

7.50 If it is impossible to take any considerations related to suitability or capacity into account at award stage, this makes it more difficult for a wide range of businesses to compete. In procedures with a separate selection stage, it means that such matters must be dealt with exhaustively prior to candidates even having an opportunity to tender. This runs contrary to the aim of the 2014 directives to streamline selection processes and reduce the burden placed on suppliers at this stage. This tendency will be reinforced where the link to the subject-matter requirement is interpreted as meaning that no matters relating to general corporate practices may be revisited later in the process—for example, in contract performance clauses which create a general requirement for an operator to pay its taxes or observe environmental law, as opposed to just do these things in respect of the contract awarded.[93] There is likely to be a trade-off between the strictness with which the subject-matter link is interpreted, and the strictness with which suitability is assessed prior to contract award. This brings us back to the question of whether contracting authorities are free to define the subject-matter of the contract in a way which includes their specific interest in only dealing with companies which are responsible in their wider practices.

7.51 The restrictive interpretation of the subject-matter link may be traced back to a false syllogism at the heart of the *Concordia* decision:

> Since a tender necessarily relates to the subject-matter of the contract, it follows that the award criteria which may be applied in accordance with [the provisions on award criteria set out in the directives] must themselves also be linked to the subject-matter of the contract.[94]

While it is true that a tender relates to the subject-matter of the contract, it may also relate to other things. For example, it will normally contain a description of the tenderer's business, staff, and resources and an indication of acceptance of any proposed contract terms. It is clear that where matters have already been assessed

---

[92] Annex XII, Pt II(d) and (g) Public Sector Directive, which may be applied under Art 80(1) Utilities Directive and Art 38(7) Concessions Directive.

[93] It is possible that the general duty placed on Member States to ensure observance of applicable environmental, social, and labour laws in the execution of public contracts under Art 18(2) could be cited as justification for such conditions. However, the requirement for a subject-matter link in Art 70 may be considered to be a more specific obligation, and one which rests directly on contracting authorities.

[94] Case C-513/99 *Concordia*, para 59.

at selection stage, they cannot form part of award criteria. However, as indicated above, the view that questions of capacity or experience can never be assessed at award stage—that promoted in *Lianakis*—has been rejected in the 2014 directives. This refers to the experience of staff proposed for a contract as opposed to general corporate experience, but still contradicts the idea that award criteria can only concern characteristics of what *will be* performed, as opposed to what has already occurred. The link to the subject-matter requirement, if strictly construed, can be detrimental both to the realization of environmental and social objectives and to the ability of the market to deliver these. To understand this, it is worth taking a few examples of how environmental and social criteria may affect the market in the context of procurement procedures.

In the case of renewable electricity, the requirement that specifications, award **7.52** criteria, and contract performance clauses be linked to the subject-matter of the contract would likely preclude broader schemes designed to encourage investment in renewable electricity via the award of public contracts. A contracting authority is free to insist that all or a given percentage of the electricity it purchases is produced from renewable sources, but not to use its award of contract as a means of distinguishing between suppliers who produce or supply a greater percentage of renewable energy overall, or who invest in new renewable facilities—unless this in some way affects the electricity which it is purchasing. Public sector demand for renewable electricity may push prices up, due to limitations on production capacity. Eventually, supply should increase to meet this demand; however, as is well recognized by the Court in its case law on green certificates, the normal rules of supply and demand are insufficient to develop the level of renewable energy capacity needed to meet Europe's 2020 target. Award criteria or contract performance clauses which target the development of additional renewable energy capacity may be more effective in contributing to this target than those which relate solely to the electricity consumed by the authority.

A second example of how a narrow link to the subject-matter requirement can be **7.53** detrimental is where life-cycle costing or other award criteria include a direct comparison of greenhouse gas emissions between tenders. For a supply contract, this may include the emissions associated with transport of the goods from a warehouse or production facility to the point of consumption. A tenderer with a warehouse or production facility closer to the point of consumption would therefore attain higher marks than one with identical facilities which are further away—even if the closer supplier is less environmentally efficient overall—for example, because of longer delivery routes to its other clients. If a company's overall emissions are not considered to be linked to the subject-matter, then they cannot be taken into account—limiting the effectiveness of criteria intended to address climate change *and* discriminating against suppliers who are located at a greater geographic distance from the contracting authority.

7.54 On the social side, similarly counterproductive effects can be seen to arise where contracting authorities are unable to take general corporate practices into account. One of the arguments made against living wage or fair trade schemes is that they may push local costs and prices up, with a negative impact on those who are not covered by such schemes. This effect—which admittedly is difficult to measure—would be compounded where contracting authorities are obliged to focus only on the goods, services, or works they are purchasing, as opposed to looking at the broader practices of tendering firms. As for schemes promoting employment or apprenticeships, award criteria or contract clauses which only focus on these to the extent that they are specific to the contract being awarded are both less likely to be efficient in promoting their objectives (as it may make more sense for firms to employ apprentices or long-term unemployed people on another contract) and more likely to be discriminatory against non-domestic undertakings than those which allow 'credit' for the operation of such schemes as part of general corporate practices.[95]

7.55 There are at least three reasons, then, for questioning the value of a strict link to the subject-matter requirement for technical specifications, award criteria, and contract performance clauses. The first is that it tends to counteract attempts to reduce the burdens placed on suppliers at selection stage. The second is that it may specifically undermine the environmental or social objectives which contracting authorities wish to pursue via their procurement, many of which are endorsed at Union level. The third is that it is more likely to result in market fragmentation and to impede the free movement of goods and services, as well as the efficient allocation of resources which is the ultimate aim of these freedoms, than approaches which are not specific to the subject-matter of the contract.

7.56 These arguments may be put to one side by those who consider that the purpose of procurement is not to influence the general corporate policies of undertakings delivering public contracts, but simply to obtain goods, services, or works on specific terms. This view has some conceptual appeal and may even be endorsed by those who support the application of contract-specific sustainability measures. It must be recognized, however, that this narrower view of the function of public procurement has its conceptual origins in comparisons with private consumption, relying on the premise that in its commercial function government should behave as a private actor on the market does. It need only be pointed out that concerns about overall corporate social responsibility—from tax compliance to environmental stewardship and community benefits—are increasingly prevalent both within procurement decisions by private companies and consumption decisions by private citizens. The idea that the public sector should be uniquely restrained from acting on such concerns is anomalous.

---

[95] Assuming that, for the most part, undertakings will be better placed to offer sheltered employment programmes or apprenticeships in the country of their establishment.

A better argument against loosening the link to the subject-matter requirement **7.57** might be that this puts the 'additionality' of sustainable procurement at risk. For example, if marks can be awarded for a supplier's efforts to increase its overall production of renewable energy instead of just that which is produced for a particular contract, can it be claimed that there is an additional positive impact from the award of the contract itself? This depends on whether criteria which target general corporate practices are combined with those which apply to the specific goods, services, or works being purchased, or replace them. Obligations imposed at the organizational level do require a robust approach to verification to ensure that they are not met by vague policies which are effectively business as usual. However, in cases where they reinforce contract-specific sustainability commitments and help to avoid the problems which a narrow view of the subject-matter engenders, they can be of clear additional benefit.

Could the principle of proportionality provide a more appropriate test than the **7.58** link to the subject-matter in determining the legitimacy of environmental and social criteria? Proportionality affords a high degree of discretion to courts to carry out a balancing exercise based on the facts before them. This can have advantages in areas where courts are tasked with reviewing complex decisions, as those relating to sustainable procurement usually are. The main disadvantage associated with application of a proportionality test is that it does not afford very much legal certainty regarding which factors the Court will take into account and how these will be weighed. However, this criticism may also be applied to the subject-matter of the contract test, given that there have been relatively few judgments applying the test in practice. The increased reference to the test in the 2014 directives may lead to further case law on this point, but in the interim contracting authorities will still find themselves in the quandaries set out above.

Recommended Approaches

While the above discussion has identified some potential shortcomings with cur- **7.59** rent EU law in respect of sustainable procurement, there are still a number of avenues available to contracting authorities wishing to procure responsibly. The following recommended approaches can be identified from the existing literature and practice across Europe.

Prioritization of product and service groups

Most contracting authorities procure a range of supplies, services, and works, **7.60** sometimes employing a category management approach. One-off projects may be subject to a separate management structure, and different procedures may apply where a central purchasing body or framework is being used. While sustainability commitments and targets are often government-wide or set at EU level, individual organizations will be responsible for implementing them via their procurement. This usually requires a process of prioritization, so that authorities can focus their efforts on procurement categories where real sustainability gains can be made. The available gains may be limited for products or services where the authority has little influence over the market—for example, because of the small size of its spend, or because of high degrees of standardization in the sector. They may also be limited if the authority has already taken significant steps to address impacts in that sector, or if it is particularly constrained from an operational or budgetary perspective.

7.61 Prioritization exercises in respect of sustainable procurement take various forms. One approach is to assign scores to a range of factors which then determine the order of focus for different products and services. These factors may include the specific environmental and social risks associated with a given category, in addition to the size and nature of procurement spend, level of influence which the contracting authority has, and its ability to do more.[96] Such an exercise can help to identify procurement categories which offer 'quick wins', in that changes to criteria or other purchasing decisions can be expected to result in measurable impacts against the targeted objectives in the short term. Others may be identified as longer-term projects which will require a greater investment of time. The organization is then able to plan its resources in a way which balances short- and longer-term progress towards its sustainability goals. An example of how such prioritization may function is shown in Table 7.5.

Table 7.5 Sample prioritization exercise for sustainable procurement

Prioritization factor	Category Paper and stationery	Vehicles	Cleaning services	Building works	Textiles
Procurement spend	1	3	3	5	2
Frequency of contract award	5	3	3	1	2
Environmental risk factors	2	4	3	5	2
Social risk factors	1	1	4	4	5
Influence on market	1	1	4	3	2
Ability to do more	4	3	4	2	1
Availability of criteria	5	3	3	4	3
Totals	19	18	24	24	17

Scoring scale: 1 = very low; 2 = low; 3 = medium; 4 = high; 5 = very high.

In this particular example, the contracting authority would identify cleaning services and building works as the highest priorities for its sustainable procurement

---

[96] These are among the factors taken into account in the Marrakech Approach to Sustainable Public Procurement prioritization methodology. See <http://www.unep.fr/scp/procurement/publications>.

efforts. A more sophisticated methodology would distinguish between quick wins and longer-term projects, and might weight factors differently depending on their relative importance to the authority. This type of exercise can be repeated where any of the underlying factors changes—for example, procurement spend goes up or new criteria become available.

Application of common criteria and use of labels

Although prioritization in respect of sustainable procurement may be specific to a **7.62** contracting authority, the criteria applied to target environmental and social considerations need not be. The development of common criteria has been one of the major projects supporting GPP at EU level, and similar criteria have been adopted at national or regional levels in many countries.[97] Alignment with the EU Ecolabel or national eco-labels has been part of the process, contributing to the ability of suppliers to demonstrate that products or services meet the criteria developed and facilitating the verification process for authorities. The existence of common criteria, like the use of standards in many sectors, can help to lower the costs of demonstrating compliance with environmental requirements in particular.

There is also an argument made against standardization, namely, that it can serve **7.63** to stifle innovation. However, the evidence to support this argument appears relatively weak.[98] In most cases, GPP criteria are based on state-of-the-art environmental performance in the sectors they cover, and are revised regularly to reflect developments in those sectors. They also often combine technical specifications based on standards or prescribed processes with those based on function or performance, together with award criteria and contract performance clauses. This means that they afford scope for variations in the market, while still guaranteeing a degree of improvement in environmental factors over the status quo. Any innovation-inhibiting effect of common criteria may also be balanced by the advantages associated with a more harmonized approach to demand for green goods and services, in terms of reduced prices and greater product availability. While no set of criteria is perfect, the work done to identify and address the main impacts of different products and services has helped to take much of the 'mystery' out of sustainable procurement criteria.

In the social arena, common criteria and labels are less frequently encountered, **7.64** with the exception of fair trade. Approaches to socially responsible procurement tend to be local, regional, or national in character—and for this reason they have often been viewed with some suspicion from the perspective of the internal market.

---

[97] Links to the EU and national/regional criteria sets are available at: <http://www.sustainable-procurement.org/resources/procurement-criteria/>.

[98] For an overview of micro- and macro-economic evidence on this question, including in the procurement context, see Knut, B. (2013) *The Impact of Standardization and Standards on Innovation: Compendium of Evidence on the Effectiveness of Innovation Policy Intervention* (Manchester: Manchester Institute of Innovation Research / Nesta).

However, there are also many approaches to social value in procurement which are not protectionist in nature and these may be considered to hold particular potential for use under the 2014 directives. Work done to develop common methodologies to measure social return on investment (SROI)[99] and social life-cycle assessment[100] of different products and services may also mean that such approaches are explicitly referenced in future revisions of the directives.

Adaptation of procurement systems and monitoring

7.65 As is evident from the discussion so far in this chapter, implementation of sustainable procurement may involve changes to multiple stages of the procurement process from contract definition through to monitoring of performance. Such transformation can be facilitated both by overall policies and by specific changes to standing orders or procedures on procurement. Success is more likely where the implications of changes to criteria have been discussed with suppliers in advance and the measures needed to verify compliance—for example, labels, test reports, or other third-party certification—have been identified in a prior information notice or other means of communicating with the market. An explicit policy on sustainable procurement, as opposed to ad hoc application of criteria, can help to ensure that such measures are seen as part of a longer-term commitment which justifies investment in means of proof. On the contracting authority side, there may also be a need to invest in staff training and adaptation of systems.

7.66 In particular, e-procurement systems should be adapted so that they allow for the tracking of sustainability requirements in tenders. At the time of writing, there appears to be considerable scope for innovative developments in such systems which assist with the verification of environmental and social criteria. For example, e-procurement systems could assist in cross-referencing the contents of different certificates and labels submitted by candidates or tenderers to determine whether they are equivalent and match the requirements specified by the contracting authority. Likewise, the computation of life-cycle costs, including the application of common EU methodologies and insertion of costs attributed to environmental externalities, is an area with obvious potential for enhanced use of technology. With the move to mandatory fully electronic tendering by 2018, the growth in the market for such applications seems certain to stimulate their advancement.

---

[99] See <http://www.thesroinetwork.org> for an explanation of social return on investment methodologies.

[100] Social life-cycle assessment has been advanced by the United Nations: see <http://www.unep.fr/scp/publications/details.asp?id=DTI/1164/PA>.

8

REMEDIES AND IMPLICATIONS FOR PRACTICE

Public procurement for the most part takes place at some distance from the courts. **8.01**
It is easy to forget, given the focus on case law in the preceding chapters, that judicial resolution of challenges to procedures is rare, and successful claims even rarer.
Nevertheless, the evolution in the substantive scope of the procurement directives
has been accompanied by a strengthening of the ability of private applicants to
bring claims, notably by the amendment of the Remedies Directives in 2007. In
addition, the Commission has been an active enforcer of the public procurement
rules, bringing over 60 infringement proceedings against Member States relating
to procurement matters between 2009 and 2012 alone.[1] It is, of course, more difficult to track the frequency of claims or complaints which are resolved outside of
courts or tribunals, but which may have regard to decided cases and bind the parties to take or refrain from a certain course of action.

The volume of private applicant challenges to procurement procedures varies **8.02**
greatly between Member States.[2] France, Italy, and Sweden are on the higher end of
the scale, England and Ireland at the lower, and Germany and Poland somewhere
in the middle.[3] This probably reflects the influence of a range of factors: level of
compliance with the directives, market dynamics, cost of access to remedies, time
limits, willingness of the courts to award specific remedies, and the culture surrounding challenges to public contracts. Even within the four neighouring jurisdictions of England and Wales, Scotland, Northern Ireland, and Ireland, marked
differences in the volume and nature of claims, as well as their outcomes, can be
observed. One feature shared by these jurisdictions is a high level of judicialization

---

[1] European Commission (2012), *Annual Public Procurement Implementation Review*, p 28.
[2] Research by the European Commission in 2011 indicated that an average of 8.5 per cent of
procedures advertised were subject to review, ranging from 1 per cent in Cyprus to 19 per cent in
Sweden. These figures should, however, be treated with some caution given the variations in available statistics and the nature of review proceedings between Member States. European Commission
(2012), *Annual Public Procurement Implementation Review*, p 31.
[3] Fairgrieve, D. and Lichère, F. (eds) (2011) *Public Procurement Law: Damages as an Effective
Remedy* (Oxford: Hart Publishing), p 192.

of procurement disputes: that is, there are no bodies other than the courts competent to deal with claims. This makes procurement challenges expensive, although
successful claimants will usually be compensated for costs. It also means that in
most cases a full written record in respect of decided cases is available, and that
precedent is acknowledged, if not always followed.

8.03   This chapter provides an overview of the remedies regime both at EU level and
within the United Kingdom and Ireland. The Remedies Directives form the foundation for challenges to public procurement procedures and some consideration
is given to their origin and scope as well as their interpretation in case law of the
Court of Justice. I then turn to the application of remedies in the UK courts, looking at the approach taken to time limits, disclosure, interim relief, resolution of
substantive claims and the award of damages, set aside, and declarations of ineffectiveness. A similar analysis is undertaken for Ireland. While the number of decided
cases in Ireland is still relatively small, recent judgments indicate a less restrictive
approach towards access to interim relief than that which applies in the United
Kingdom, including maintenance of the automatic suspension of contract award
until substantive proceedings are complete.[4] Important judgments were issued by
the Supreme Courts of both the UK and Ireland during the summer of 2014,[5]
and I consider how these, together with the implementation of the new directives,
may affect future cases. Preliminary references to the CJEU and infringement
actions brought by the European Commission also figure prominently in the remedies landscape, and their role in shaping procurement practices is given some
attention here.

The Remedies Directives

8.04   The need to provide for certain minimum common standards for the enforcement of the public procurement rules was recognized by the mid-1980s. This was
achieved initially by Directive 89/665/EEC covering the public sector and by
Directive 92/13/EEC for the utilities sector (the Remedies Directives). In *Alcatel*,
the Court observed that the purpose of Directive 89/665/EEC is 'to establish effective and rapid procedures to review unlawful decisions of the contracting authority
at the stage where infringements may still be rectified'.[6] The Remedies Directives

---

[4] Following the Supreme Court judgment in *OCS One Complete Solution Ltd v Dublin Airport
Authority Plc* [2014] IESC 51, in which it held that the Irish Utilities Remedies Regulations did not
confer on the courts a jurisdiction to entertain an application by the contracting entity concerned
to be permitted to conclude the relevant contract prior to the determination of the application for
review.

[5] In *Healthcare at Home Ltd (Appellant) v The Common Services Agency (Respondent) Scotland*
[2014] UKSC 49; and *OCS*.

[6] Case C-81/98 *Alcatel Austria AG and Others v Bundesministerium für Wissenschaft und Verkehr*
[1999] ECR I-07671, para 38.

require that Member States make review procedures available 'at least to any person having or having had an interest in obtaining a particular contract and who has been or risks being harmed by an alleged infringement'. Concern with illegal direct award of contracts in particular drove the development of amending Directive 2007/66/EU, which implemented the following main changes to the remedies regime:

   (i) placing the standstill period on legislative footing;
  (ii) requirement to notify candidates and bidders of the reasons for decisions and of the standstill period which applies;
 (iii) 30-day minimum time limit for bringing claims;
 (iv) new remedy of ineffectiveness; and
  (v) provision for a 'voluntary ex ante transparency notice' (VEAT).

Each of these now plays an important role in the availability of remedies at national **8.05** level. To date, only minor changes to the remedies regime have been introduced to reflect the 2014 reform, and these are found in Articles 46 and 47 of the Concessions Directive. They simply replace references to the 2004 directives with references to the 2014 directives within 89/665/EEC and 92/13/EEC. Given the more substantive update which took place in 2007, with Member States only implementing the changes in national law thereafter, it was perhaps felt too soon to revisit the effectiveness of remedies or attempt further reform. However, in one area at least, the Remedies Directives would have benefited from a more substantive update, that is to clarify the availability of remedies where illegal modifications to contracts take place.[7] It is possible that some Member States may opt to clarify the application of existing remedies in this situation at the same time that they implement the non-substantive updates mentioned in this paragraph, but most probably will not.

In terms of scope, the Remedies Directives apply to all contracts and concessions **8.06** 'referred to' in the 2014 directives, provided they do not fall under a specific exclusion.[8] Contracts and concessions awarded by contracting authorities are subject to Directive 89/665/EEC and contracts awarded under the Utilities Directive and concessions award by contracting entities are subject to Directive 92/13/EEC. This includes contracts governed by the Title III regime for social, health, and related services, but excludes public service contracts awarded to a central purchasing body for the provision of centralized purchasing activities.[9] As previously, Member States may invoke a derogation from the standstill period in respect of contracts awarded under framework agreements and dynamic purchasing systems,

---

  [7] See discussion at paras 5.50–5.51.
  [8] Arts 46 and 47 Concessions Directive. The phrase 'referred to' is perhaps intended to ensure the transitional continuity of the remedies regime, as it does not explicitly require that contracts be *subject to* the 2014 directives. Contracts awarded under the 2004 directives will still be subject to the Remedies Directives after the deadline for transposition of the 2014 directives has passed.
  [9] Arts 46(1) and 47(1) Concessions Directive.

although breaches of the rules on awarding contracts under these arrangements are subject to a declaration of ineffectiveness if the contract is valued above the relevant EU threshold.[10]

8.07 The Remedies Directives require that procedures are available to: (i) take interim measures to correct alleged infringements or prevent further damage to the interests concerned by suspending award procedures or the implementation of any decision; (ii) set aside any decisions taken unlawfully, including discriminatory technical, economic, or financial specifications; and (iii) award damages to any person harmed by an infringement. In addition, ineffectiveness must be available as a remedy in situations where there has been an illegal direct award of a contract (ie no contract notice has been published) or there has been a breach of the suspension or standstill period together with a substantive breach.[11] Ineffectiveness would thus be the appropriate remedy in cases of illegal modifications to contracts or direct award to an in-house or other public body where this is not covered by the *Teckal/Hamburg* exemptions. The meaning of ineffectiveness is defined under national law, and may mean retrospective or prospective cancellation of contractual obligations. Derogations from ineffectiveness are possible where justified by overriding reasons in the general interest, as distinct from economic interests directly linked to the contract, such as the cost of delays or of running a new procurement procedure. Where this derogation is applied, and also where ineffectiveness results only in cancellation of prospective obligations, Member States must provide for alternative penalties in the form of fines on the contracting authority or shortening the duration of the contract.[12]

8.08 Publication of a voluntary ex ante transparency notice (VEAT) provides a means of safeguarding contracts against a declaration of ineffectiveness. If a contracting authority considers that the publication of a contract notice is not required—for example, because the contract is excluded from the scope of the directives or eligible for application of the negotiated procedure without prior publication of a notice—then a VEAT can be published setting out the scope and value of the contract together with the justification for derogating from competition.[13] A period of at least ten days must be allowed from the date after publication of the notice prior to concluding the contract.[14] This mechanism has been widely adopted in several Member States such as France (30,600) and Poland (4,000), although it is

---

[10] Arts 46(3) and 47(3) Concessions Directive amending Art 2(b) Directive 89/665/EEC and Art 2b of Directive 92/13/EEC—although note that for the utilities sector both the derogation from standstill and remedy of ineffectiveness appear to only apply in respect of contracts awarded under dynamic purchasing systems, and not under frameworks.

[11] Art 2db Remedies Directives. The breach of the suspension or standstill period must also have deprived the applicant of the possibility of pre-contractual remedies and the substantive breach must have affected their chances of winning the contract.

[12] Art 2e Remedies Directives.

[13] Art 3a Remedies Directives.

[14] Art 2d4 Remedies Directives. A longer period may be provided for in national law.

less frequently used in the UK (2,130) and Ireland (33).[15] The CJEU has confirmed that a VEAT must serve to protect the award of contract from a declaration of ineffectiveness where the conditions for its use are fully met by a contracting authority, including the publication in the notice of clear and unequivocal reasons justifying the direct award of the contract.[16]

Equivalence and effectiveness

Although the Remedies Directives provide only a limited degree of harmoniza- **8.09**
tion, two general principles of EU law serve to buttress their presence in national legal systems. The principle of equivalence requires that the procedural rules governing actions for safeguarding an individual's rights under EU law must be no less favourable than those governing similar domestic actions. The principle of effectiveness requires that procedural rules must not render the exercise of rights conferred by EU law 'practically impossible or excessively difficult'.[17] While the former principle has undoubtedly influenced the manner in which domestic courts interpret and apply the remedies regime, the CJEU has primarily been concerned with effectiveness in its superintendence of the remedies available at national level. Three of its judgments in particular have served to emphasize the importance of the principle of effectiveness of remedies.

The first, *Alcatel*, concerned the award of a contract for an electronic information **8.10**
system to be installed on the Austrian motorway network. The contracting authority had signed the contract on the same day that the successful tenderer was identified, with the other bidders only receiving news of this later via the press. Their application for the suspension of the contract was rejected, but their substantive claim that a breach of the procurement rules had taken place later succeeded. In this situation, under Austrian law a court could only award damages and not set aside the awarded contract. The CJEU held that the Remedies Directives required that a contracting authority's decision on which bidder to award a contract to must be open to review prior to the conclusion of the contract.[18] This led to Member States making provision for a standstill period between notification of results of a competition and entering into a contract. The standstill period was fixed at a minimum of ten calendar days when Directive 2007/66/EU was adopted.[19]

---

[15] The figures in brackets refer to the number of VEAT notices published on Tenders Electronic Daily for each country between December 2009 and August 2014.

[16] Case C-19/13 *Ministero dell'Interno v Fastweb SpA*, not yet reported, paras 45–54.

[17] Case C-568/08 *Combinatie Spijker Infrabouw-De Jonge Konstruktie and Others v Provincie Drenthe* [2010] ECR I-12655, para 91 and case law cited.

[18] Case C-81/98 *Alcatel*, para 43.

[19] Art 2a(2) Remedies Directives, as inserted by Directive 2007/66/EU. The ten-day minimum period applies provided notification is sent electronically; if other means are used, then the minimum is set at 15 days or ten days beginning the day after receipt of the notification.

8.11 The *Lämmerzahl* case concerned time limits applied under a restrictive interpretation of a German law regarding challenges to procurement breaches. This meant that where an alleged breach was identifiable based on the contract notice or invitation to tender, a complaint had to be raised during the tender period and not subsequent to it. The contracting authority in *Lämmerzahl* had failed to state the total quantity or scope of software licences which it was purchasing, which brought the value of the contract above the EU threshold. The claimant had sought to clarify the volume of licences required, but had received a non-committal response from the contracting authority. In this situation, the Court held that the application of the German law deprived it of an effective remedy. A time limit for bringing claims might end on the date of tender submission provided it applies only in respect of breaches which could be identified during this period and not those which arise later.[20] The recent *Idrodinamica* case confirmed that time limits must begin again where a new decision—in that case the authorization of a change in the composition of the winning consortium—is adopted after the initial award decision, but prior to the signing of a contract.[21]

8.12 In *Uniplex*, the time limits placed on applications for review in England and Wales were challenged. The requirement then in place under the Public Contracts Regulations for proceedings to be brought 'promptly and in any event within three months from the date when grounds for the bringing of the proceedings first arose' was found by the CJEU to introduce an unacceptable element of uncertainty regarding access to remedies.[22] While it was up to each Member State to determine the time limits for applications to review procurement decisions (taking into account the 30-day minimum), these must not undermine the effectiveness of EU law.[23] The Court emphasized that merely informing an unsuccessful bidder that its tender had been rejected did not place it in a position whereby it could bring proceedings, and that it is only where the reasons for such a decision have been furnished to it by the contracting authority that it is effectively in such a position. The time limits for review of decisions could only begin to run from the date on which the claimant knew or ought to have known about an alleged infringement.[24]

8.13 *Alcatel, Lämmerzahl*, and *Uniplex* all served to demonstrate the importance placed by the Court on the effectiveness of remedies at national level. Together with the 2007 reform, these judgments meant that Member States were obliged to examine their procedures to ensure they offered adequate access to remedies to claimants in

---

[20] Case C-241/06 *Lämmerzahl GmbH v Freie Hansestadt Bremen* [2007] ECR I-08415, para 58.

[21] Case C-161/13 *Idrodinamica Spurgo Velox srl and Others v Acquedotto Pugliese SpA*, not yet reported, para 41.

[22] Case C-406/08 *Uniplex (UK) Ltd v NHS Business Services Authority* [2010] ECR I-00817, para 42. A similar provision existed under the Irish Rules of the Superior Courts, which the Commission successfully challenged in Case C-456/08 *Commission v Ireland* [2010] ECR I-00859.

[23] Case C-406/08 *Uniplex*, para 40.

[24] Case C-406/08 *Uniplex*, paras 26–32.

procurement cases. Review procedures must be available in respect of all decisions taken by contracting authorities which are subject to the EU rules on public procurement, regardless of the nature and content of those decisions.[25] The Court has held that the remedy of damages cannot be contingent on the claimant showing that the contracting authority was at fault in committing the breach.[26] However, it has also evinced reluctance to interfere with the principles governing award of damages under national law—conscious of the limited level of harmonization provided for under the Remedies Directives and the differences inherent in national legal systems in this area.

Discretion of Member States over remedies

This can be seen most clearly in *Combinatie Spijker Infrabouw*, a preliminary ref- **8.14** erence from a Dutch court regarding award of a contract for the renovation of two canal bridges.[27] The court dealing with interim measures had issued an order preventing the contracting authority from awarding a contract to any party other than the originally identified preferred bidder. The contracting authority chose on this basis to award a contract to that bidder, despite the ongoing substantive challenge from Combinatie (an unsuccessful bidder), who argued that the bid in question was invalid. The court which heard the substantive case referred a number of questions to the CJEU, concerned that the effect of any order in the claimant's favour would be limited given the outcome of the interim proceedings.[28] The CJEU declined to respond to several of the questions on the basis that they were hypothetical to the case at hand.

However, the CJEU did address the questions of whether interim measures could **8.15** be entirely independent from substantive proceedings (meaning that a claimant's failure to succeed on substantive points would not undo a court's interim orders) and whether Directive 89/665 placed any constraints on the manner in which liability is determined and damages calculated under national law. These matters had potentially far-reaching consequences for the implementation of the remedies regime, given the diversity of procedural rules in place in Member States. In the

---

[25] Case C-249/01 *Hackermüller* [2003] ECR I-6319, para 24 and the case law cited.

[26] In Cases C-70/06 *Commission v Portugal* [2008] ECR I-00001 and C-314/09 *Stadt Graz v Strabag AG and Others* [2010] ECR I-08769. This view was also endorsed by McCloskey J in *Easycoach Ltd v Department for Regional Development* [2012] NIQB 10, para 88. In *Baxter*, Peart J in the Irish High Court had to determine whether a typo in a notification letter (incorrectly identifying the successful bidder) constituted a manifest error, and dismissed this idea without disavowing that a faultless error could in some cases be a manifest one. This finding, while undoubtedly correct, could more easily be justified if the requirement of causation was explicitly applied (*Baxter Healthcare Ltd v Health Service Executive* [2013] IEHC 413, paras 48–9).

[27] Case C-568/08 *Combinatie Spijker Infrabouw* [2010] I-2655.

[28] Clearly, such a situation could also arise in the UK or Ireland if the automatic suspension is lifted, in which case the claimant's remedy would be in damages, unless an order of ineffectiveness is made under the limited circumstances allowing for this under the remedies regulations.

event, both the Advocate General and Court held that Directive 89/665 conferred a broad discretion on Member States regarding the organization of interim and substantive proceedings, and declined to interfere with questions of determination of liability or calculation of damages.

8.16 The Advocate General also considered the meaning and effect of Article 2(7) of the Utilities Remedies Directive, which provides that where damages are sought in relation to bid costs, claimants need only prove a breach of the applicable procurement rules, that they had a real chance of winning the contract, and that chance was adversely affected by the breach in question.[29] In other words, they need not establish that 'but for' the breach they would have won the contract, or that it eliminated entirely their chances of doing so. This provision is important both for its absence from Directive 89/665[30] and for its limited applicability: it does not apply to the remedies of set aside or ineffectiveness, and only applies to damages inasmuch as these relate to bid costs. The Advocate General inferred from this that the legislature wished to leave it open to Member States to apply different approaches to causation in other situations.[31]

8.17 The Court for its part held that:

(i) The Remedies Directives do not prescribe the form or nature of interim proceedings, nor that they must be part of the same decision-making process as the substantive proceedings.

(ii) A court hearing an application for interim measures is not precluded from interpreting substantive provisions of the procurement rules, notwithstanding that this interpretation may be found to be erroneous in later substantive proceedings.

(iii) Individuals harmed have a right to redress where the rule of EU law which has been infringed is intended to confer rights on them, the breach of that rule is sufficiently serious, and there is a direct causal link between the breach and the loss or damage sustained by the individuals. Liability in other cases is at the discretion of Member States, subject to the principles of equivalence and effectiveness.[32]

---

[29] Case C-568/08 *Combinatie Spijker Infrabouw*, Opinion of AG Cruz Villalón, paras 93–7.

[30] Obviously Directive 89/665 precedes Directive 92/13; however, on none of the three occasions of its amendment (in 1992, 2007, and 2014) has the opportunity been taken to include an equivalent provision.

[31] The legislative history of Art 2(7) Directive 92/13 clearly indicates that the drafters wished to distinguish between bid costs and other headings of damages such as loss of profit, and not to interfere with national rules regarding proof and causation in the latter case. See Hebly, J. (ed) (2011) *European Public Procurement: Legislative History of the 'Remedies' Directives 89/665/EEC and 92/13/EEC* (Alphen aan den Rijn: Kluwer Law International), pp 375–90.

[32] Case C-568/08 *Combinatie Spijker Infrabouw*, operative part of judgment. The third point is a statement of the general *Francovich* principles governing State liability for breaches of EU law (Joined Cases C-6/90 and C-9/90 *Andrea Francovich and Others v Italian Republic* [1991] ECR I-5357).

In *Fastweb*, an Italian court was faced with a situation where there were only two **8.18** bidders for a contract and both had submitted tenders which the court determined did not meet the technical specifications. The unsuccessful bidder sought a review of the award procedure, whereas the successful bidder entered a counterclaim to prevent the review, on the basis that the unsuccessful bidder lacked standing to initiate the review because its bid had been inadmissible. The court was inclined to rule that in such a situation the award of contract must be annulled. However, it felt constrained by an earlier ruling of the *Consiglio di Stato* (Italy's highest administrative court), which held that where a challenge to standing was entered, this must be considered before the substantive review of the contract.

The CJEU held that such a rule was not permissible 'in the absence of a finding **8.19** as to whether th[e] technical requirements are met both by the bid submitted by the successful tenderer, which won the contract, and by the bid submitted by the tenderer which brought the main action for review'.[33] This judgment is important primarily for what it does not say—which is that review procedures must in general be available to all operators with an interest in obtaining a contract, as opposed to only those who can show specific harm caused by a decision. It was only in the limited situation 'where the validity of the bid submitted by each of the operators is challenged in the course of the same proceedings and on identical grounds' that the CJEU considered that review procedures must be available in the absence of specific harm being shown.[34]

To hold otherwise would contradict the explicit wording of the Remedies **8.20** Directives, which state that review procedures must be available 'at least to any person having or having had an interest in obtaining a particular contract and who has been or risks being harmed by an alleged infringement'. The idea of harm, whether actual or potential, is thus central to availability of remedies under the EU directives—albeit that this forms a minimum standard and Member States are free to go further in their national provisions. Can a causal link between the alleged breach and the actual or potential harm be a prerequisite for damages? This very question was referred to the Court in the *GAT* case, but it was declared inadmissible as the Austrian court making the reference did not itself have jurisdiction to award damages.[35] The Court did hold that an applicant could not be denied damages simply on the basis that another illegality discovered by the Court would have in any case deprived it of the opportunity to win the contract.[36]

---

[33] Case C-100/12 *Fastweb SpA v Azienda Sanitaria Locale di Alessandria*, not yet reported, para 34.

[34] Case C-100/12 *Fastweb*, para 33.

[35] Case C-315/01 *Gesellschaft für Abfallentsorgungs-Technik GmbH (GAT) v Österreichische Autobahnen und Schnellstraßen AG (ÖSAG)* [2003] ECR I-06351, paras 22 and 39.

[36] Case C-315/01 *GAT*, para 54.

8.21 This accords with the general legal principle that a party should not be able to rely on its own wrongful act to deny a remedy. Again, however, it is notable that it does not mean that proof of causation cannot be required in other circumstances, where there is no other illegality or the remedy sought is to set aside the contract. Treumer has argued that the same principles which apply generally to the determination of State liability for infringement of EU law and which have been developed in the Court's case law should be applicable for breaches of the public procurement rules, namely that: the rule of law infringed must be intended to confer rights on individuals; the breach must be sufficiently serious; and there must be a direct causal link between the breach and damage sustained.[37]

8.22 While the spirit of *Alcatel, Lämmerzahl, Uniplex*, and the Remedies Directives is without doubt to ensure that effective remedies are available where breaches of the substantive rules occur, the Remedies Directives do not make any provision for a general 'public interest' enforcement of the procurement rules—other than by the European Commission, as discussed in paragraphs 8.77 and 8.78. They therefore do not require, if a breach is committed in the application of award criteria, for example, that an action be available to a bidder who does not meet one of the exclusion or selection criteria, or has put in a bid which is not in conformity with the technical specifications—if the breach could not have affected their position. In practice, national systems place a varying degree of emphasis on the question of causation, and the point in proceedings at which this is determined.[38] In many cases, this follows from established rules in respect of similar proceedings under national law—in accordance with the principle of equivalence. However, it is not always obvious which type of national proceedings should be considered equivalent to actions for breach of the public procurement directives, given that these rest at the intersection of public and private law.[39]

---

[37] Treumer, S. (2011) 'Basis and Conditions for a Damages Claim for Breach of the EU Public Procurement Rules' in Fairgrieve and Lichère, *Public Procurement Law*, p 157. These principles were stated by the Court in Joined Cases C-46/93 and 48/93 *Brasserie de Pêcheur and Factortame III* [1996] ECR I-1029. Treumer also discusses the alternative view that strict liability should apply as for breaches of gender discrimination law, or that the conditions for liability for procurement cases should be determined under national law (pp 156–8).

[38] See Caranta, R. (2011) 'Damages for Breaches of EU Public Procurement Law: Issues of Causation and Recoverable Losses' in Fairgrieve and Lichère, *Public Procurement Law*, pp 167–84. Liability and causation can be particularly difficult to establish if the claimant has been (wrongfully) excluded at an early stage, as it will not be possible to know what, if any, chance their tender would have had to succeed.

[39] See the discussion of HHJ Humphrey Lloyd QC in *Harmon CFEM Facades (UK) Ltd v The Corporate Officer of the House of Commons* [1999] EWHC Technology 199, regarding the application of contractual vs tortious liability in procurement cases and the attendant rules on causation (paras 257–61 of judgment). Arrowsmith has argued that 'analogous provisions' for the purpose of equivalence may have to relate to procurement, following from the Court's judgment in Case C-225/97 *Commission v France* [1999] ECR I-03011. See Arrowsmith, S. (2005) *The Law of Public and Utilities Sector Procurement* (London: Sweet & Maxwell), p 1387.

Remedies in the United Kingdom

The Remedies Directives are implemented within the body of the Public Contracts **8.23**
Regulations (PCR) and Utilities Contracts Regulations (UCR) which apply in
England, Wales, and Northern Ireland, and the separate regulations which apply
in Scotland. These regulations were amended in 2009 and 2011 to reflect the 2007
changes to the Remedies Directives and the impact of the *Uniplex* judgment.[40] The
remedies provisions are set out in Part 9 of each of the relevant sets of regulations,
which will be replaced by those implementing the 2014 directives. The Scottish
regulations, which are for the most part similar to those in place in the rest of the
UK, were updated in 2012 to include the remedies provisions.[41] In light of the discussion on causation in paragraphs 8.20 to 8.22, it is worth noting that the PCR,
UCR, and Scottish regulations all make actions available only to economic operators who suffer or risk suffering loss or damage 'in consequence' of breaches of the
substantive rules.[42] However, as will be seen, the UK courts have at times seemed
to underplay this requirement, while applying relatively stringent rules in respect
of time limits and interim measures.

Over 60 reported procurement judgments have been delivered by UK courts since **8.24**
2006, either at the interlocutory stage, in substantive proceedings, or both. There
is thus an ample body of domestic case law upon which courts may draw in determining new matters placed before them, in addition to the rather larger volume of
European cases. However, many of the domestic cases have not proceeded to full
trial on the merits, due to the impact of interim measures or the decision of the
parties to settle. Only a handful of recorded cases show damages being awarded
to claimants. In England and Wales, an increasing number of procurement claims
are heard in the Technology and Construction Court (TCC), which has developed a degree of judicial expertise in the specialized nature of procurement challenges. In Scotland, the Sheriff Court and Court of Session are both competent
to hear procurement claims, and in Northern Ireland the High Court and Court
of Appeal have heard a disproportionately high number of procurement cases,
perhaps reflecting the particular economic importance of public contracts in that
jurisdiction, among other factors. The main contours of this jurisprudence are outlined in paragraphs 8.25 to 8.55, although naturally an exhaustive account cannot
be given here.

---

[40] By the Public Contracts (Amendment) Regulations 2009, Utilities Contracts (Amendment)
Regulations 2009, and Public Procurement (Miscellaneous Amendments) Regulations 2011.
[41] The Public Contracts (Scotland) Regulations 2012, The Utilities Contracts (Scotland)
Regulations 2012, and the Public Contracts and Utilities Contracts (Scotland) Amendment
Regulations 2012.
[42] Reg 47C PCR; Reg 45C UCR; Reg 47(5) PC(S)R; and Reg 44(4) UC(S)R.

Time limits

8.25 The PCR, UCR, and Scottish regulations all require that claims be brought within 30 days of the date when the economic operator first knew or ought to have known that grounds for starting the proceedings had arisen.[43] Courts are able to grant extensions to the time limits where they see good reason to do so, up to a maximum of three months. In respect of applications for the remedy of ineffectiveness, a longer time limit of six months applies.[44] The question arises of when time begins to run, whether from the moment when a candidate or tenderer is notified of rejection and given reasons, or from some other point in time. In *SITA v Manchester Waste Management Authority*, the Court of Appeal, applying *Uniplex*, held that:

> Once the prospective claimant has sufficient knowledge to put him in a position to take an informed view as to whether there has been an infringement in the way the process has been conducted, and concludes that there has, time starts to run...[45]

and that:

> the standard ought to be a knowledge of the facts which apparently clearly indicate, though they need not absolutely prove, an infringement.[46]

8.26 There are several examples of cases in which this has meant a claim is out of time even where it has been made within 30 days (or, formerly, three months) of notification of the outcome of a procedure. In *Mears v Leeds City Council*, Ramsey J referred to a number of cases in which the court had to determine the date on which the grounds for a challenge first arose, finding effectively that this was a moveable feast which might fall before or after the date of notification depending on the knowledge available to the claimant. In the case at hand, two of the applicant's grounds of challenge which related to an approach to evaluation of pricing, of which it had been informed during the tender period, were time-barred.[47]

8.27 In *Turning Point Ltd v Norfolk County Council*, the claimant submitted a bid excluding any potential liability arising under the Transfer of Undertakings rules, on the basis that it had not received sufficient information from the contracting authority about this liability. Its bid was rejected as non-compliant. Akenhead J held that the claim was out of time, as the claimant had been aware of the alleged lack of clarity during the tender period. These rulings, while they may seem harsh on claimants, appear to be consistent with *Lämmerzahl* and *Idrodinamica*, as well as *Uniplex*. In each of those cases, the CJEU specifically contemplated that time limits may run from a point other than that at which bidders are notified of the

---

[43] Reg 47D PCR; Reg 45D UCR; Reg 47(7)(b) PC(S)R; and Reg 44(6)(b) UC(S)R.

[44] Reg 47E PCR; Reg 45E UCR; Reg 47(7)(a) PC(S)R; and Reg 44(6)(a) UC(S)R. This period can be reduced to 30 days by contracting authorities if they notify the economic operator of the decision in question and the reasons for it, or publish a contract award notice in the OJEU.

[45] [2011] EWCA Civ 156, per Elias LJ, para 22.

[46] *SITA*, para 27.

[47] *Mears Ltd v Leeds City Council (No 1)* [2011] EWHC 40 (QB), paras 59–71.

outcome of their tenders, provided that it is a point at which the requisite knowledge of an alleged breach was available to the claimant.

The UK courts have also been reluctant to exercise their discretion to extend time lim- **8.28** its for procurement challenges. In *Mermec UK Ltd v Network Rail Infrastructure Ltd*, Akenhead J refused to grant an extension in circumstances where there was no explanation for why the claim could not have been drafted at an earlier date. He considered that a good reason such as the illness or detention of relevant personnel would have to be advanced even where the extension in question was only for a short period.[48] If the claimant's legal advisers had been negligent in causing the delay, then a separate claim might lie against them, but that did not affect the time limit for the claim against the defendant. In *Montpellier Estates v Leeds City Council*, the claimant argued for an extension of time on the basis that: it had acted promptly; the knowledge it had about the alleged breach had increased considerably after the date upon which the time limit was held to begin; the defendant had concealed certain details from it; and no prejudice had been caused to the defendant during the ensuing period.[49] These arguments were rejected by Supperstone J, who relied in part on evidence that the claimant had specific knowledge of certain grounds of its claim at any early stage.[50]

Connected to the application of time limits and extensions is the question of when **8.29** a claimant may be permitted to amend its statement of claim to include matters which were not explicitly included in the original statement. In *Corelogic*, the original claim form only alleged a failure on the part of the contracting authority to provide certain information, whereas the claimant later sought to amend this to add claims of manifest error of assessment and application of an undisclosed award criterion.[51] The application to amend was refused, as was the request for an extension of time, as the claimant had not put forward a good reason for this. Based on this judgment, it appears that if a claimant is to succeed in an application to amend its claim, it must argue that: (i) the amendment does not constitute a new claim;[52] (ii) if it is a new claim, it is in time; and (iii) if it is not in time, there is a good reason for the court to extend the time period. A claimant may also seek to have the starting point for the time limit shifted where an apparently new ground of claim comes to its attention—for example, due to the disclosure of primary evaluation documents or other evidence. In a recent challenge by a firm of solicitors to the award of a framework agreement by the Insolvency Service, the Court of Appeal allowed the claimant to amend its particulars of claim on the basis of further evidence disclosed by the defendant.[53]

---

[48] [2011] EWHC 1847 (TCC), para 23.

[49] [2013] EWHC 166 (QB), para 431.

[50] *Montpellier Estates*, para 435.

[51] *Corelogic Ltd v Bristol City Council* [2013] EWHC 2088 (TCC).

[52] This argument succeeded in *Nationwide Gritting Services Ltd v The Scottish Ministers* [2014] CSOH 41.

[53] *DWF LLP v Secretary of State for Business Innovation and Skills, Acting on Behalf of the Insolvency Service* [2014] EWCA Civ 900.

Disclosure

8.30   Contracting authorities are required to notify unsuccessful candidates and bidders
of decisions taken and the reasons for rejection of their application or tender. In
the case of tenderers, the authority is also obliged to provide the name, scores, and
characteristics and relative advantages of the designated successful tenderer, as well
as information about the standstill period which will apply.[54] As the statutory duty
to disclose information about the evaluation is limited, claimants often face difficulty in establishing the merits of their case. In this area, the UK courts have been
more willing to assist claimants than they have been in relation to time limits and
extensions. In *Alstom Transport v Eurostar International Ltd*, Vos J made an order
for specific disclosure of the defendant's completed evaluation templates and other
documents identifying the detailed scores produced by evaluators.[55] In *Amaryllis
v HM Treasury*, the idea that the contracting authority's internal documents, as
opposed to those of third parties, attracted public interest immunity or confidentiality was rejected in strong terms by Coulson J.[56] In *Croft House Care and Others
v Durham County Council*, the claimants' application for disclosure of the submissions of other participants in the procedure was opposed on the basis that this
would divulge sensitive commercial details and thereby prejudice any rerun of the
procedure, and that there were practical difficulties with establishing a confidentiality ring. The judge, however, did not consider such problems insurmountable and
ordered disclosure of seven categories of documents, including pre-qualification
and tender submissions from other bidders, subject to redactions.[57]

8.31   A series of disclosure rulings in 2013 and 2014 further illustrate the situations
in which UK courts will be sympathetic to such applications from claimants. In
Roche Diagnostics, the defendant resisted disclosure of its primary evaluation documents, instead providing certain spreadsheets produced after the evaluation was
complete, which contained errors and inconsistencies. Coulson J emphasized the
importance for claimants of having early access to the primary evaluation documents and granted disclosure of those which were germane to the case being
pleaded, including information about the interim contract which the authority
had entered into pending resolution of the substantive proceedings.[58] By contrast,
in *Pearson* and *Covanta*, Akenhead J displayed a markedly more conservative
approach to early specific disclosure in the context of interim proceedings, refusing
to grant this where the claimants had not shown that the documents in question

---

[54] Reg 32(2)(d) PCR; Reg 33(2)(d) UCR; Reg 32(2)(f) PC(S)R; and Reg 33(3)(f) UC(S)R.
[55] [2010] EWHC B32 (Ch).
[56] *Amaryllis Ltd v HM Treasury No 2* [2009] EWHC 1666 (TCC).
[57] [2010] EWHC 909 (TCC).
[58] *Roche Diagnostics Ltd v The Mid Yorkshire Hospitals NHS Trust* [2013] EWHC 99 (TCC). The
case was cited with approval by the Northern Ireland High Court in *John Sisk and Son (Holdings)
Ltd v Western Health and Social Care Trust* [2014] NIQB 56; however, only limited disclosure was
granted to the plaintiff in that case.

were necessary to argue the interim points, as opposed to just relevant to their broader case.[59] In *Wealden Leisure Ltd v Mid-Sussex District Council*, disclosure of the final tenders received was ordered to allow the claimant to plead its case that the successful tender may have been abnormally low.[60]

The voluntary disclosure of primary evaluation documents by a contracting **8.32** authority where it faces a potential or actual challenge to its procurement decisions is a strategic decision. In theory, if the authority is confident that no breach has occurred, then early and comprehensive disclosure appears likely to work in its favour, inasmuch as it will make it difficult for a claimant to argue that there is a serious issue to be tried for the purpose of maintaining a suspension—and may dissuade it from proceeding any further. Unfortunately, even where procedures are run carefully and there is no evidence of prejudice, there may be a lack of confidence on the part of the authority regarding the correct application of the procurement rules to all aspects of an evaluation. In most cases, minor errors will not be such as to alter the outcome of a procedure. While it is very difficult for a claimant or judge to make out the merits of a claim based on incomplete information, it can be equally difficult for an authority to know whether such disclosure will be necessary to defend itself. In addition to confidentiality concerns (which may be allayed by the creation of a confidentiality ring), the disclosure of information about other bids in particular can be prejudicial to future competitions, as recognized by the CJEU in the *Varec* judgment.[61]

There are thus often good reasons on both sides for contesting disclosure, but it **8.33** may be wise for contracting authorities to engage in a higher level of disclosure than that required under the regulations as a matter of course—for example, by providing evaluators' comments in respect of each score assigned. This has several potential advantages which go beyond defensive strategy. The provision of detailed scoring information and comments as part of notification letters can create an incentive for contracting authorities to double- or triple-check their evaluation, knowing that it will be subject to immediate scrutiny. This can help to avoid simple errors or omissions which, while they will not change the overall outcome of the evaluation, may nevertheless provide fodder for a claim. The provision of such information, together with voluntary debriefing of bidders, can also help to improve the quality of future bids, and to create confidence in the transparency of procedures. The importance of consistency between information provided in notification letters and any comments made during debriefing sessions cannot be emphasized enough. Voluntary disclosure and debriefing are considered further in paragraph 8.89.

---

[59] *Pearson Driving Assessments Ltd v The Minister for the Cabinet* [2013] EWHC 2082 (TCC); and *Covanta Energy Ltd v Merseyside Waste Disposal Authority* [2013] EWHC 2964 (TCC).
[60] High Court, Chancery Division, judgment of Andrew Hochauser QC of 16 July 2014.
[61] Case C-450/06 *Varec SA v Belgian State* [2008] ECR I-00581.

Interim relief

8.34 Where a contracting authority or entity is notified of a claim under the PCR, UCR, or Scottish regulations, an automatic suspension comes into effect which prevents it from concluding the contract.[62] The contracting authority can apply to court to have the automatic suspension lifted, and the court may make interim orders to end, modify, or restore the suspension or to suspend the implementation of any other decision or action.[63] Whereas the PCR and UCR state that the court must determine if it would be 'appropriate' to grant the suspension in the absence of the statutory requirement to do so, under the Scottish regulations courts must determine if 'the negative consequences of such an order are likely to outweigh the benefits', having regard to the need for effective and rapid review of decisions, the probable consequences for the interests at stake, and the public interest.

8.35 In *Letting International*, the Court of Appeal held that application of the *American Cyanamid* principles governing the grant of injunctions was appropriate for determining the availability of interim measures in cases coming under the Public Contracts Regulations.[64] These are:

  (i)   whether there is a serious issue to be tried; if so
  (ii) would damages be an adequate remedy (for either party); and
  (iii) does the balance of convenience favour granting or refusing interim relief?

8.36 In *Letting International*, which preceded the introduction of the new remedies regime, the Court of Appeal ordered that the suspension of the contract award be maintained. Interestingly, this has not been the result in the majority of cases taking place since the introduction of the new remedies rules. The operation of the *American Cyanamid* test has in most cases resulted in the automatic suspension being lifted where a contracting authority has applied for this.[65] That does not give a full picture of the prevalence of interim measures, as there are further cases in which the contracting authority has not applied for lifting of the suspension. Nevertheless, it seems that the *American Cyanamid* test sets a relatively high bar for maintaining suspension, and it is notable that the Irish courts have rejected its application on the ground that it introduces impermissible restrictions on the availability of interim measures as envisioned under the Remedies Directives.[66]

---

[62] Reg 47G PCR; Reg 45G UCR; Reg 47(9) PC(S)R; and Reg 44(8) UC(S)R.
[63] Reg 47H PCR; Reg 45H UCR; Reg 48 PC(S)R; and Reg 45 UC(S)R.
[64] *Letting International Ltd v London Borough of Newham* [2007] EWCA Civ 1522, para 12.
[65] However, several judgments upholding the automatic suspension were delivered in the second half of 2014: *DWF LLP v Secretary of State for Business Innovation and Skills, acting on behalf of the Insolvency Service* [2014] EWCA Civ 900; *Edenred (UK Group) Ltd v HM Treasury and Others* [2014] EWHC 3555 (QB); and *NATS (Services) Ltd v Gatwick Airport Ltd and Another* [2014] EWHC 3133 (TCC). In *NATS*, Ramsey J seemed to consider that establishing the inadequacy of damages was not a separate requirement for interim relief, but formed part of the overall balance of convenience question (para 25 of the judgment).
[66] In *OCS One Complete Solution Ltd v Dublin Airport Authority Plc* [2014] No 177 J R, discussed in para 8.57.

In *Harmon*, HHJ Humphrey Lloyd QC also considered that application of the *American Cyanamid* principles might not be appropriate in respect of procurement claims, inasmuch as they made the availability of relief contingent on demonstrating the inadequacy of damages and the availability of a cross-undertaking in damages from the claimant.[67]

There are a few examples of an automatic suspension or injunction against a contract being maintained where the court has found that damages would not be an adequate remedy for the claimant. In *Morrisons Facilities Services v Norwich City Council*, the inadequacy of damages for the claimant was held to outweigh their potential inadequacy for the Council.[68] In *Covanta*, which concerned the award of a major waste-to-energy contract, the injunction was left in place on the basis that: (i) damages would not be an adequate remedy for the claimant due to their assessment being 'virtually impossible' based on the complex facts of the case; (ii) while damages would not be an entirely adequate remedy for the defendant (due to the environmental damage which would result from the ongoing suspension of the contract), this was insignificant in light of the delays to the project which had already occurred; and (iii) the overall balance of convenience favoured maintaining the injunction. In addition to the delay which had already taken place, Coulson J considered the public interest loss which would arise if the authority concluded the contract and was then compelled to pay damages to the claimant.[69] In *DWF*, the Court of Appeal agreed to lift an automatic suspension in part, allowing another lot of the disputed framework to be awarded and the undisputed places taken up.[70] **8.37**

One criticism of the application of the *American Cyanamid* principles at interim stage in procurement cases is that it places too much emphasis on the possible award of damages, to the exclusion of other remedies. Remedies are to be available to those who risk being harmed, as well as those who have been harmed, and interim measures should be available 'with the aim of correcting the alleged infringement', as well as preventing further harm. To achieve this, interim declarations may be appropriate in some cases—for example, to declare that a particular criterion or evaluation methodology is unlawful. Such remedies might also prove more accessible to claimants without deep pockets, as they would not require a cross-undertaking in damages, and—importantly—could also be less prejudicial to other bidders. **8.38**

---

[67] *Harmon*, para 253.
[68] [2010] EWHC 487 (Ch), para 47.
[69] *Covanta Energy Ltd v Merseyside Waste Disposal Authority* [2013] EWHC 2922 (TCC), paras 50–77.
[70] *DWF LLP v Secretary of State for Business Innovation and Skills, Acting on Behalf of the Insolvency Service* [2014] EWCA Civ 900. The case raises an interesting substantive point on scoring of award criteria relative to other lots in a tender, which had not yet been subject to judgment at the time of writing.

8.39   Naturally, however, there is a reluctance on the part of many bidders to challenge a process while they still have a chance of winning. This may appear to be a boon to contracting authorities, but it can also mean that they are able to proceed on an erroneous basis and thereby prejudice multiple bidders—for example, where an illegal selection or award criterion is indicated in the procurement documents. This may begin to shift with the more extensive publication requirements provided for in the 2014 directives, which mean that (in theory) all bidders or potential bidders will have sight of tender documents from the outset of a procedure. Time in respect of any challenge to the content of these documents would begin to run from the date of their publication, unless there is a subsequent departure from them in the conduct of the procedure or evaluation. Shifting the timing and focus of claims to an earlier point in procedures should be beneficial to both claimants and defendants, inasmuch as it reduces the legal and other costs associated with suspension of contract award and payment of damages.

Substantive claims

8.40   Focus in the UK courts on the interim relief stage has to some extent detracted from the resolution of substantive claims. A large number of cases appear to have been settled out of court in the aftermath of preliminary proceedings. Nevertheless, there is a growing body of case law relating in particular to the following points:

   (i)   disclosure and application of selection and award criteria;
   (ii) clarification of expressions of interest and tenders;
   (iii) provision of information to bidders about broader strategies;
   (iv) reliance on exemptions from the directives, such as for public-public cooperation; and
   (v)   establishment and operation of framework agreements.

8.41   Assorted claims on a wide range of other matters have also been heard in the higher courts, but it is the disclosure and application of award criteria which has been challenged most often. While there is not space here to discuss each of the above aspects (interesting as they are), it is worth examining the UK courts' jurisprudence on the first two points.

Award criteria

8.42   Challenges to the way in which award criteria are applied occur with particular frequency for a number of reasons. First, there will often be a clear line of causation between an unsuccessful bidder's score against the award criteria and its failure to win the contract. Second, as noted in Chapter 4, award criteria typically form the linchpin of a procedure and there is understandable focus on them by both sides. There is also often a perceived element of subjectivity in the way in which award criteria are applied—although, as discussed in paragraph 8.43, this is permissible under the procurement rules provided any such discretion is exercised within predetermined boundaries. Finally, challenges to the manner in which award criteria are applied (as opposed to their formulation), or to the introduction of an undisclosed criterion, are less likely to be out of time than claims which relate to selection criteria or technical specifications. However, it should be noted that contracting authorities enjoy a greater degree of discretion over award criteria than either of these other elements of tender procedures, a fact which for the most part has been recognized by the UK courts.

The Supreme Court's judgment in *Healthcare at Home* will likely shape the way in **8.43** which future challenges to award criteria are argued. In that case, the claimant had challenged both the clarity of the award criteria applied and the adequacy of the reasons given for its rejection.[71] The Supreme Court focused on the interpretation of the 'reasonably well informed and normally diligent tenderer' test set out by the CJEU in *SIAC*, finding that this required the court to apply an objective standard rather than engage in a purely empirical enquiry.[72] Although this affirmed the approach of the Scottish courts in the case, some earlier cases had appeared to apply an empirical approach to interpreting award criteria, drawing on the evidence of other tenderers for that purpose.[73] The requirement that evaluation of tenders be done according to fixed, transparent criteria which are known in advance to tenderers and which are objectively capable of being interpreted in the same way by each of them does not mean that there is no element of comparison or relativity in the way in which scores are assigned against those criteria. Tenders are not evaluated in a vacuum, but in a competitive environment, and scoring will reflect this. This is most obviously the case in relation to cost criteria, where the score obtained by each bidder will reflect the difference between their tendered cost and the lowest valid and responsive tender. But it is also true in respect of qualitative criteria, where performance may be assessed in relation to other bids, provided this is within the scope of the criteria set out.

In *Clyde Solway Consortium v Scottish Ministers*, the court accepted that there was **8.44** a distinction between the transparency requirement in respect of the formulation of award criteria and the transparency requirement in respect of evaluation methodology.[74] However, Silber J in *Letting International* rejected this approach, citing the CJEU judgments in *Universale-Bau*, *ATI*, and *Lianakis*, which had been delivered since *Clyde Solway*, and which in his view required that all of the elements to be taken into account by the contracting authority, and their relative importance be disclosed in advance. It was thus unimportant whether the challenge was to sub-criteria or a scoring methodology, as the same disclosure obligation applied to

---

[71] *Healthcare at Home Ltd v Common Services Agency* [2013] CSIH 22.
[72] *Healthcare at Home*, para 27.
[73] Eg the Northern Ireland Court of Appeal in *William Clinton t/a Oriel Training Services v Department for Employment and Learning and Department for Finance and Personnel* [2012] NICA 48.
[74] *Clyde Solway Consortium v Scottish Ministers and Others* [2001] ScotCS 15, paras 36–9.

each.[75] It was only in the narrow circumstances set out in *ATI*—where disclosure of sub-criteria or weightings could not have affected the preparation of bids—that non-disclosure was permissible.[76] The required level of transparency had not been provided by the contracting authority and Silber J did not consider the question of causation (ie whether the claimant would have succeeded in its bid but for the lack of disclosure) to be essential to the case.[77]

8.45 In *Mears Ltd v Leeds County Council*, the claimant successfully challenged the authority's non-disclosure of weightings for certain sub-criteria. The trial judge considered that the claimant need only show that it had a real or substantial chance of being selected for the next stage if the weighting been disclosed, as opposed to one which was merely 'fanciful'.[78] Similarly, the Scottish Court of Session found a breach of transparency in relation to the scoring of award criteria in *BT v Common Services Agency*. In that case, although the defendant had disclosed all of its sub-criteria and their respective weightings, it had not disclosed the scoring system which was applied in respect of each. Under the system applied, if a tender omitted to address one of the requirements under a sub-criterion, it could achieve only one-fifth of the marks available for the sub-criterion. This approach was not clearly set out in the tender documents. Full knowledge of the scoring methodology would likely have had an impact on the pursuer's preparation of its bid.[79]

8.46 In terms of the appropriate remedy, having reviewed several authorities Lord Malcolm considered that given that (i) the nature of the breach was not on the more serious end of the scale and (ii) the pursuer had not shown that, but for the breach, it would have won the contract, set aside would not be a proportionate remedy.[80] Taking into account the clear public interest in allowing the contract (which was for the Scottish Wide Area Network) to proceed, and the difficulties associated with any rerun of the procedure, damages were an adequate, proportionate, and effective remedy.[81] The approach to causation in the case is of note, as Lord Malcolm considered it as one of the factors which determines the appropriate remedy, rather than as a prerequisite to any action under the Regulations. He appears to have been influenced by the judgment in *Mears* in this regard.

---

[75] *Letting International Ltd v London Borough of Newham* [2008] EWHC 1583 (QB), paras 81–4.
[76] Case C-331/04 *ATI EAC and Viaggi di Maio v ACTV Venezia SpA* [2005] ECR I-10109. The Court set out a three-pronged test for when non-disclosure of sub-criteria is permissible: if they (i) do not alter the main criteria; (ii) do not contain elements which could have influenced the preparation of bids; and (iii) do not give rise to discrimination against any tenderer (paras 26–32 of the judgment).
[77] *Letting International*, paras 142–8.
[78] [2011] EWHC 2694 (TCC), para 206.
[79] *British Telecommunications Plc v Common Services Agency* [2014] CSOH 44, para 33.
[80] *British Telecommunications*, paras 27–33.
[81] *British Telecommunications*, para 38.

In *McLaughlin and Harvey*, the court found that the contracting authority had   **8.47**
failed to disclose some 39 sub-criteria along with their weightings, and that this
had a material effect both on the claimant's preparation of its tender and on the
outcome of the competition.[82] The establishment of a high-value framework agreement was accordingly set aside. In *Varney*, Flaux J held that the defendant's evaluation of certain return schedules did amount to undisclosed sub-criteria, but as
knowledge of the scores assigned to these could not have affected the preparation of
the claimant's bid, they were permissible under the *ATI* test.[83] Interestingly, Flaux J
also accepted that the defendant's application of a financial stability test at award
stage without providing for this in the tender documents did constitute a breach
of the principle of transparency, but as there was no causal link between this and
the claimant's loss, it did not attract any remedy.[84] The judgment in *Varney* broadly
accords with the CJEU's approach in the later *Evropaiki Dynamiki v EMSA* case,[85]
which can be seen as moving away from a narrow interpretation of *Lianakis* and
ATI, which would leave contracting authorities with very little discretion in the
application of award criteria.

Clarifications

The second substantive matter which has arisen in many of the UK cases is the   **8.48**
extent to which contracting authorities may be obliged to seek clarification of
information submitted by candidates or tenderers. No such general obligation to
seek clarification arises under the procurement directives—however, the principles
of equal treatment and proportionality may operate to create such an obligation in
specific cases. The precise wording of any provisions in the tender documents relating to clarifications is also important, as can be seen from the CJEU judgment in
Manova.[86] In *All About Rights*, one of a series of cases stemming from the award of
legal aid contracts by the Legal Services Commission, the claimant had submitted
a mandatory form which was blank.[87] Carr J considered both the European and

---

[82] *McLaughlin & Harvey Ltd v Department of Finance & Personnel (Nos 2 and 3)* [2008] NIQB
91, [2008] NIQB 122.

[83] *J Varney & Sons Waste Management Ltd v Hertfordshire County Council* [2010] EWHC 1404
(QB), para 99.

[84] *Varney*, para 131.

[85] Case C-252/10 P *Evropaïki Dynamiki v Agence européenne pour la sécurité maritime (EMSA)*
[2011] ECR I-00107.

[86] Case C-336/12 *Ministeriet for Forskning, Innovation og Videregående Uddannelser v Manova
A/S*, Judgment of the Court (Tenth Chamber) of 10 October 2013, not yet reported. The importance of applying provisions expressed as mandatory in procurement documents was again emphasized by the CJEU in Case C-42/13 *Cartiera dell'Adda SpA v CEM Ambiente SpA*, not yet reported.

[87] *All About Rights Law Practice, R (on the application of) v Legal Services Commission* [2011]
EWHC 964 (Admin). Other cases arising from the same procedures include: *Hossacks (A Firm of
Solicitors), R (on the application of) v Legal Services Commission* [2012] EWCA Civ 1203; and *The
Law Society, R (on the application of) v Legal Services Commission and Others* [2007] EWHC 1848
(Admin). Note that these cases proceeded by way of judicial review rather than under the statutory
remedies regime.

domestic authorities on the clarifications and came to the conclusion that the pool of comparators for determination of compliance with the equal treatment duty should be limited to those who had participated in the same tender procedure and had submitted blank versions of the same essential document at tender stage. As those tenders had also been rejected, the claimant's case failed. Carr J's approach seems to give effect to the CJEU's jurisprudence on this question, which has never pointed towards a general obligation to clarify incomplete tenders.[88]

8.49 A conflicting view has been taken in several cases in Northern Ireland, whereby the courts have appeared to find an obligation to clarify in certain situations. In *First4Skills v Department for Employment and Learning*, a claimant who had failed to submit a required spreadsheet as part of its tender succeeded in having the automatic suspension maintained. McCloskey J found that there was a serious issue to be tried as to whether the authority had breached the principles of proportionality and equal treatment by refusing to seek clarification in respect of the omission.[89] In a second case arising out of the same procurement, McCloskey J held that the defendant's failure to seek clarification was in breach of its obligations arising both under the specific terms of the tender documents and under EU law.[90] Central to this finding was the fact that the defendant had engaged in clarifications with 13 other bidders. The Northern Ireland Court of Appeal upheld this judgment, although Sir Anthony Hart dissented on the question of the defendant being under a duty to clarify in the circumstances, finding that this conflicted with the relevant EU and UK authorities.[91]

Damages

8.50 The availability of damages in respect of breaches of procurement law was considered in the *Harmon* case, which concerned the award of a fenestration contract for a high-profile parliamentary building in London. In that case, Humphrey Lloyd QC held that the contractual approach to calculation of damages was applicable to breaches of procurement law, based on the claimant's loss of chance to win the contract.[92] Applying the principle set out in *Brasserie de Pêcheur*,[93] he found that this should take account of the loss of profit which the claimant has suffered, but discounted by their chance of winning the contract. It does not require the claimant to prove that, but for the breach complained of, it would have won the contract.

---

[88] See discussion of the *Tideland Signal* at para 2.44 and Case C-599/10 *SAG Slovensko and Others v Úrad pre verejné obstarávanie* [2012] WLR (D) 103.

[89] [2011] NIQB 59, paras 19–21.

[90] *Clinton (t/a Oriel Training Services) v Department for Employment & Learning* [2012] NIQB 2, paras 42–7.

[91] *Clinton (t/a Oriel Training Services) v Department for Employment & Learning* [2012] NICA 48, paras 59–64.

[92] *Harmon*, para 259.

[93] Joined Cases C-46/93 and 48/93 *Factortame III*.

As in several other jurisdictions, bid costs cannot normally be recovered in the UK, on the logic that these would have been incurred regardless of whether the tenderer was successful and will in any event be included in the amount of lost profits.[94]

In *European Dynamics v HM Treasury*, Akenhead J set out how damages could **8.51** be calculated based on loss of chance. This involves looking at projections and/or historical data to determine the value of the contract(s) in question, and in the case of a framework agreement taking account of the share of the work that the claimant might have expected to win. The percentage profit which the claimant would have earned on this amount is then calculated with reference to its actual pricing and accounts or other available evidence, and this amount discounted to reflect the payment of damages in advance of when amounts under the contract would have been paid.[95] This contrasts with the approach applied by the Scottish Court of Session in *Aquatron v Strathclyde Fire Board*, where no discount was applied either on the basis of loss of chance (admittedly there were only two bidders in that case) or on the basis of early payment—in fact, interest was added to the amount payable by the authority.[96] Damages were also awarded by the Court of Session in *BT v Common Services Agency*.[97] In *Risk Management Partners*, the High Court determined that the claimant was entitled to damages in respect of the illegal direct in-house award of a contract, but this was overturned by the Supreme Court.[98]

The number of cases in which UK courts have awarded damages in respect of **8.52** procurement breaches remains low. One possible reason for a large number of claims being settled prior to damages being determined is that claimants may be reluctant to disclose to a court their projected profit margin for public contracts. Another may be that at the interim stage, in order to maintain the suspension of the contract, claimants must show that damages would not be an adequate remedy. Conceptually, it is possible to distinguish between difficulties in the calculating the quantum of damages and their adequacy as a remedy. However, in practice, courts have effectively conflated the two questions at interim stage—finding that where there is sufficient uncertainty associated with the calculation of damages, this renders them an inadequate remedy.[99] Such uncertainties, while assisting the claimant at interim stage, would also make an award of damages more difficult if they are not successful in obtaining other remedies or a settlement.

---

[94] See Arrowsmith, *The Law of Public and Utilities Sector Procurement*, para 21.19; Donnelly, C. (2011) 'The New Remedial Landscape: Ireland' in Fairgrieve and Lichère, *Public Procurement Law*, p 31; and Fairgrieve and Lichère, *Public Procurement Law*, p 181.

[95] *European Dynamics SA v HM Treasury* [2009] EWHC 3419 (TCC), para 22.

[96] *Aquatron Marine (t/a Aquatron Breathing Air Systems) v Strathclyde Fire Board* [2007] ScotCS CSOH 185.

[97] [2014] CSOH 44.

[98] *Risk Management Partners Ltd v Council of the London Borough of Brent* [2008] EWHC 1094 (Admin).

[99] See, eg, *Morrisons Facilities Services* [2010] EWHC 487 (Ch); and *Covanta* [2013] EWHC 2964 (TCC).

Other remedies

8.53 *Alstom Transport v Eurostar International Ltd* was the first recorded UK case in which a declaration of ineffectiveness was sought. The case concerned the award of a rolling stock contract by the entity operating the Channel Tunnel railway.[100] The ground for ineffectiveness was that the contract entered into by the parties differed materially from that which had been the subject of the tender competition, in which Alstom was unsuccessful. Alstom argued that the modifications amounted to a new contract in respect of which a new notice was required. Mann J rejected this argument on the basis that the defendant had used a notice on the existence of qualification system, which offers greater flexibility than a normal contract notice.[101] In *Varney*, Flaux J considered (obiter) that if the claim of an illegal modification had been made out, the only available remedy was a judicial review order to quash those changes.[102] Judicial review has continued to be used as an alternative avenue for some procurement claims—for example, where an applicant might not be considered eligible to bring an action under the PCR because it is not an economic operator. This route was used by the Law Society and other claimants in respect of the Legal Services Commission tenders, without any appreciable difference in the standard of review applied compared to the PCR.[103] However, it is submitted that if an illegal modification to a contract after its award results in a new contract which would be covered by the directives, the correct remedy is a declaration of ineffectiveness.[104] Importantly, the longer six-month time limit would also apply in such cases.[105]

8.54 The remedy of set aside has been granted with noticeable frequency by the Northern Irish courts.[106] The Scottish courts have at times taken a more limited view of when a contract can be set aside, appearing to restrict this to situations in which it can be shown that the outcome of the procedure would have been different but for the breach complained of.[107] This more restrictive approach can still be seen to vindicate the requirement for effective review as set out in the Remedies Directives and the CJEU's case law discussed in paragraphs 8.09 to 8.22. If an unsuccessful bidder cannot show that its interests have been actually or potentially damaged by an unlawful decision, then the Remedies Directives do not require that any remedy be

---

[100] [2011] EWHC 1828 (Ch).

[101] *Alstom*, paras 33–43.

[102] *Varney*, para 231.

[103] *The Law Society, R (on the application of) v Legal Services Commission* [2007] EWCA Civ 1264.

[104] This follows from Art 2d(1)(a) Remedies Directives.

[105] Art 2f(1)(b) Remedies Directives.

[106] Including *Henry Bros (Magherafelt) Ltd and Others v Department of Education for Northern Ireland* [2008] NIQB 105; *McLaughlin and Harvey; Resource (NI) v Northern Ireland Courts & Tribunals Service* [2011] NIQB 121; and *Easycoach v Ltd Department for Regional Development* [2012] NIQB 10.

[107] See *BT v Common Services Agency*, in which Malcolm LJ declined to set aside the award of contract, finding that damages were an adequate and proportionate remedy.

available to it. Evidence that a claimant had no possibility of obtaining a contract even if the alleged breaches have taken place would contradict the existence of such real or potential harm. This may be the case where a claimant submits a bid which is late, non-compliant with the technical specification, abnormally low, or priced so high in comparison to other bids that it had no chance of winning. If the alleged infringement of the rules does not relate to any of these factors, then it is difficult to see why the claimant should have a remedy available to it.

Where the remedy sought is for the disputed contract to be set aside, failure to **8.55** ask whether the claimant's position was in fact prejudiced by the decision complained of opens the door to procedures being rerun when in fact the breach did not affect the outcome. This has implications not only in terms of the efficiency of public contracts, but also in terms of fairness to the other bidders whose position is cast into doubt. The availability of remedies in procurement cases in several other European jurisdictions is made explicitly dependent on the claimant showing a causal link between the breach complained of and its failure to win the contract.[108] The Remedies Directives assign the role of enforcing the rules in the abstract—that is, where there is no party immediately harmed by the breach—to the European Commission.[109] This does not prevent Member States from allowing broader public interest enforcement of the rules within their domestic systems, for example, via judicial review. There is perhaps a risk associated with this approach, however, as the principle of equivalence means that any procedural advantages associated with alternative remedies should also be extended to claimants under the statutory regime.

Remedies in Ireland

The Remedies Directives are implemented in Ireland by two separate 2010 regula- **8.56** tions covering the public and utilities sectors.[110] Some 20 recorded cases have been decided by the High and Supreme Courts between 2006 and 2014, with a small but discernible increase in the period after the implementation of the new regulations. A notable feature in relation to the decided cases is that many of them do not relate to fully covered public sector contracts, but to those designated as non-priority services under the 2004 directives,[111] those awarded by entities covered by the Utilities

---

[108] See Caranta, 'Damages for Breaches of EU Public Procurement Law', pp 169–75. France, Italy, and Sweden all have explicit causation requirements.

[109] Via the 'corrective mechanism' set out in Art 3 Remedies Directives, which supplements the Commission's ability to bring infringement proceedings under the Treaty.

[110] SI 130 of 2010 *European Communities (Public Authorities' Contracts) (Review Procedures) Regulations 2010* and SI 131 of 2010 *European Communities (Award of Contracts by Utility Undertakings) (Review Procedures) Regulations 2010* (hereinafter, the 'Remedies Regulations').

[111] *Release Speech Therapy Ltd v Health Service Executive* [2011] IEHC 57; *Fresenius Medical Care (Ireland) Ltd v Health Service Executive* [2013] IEHC 414; and *Baxter Healthcare Ltd v Health Service Executive* [2013] IEHC 413.

Regulations or other less prescriptive rules,[112] or those below the EU thresholds.[113] At times, the significance of the different rules which apply in each case appears to have been underplayed by the Irish courts,[114] although this may reflect the tendency of applicants to frame challenges in terms of breaches of the general Treaty principles of transparency, equal treatment, and proportionality, instead of relying on the detailed rules applicable to a contract. An increasing number of claims are being routed through the Commercial Court, which has helped to expedite procedures and ensure effective case management.

Time limits

8.57 A very similar situation pertained in Ireland as that which existed in the UK prior to the *Uniplex* judgment, whereby proceedings had to be brought 'at the earliest opportunity and in any event within three months'. This has now been replaced by a 30-day time limit in the Remedies Regulations, or six months in the case of an application for ineffectiveness unless specific notification measures have been taken at the time of award.[115] A party wishing to challenge a decision must in the first instance notify the contracting authority, providing a statement of the matters which in his or her opinion constitute the infringement and the intention to make an application to the High Court.[116] Once an application to the High Court has been made for review of a contracting authority's or entity's decision to award a contract, an automatic suspension comes into effect so that the contract cannot be concluded until the Court has determined the matter or made an order to lift the suspension, or the proceedings are withdrawn or otherwise disposed of.[117] In *OCS*, the Supreme Court clarified that the application need not be made within the standstill period, and that it was not necessary for the applicant to specifically request suspension. It also reached an interesting conclusion on the possibility of lifting the suspension, discussed in paragraphs 8.65 and 8.66.[118]

---

[112] *Ryanair Ltd v Minister for Transport and Another* [2009] IEHC 171; *OCS; Veolia Water UK Plc and Others v Fingal County Council* [2006] IEHC 240; and *Student Transport Scheme Ltd v The Minister for Education and Skills and Another* [2012] IEHC 425.

[113] *QDM Capital Ltd v Athlone Institute of Technology* IEHC, Birmingham J, 3 June 2011; *QDM Capital Ltd v Galway City Council* [2011] IEHC 534; *Gaswise Ltd v Dublin City Council* [2014] IEHC 56; and *O'Kelly Bros Civil Engineering Company Ltd v Cork City Council and Another* [2013] IEHC 159.

[114] Eg in *Danninger v Bus Átha Cliath* [2007] IEHC 29, the court did not consider whether the contract, which was awarded by a contracting entity carrying out activities in the transport sector, might be subject to the rules for award of works contracts by utilities set out in Directive 90/531/EEC. On the facts of the case, this would have been significant to the question of whether the respondent was entitled to engage in negotiations, although not such as to suggest a different result.

[115] Reg 7 Remedies Regulations.

[116] Reg 8(4) Remedies Regulations.

[117] Reg 8(2) Remedies Regulations.

[118] [2014] IESC 51.

Order 84A of the Rules of the Superior Courts (RSC) allows for the time limit to **8.58** be extended with good reason, and unlike the UK provisions this is not capped at three months. The Irish courts have perhaps been somewhat more willing to contemplate time extensions than their UK counterparts. In *Dekra Eireann Teoranta*, an extension was granted in the High Court, but the Supreme Court overturned this on the basis that no good reason had been advanced and the general scheme of the Remedies Directives required that claims be brought rapidly.[119] The fact that an applicant confined itself to seeking a remedy in damages was not a factor militating in favour of extending time. In *Veolia v Fingal County Council*, Clarke J agreed to extend time in respect of two of the applicant's three grounds of claim, on the basis that the applicant's lack of knowledge of these grounds could be attributed to the contracting entity's failure to answer questions in a transparent manner.[120] In *Danninger v Bus Átha Cliath*, the time issue was not decisive; however, Charleton J on review of the relevant authorities considered that time began to run from one month after the applicant had received the tender documents which contained the alleged breach, as this was a reasonable time in which to obtain legal advice.[121]

The question of when time begins to run in respect of procurement claims has **8.59** also received attention in the Irish courts. In *SIAC v Mayo County Council*, Kelly J emphasized that time must begin to run at the point when the grounds for the application arose, rather than any later point. He considered that allowing for delay until the applicant learns of the outcome of the procedure would risk undermining the effectiveness of EU law, given the emphasis placed on rapidity and the availability of remedies prior to contract award.[122] It should be noted that each of the above cases was decided prior to the CJEU's judgment in *Uniplex*, which made clear that time could not begin to run against an applicant in the absence of its actual or constructive knowledge of an alleged breach. While this is now reflected in the wording of the Remedies Regulations, it is also accompanied by the shorter general time limit of 30 days. To date, there has been limited jurisprudence to indicate how this may impact decisions about when time begins to run, or indeed the possibility of granting an extension under Order 84A. At least one commentator has questioned whether the wording in the Remedies Regulations is sufficiently clear to allow applicants to discern their position.[123]

---

[119] *Dekra Eireann Teoranta v Minister for the Environment and Local Government* [2001] IEHC 154; [2003] IESC 25.

[120] [2006] IEHC 137. Note that the question of lack of knowledge, and blame therefore, are no longer relevant considerations for the extension of time, as time does not begin to run until an applicant knew or ought to have known about an alleged breach. Failure on the part of a contracting authority to act transparently may still be a factor in determining when such knowledge did or should have arisen, and thus when time begins to run.

[121] *Danninger*, para 59.

[122] *SIAC Construction Ltd v National Roads Authority* [2004] IEHC 262.

[123] Donnelly, 'The New Remedial Landscape: Ireland', p 129.

8.60 In *Gaswise*, Finlay Geoghegan J held that the applicant's claim that a competitor fell short of the level of turnover required for the tender was not time-barred as the contracting authority had failed to fully disclose the identity of that tenderer, depriving the applicant of the requisite degree of knowledge to bring a claim.[124] In *Student Transport Scheme*, McGovern J held that the longer six-month time limit would apply in respect of an impermissible modification to a contract where no notice was published, but on the facts he found that no new contract had been awarded.[125] In *Copymoore*, the applicants were able to bring their claim outside of the time limits, but this was based on the particular facts of that case (explained in paragraph 8.69) which involved a challenge to a Ministerial Circular and was not governed by the Remedies Regulations.[126] In *Baxter*, Peart J commented that:

> It seems to me that for the purpose of effectiveness, the person who has a potentially good point, labours under precisely the same burden of moving expeditiously as the person who seeks to raise an issue which may seem less meritorious at that stage. I see nothing in the Directives, or the Regulations, or the case-law from the ECJ which suggests that the merits are a consideration in relation to whether an application has moved in time.[127]

Disclosure

8.61 Few of the recorded judgments in Ireland deal with the question of disclosure. If voluntary disclosure has not been satisfactory, an applicant may seek discovery of documents under Order 31 of the Rules of the Superior Courts. Where discovery of confidential documents is sought, the court will apply a proportionality test to determine if disclosure is necessary.[128] Redaction and the creation of confidentiality rings are both possible in order to achieve a balance between the interests at stake. It appears that applicants in some cases have had relatively little information available to them, at least during the preliminary stages, but this does not seem to have been the subject of formal challenge. However, in at least one case, *Gaswise*, the applicant had access to both unsuccessful and successful tenders.

8.62 Decisions of the Information Commissioner have cast some light on the role which the Freedom of Information Act may play in facilitating access to documents for the purpose of procurement claims. In *McKeever Rowan Solicitors v Department of Finance*, the Commissioner held that there was only limited scope to exempt tenders from disclosure under the Act, notwithstanding that information within them may have been expressed as being commercially confidential.[129] Once fee rates and other details of tenders became part of a contract, no general exemption

---

124 *Gaswise*, paras 49–59.
125 *Student Transport Scheme*, para 31.
126 *Copymoore Ltd and Others v The Commissioner of Public Works in Ireland* [2013] IEHC 230.
127 *Baxter Healthcare Ltd*, para 96.
128 *Telefonica O2 Ltd v Commission for Communications Regulation* [2011] IEHC 265.
129 Case 99183 of 21 January 2003, citing earlier decisions in Cases 98188 and 98049.

on confidentiality grounds applied and these were ordered to be disclosed. Certain details in relation to unsuccessful tenders were also released, although where specific objections had been raised, information could be withheld. Arguably, this approach does not fully reflect the risks to competition from disclosure of confidential tender information which the CJEU emphasised in *Varec*.

Interim relief

In *O'Kelly Brothers*, the High Court refused an application for an interlocutory **8.63** injunction to suspend the performance of a below-threshold contract for the demolition of unoccupied dwellings as part of an urban regeneration project in Cork.[130] It applied the *Campus Oil* principles adopted by the Irish Supreme Court which mirror the *American Cyanamid* test.[131] On the facts at hand, it found that damages would be an adequate remedy for the applicant and that the balance of convenience favoured proceeding with the contract. In *QDM Capital Ltd v Athlone Institute of Technology*, the High Court considered for the first time an application by a contracting authority to lift the automatic suspension introduced by the 2010 regulations, and granted this.[132] The contract was for the refurbishment of buildings and the applicant was unsuccessful in its claim that this should be categorized as a mixed supplies/services contract as opposed to works.

In *OCS*, Barrett J explicitly declined to apply the *Campus Oil/American Cyanamid* **8.64** test to determine the availability of interim relief under the 2010 regulations. He considered that to do so would contravene the wording of both the regulations and Remedies Directives and introduce limitations on the availability of interim measures not envisioned by those instruments, namely by requiring the claimant to demonstrate the impossibility of calculating damages and to itself provide a cross-undertaking in damages.[133] The Court was instead required to evaluate the probable consequences of interim measures for all interests likely to be harmed, as well as the public interest, and to determine whether the negative consequences of lifting an automatic suspension would outweigh the benefits. The burden of proof rested on the contracting entity to establish that the suspension should be lifted.[134]

On appeal, the Supreme Court confirmed that automatic suspension of contract **8.65** award was triggered by an application for review even where this was made after the expiry of the standstill period. It also held, surprisingly, that the courts had *no* jurisdiction under the 2010 regulations to lift the automatic suspension. This appears to have been[135] based on interpretation of Regulation 8(2), which provides that:

---

[130] [2013] IEHC 159.
[131] *Campus Oil Ltd and Others v Minister for Industry and Energy and Others* [1983] IESC 2.
[132] [2011] IEHC 387.
[133] *OCS One Complete Solution Ltd v Dublin Airport Authority Plc* [2014] IEHC 306, para 34.
[134] *OCS* [2014] IEHC 306, para 33.
[135] Full judgment in the case has not been issued at the time of writing.

If a person applies to the Court under paragraph (1), the contracting authority shall not conclude the contract until—

(a) the Court has determined the matter, or
(b) the Court gives leave to lift any suspension of a procedure, or
(c) the proceedings are discontinued or otherwise disposed of.

Article 8(2)(b) can be construed as referring to a suspension put in place prior to the decision on award of a contract, rather than one which takes effect after that decision, but prior to the contract being entered into.

8.66 This interpretation may be seen to place contracting authorities at risk of frequent, significant delays in executing contracts where ill-founded claims are advanced, given that there will be no assessment of whether a 'serious issue to be tried' exists at the preliminary stages. However, this risk should probably not be over-emphasized, due to two practical considerations. The first is that Order 84A requires that applications be accompanied by a detailed grounding statement and affidavit encompassing such matters as the alleged infringement, the applicant's interest or harm, the relief sought, and grounds for relief.[136] Applicants who are merely interested in delaying the award of a contract may have difficulty in providing such statements and affidavits. The second is the near certainty of costs being awarded against any unsuccessful applicant, which may be sizeable given that such applications must be brought in the High Court. Weighted against these factors is the absence of any requirement for applicants to provide a cross-undertaking in damages. It remains to be seen whether this situation will lead to a measurable increase in the number of claims, or indeed to revision of the Irish Remedies Regulations to allow for automatic suspensions to be lifted.

Substantive claims

8.67 The relative ease of obtaining interim relief in Ireland should not be confused with a greater willingness on the part of the courts to grant remedies in respect of substantive claims. In fact, only a handful of challenges to procurement decisions have been successful. In *Advanced Totes*, a contract for totalizer services at a greyhound racing track was set aside, on the basis that the defendant had applied an undisclosed award criterion and failed to act transparently.[137] In subsequent proceedings, an injunction was granted to prevent the authority from using the totalizer equipment which had been delivered under an interim contract.[138] In *Gaswise*, the applicant successfully challenged its exclusion from a framework on the basis that it was entitled to rely on a checklist provided by the contracting authority, despite certain contradictory statements in the tender documents. Finlay Geoghegan J explicitly

---

[136] Rules of the Superior Courts, Order 84A(3).
[137] *Advanced Totes Ltd v Bord na gCon* [2006] IESC 17.
[138] *Advanced Totes v Bord na gCon (No 2)* [2006] IEHC 161.

referred to the interpretation of other tenderers in reaching the conclusion that the requirement in question was not adequately transparent, which contrasts with the approach of the UK courts in *Healthcare at Home*. However, it should be noted that in *Gaswise* the evidence indicated that the contracting authority had not treated all tenderers equally in respect of the disputed exclusion criterion.[139] The applicant was also successful in its claim that a turnover requirement lacked the necessary transparency.

In *Whelan Group v Ennis*, a selection criterion requiring at least one contract valued **8.68** above £10 million to have been completed in the five years prior to the tender was upheld as proportionate in the High Court.[140] In *Baxter* and *Fresenius*, both cases concerning the award of contracts by the Health Service Executive for renal dialysis services, the claimants alleged that a number of manifest errors had occurred in the course of a competitive dialogue procedure. The High Court rejected these claims, appearing to apply a relatively high threshold for manifest error in evaluation of tenders. Peart J considered that a margin of appreciation existed for contracting authorities charged with the evaluation of bids, which was not to be lightly interfered with.[141] This included the contracting authority's decision not to clarify the applicant's lack of a response in respect of one of the award criteria, a situation which Peart J distinguished from that in *Tideland Signal*, which concerned a more superficial omission. In *Smart Telecom Plc v Radio Teilifís Eireann*, the High Court held that a response to a request for clarification did not need to be communicated to all bidders if it merely reiterated information which had already been provided.[142] Such points are of great practical significance to contracting authorities in determining when an obligation to seek or provide clarification may arise.

In contrast with the Northern Irish cases discussed in paragraph 8.49, the Irish **8.69** High Court has placed greater emphasis on the discretion which contracting authorities have over clarifications.[143] It has also considered the standing requirements derived from the Remedies Directives, based on the definition of an 'eligible person' for the purpose of reviews brought under the 2010 regulations. In *Copymoore*, a group of applicants brought a challenge against a framework agreement for managed print services for which none of them had tendered. Their case arose when a Ministerial Circular instructed contracting authorities to use the framework, effectively making its use mandatory rather than voluntary as had been the case at the time the procurement procedure was run. Hogan J held that the applicants could not be considered eligible persons within the meaning of

---

[139] *Gaswise*, paras 24–6.

[140] *Whelan Group (Ennis) Ltd v Clare County Council* [2001] IEHC 33.

[141] *Fresenius*, para 41.

[142] [2006] IEHC 176. Note, however, that this was not a procurement case, but a challenge to the award of a sponsorship contract by the State broadcaster.

[143] As per the Supreme Court judgment in *SIAC Construction Ltd v County Council of the County of Mayo* [2002] IESC 39, para 36; *Baxter* and *Fresenius*; and *Release Speech Therapy*.

the Remedies Regulations, following the approach of the CJEU in *Grossman Air Services*.[144] However, they were entitled to challenge the subsequent administrative decision which amounted to a de facto material change to the framework, and were successful in having this quashed.[145]

8.70 *Student Transport Scheme* concerned a long-standing arrangement between the Minister for Education and a semi-State body to provide school transport services.[146] The applicant wished to tender for the services and brought a claim on the occasion of arrangements for the operation of the service in 2011/12 being agreed between the parties. The evidence was that the operator of the service, which is entirely independent of the Minister for Education, was paid the direct costs of running the service plus a 13 per cent overhead charge. McGovern J in the High Court held that the applicant had not established that this was a contract for pecuniary interest, and that even if it was the applicant had not established a material change which would bring the contract within the procurement rules (the original arrangement having been entered into prior to Ireland's accession to the EU). He also considered that any such contract would fall within the *Teckal* exemption, although this was mentioned only in passing and without consideration of the further case law regarding public-public cooperation.[147] Overall, the judgment appears to underplay the CJEU's expansive definition of public contracts as discussed in Chapter 1 and it is questionable whether this approach would withstand the more detailed rules on modifications to contracts and in-house awards now in place. At the time of writing, it is under appeal to the Supreme Court.

8.71 In *Ryanair v Minister for Transport*, the High Court had to consider the correct course of action where the designated successful bidder is unable to perform a contract.[148] In that case, it held that awarding the contract to the next runner-up from the competition did not amount to a material change. However, it should be noted that the contract related to a public service obligation and so was not subject to the procurement directives. The approach to standing in the case, whereby the applicant was found to have sufficient interest despite not having submitted a tender in respect of the lot complained of, is probably more generous than that which would apply under the Remedies Regulations. Order 84A allows a contracting authority or notice party to apply to have proceedings dismissed on the basis that an applicant is not an 'eligible person' within the meaning of the Remedies Regulations[149]—which may come into greater use in the case of challenges to

---

[144] Case C-230/02 *Grossmann Air Service, Bedarfsluftfahrtunternehmen GmbH & Co KG v Republik Österreich* [2004] ECR I-01829.

[145] *Copymoore*, para 63.

[146] *Student Transport Scheme* [2012] IEHC 425.

[147] *Student Transport Scheme*, para 28.

[148] [2009] IEHC 171.

[149] Rule 6(2), Order 84A RSC.

modifications to contracts or in-house awards following implementation of the 2014 directives.

Damages

Although the Remedies Regulations create a broad power for the courts to award **8.72** damages in respect of breaches of EU law or the Irish implementing measures, this power has not yet been much exercised. As in the UK, a preference on the part of claimants for decisions to be set aside appears to exist, and so there has been little consideration of the basis on which damages fall to be calculated in procurement claims. In *Clare Civil Engineering*, damages were awarded to the applicant based on a finding that, but for the unlawful rejection of its tender, it would have been awarded the contract in question.[150] However, no judgment on quantum was entered. In *Vavasour*,[151] the High Court set out principles for the calculation of loss of profit which might well apply to procurement claims, although the percentage reduction based on loss of chance would fall to be determined where the applicant could not show a certainty that it would have won the contract as in *Clare Civil Engineering*.

Other remedies

The Remedies Regulations provide that the Court may vary, set aside, or affirm **8.73** any decision falling within their scope, and may declare a contract ineffective or impose alternative penalties.[152] In *Advanced Totes*, the contract was set aside and an additional order was made to prevent the respondent from using the disputed equipment. In *Release Speech Therapy*, the defendant contracting authority argued that the order of *certiori* requested by the applicant in respect of its decision to reject the tender was not an appropriate remedy, as the applicant could not receive any benefit from such an order.[153] While the judgment does not address this argument squarely, McMahon J did consider that if the applicant could not have provided the service in question (due to inability to meet the specification), errors in the marking scheme for award criteria were not relevant to its case.[154] This approach suggests that real or potential harm is a prerequisite for procurement decisions being set aside, an approach which the UK courts appear to have rejected for the most part, but which I argue in paragraphs 8.20 to 8.22 may have merits and reflect the intention of the EU Remedies Directives without going beyond them.

In *Gaswise*, the entire procurement process was quashed based on the High Court's **8.74** finding of multiple breaches of transparency as described in paragraph 8.67. The

---

[150] *Clare Civil Engineering Ltd v Mayo County Council* [2004] IEHC 135.
[151] *Vavasour v O'Reilly and Others* [2005] IEHC 16.
[152] Reg 9(1) Remedies Regulations.
[153] *Release Speech Therapy Ltd v Health Service Executive* [2011] IEHC 57, para 3.
[154] *Release Speech Therapy*, para 21.

defendant had contended that the more limited remedy of an order setting aside the decision to exclude the applicant would be both effective and proportionate. In rejecting this argument, Finlay Geoghegan J pointed to the need for the applicant's tender to be evaluated by a fresh evaluation team, given the evidence of unequal treatment in the initial evaluation. She also considered that merely quashing the applicant's exclusion would be likely to lead to further litigation, and that it was proportionate in light of the interests of the other tenderers to quash the entire procedure.[155]

8.75 The Irish Remedies Regulations provide that a declaration of ineffectiveness will have prospective effect only.[156] They also include provision for alternative penalties where the court declines to declare a contract ineffective for overriding reasons related to a general interest.[157] In *Student Transport Scheme*, the applicant sought a declaration of ineffectiveness based on the illegal modification of a contract, but as noted in paragraph 8.70 the claim was dismissed. As in the UK, further cases in which a declaration of ineffectiveness is sought may be expected to arise based on the implementation of the rules on modifications to contracts and public-public cooperation set out in the 2014 directives.

Preliminary References to the CJEU

8.76 Article 267 of the Treaty sets out the procedure for national courts to make references to the Court of Justice for a preliminary ruling. The UK and Irish courts have been relatively reluctant to use this mechanism in procurement cases, with only two such references recorded in the period from 2000 to 2014.[158] As the discussion in paragraphs 8.23 to 8.75 indicates, there are currently noticeable variations between the English, Scottish, Northern Irish, and Irish courts in the interpretation of certain substantive rules and principles, such as those relating to disclosure of evaluation methodologies and clarifications of tenders. It is perhaps unfortunate that greater recourse to the Article 267 mechanism has not been made in respect of such matters, given that they are important points which recur frequently in the cases heard. In *Gaswise*, Finlay Geoghegan J considered referring the question of whether a tenderer could rely on other entities in order to meet a minimum turnover requirement to the CJEU, but decided against this on the basis that it was not necessary to resolve the case at hand and would delay the proceedings.[159] While the delay inherent in making a preliminary reference can be seen as inimical to the

---

[155] *Gaswise*, paras 73–84.
[156] Reg 12 Remedies Regulations.
[157] Reg 13 Remedies Regulations.
[158] In Case C-19/00 *SIAC v Mayo County Council* [2001] ECR I-07725; and Case C-406/08 *Uniplex*.
[159] *Gaswise*, para 70.

need to resolve procurement challenges rapidly, the length of trials and appeals may in some cases make this a false economy.

Enforcement by the European Commission

The European Commission plays a central role in enforcement of the procure-   **8.77**
ment rules by bringing infringement actions against Member States in respect
of alleged breaches. Under Articles 258 and 260 TFEU, the Commission must
formally notify the Member State of the alleged infringement, allow it to submit
its observations, and deliver a reasoned opinion which takes these into account. If
the Member State does not comply with the reasoned opinion within a designated
period, the Commission may bring the matter before the CJEU, which is empow-
ered to impose a lump-sum or penalty payment if it finds against the Member
State. Infringement actions relate to: a failure to notify the Commission of implementing measures by the required deadline; cases of non-conformity, where the
transposition measure is not in line with EU law; or cases of incorrect application,
where the infringement takes the form of some action or omission attributable
to the Member State. The latter two categories account for the vast majority of
infringement actions in the procurement field, and within these categories direct
award of contracts without competition and use of the negotiated procedure are
the most frequent source of actions.[160]

The Commission typically acts on complaints from private parties in initiating   **8.78**
such actions, including frustrated bidders and citizens with an interest in public
contracts, but may also bring actions on its own initiative. More than half of all
infringement actions relating to procurement are resolved prior to or at the reasoned opinion stage. Those which are not are referred to the Commission's legal
service, which then initiates proceedings in the CJEU. The average time from initial notification to proceedings being registered is over two years, with typically
another two years being taken for judgment to be issued (usually preceded by the
opinion of the Advocate General appointed to the case).[161] Given that the initial
complaint may have been lodged some time after the decision complained of, it is
not uncommon for periods of more than five years to elapse between notification
and judgment being issued in infringement cases. This means that many judgments concern directives no longer in force; however, the Court's interpretation
is often equally applicable under more recent directives which include similar or
identical provisions.

---

[160] European Commission SEC (2011) 853 final *Evaluation Report: Impact and Effectiveness of EU Public Procurement Legislation* (Pt 1), p 50.
[161] European Commission (2012) *Annual Public Procurement Implementation Review*, p 29.

Implications for Procurement Practice

8.79 The case law discussed so far in this chapter has implications for procurement practice in three areas in particular: clarification of submissions by candidates and tenderers; evaluation and scoring procedures; and notification and debriefing of tenderers. These are considered briefly here, with some suggestions for how procedures may be conducted to reduce the risk of legal challenges on these points.

Clarification

8.80 Contracting authorities should make it abundantly clear in their procurement documents that clarification may be undertaken at their discretion. Where clarification is requested from a candidate or tenderer, the scope of information which will be taken into account should be stated—excluding the possibility that any new information which post-dates the original deadline for submission can be provided. The guiding principle in respect of clarifications must be that of equal treatment, meaning that similar situations are not treated differently and different situations are not treated in the same way, unless there is an objective justification for this. What this means in practice will depend very much on the particular circumstances of a competition. For example, at selection stage, contracting authorities are often faced with a large number of expressions of interest which are missing one or more of the requested elements. Possible approaches are to refuse to seek clarification in respect of any, to clarify all, to clarify with some candidates and not others, or to clarify certain elements and not others. There is no one solution to this question, but the authority must be conscious of the policy it has set out in its published documents, as well as the overall proportionality of the approach it adopts.

8.81 On the related issue of clarifications requested by candidates or tenderers, failure to provide full responses to questions may stand against a contracting authority. This is true not only in respect of potential breaches of the transparency principle, but also if a court has to determine when time began to run in respect of any alleged breaches or ambiguities in tender documents. An incomplete or misleading response will allow a claimant to argue that time did not start to run against them. In general, it is necessary to provide clarifications to all candidates or bidders who are involved in a procedure. While this is normal practice for most contracting authorities, some care needs to be taken regarding the scope of information provided in the course of clarifications, to ensure that this does not inadvertently disclose confidential information provided by participants or prejudice competition in any way. This is particularly true in relation to competitive dialogue and negotiated procedures, where the contracting authority may be in possession of considerable information about bidders' proposals and strategies prior to the final tender stage.

Evaluation

As the procurement directives are largely silent on how evaluation is to be carried **8.82** out, national courts and, to a lesser extent, the CJEU, have had to consider whether various evaluation methodologies uphold the basic principles of transparency and equal treatment. In the UK and Ireland, this enquiry has often been inflected with principles derived from the judicial review of administrative decisions, such as reasonableness and fairness of procedures. In certain cases, legitimate expectations or the idea of an implied contract existing under the procurement documents has also influenced decisions on evaluation practices—however, the implementation of the 2007 remedies reform appears to have largely superseded this approach. The following guidelines might be distilled from the judgments reviewed so far in this chapter:

(i) All criteria, sub-criteria and weightings should be disclosed in procurement documents, and not altered during the evaluation process. Information about the way in which criteria will be assessed should be given, identifying the factors which will contribute to marks being obtained. It should be made clear in the tender documents if those factors are not listed exhaustively, meaning that additional considerations which are directly relevant to the criterion may be taken into account.[162]

(ii) The evaluation methodology should make it possible for the full range of scores under both the cost and qualitative criteria to be used, and the intervals which will be applied in respect of qualitative scores (e.g. no response, poor, reasonable, good, very good, excellent—each with an associated percentage of the total available marks) made known in advance and followed. It should be clear that performance will be assessed relative to other tenders.

(iii) Both consensus scoring and silo scoring are permissible, but the former may help to forestall certain grounds of challenge. Consensus scoring means that the evaluation panel assigns marks for each criterion as a whole, whereas silo scoring means that different individuals are responsible for scoring different criteria. While the latter approach may be more effective where specialist knowledge is needed to assess certain criteria, it is important that overall consistency in the approach to scoring is maintained and documented. Scoring should take place at the end of the evaluation process, once all relevant considerations have been taken into account, to avoid instances of 'marking up' or 'marking down' to the extent possible—as these may be the basis for a challenge even where they are undertaken in good faith and in accordance with the stated award criteria.

(iv) Existence of multiple iterations of evaluation documents should be avoided inasmuch as it may raise doubts about the uniformity of the approach taken and its

---

[162] It is important to distinguish here between listing all award criteria and sub-criteria and listing all considerations which may be relevant to the assessment of those criteria. The latter does not appear to be required under EU law: see in particular the CJEU's judgment in Case C-252/10 P *Evropaïki Dynamiki v EMSA*, paras 32–6.

conformity with the methodology described in the procurement documents. A single, authoritative evaluation matrix which is free of mistakes can provide a high level of protection against claims both at the preliminary stages and during any eventual trial of substantive issues. This must be a true record of the evaluation undertaken and fully reflect the information provided to bidders.

8.83 Under the remedies rules as currently applied in the UK and Ireland, it is usually better for a contracting authority to include exhaustive information about its criteria and evaluation methodology in the procurement documents—*even if these contain elements of illegality*—than to introduce any additional considerations or decisions at the evaluation stage. This is because time in respect of any challenge to those criteria will be more likely to run from the date of publication if they are fully explained and subsequently followed in the evaluation. This is somewhat unfortunate from the perspective of good procurement, as it is often not possible or desirable to have full foresight of the factors which will distinguish bids or the fairest and most efficient way of conducting an evaluation. While a wide range of situations can and should be anticipated in procurement documents—for example, how consortium bids will be treated, the approach to clarifications, and the procedures to be followed where an abnormally low tender is detected—some matters must be subject to flexibility based on the actual expressions of interest and tenders received.

8.84 For example, where an output- or performance-based specification is used, the costs associated with each bid will sometimes take different forms. If an authority is purchasing IT equipment, it may wish to take account of upgrades, maintenance, warranties, disposal costs, training, or any other necessary ancillaries. While the general headings for such costs can be anticipated in tender documents, it is not always possible to specify in precise detail the quantity of each which will need to be taken into account to ensure bids are compared on a like-for-like basis. In such cases, it may be advisable where decisions are made during evaluation which were not specifically envisioned in tender documents to notify all bidders of the decision prior to the results being finalized—if this can be done in a way which preserves the confidentiality and integrity of the evaluation process.[163]

8.85 If 50 marks are available for quality, then it should be possible for a tender to score anything between 0 and 50. Unlike cost criteria, it is not normally the case that the worst tender will score 0 and the best 50—although there is nothing in the CJEU jurisprudence on award criteria to prevent such an approach provided it is clearly set out in the tender documents. However, it may not be proportionate if the bids are in fact relatively close in quality. A score of zero would normally be reserved for a tender which did not respond at all to the criterion—although in that case it may also fail to comply with the specification. Unfortunately, in many legal challenges

---

[163] This was in fact the approach of the contracting authority in *Mears v Leeds City Council*, in which a claim regarding evaluation of costs was found to be out of time ([2011] EWHC 40 (QB)).

to award criteria, it appears that contracting authorities have adopted an evaluation approach which leads to only a very small number of marks, sometimes less than one, separating bids. In certain cases, this may be justified by the similar quality of the tenders, but in others it may simply reflect a failure to 'use' all of the marks available within a criterion to properly distinguish between tenders.[164] Unsuccessful bidders are naturally prone to question results if there is apparently only a very small distance separating them from the successful bid.

It may also pose a problem with regard to the principle of equal treatment. This **8.86** arises where the recommended approach to evaluating costs described in Chapter 6 is applied, meaning that the lowest valid and responsive tender receives full marks under the cost criterion, and other bids are scored proportionately. If a tender which is twice as expensive receives half as many of the available marks under the cost criterion, then it should also be possible for it to receive twice as many of the available quality marks, if it is in fact twice as good. The relative importance of cost and quality to the contracting authority is already reflected in the weighting assigned to criteria. If only a small range of the available marks for quality are used, this places the better quality, more expensive bid at a disadvantage which does not reflect the weighting of the award criteria as advertised. Ultimately, it is up to contracting authorities to determine their evaluation approach and make this known in advance to tenderers. Assigning clear intervals for scoring—so that if, for example, a tender performs relatively poorly under a particular qualitative criterion it only obtains 10 to 20 per cent of the marks available—is generally advisable in order to both identify the bid which is truly most advantageous based on the criteria and weightings, and forestall potential challenges.

Notification letters

It may seem trite to emphasize it, but notification letters should be minutely **8.87** checked to ensure they are correct in every detail and leave no room for misinterpretation. The requirement is to provide the name of the successful bidder, the scores achieved by it and the bidder being notified, and the characteristics and relative advantages of the successful tender.[165] This may be done by providing an extract from the scoring sheets together with commentary on any specific areas where the successful tender scored more highly than the bid in question. Both the

---

[164] In some cases, this appears to derive from the fact that contracting authorities are actually assessing compliance with their requirements (technical specifications) under the award criteria, whereas they should be assessing performance above and beyond the specification, as discussed in Chapter 4.

[165] Reg 32 PCR and Reg 6 Remedies Regulations (Ireland)—assuming the tender is admissible in the sense of complying with the specification and other mandatory requirements. In other cases, the requirement is to provide a statement of the reasons for rejecting the tender, but it is not necessary to give any information about the successful bidder. There is also a general ability to withhold information if this would impede law enforcement or otherwise be contrary to the public interest, or prejudice the legitimate commercial interests of other economic operators or fair competition.

scores and comments should be clearly linked to the criteria and evaluation methodology as previously notified to tenderers, and not concern any extraneous matters. The notification letter should allow an unsuccessful tenderer to fully appreciate the reasons for rejection without going beyond what is necessary for this purpose. In general, it is neither necessary nor advisable to provide the unsuccessful bidder's rank or any information about tenders other than its own and that of the successful bidder—this may both breach the duty of confidentiality owed to other bidders and invite challenges based on rank.

8.88 If an error is discovered after letters have been sent out but prior to finalizing the contract, how should the contracting authority proceed? Arguably, this depends on whether the error has the potential to alter the outcome of the procedure. If it does, then award of the contract should be suspended, the designated successful bidder and any other concerned bidders informed, and re-evaluation undertaken. The scope of any such re-evaluation must relate only to the discovered error and not take account of any new information which post-dates original tender submission. The new outcome should be notified to all bidders and a new standstill period applied. If, however, the error is such that it could not have altered the outcome, it may not be necessary to notify all bidders, but simply to correct the evaluation of the bidder concerned and apply a new standstill period from the date on which it is notified of its correct scores.

8.89 Given the possibility of such a situation occurring, it is vital that the notification letter to the designated successful bidder is provisional only and makes clear that no contract can be formed between the parties until the standstill period has elapsed and documents have been executed. There is nothing to prevent the contracting authority from meeting with the designated successful bidder during the standstill period, although it may wish to prioritize debriefing sessions for any unsuccessful bidders who request this. Such debriefing is voluntary, but can be worthwhile in order to gather feedback from bidders on their perception of the procedure and any factors which may have influenced their bidding strategy. Some contracting authorities engage in debriefing as a matter of course, whereas others only offer this where there has been an unusual investment in process by bidders or if there are specific concerns which they wish to allay. There is always some risk that debriefing sessions become 'fishing expeditions' or that comments can be misconstrued or made in error. The voluntary and ancillary nature of debriefing sessions should be emphasized for this reason.

Conclusion

8.90 Just as the substantive rules on public procurement represent a fascinating nexus between public and private interests, the question of remedies in procurement cases lies at the intersection of public and private law.[166] As seen in this chapter, the

---

[166] See Arrowsmith *The Law of Public and Utilities Sector Procurement*, paras 2.63–2.67 for the

decisions taken at national level regarding time limits, disclosure, interim measures, and the availability of specific remedies influence the effectiveness of the remedies regime just as clearly as the framework provided by the Remedies Directives. With the introduction of new substantive rules under the 2014 directives, courts can expect to see a variety of claims advanced which present novel or untested points of law. Modifications to contracts, public-public cooperation, subcontracting arrangements, abnormally low tenders, and verification of exclusion and selection criteria may all become more fertile sources of claims.

What is the impact of the availability of remedies on costs and compliance within **8.91** public procurement? The theory that rapid, effective remedies encourage fairer procedures has logical weight, but may not be supported by robust evidence. Although some valuable comparative work has been done since the introduction of the 2007 reform,[167] it remains difficult to disentangle the volume of cases and their outcomes from the multiple factors which influence these at domestic level, mentioned at the outset of this chapter. Making links to longer-term improvements in procurement practices requires additional inferences, such as that contracting authorities or their legal advisers are aware of decided cases, that those operators who exercise their right to avail of remedies are those with good cases, and that courts are correct in their interpretation of EU law. Given these uncertainties, it is legitimate to ask whether the remedies regime as applied in the UK and Ireland does more harm than good.

The obvious advantages are that it provides a means for the substantive procure- **8.92** ment rules to be enforced and for the rights of economic operators to be vindicated. It may also indirectly contribute to public interest objectives such as transparency and accountability in government decisions, and the prevention of corruption—although again this requires a number of inferences to be made about how contracting authorities react to the possibility of legal challenges. Conversely, it may be argued that the remedies regime actually encourages less transparency and openness in decision making, due to fear of challenges. For example, it may be a factor in decisions to seek a derogation from the application of the directives or to award smaller value contracts which will not be subject to the substantive directives and therefore to the remedies rules.[168]

---

arguments for and against requiring a specific public law element in order for public contracts to be amenable to judicial review.

[167] See in particular Bianchi, T. and Guidi, V. (2010) *Comparative Survey on the National Public Procurement Systems across the PPN* (Rome: Public Procurement Network); Treumer, S. and Lichère, F. (eds) (2011) *Enforcement of the EU Public Procurement Rules* (Copenhagen: DJØF); and Fairgrieve and Lichère, *Public Procurement Law.*

[168] It is notable in this regard that the UK and Ireland are among a very small number of Member States in which the remedies regime is restricted to above-threshold contracts. See European Commission SEC (2011) 853 final *Evaluation Report: Impact and Effectiveness of EU Public Procurement Legislation* (Pt 1), p 67.

8.93 There is also a specific risk that the way in which the remedies regime is implemented in the UK and Ireland places smaller companies bidding for public contracts at a disadvantage. Unlike other jurisdictions where administrative or specialized review bodies exist to deal with procurement claims, in the UK and Ireland this function is reserved to the higher courts—with associated high costs of litigation. In England, this is further compounded by the requirement for claimants to provide a cross-undertaking in damages where they wish to maintain the suspension of contract award. The expense of bringing claims means that smaller bidders are less likely to challenge procedures, and may in turn foster a reluctance on the part of contracting authorities to take procurement decisions against large or well-resourced companies.

8.94 While the overall purpose of the remedies regime should be to improve the quality of decision making and provide a fair and accessible means of redress when things go wrong, it may also distort procurement decisions in favour of those who are most likely to bring claims. This effect is exacerbated where courts are not in a position to rapidly dismiss unmeritorious claims—whether due to a lack of disclosure on the part of the contracting authority, procedural rules on interim measures, or simply due to the complex nature of procurement law. Arguably, the UK courts have gone too far in the direction of restraining access to interim measures, while applying a relatively low standard for the award of substantive remedies, given that this does not appear to require a causal link to be shown between an alleged breach and harm to the claimant. The situation regarding access to interim relief in Ireland is notably more favourable to claimants than that which applies in the UK; however, the standard of review for claims may also be tougher.

8.95 Although it appears that substantive amendments to the remedies regulations will not be undertaken as part of the implementation of the 2014 directives, there may well be a need in the near future to revisit the statutory basis for remedies in both jurisdictions, in order to ensure the appropriate balance between the rights of claimants and defendants, as well as the numerous aspects of public interest which arise in procurement cases. Increased use of the jurisdiction to vary a decision or set it aside in part only (for example, to remove a discriminatory specification) would also assist in the development of a sophisticated and fit-for-purpose remedies regime which adequately balances the interests of the parties concerned—including other candidates or tenderers involved in a procedure—and the public interest.

INDEX

References are to Paragraph Number apart from the Introduction when Roman Numerals are used.